The Politics of the Bench
and the Bar

THE POLITICS OF THE BENCH AND THE BAR

Judicial Selection Under the Missouri Nonpartisan Court Plan

RICHARD A. WATSON

RONDAL G. DOWNING

University of Missouri

John Wiley and Sons, Inc.

New York · *London* · *Sydney* · *Toronto*

10 9 8 7 6 5 4 3 2 1

Library of Congress Catalog Card Number: 69-16133
SBN 471 92220 x
Printed in the United States of America

TO

Joan and Virginia

ACKNOWLEDGMENTS

A study of this broad scope could have been conducted only with the cooperation of a large number of persons who assisted us at all stages of the six year project. We hope that the final product justifies the energies and resources they devoted to the task. While acknowledging their contributions, we also absolve them of errors of fact or interpretation contained in the study.

We are especially indebted to the Social Science Research Council and its Committee on Political Behavior. Their generous grant, under the Council's program for research on American Governmental and Legal Processes, made possible the initiation of the study in the summer of 1962 and the collection of virtually all the data utilized. The Research Center of the University of Missouri School of Business and Public Administration (Columbia) also helped finance our efforts, particularly in the latter years of the study when we were engaged in data analysis and the preparation of the manuscript. For this assistance, and for his personal support and encouragement, we wish to thank Robert Paterson, Director of the Center.

Two individuals contributed in a major way to the gathering and analysis of our data. Our colleague Frederick Spiegel was originally a co-investigator in the research and worked along with us in the personal interviews we conducted early in the project. However, at a crucial point in the study he was asked to assume administrative duties at the University of Missouri and these prevented his continuing with the project during its analysis and writing stages. The other person to whom we are particularly indebted is William Reid,, formerly a graduate student in political science at the University of Missouri and now Assistant Professor at the University of Maine, who participated in a very real way in all phases of the study. He performed most of the tasks of analyzing the survey and related data, and it is no exaggeration to say that without his very able assistance this book could never have been written in its present form.

In addition to Mr. Reid, other graduate assistants in the Research Center at the University of Missouri aided us at various times. Among them were James Culpepper, Nicholas Filapello, Kenneth Johnson, Thomas Lagnow, William McCauley, David Schaub, Gregory Snider, and Elmer Williams.

The Center's secretarial staff also performed ably and with dispatch a wide variety of tasks associated with the typing and filing of interview protocol notes and other data collected for the study, as well as the laborious task of typing the successive drafts of the manuscript itself. Among those most importantly involved in the project over the years have been Mrs. Carolyn Alhashimi, Miss Linda Fox, Mrs. Carol Kreiger, Mrs. Ruth Berry Long, Mrs. Elizabeth Miederhoff, Miss Lila Stemmons, Mrs. Betty Stone, and Mrs. Claire Thomas.

Many others have contributed to the substance and methodology of our study. Professors Joel Grossman and Herbert Jacob of the University of Wisconsin read the manuscript in its entirety and made valuable suggestions concerning its improvement. Our colleagues in the University of Missouri Department of Political Science helped immensely, not only by offering advice about how we might best cope with specific problems encountered in the study but even more importantly by affording the kind of congenial and stimulating intellectual environment essential for scholarly work. We also received help from members of the Law School faculty of the University of Missouri on some aspects of the study. Professor Kenneth Vines of the University of Buffalo provided information about his own research that was useful to us.

During 1965–1966 Mr. Watson was a Fellow at the Center for Advanced Study in the Behavioral Sciences at Stanford, California. He wishes to thank Dr. Ralph Tyler, Director of the center, his capable staff, and several Fellows including Donald Reich, Nelson Polsby, Martin Trow, Max Rheinstein, Amitai Etzioni, Julian Stanley, John Holland, Bert Green, Seymour Mandelbaum, Herbert Stein, and Kenneth O'Connell, Justice of The Oregon Supreme Court, for their assistance. While in California he also consulted with Professor Jerome Carlin of the Center for the Study of Law and Society, and visiting Professor of Political

Science, Deil Wright, at the University of California at Berkeley. He also expresses his appreciation to his secretary Mrs. Anna Tower, who served as his "girl Friday" during this delightful year at the Center, as well as Mrs. Katherine Holbrook, Jack Nadler, and Ted Cooper of the Center staff who provided valuable assistance in analyzing data for the project.

This study could never have been conducted without the cooperation of more than 200 lawyers, judges, public officials, and laymen in Missouri who took time from busy schedules to tell us in personal interviews their experiences with the operation of the Plan. It is a testimony to their cooperation that not one of those we sought to interview refused; the interviews averaged over one hour in length and some lasted as long as six hours. We have respected the request that their remarks be anonymous, but we want them to know how much we appreciate their helpfulness. The same is true of the more than 1200 lawyers in the state who responded to our mail questionnaire.

Some members of the Bar who assisted us can and should be identified. We are particularly grateful to Wade Baker, Executive Director of the Missouri Bar Association, its President, Orville Richardson, as well as the members of its governing board in 1964, who facilitated our taking the mail survey that year by providing us with the membership list of the organization. We also wish to acknowledge in particular the information provided us by other members of the legal profession, who included Glenn Winters, Executive Secretary of the American Judicature Society, Elmo Hunter, Federal District Judge for the Western District of Missouri, William Braithwaite, Research Attorney of the American Bar Foundation, William Cunningham, Executive Secretary of the Judicial Conference of Missouri, Russel Niles, President of the Bar of the City of New York, and Ronald Foulis of Washington, D.C.

Although most of our data came from personal interviews and mail surveys, we also gained much valuable information from documentary sources. In this regard we should like to thank the research staffs of *The Kansas City Star, The St. Louis Post Dispatch,* The Missouri University General Library and Law Library, The Missouri State Supreme Court Library, and The Missouri Historical Library for their valuable assistance. We also appreciate the help provided by persons at Community Studies, Inc., of Kansas City, the Governmental Research Institute of St. Louis, and the Data Processing Center of the University of Missouri (Columbia).

Some parts of the book have already appeared in articles in the *American Bar Association Journal,* the *American Political Science Review,* and the *American Journal of Sociology*. We are grateful to the editors of these publications and the University of Chicago Press, which publishes the last journal, for permission to use material from these articles here.

Finally, we should like to thank our wives Joan and Virginia for their patience and tolerance during the long periods of this study when we had to absent ourselves for personal interviewing, as well as the lonely nights of writing. It is to them that this book is dedicated.

R. A. W.
R. G. D.

CONTENTS

TABLES

The Politics of the Bench
and the Bar

INTRODUCTION

One of the key issues in any society is the manner in which individuals come to occupy positions of public leadership. The identification of recruitment as one of the basic functions that must be performed in any political system[1] has stimulated a spate of studies in recent years, which have inquired into how persons are selected for governmental posts. These inquiries have ranged broadly from Theodore White's exciting chronicles of "The Making of the President, 1960 and 1964" to detailed investigations of the recruitment of city councilmen and local party officials. Moreover, similar investigations are being conducted to an increasing extent by scholars of foreign political systems.

An analysis of such investigations indicates, however, that the overwhelming number of them concentrate on legislative and executive officials. The choosing of judges constitutes the "dark continent" of recruitment studies. A preoccupation with the decision-making portion of the judicial process, and even more particularly with Supreme Court cases,[2] means that we have only bits and pieces of information on how members of the judiciary come to office. Analyses of social backgrounds and career routes of both federal and state judges have been published in recent years,[3] but they merely indicate "who" has made it to the top, not "why"

---

[1] For a study that emphasizes the importance of recruitment as a political function, see Gabriel Almond and James Coleman, *The Politics of the Developing Areas* (Princeton: Princeton University Press, 1960), pp. 26 ff.

[2] The study of public law traditionally has concentrated on the analysis of Supreme Court decisions. However, in recent years, a number of judicial "behavioralists" have considered the entire judicial process to be their proper field of study. In keeping with this broader focus, they have begun to inquire into such matters as the "environment" in which courts and judges operate, the "roles" they assume in carrying out their functions, and the "impact" that judicial decisions actually have on the behavior of individuals and groups in society.

[3] One such study is John R. Schmidhauser's "The Justices of the Supreme Court: A Collective Portrait," *The Midwest Journal of Political Science*, 3 (1959), 1–50.

they were successful or "how" the recruitment process works in actual operation. For the most part judgments about these matters can be gleaned only from case studies of individual judicial appointments[4] (which may or may not be typical of the process generally) or, in the case of lower court federal judges, from investigations into the role the American Bar Association has assumed in recent years in the selection of the members of these benches.[5] Only one study, an exploratory one by Henderson and Sinclair, makes any systematic attempt to analyze the selection process at the state level.[6] There are no studies at all of what motivates some lawyers to seek to go on the bench and others to remain in the practice of law. Thus we are in the same situation with respect to judges as Max Lerner described some years ago concerning judicial decisions: we know they aren't brought by storks,[7] but we have little knowledge of the forces that actually do produce them.

It is difficult to account for this neglect of judicial recruitment as a field of study, particularly as it relates to positions in the state judiciary. Without minimizing the importance of the federal courts in our system of government, it remains a fact of life that the overwhelming amount of litigation in our society is processed at the state and local level; that handled by the national courts is like the tip of an iceberg that appears above the water. Moreover, no other groups of officeholders are chosen by such a variety of methods. At the present time no less than five distinct techniques are used by states to select their judges: executive and legislative appointment; popular election by partisan and nonpartisan ballots, and the Nonpartisan Court Plan (also known as the "Missouri" and "Merit" Plan). The last was developed by the American Bar Association and allied groups and provides for judges to be nominated by commissions composed of lawyers, other judges and laymen, and appointed by the governor of the state from among the three nominees.[8] Despite the research potentialities of this range of experiences

---

[4] An excellent study of the appointment of Pierce Butler to the Supreme Court is David J. Danelski's, *A Supreme Court Justice is Appointed* (New York: Random House, 1964).
[5] See Joel B. Grossman, *Lawyers and Judges: The ABA and the Politics of Judicial Selection* (New York: John Wiley and Sons, 1965).
[6] Bancroft C. Henderson and T. C. Sinclair, *Judicial Selection in Texas: An Exploratory Study*, University of Houston Studies in Social Science (Houston: Public Affairs Research Center, 1964).
[7] See his *Ideas for the Ice Age: Studies in a Revolutionary Era* (New York: The Viking Press, 1941), p. 259.
[8] The five methods are associated with basic historical trends in the nation: executive and legislative appointment of judges came from early colonial and state practice;

(certainly one of the relatively few instances in which the states in our federal system do actually serve as "laboratories" for governmental experimentation), we have no systematic studies of how such procedures actually work, that is, who is influential in choosing judges under the various methods. As Herbert Jacob, one close student of the subject has suggested, "the debate over judicial selection continues in a factual vacuum."[9]

This study focuses on the operation of the Nonpartisan Court Plan in Missouri, the state where it was first accepted by the electorate in 1940. As described later, the Plan has recently become the object of a nation-wide crusade that has seen its adoption, in whole or in part, in fourteen other states, its voluntary use in four more, and its current consideration by bar associations and state legislatures throughout the United States. Therefore an empirical study of the operation of the Plan in its mother state over the period of a quarter century provides much-needed information on a vital issue of present-day public policy. Hopefully, it helps to fill the "factual vacuum" in judicial selection to which Jacob refers.

The study, however, has a more inclusive purpose: it explores broadly Bench-Bar relationships pertaining to the state judiciary. Despite the fact that judges are recruited from a particular subculture in our society (i.e., the legal community), no one has systematically studied such basic matters as the motivations behind lawyers' seeking a judicial position; the stumbling blocks to such candidacies; the "stakes" other members of the Bar perceive in the question of who should sit on the bench; social cleavages in the Bar on the issue of state judicial selection; and the interest that sitting members of the judiciary take in the process by which their future colleagues are chosen. An analysis of the operation of the Nonpartisan Court Plan lends itself ideally to the exploration of such basic inquiries, since the formal role the legal community assumes in this particular process institutionalizes and brings to the surface the web of Bench-Bar relationships and forces which are present at

---

partisan election stemmed from the Jacksonian Revolution in the middle of the 1800's; the use of nonpartisan judicial ballots was a part of the Progressive movement of the early part of this century; and, as discussed subsequently, the beginnings of the Nonpartisan Court Plan can be traced to the period immediately preceding World War II. The classic historical study of the subject is Evan Haynes' *The Selection and Tenure of Judges* (New York: The National Conference of Judicial Councils, 1944). For a summary of present state practices with respect to judicial selection, see *The Book of the States, 1966–1967* (Chicago: Council of State Governments, 1966), p. 116 f.
[9] See his *Justice in America* (Boston: Little, Brown and Company, 1965), p. 207.

a subterranean level in other judicial selection systems as well.[10] It also reveals the other parties concerned with the actions of the courts, such as social and economic institutions in the state, and the way in which Bench and Bar politics blends with gubernatorial politics as components of the state political system.

The operation of the Court Plan in Missouri is complicated by the fact that separate Commissions nominate judges for the trial bench in Jackson County (Kansas City is its major city and most of its lawyers practice there), a similar judiciary in St. Louis City (suburban St. Louis County still elects its judges), and for all appellate courts in the state. This situation, in turn, produces three distinctive selection processes. Although this development makes our research task a more difficult one, it also permits us to employ a comparative approach in our analysis. In doing so we use a common conceptual framework to determine the similarities and differences that exist in the operation of the three selection processes under study.

The student of judicial recruitment and selection must try to understand not only the *dynamics* of the process but also another equally important issue: the *consequences* that are associated with the operation of a particular system. The literature on judicial selection is replete with statements about the kinds of judges a given method produces. Thus Herbert Brownell, former Attorney General of the United States, has bemoaned what he refers to as, the "gray mice" of the judicial establishment, the "ordinary likeable people of small talent," who come to the bench as a result of partisan political forces, which govern the choice of judges under either popular elections or executive appointment.[11] In the opposite vein are the assumptions concerning the products of the Nonpartisan Court Plan as articulated in the following ditty:

> Oh, the Old Missouri Plan
> Oh, the Old Missouri Plan
> When Wall Street lawyers all judicial candidates will scan

---

[10] One author has expressly used this term to describe the process by which a state supreme court judge was appointed. See John E. Crowe, "Subterranean Politics: A Judge is Chosen," *Journal of Public Law*, 12 (1963), 275–289. Other studies that stress the importance of the role of the legal profession in the selection of judges, even under a partisan selection system, are Henderson and Sinclair, *op. cit.*, Vol. 1, p. 19, and Kenneth N. Vines, "The Selection of Judges in Louisiana," in Vines and Herbert Jacob, *Studies in Judicial Politics*, Vol. XIII, Tulane Studies in Political Science (New Orleans: Tulane University Press, 1962), p. 119.

[11] See his article, "Too Many Judges Are Political Hacks," which originally appeared in the April 18, 1964 issue of the *Saturday Evening Post*, reprinted in *Source Materials on Modern Courts for Oklahoma* (Committee on Administration of Justice of the Oklahoma Bar Association), at p. 14.

If you're not from Fair Old Harvard
They will toss you in the can . . .
Oh, the Old Missouri Plan
Oh, the Old Missouri Plan
It won't be served with sauerkraut nor sauce Italian
There'll be no corned beef and cabbage
And spaghetti they will ban
There'll be no such dish
As gelfilte fish
On the Old Missouri Plan.[12]

Provocative or amusing as such observations may be, it is also possible that these judgments about our judiciary are highly inaccurate, since they are based only upon limited personal impressions. Even if we concede that a group of judges in one state is superior to those in another, the question remains whether it is the selection system itself that produces the differences among members of the bench or whether other factors (such as the total political environment or general caliber of political leadership in the two states) contribute more to the disparities between their judges.

A study of judicial selection in Missouri permits us to do a comparative analysis of different selection methods that have been employed within one state. The Nonpartisan Court Plan succeeded the partisan election system that was formerly used to choose trial court judges in Jackson County and St. Louis, as well as judges to the three intermediate courts of appeal and the Supreme Court of the state. Thus the results of the changeover which took place in these jurisdictions in 1940 can be analyzed. Moreover, judges in "outstate" Missouri, as well as those serving in urban St. Louis County, are still chosen in partisan contests, so that comparisons can be made between these present-day elective jurists and the Plan judges who now serve in the two major cities of the state.

We have taken a range of considerations into account in assessing the consequences of the two systems. We examine the social backgrounds of the two sets of judges to see whether the stereotype of the Plan jurist expressed in the above ditty is accurate; we also compare the quality of all Missouri jurists to test Brownell's assertion that elective judges are more likely to be "people of small talent" than are Plan ones. An analysis is made of how the two groups of judges behave on the bench, and their respective tendencies to remain in office for

---

[12] The ditty was from a judicial minstrel of the Bar Association of the City of New York and was sung by Judge James Garrett Wallace. See Charles E. Clark and David M. Trubek, "The Creative Role of the Judge: Restraint and Freedom in the Common Law Tradition," *Yale Law Journal*, 71 (1961), 272, footnote 59.

life or to leave the judiciary on a voluntary or involuntary basis are also compared.

Because we were interested in a wide range of substantive matters relating to both the dynamics and consequences of selection, we cast our conceptual and methodological nets broadly, utilizing a variety of approaches and materials. We have been intentionally eclectic in employing a number of concepts from role and systems analyses, as well as "political culture," to help us view and order different types of data. In gathering such data, we first examined newspaper and journal accounts of developments under the Plan to gain valuable background information for our personal interviews. More than 200 open-ended interviews were held with lawyers, judges, and political figures in the state to obtain detailed data on individual judicial appointments and the specifics of the recruitment and selection process. Following these interviews we conducted a survey by using a mailed questionnaire to examine the general thinking and attitudes of a random sample of lawyers in the state on the general operation of the Plan, the performance of all judges before whom they practiced, and the qualities they looked for in a good judge. The disposition of lower court cases appealed to the Supreme Court was checked to determine the affirmance-reversal rates of individual trial court judges, and Supreme Court decisions were analyzed to assess the liberal-conservative predilections of individual judges. Finally, we examined social-background and tenure information on Plan judges (including voting statistics relating to Bar polls and elections held in conjunction with the Plan) and compared it with similar data on elected judges.

The empirical findings of the study show that many of the assumptions made about the dynamics of the selection process by both proponents and opponents of the Plan are erroneous. The Plan has not eliminated political forces from the selection of judges, as its supporters claim; nor has it meant that the "bluebloods" of the legal profession (the large-firm lawyers representing the affluent and prestigious institutions in society) decide who will sit on the bench, as feared by many persons who attack the Plan. Instead, the selection system, as it has evolved in practice, is a highly pluralistic one that reflects diverse interests: upper- and lower-status lawyers; a range of social and economic institutions; sitting members of the judiciary; and the factions and gubernatorial followings of state politics. The study also shows that the Plan has not brought all the results, either in terms of kind of personnel recruited or performance on the bench, that its founders intended.

The study is divided into three major parts. First, Chapters 1 to 5 analyze the dynamics of the recruitment and selection process. Second,

Chapters 6 to 9 deal with the consequences of the Plan; and, finally, the last chapter contains some concluding comments on the study and its implications for future research. Before examining these matters, however, let us explain the development and general nature of the Nonpartisan Court Plan.[13]

THE DEVELOPMENT AND NATURE OF THE NONPARTISAN COURT PLAN

The roots of the Nonpartisan Court Plan can be traced to conditions fostered by the Jacksonian Revolution that occurred in the middle of the last century in the United States. Before that time, our state judges were generally appointed by the governor and confirmed by a council or the legislature, or were chosen by the legislature itself.[14] However, the philosophical egalitarianism of Jacksonian Democracy led existing states to abandon the appointive method for popular election of judges along with other public officials: New York led the way in 1846 and, within a decade, 15 of the 29 states in existence at that time followed suit. Moreover, new states entering the Union after 1846 adopted the popular election of all or most of their judges.[15]

For a time there appeared to be little agitation for change in the method of choosing our state judges, but the rise of the urban political machines in the immediate post-Civil War period in the United States resulted in the choice of judges actually being made by party leaders, whose decisions the voters merely ratified. Lawyer resentment over Boss Tweed's control of the courts led to the establishment of the first modern bar association in the nation: the Bar of the City of New York, in 1870. Within the decade that followed, a number of similar associations, including the American Bar Association, were formed to improve the administration of justice in the United States. Thus the growing profes-

---

[13] In addition to Haynes, *op. cit.*, other studies treating general trends in judicial selection in the United States, and the development of the Nonpartisan Court Plan, include James W. Hurst, *The Growth of American Law: The Law Makers* (Boston: Little, Brown and Company, 1950); Jack W. Peltason, *The Missouri Plan for the Selection of Judges*, Vol. XX, No. 2, *The University of Missouri Studies* (Columbia: University of Missouri Press, 1945); and Glenn R. Winters, "Selection of Judges—an Historical Introduction," *Texas Law Review*, 44, No. 6 (June, 1966), 1081–1088.

[14] The exceptions were Georgia, Indiana, and Michigan which provided for the popular election of some of their judges, and Mississippi which adopted this method for its entire judiciary in 1832. Hurst, *op. cit.*, p. 122.

[15] *Ibid.* This situation prevailed until Alaska and Hawaii entered the Union.

sionalization of the legal community was clearly linked to the issue of judicial selection.[16]

Initially, the leaders of the Bar worked within the framework of popular elections to accomplish their reforms. In doing so they pursued two separate strategies. One involved minimizing the power of political party organizations in electing judges through such devices as separate judicial nominating conventions, nonpartisan ballots, direct primaries, and separate judicial elections. The other strategy called for maximizing the influence of the legal profession in judicial selection by means of referenda in which bar associations evaluated the capabilities of the various judicial candidates and publicized their recommendations for the benefit of the general public.[17] However, neither strategy was successful, since political party leaders continued to operate effectively no matter which type of judicial election method was employed, and the voters took their cues in judicial elections from political party leaders rather than from the organized Bar.

Shortly after the turn of the century, a number of Bar leaders concluded that no meaningful improvements in judicial selection could be accomplished as long as judges were popularly elected. In 1906 Roscoe Pound, a young professor at the University of Nebraska, delivered an address before the American Bar Association, in which he charged that such elections were destroying the respect for the judiciary.[18] Seven years later, ex-President William Howard Taft told the same Bar group that nonpartisan elections of judges were a failure. That same year (1913), the American Judicature Society was founded to work for the improvement of justice; one of its main objectives was to secure some method of selection more satisfactory than popular election.[19]

Proclaiming dissatisfaction with the elective method was one thing; devising a feasible substitute for it was another. However, the very next year (1914), a founder and director of research for the Society, Albert Kales, developed a plan that incorporated elements of both the election and appointment of judges. The system called for the election, for a short term, of a Chief Justice of a metropolitan court district;

---

[16] Roscoe Pound, *The Lawyer from Antiquity to Modern Times* (St. Paul: West Publishing Co., 1953), Chapter IX.

[17] For example, Chicago conducted its first Bar primary in 1887. For an analysis of this and subsequent primaries in this metropolitan community, see Edward M. Martin, *The Role of the Bar in Electing the Bench in Chicago* (Chicago: University of Chicago Press, 1936).

[18] Printed in the *Journal of the American Judicature Society*, 46 (1962), 55 ff., cited in Winter, *loc. cit.*, footnote 14.

[19] Peltason, *op. cit.*, p. 36.

the Chief Justice would then appoint other judges on the court as vacancies occurred. Also included in the plan was a proposal that a Judicial Council, composed of the presiding judges of various divisions of the metropolitan court, compile a list of lawyers practicing before them who they felt would make good judges; the Chief Justice would then be required to make at least every other judicial appointment from that list. Finally, the Kales Plan provided for appointed judges going before the electorate periodically with no opponents, being retained or voted out of office on the basis of their records.[20] In 1926 Harold Laski, the English political scientist and economist, proposed a variant of the Kales Plan for choosing American state judges. He substituted the Governor of a state for the Chief Justice as the appointing agent, and added the state Attorney General and the President of the state Bar Association to the judicial members of the nominating commission.[21]

The Kales-Laski proposal thus contained the basic features on which subsequent plans for judical reform have been based: (a) a commission to nominate candidates for the bench; (b) an elected official who makes his appointments from that list; and (c) subsequent elections in which appointed judges run on their records with no opponents. California adopted the latter feature of the Plan in 1934, but the enactment there gave the governor's advisory body, a confirming, rather than a nominating, function to perform in the selection process.[22] A selection plan closer to the Kales-Laski model was adopted by the House of Delegates of the American Bar Association in 1937. Beyond this, similar plans were proposed in Ohio and Michigan in the late 1930's, but both were defeated by the voters. This set the stage for the adoption of the Nonpartisan Court Plan by the voters in Missouri in November of 1940.

The Campaign for the Plan in Missouri

It is difficult to determine the precise reasons why Missouri became the first state to adopt the Plan favored by the American Judicature Society and American Bar Association, but certain factors contributed

---

[20] *Annals of the American Academy of Political and Social Science,* Vol. LII (March, 1914), 1–12, cited in Winter, *loc. cit.,* footnote 15.

[21] "Technique of Judicial Appointment," *Michigan Law Review,* 24 (April, 1926), 526–543, cited in Peltason, Chapter II, footnote 19.

[22] The California Plan vested the appointment power in the governor with confirmation by a Commission on Qualifications composed of the Chief Justice of the Supreme Court, a Presiding Judge of the appropriate District Court of Appeals and the Attorney General of the state.

greatly to the successful campaign waged there. One was the general political climate of the times.[23] The Pendergast and Shannon factions of the Jackson County Democratic party (these factions are discussed more fully in Chapter 3) fought a bitter intraparty battle in the state Supreme Court primary contest in 1936 and, two years later, they joined forces in an unsuccessful effort to unseat an able and popular incumbent Supreme Court justice who was reputed not to have voted Pendergast's way in certain litigation before the Court. The blatant injection of party factional fights into the selection of judges for the highest court in the state alarmed many lawyers and many prominent citizens in Missouri. On the other side of the state, ward leaders succeeded in getting a person elected to the St. Louis Circuit Court who had never really practiced law but had served as a pharmacist in a St. Louis hospital in the years preceding his election to the circuit bench. Despite the fact that he rated at the bottom of the list in the Bar poll in 1934, he was elected to the Circuit Court.[24] His subsequent service on the court during the next six years was severely criticized by the St. Louis press. Thus the public in Missouri was exposed in the late 1930's to unfavorable stories about the selection of judicial candidates in the state, and this undoubtedly helped to pave the way for the reform campaign that followed.

On the positive side the campaign for the adoption of the Plan in Missouri was well-organized and executed. The leadership of the Bar Association of St. Louis first developed a concrete plan for judicial selection;[25] the Missouri State Bar Association and the newly formed Lawyer's Association of Kansas City worked closely with the St. Louis group in refining its provisions, and in building support for it among lawyers in the State.[26] Perhaps even more important for the eventual adoption

---

[23] The information on political conditions as they related to the Missouri judiciary was taken from an unpublished manuscript by Charles P. Blackmore, *Has Missouri Found the Answer?: A Historical Study of the Missouri Non-Partisan Court Plan.*

[24] Another factor strengthening the influence of the ward leaders in the primaries was the fact that circuit judges contested for vacancies "at large" rather than by division. In the last election preceding the adoption of the Plan, 27 Democratic candidates, including 8 incumbents, and 18 Republicans filed for the 9 vacancies on the St. Louis circuit bench.

[25] Preliminary Report of the Committee of Judicial Selection and Tenure of the Bar Association of St. Louis, September 20, 1937. We are indebted to Ronald J. Foulis, Chairman of the Committee, for furnishing us with a copy of this report.

[26] Some groups did oppose it, however, including the bar associations of Kansas City, St. Louis County, and Jasper County, along with the Lawyers' Association of St. Louis. Peltason, *op. cit.*, p. 54. See Chapter 1, *infra*, for an analysis of the bar rivalries in Kansas City and St. Louis.

of the Plan was the development of a state-wide organization—the Missouri Institute for the Administration of Justice—which brought prominent lay persons in the state into the campaign for the Plan. When the Missouri state legislature failed to submit to the people a constitutional amendment incorporating the Plan, it was this organization that was responsible for gathering the signatures necessary to get the Plan on the ballot under the initiative provisions of the Missouri Constitution.[27] It was this same group, organized in counties throughout the state, that led the ratification campaign which came to a successful conclusion in November of 1940. Those who worked for the Plan in Missouri benefitted from the unsuccessful experiences in Ohio and Michigan which pointed to the importance of involving the lay community in battles for judicial reform.[28] The rallying of a host of citizen's groups (business, elements of organized labor,[29] women's groups, religious and educational organizations, and metropolitan newspapers) all helped to blunt the charge that the Plan was merely the creature of the Bar.

The Plan had scarcely been adopted, however, when its opponents moved to kill it. The Democratic floor leader of the House of Representatives, H. P. Lauf, was successful in steering a proposed constitutional amendment through that body, as well as the state Senate, which provided for the repeal of the Plan. In the campaign that followed, its opponents (the "repealists") were better organized than they had been when the Plan was first proposed. Opposition was particularly strong in the St. Louis area where a Committee of One Thousand Lawyers, formed to support the Lauf amendment, attacked the Plan as a device of the press, insurance companies, and railroads to control the bench. Despite these efforts, however, the Lauf amendment was defeated, and the Plan was supported by a more favorable vote than had attended its original adoption two years previously.[30]

---

[27] Signatures of 5 percent of the voters of two-thirds of the Congressional districts amounting to about 50,000 names were required to place the Plan on the ballot. The Institute actually gathered 74,075 signatures. Ibid., p. 53.

[28] Two individuals interested in the unsuccessful attempts to bring judicial reform in Ohio and Michigan, Howard L. Barksdull and George E. Brand, respectively, warned the Missouri proponents of the Plan that an educational campaign would be necessary to gather public support. Ibid., pp. 40 and 53.

[29] The State Industrial Union Council of the C.I.O. supported the Plan, but the Central Trades and Labor Union of the A.F. of L. opposed it. Ibid., p. 55.

[30] The vote in 1940 was 535,642 for and 445,194 against, but the amendment received majority support in only 22 counties plus the City of St. Louis, with 92 counties voting against it. In 1942, the Lauf amendment was defeated by a 389,065 to 216,544 margin with only 3 counties voting in favor of it. Ibid., pp. 56 and 63.

The situation with respect to the Plan has not changed markedly in Missouri since 1942. It has continued to have its major support in Jackson County and St. Louis where the Plan applies to the circuit and probate courts, as well as the Court of Criminal Correction in St. Louis.[31] In 1967 residents of St. Louis County, whose trial judges have continued to be elected by partisan ballots, were successful in securing enabling legislation permitting them to vote on the adoption of the Plan in their county.[32] There has been no serious effort to extend the provisions of the Plan to the outstate areas of Missouri, which appear to be satisfied with their partisan-elected, trial judges. Finally, there has been no attempt to eliminate the use of the Plan in the appellate courts of the state (that is, the Supreme Court and the three intermediate courts of appeals in Kansas City St. Louis, and Springfield). As we indicate in Chapter 7, outstate, lawyers and metropolitan lawyers, overwhelmingly support the Plan for selecting appellate judges in Missouri.

The Adoption of Nonpartisan Court Plan in Other Jurisdictions

After the successful adoption of the Court Plan in Missouri in the early 1940's, its proponents looked forward to its adoption in other states. However, judicial reform was delayed by World War II, and it was not until 1956 that the Plan achieved its first major success in Alaska when the new state provided in its constitution for the Plan's use in all major courts.[33] The only other significant victory in the 1950's occurred in Kansas in 1958 when that state abandoned the partisan election of its Supreme Court judges in favor of the Plan.

If the seeds of judicial reform fell primarily on fallow ground in the two decades following the adoption of the Plan in Missouri in 1940, the movement picked up considerable momentum in the 1960's. States legally adopting the Court Plan since 1962 include Colorado, Iowa, Nebraska, Oklahoma (appellate courts only), Utah, and Vermont. In addition, in Arizona, Idaho, Massachusetts, and Montana, governors have voluntarily agreed to use nominating commissions to screen candidates for the state bench. The last two mayors of New York City, as well as a former mayor of Philadelphia, have followed a similar practice

---

[31] The probate courts and the St. Louis Court of Criminal Correction were added as Plan Courts in the new Missouri Constitution adopted in 1945.

[32] In 1950 the Missouri Supreme Court ruled that the Plan could not be adopted by other jurisdictions of the state without enabling legislation. See *State ex rel. Miller v. Toberman,* 360 Mo. 1101, 232 SW 2d 904 (1950).

[33] In 1950 provisions of the Plan were adopted for the Circuit Court of Jefferson County (Birmingham), Alabama.

for their judicial appointments. The Plan also has been adopted legally at the local level in Dade County, Florida, Denver, Colorado, and Tulsa, Oklahoma. Finally, Illinois and Pennsylvania, although maintaining popular election for the initial selection of their judges, have followed California in adopting the tenure features of the Plan by which members of the bench run for reelection on their records without an opponent.[34]

A major force in judicial reform in recent years has been the American Judicature Society. Utilizing the strategy first employed successfully in Missouri, the Society has been working closely with state and local bar associations in organizing Citizens' Conferences to bring important lay participation and support into the movement for better courts. At the time this book goes to press a national campaign on the Plan's behalf is being conducted before bar associations, state legislatures, and citizens' groups in virtually every state in the nation.[35]

The Major Provisions of the Missouri Nonpartisan Court Plan

Before analyzing the dynamics of the Missouri Nonpartisan Court Plan, particular features of that Plan must be explained briefly.

1. A key component of the Plan is the nominating commission. There are three of these commissions in Missouri. Two separate commissions nominate candidates for the circuit courts in Jackson County and St. Louis City, respectively.[36] Each such commission is composed of five members—two lawyers elected by attorneys residing in the court's jurisdiction, two resident laymen appointed by the governor of the state, and the presiding judge of the court of appeals of the area, who serves as *ex officio* chairman of the circuit nominating commission. A third, or appellate, commission nominates judges for the Supreme Court, as well as the three courts of appeals in Kansas City, St. Louis, and Springfield. The appellate commission consists of seven members—three lawyers elected by attorneys residing in each of the three courts of appeals jurisdictions into which the state is divided; three laymen residing in

---

[34] For a summary of the Plan's use through the end of 1967, see Glenn R. Winters (eds.), *Selected Readings on Judicial Selection and Tenure* (Chicago: American Judicature Society, 1967), Appendix 3. Winters provided us with an even more up-to-date record of the Plan in a telephone conversation on May 27, 1968.

[35] Recently, Senator Hugh Scott of Pennsylvania introduced a measure to provide for the use of the Plan to choose federal judges as well, but to date nothing has come of his proposal.

[36] As already indicated, these circuit commissions also nominate candidates for the Jackson County and St. Louis City probate courts, as well as the St. Louis Court of Criminal Correction.

the same three jurisdictions who are appointed by the governor, and the chief justice of the Supreme Court who is *ex officio* chairman of the appellate commission.[37]

2. When new judgeships are created or vacancies occur in any of the above courts, the appropriate nominating commission sends a list of three candidates for the judicial position to the governor of the state. The chief executive must make his appointment from among the persons who appear on this list of candidates.

3. After one year's service on the bench each of the judges appointed under the Plan goes before the people at the next general election to secure their approval for his continuance in office. He runs on his record with no opponent, with the electorate voting on the question, "Shall Judge _____ be retained in office?" If the majority of those voting on the question vote "Yes," he remains in office for his regular term (six years for circuit judges and twelve years for judges of the three courts of appeals and the Supreme Court).[38] If a judge fails to receive such an affirmative vote, a vacancy is created for his judicial position, and the nomination and appointment process described above is put into effect to choose his successor.

With this background information in mind, we can analyze the recruitment and selection process as it evolved in Missouri during the quarter century following the Plan's adoption in 1940.

---

[37] All lawyer and lay nominating commission members serve six-year terms. They may not succeed themselves in office.

[38] The terms of probate judges and judges of the St. Louis Court of Criminal Correction are four years.

PART I

THE RECRUITMENT AND

SELECTION PROCESS

As already suggested, the number of studies devoted to the recruitment of political decision makers has burgeoned in recent years. However, Herbert Jacob, in a recent review of studies of elected officials in the United States, suggests that "too little of this research has concerned itself with the whole of the recruitment process."[1] Instead, he says, we have "excellent descriptions of isolated fragments" of the process, including a few which concentrate on psychological factors which lead certain persons to such public office; a substantial number which trace the social backgrounds and career ladders of officials; and numerous investigations into the political institutions (groups, parties, election systems) which constitute what he calls, "the final phase of the recruitment process in a democracy."[2] Lester Seligman, a close student of the subject, identifies another basic defect in recruitment studies: their failure to explore what he calls the "blocks to the free recruitment of leadership in our society."[3] A preoccupation with studying those who have made it to the top means that we have virtually no information on the negative features of recruitment, that is, the factors which lead persons not to consider a public career,[4] or which serve to screen out those that would like to occupy such positions if they had the opportunity to do so.

---

[1] See his article, "Initial Recruitment of Elected Officials in the U.S.," *The Journal of Politics,* 24 (November, 1962), 703.

[2] *Ibid.*

[3] See Lester Seligman, "The Study of Political Leadership," *The American Political Science Review,* XLIV (1950), 908.

[4] For a discussion of both negative and positive attitudes of the public toward careers in public life, see William C. Mitchell, "The Ambivalent Social Status of the American Politician," *The Western Political Quarterly,* XII (September, 1959), 683–698.

Although the criticisms of Jacob and Seligman are directed primarily against studies of elected legislative and executive officials, they apply to an even greater extent to those relatively few investigations which have concerned themselves with the recruitment of judges. As noted before, there are a limited number of works that analyze the social backgrounds and career routes of members of the Bench,[5] and even fewer that attempt to describe the process by which judges are chosen.[6] And there are no studies of what leads certain lawyers to seek to go on the bench and others to remain in private practice.

We have taken these basic defects into account in formulating the framework for the analysis that we utilize in our study of the recruitment of judges under the Nonpartisan Court Plan. We have attempted to meet Jacob's call for an "integrated" approach to the study of the recruitment process by first delineating the various components of the process, and then relating them to each other; we have also sought to explore the "blocks to free recruitment," which Seligman speaks of, by identifying the various factors that serve to prevent most lawyers from becoming judges.

Conceptually, we have developed a rough model for choosing judges under the Nonpartisan Court Plan which analyzes recruitment as a progressive, winnowing process. At the one end of the process, we have the "particular subculture"[7] from which judges are drawn, that is, the legal community consisting of persons admitted to the Bar.[8] At the other

---

[5] An early study of the backgrounds of justices of the United States Supreme Court and state supreme courts is an article by Rodney L. Mott, Spencer D. Albright and Helen R. Semmerling entitled, "Judicial Personnel," *Annals of the American Academy of Political and Social Science*, 167 (1933), 143–155. Others include Todd Hoopes, "An Experiment in the Measurement of Judicial Qualifications in the Supreme Court of Ohio," *Cincinnati Law Review* 18 (1949), 417–466; John R. Schmidhauser, "The Justices of the Supreme Court: A Collective Portrait," *The Midwest Journal of Political Science*, 3 (1959), 1–50; Bancroft C. Henderson and T. C. Sinclair," *Judicial Selection in Texas: An Exploratory Study*, University of Houston Studies in Social Science (Houston: Public Affairs Research Center, 1964), Vol. 1, Chapter V; Joel B. Grossman, *Lawyers and Judges: the ABA and the Politics of Judicial Selection*, (New York: John Wiley and Sons, 1965), pp. 198–206 and Sheldon Goldman, "Characteristics of Eisenhower and Kennedy Appointees to the Lower Federal Courts," *The Western Political Quarterly*, XVIII (December, 1965), 755–762.

[6] A study that describes the process for selecting federal and state judges in Texas in Henderson and Sinclair, *op. cit.*

[7] Almond and Coleman, *The Politics of the Developing Areas* (Princeton: Princeton University Press, 1960), p. 31, use this term to describe the particular portions of the total society from which persons are recruited for specialized roles in the political system.

[8] Although membership in the Bar is frequently an informal rather than a formal

end are the lawyers who emerge as the chosen few who sit on the bench. We have examined the factors that eliminate the candidates at various stages between these two extremes. We have also integrated the recruitment process with the personnel involved in it, by comparing the characteristics of lawyers who are excluded and retained at progressive phases of the winnowing procedure.

Although the term recruitment is generally used to describe the total process whereby persons come to occupy positions of public leadership (we have utilized this meaning thus far in the discussion), for purposes here, it is helpful to divide the discussion into the separate stages of recruitment and selection. Recruitment in this context refers to the process by which certain lawyers' names are placed for consideration as judges before the commissions that initially screen candidates for the bench. Chapter 2 of the study concentrates on this phase of the screening mechanism. Selection is reserved for that part of the process whereby the commissions narrow the candidates to three nominees for each judgeship, and by which the ultimate appointing authority (the governor) makes his choice from among these three nominees.[9] Chapters 3 to 5 deal with the selection of judges for the Jackson County circuit, the St. Louis City circuit, and the appellate courts, respectively.

But before examining the actual recruitment and selection of judges under the Plan, it is necessary to look at the selection of the selectors, that is, the method by which the lawyer and lay members of the nominating commissions are chosen, for their choice determines the kinds of persons who sit on these commissions and the perspectives they bring to their deliberations. This, in turn, shapes the nature of the filtering process by which lawyers come to ascend the bench, since the nominators play such an important part in determining who will ultimately be chosen as judges. Therefore Chapter 1, the first part of this general section, discusses the procedure by which the lawyer and lay persons on the commissions are chosen and the factors that bear on their selection.

---

qualification for a judgeship, the *Constitution of the State of Missouri*, 1945, Art. V, Sec. 25, requires all judges in Missouri to be licensed to practice law in the state.

[9] Seligman distinguishes between the two concepts in analyzing the choosing of elected officials, by referring to the former as relating to "factors that affect *eligibility* for political activism, e.g., social structure, *etc.*," and the latter as "the *immediate* process of nomination or election." See his article, "A Prefatory Study of Leadership Selection in Oregon," *The Western Political Quarterly*, XII (March, 1959), 153.

1

❦

SELECTING THE SELECTORS:

CHOOSING THE MEMBERS OF THE

NOMINATING COMMISSIONS

As already explained, the commissions for the circuit courts of Jackson County and St. Louis City, as well as the Appellate Commission that nominates candidates for the Courts of Appeals and Supreme Court of the state, contain judicial, lawyer, and lay members. The judges who serve as presiding officers of the respective commissions serve *ex officio* and, therefore, there is no discretion involved in their selection. However, both the lawyer and lay persons on the commission reach their positions by virtue of prescribed methods: the lawyers emerge as choices of the legal community in elections for such posts, while the laymen are appointees of the governor. This chapter analyzes the political dynamics of both selection methods and the kinds of persons who emerge as selectees under the two processes.

First, we examine the elections of lawyer members of the circuit and appellate nominating commissions. As the discussion indicates, these elections have spawned a party subsystem operating in the legal community similar to a general party system existing within the larger political order. The succeeding sections, therefore, analyze bar politics within the conceptual framework of a general party system, that is, what bar groups constitute the competing "parties," and what are the social and ideological differences between them; how do they go about marshalling their resources in the electoral contest and what do they conceive to be the "stakes" or "pay offs" of such contests. The analysis also relates these lawyer contests to broader social interests concerned with the actions of the courts.

19

The concluding part of the chapter discusses the selection of the lay members of the commission by the governor. It assesses the factors underlying such gubernatorial appointments and the general backgrounds of persons who have been appointed to such commissions over the years.

THE ELECTION OF LAWYER MEMBERS
OF THE NOMINATING COMMISSIONS

The Nonpartisan Court Plan has most relevance for the Jackson County (Kansas City) and St. Louis areas in Missouri. Lawyers in these communities elect members to the separate commissions which nominate candidates to the trial courts in Jackson County and St. Louis City; judges in the remaining forty-one "outstate" circuits are chosen by popular election. Moreover, despite the fact that all attorneys in the state are eligible to vote for one of the three lawyer members of the Appellate Commission, those practicing in the two major cities outnumber outstate attorneys in two of the three courts of appeals districts from which the laywer commissioners are chosen. Therefore this chapter concentrates on the politics of the Kansas City and St. Louis Bars relating to judicial selection.

The Development of Cleavages in the Missouri Metropolitan Bar

Before the 1930's there was only one bar association in Kansas City and in St. Louis,[1] but lawyers in both communities developed schisms in their ranks during the depression period. Accounts indicate that a fight over the enforcement of canons of legal ethics (a matter that has caused difficulties in other metropolitan areas as well)[2] triggered the

---

[1] The Bar Association of St. Louis was established in 1874. See *The Bench and Bar of Missouri: History of the Bar Associations of St. Louis and Missouri* (St. Louis: The St. Louis Star, 1899), p. 7. The exact date of the formation of the Kansas City Bar Association is undetermined, but Roscoe Pound notes in his study, *The Lawyer from Antiquity to Modern Times* (St. Paul: West Publishing Company, 1953), at p. 315, that it was listed in an official report of the American Bar Association issued in 1887.

[2] Jerome Carlin deals with problems of legal ethics in Chicago in *Lawyers on Their Own* (New Brunswick: Rutgers Univ. Press, 1962), and in New York City in *Lawyers' Ethics: A Survey of the New York City Bar* (New York: Russel Sage Foundation, 1966).

split. A concerted campaign against "ambulance chasers" and criminal attorneys by certain leaders of the Kansas City and St. Louis Bar Associations, polarized the Bar in both cities. Lined up on one side of the issue were "plaintiffs'" lawyers (those representing injured persons in personal injury cases) and on the other side were "defendants'" lawyers (those having as clients the parties—primarily insurance companies and business concerns—being sued). Included as allies of the former were criminal attorneys; joining the ranks of the latter group were lawyers representing primarily corporations, particularly established economic institutions such as railroads, banks, insurance companies, and public utilities, in all kinds of legal matters, not just those involving personal injury cases.[3]

As a result of this cleavage in the Bar, a power struggle took place in the bar associations in both cities, with the plaintiffs' group seeking to gain influence at the expense of the established defendants' attorneys who had traditionally been in control of both organizations. In the case of the Kansas City Bar Association the plaintiffs' lawyers won the battle by joining the Association in numbers and, once in, they won its leadership positions. This caused the defendants' group to bolt the organization and form a new one called the Lawyers' Association of Kansas City. On the opposite side of the state the reverse situation occurred; the St. Louis Bar Association "establishment" succeeded in excluding many plaintiffs' lawyers from its membership altogether and maintained firm control over the key offices of the organization. This led the plaintiffs' attorneys there to form another organization, known as the Lawyers' Association of St. Louis. The end result of these developments was the division of the Bar in both communities, with the plaintiffs' lawyers in control of the Kansas City Bar Association and the Lawyers' Association of St. Louis, and the defendants' attorneys in the driver's seat of the St. Louis Bar Association and the newly formed Lawyers' Association of Kansas City.

This division of the Metropolitan Bar has had direct relevance for judicial selection in Missouri over the years. In the late 1930's, when the elective system was still in effect, the two St. Louis associations conducted separate bar polls which often resulted in the voters' securing conflicting advice from the legal profession concerning the more qualified candidates for the Bench. When the campaign for the adoption of the Nonpartisan Court Plan was launched, leaders of the defendants' orga-

---

[3] Some lawyers refer to this latter group as "defendants'" lawyers while others prefer to be more precise and call them "corporation" attorneys. In any event all parties agree that they belong with the defendants' group insofar as this division within the Bar is concerned.

nizations in both cities campaigned for its adoption, but their counterparts in the plaintiffs' groups generally opposed it.[4] Once the Plan was adopted the rivalry between the Bar and Lawyers' Association in each metropolitan community shifted so as to take place within the framework of the new selection system, with the respective bar groups backing separate candidates in the lawyer elections as discussed subsequently in this chapter.

Present-Day Divisions in the Kansas City and St. Louis Bars

These historical developments give us some important clues concerning the kinds of cleavages in the legal community which have had an impact on judicial selection in Missouri. They suggest that the plaintiff-defendant dichotomy has been a key factor in the polarization of the Metropolitan Bar. With this as a starting point, we extended our current analysis to a broad exploration of the differences between the attorneys in the respective bar associations in the two communities. In doing so we found that certain concepts developed by students of the sociology of the legal profession relating to "styles" of law practice[5] were very relevant to our study. As social and economic differences between Republicans and Democrats serve to illuminate the nature of our general party system, so similar distinctions between Bar and Lawyers' Association lawyers help explain the nature of the "two party" system that has developed in the metropolitan legal community for electing representatives to the judicial nominating commissions.

We gathered our data for this analysis from two major sources. The first was a series of personal interviews with attorneys in both communities whom we thought would have the best insight into the schism in the Bar: officers of the respective Bar and Lawyers' Associations, prominent plaintiffs', defendants', and corporation lawyers, and certain essentially "neutral" members of the legal profession whose practices tended to remove them somewhat from the conflict. We supplemented

---

[4] Peltason, *op. cit.*, Chapter III.
[5] The major studies utilized were Carlin, *Lawyers on Their Own, op. cit.*; his *Current Research in the Sociology of the Legal Profession* (New York: Bureau of Applied Social Research, Columbia University, August, 1962, mimeographed); Erwin Smigel, *The Wall Street Lawyer* (London: Free Press of Glencoe, 1964); and two articles by Jack Ladinsky, "Careers of Lawyers, Law Practice and Legal Institutions," *American Sociological Review*, 28 (February, 1963), 47–54, and "The Impact of Social Background of Lawyers on Law Practice and the Law," *The Journal of Legal Education*, 16 (December, 1963), 127–144. Richard Wells refers to these studies as relating to "styles" of practice in "The Legal Profession and Politics," *Midwest Journal of Political Science*, VIII (May, 1964), 166–190.

this information with data elicited in a mailed questionnaire to a sample survey of the Missouri Bar.[6]

The first facet of differences in the bar associations we explored related to specialties of legal practice. Our interviews indicated that the plaintiffs'-defendants' split that led to the establishment of the two associations in both Kansas City and St. Louis is still salient in Bar circles. In fact, it has been exacerbated in recent years by the formation of the National Association of Claimants' and Compensation Attorneys, an organization designed to make personal injury lawyers more effective opponents of attorneys representing employers and insurance companies.[7] The aggressive policies of this national interest group[8] and its affiliate Missouri state chapter serve to rally the plaintiffs' lawyers (the "NACCA" and "MACCA" men) and to alarm the defendants' attorneys,[9] a development that naturally intensifies the rivalries of the two segments of the Kansas City and St. Louis Bars. We also were told that the basic division of the plaintiffs' and defendants' lawyers into the respective associations still persists, although a spokesman for the defense attorneys in the St. Louis area volunteered the information that many of their group had joined the Lawyers' Association there in recent years "to keep an anchor on the plaintiffs' boys to prevent them from completely taking over the organization."

We also expanded our analyses beyond the plaintiff-defendant dichot-

---

[6] Since the Missouri Bar is integrated, we were able to use the membership of the State Bar Association as our "population." In May of 1964, we mailed a questionnaire to every other member of the Bar (3303 of 6606) and received 1233 replies, a 37 percent response. This means that almost one-fifth of the lawyers in the state are included in our sample. Moreover, a comparison of the sample with the total population of Missouri lawyers analyzed in *The 1964 Lawyer Statistical Report* (Chicago: American Bar Foundation, 1965) indicates that it is very representative on such characteristics as geographical location of practice, law school education, and kind of practice arrangement. The age composition of the sample also reflects that of the State Bar with the exception that older lawyers are slightly underrepresented. See the Appendix for a further discussion of the sample survey.

[7] The organization was established in Portland, Oregon in 1946 by 11 men, and 6 years later had a membership of 2000 lawyers located in every state in the nation. One of the leaders of the group, Samuel B. Horowitz, explains its origins, purposes and activities in "NACCA and Its Objectives," *NACCA Law Journal*, 10 (1953), 17–43. Recently the name of the organization has been changed to the American Trial Lawyers Association.

[8] In addition to the publication of its journal, NACCA has been active in establishing lectureships at law schools, writing articles for law reviews, developing a library on the rights of injured workers, and lobbying before legislative bodies. See Horowitz, *ibid.*, 25 ff.

[9] For an article expressing this concern, see Robert P. Hobson, "NACCA—As Viewed by Defense Counsel," *Kentucky State Bar Journal*, 20 (1956), 170–172.

omy to ascertain other differences in practice specialties associated with Bar and Lawyers' Association memberships. We wanted to determine whether the corporation lawyers still ally themselves with the defendants' counsel (as was true with the 1930's) and whether criminal law specialists continue to join forces with plaintiffs' attorneys as they had done when both groups were targets of the legal ethics campaign in the depression years. We also explored the possibility that other practice specialties that divide the legal profession were relevant, that is, whether lawyers handling domestic relations and labor matters for unions tend to identify with the plaintiffs' attorneys, whereas probate and trust lawyers find common cause with those on the defendants' side of the Bar schism.

Our source of data to test these matters—as well as others that follow—is the sample survey referred to above. Lawyers were asked to indicate the bar associations they belonged to, and on this basis, the respondents in the Kansas City and St. Louis areas were each divided into two groups: the Bar Association and the Lawyers' Association.[10] Information on practice specialty was elicited by an inquiry requesting each lawyer to select, from a list of ten possibilities, the fields (up to three) in which he had earned most of his income or salary since being admitted to practice.[11] Table 1.1 shows the way in which the specialties are divided between the bar groups in each city.

Table 1.1 indicates that in general the practice specialty divisions are as anticipated. Plaintiffs' lawyers constitute a greater proportion of the memberships of the Kansas City Bar Association and the Lawyers' Association of St. Louis than of their rival associations; the defendants' attorneys tend to be a more important group in the Kansas City Lawyers' Association than in the Bar Association of that city. The latter pattern

---

[10] Although there were a considerable number of lawyers in each community who belonged to both the Bar Association and the Lawyers' Association, those with overlapping memberships were similar in characteristics to those belonging to the Lawyers' Association alone. Combining the two groups, therefore, does not distort the analysis, and we did this under the category of Lawyers' Association. Apparently, as our interviews seem to indicate, the decision to join the "rebel" organization (the Lawyers' Association in each city) represents the important associational commitment on the part of a lawyer, and a simultaneous membership in the older, official Bar Association tends to be a matter of tradition and form.

[11] In addition to the ones discussed in this chapter, the fields included real property, municipal and administrative law, and negligence and/or compensation, equally for plaintiff and defendant. In developing the list, we were guided by the approach to this same subject in an official State Bar Study entitled, The Missouri Bar— Prentice-Hall Survey: A Motivational Study of Public Attitudes and Law Office Management, 1963.

TABLE 1.1

DISTRIBUTION OF SELECTED FIELDS OF LEGAL PRACTICE AMONG
MEMBERS OF MAJOR BAR ORGANIZATION IN KANSAS CITY
AND ST. LOUIS AREAS (Percent)

Field of Practice[a]	(Plaintiffs') Kansas City Bar Association (N = 137)	(Defendants') Lawyers' Association of Kansas City (N = 178)	(Plaintiffs') Lawyers' Association of St. Louis (N = 157)	(Defendants') St. Louis Bar Association (N = 260)
Plaintiffs'	44	10	43	12
Defendants'	9	23	18	17
Corporation	34	55	31	52
Domestic relations	20	6	20	7
Criminal	11	1	8	2
Probate and trust	27	36	35	41
Labor	3	2	5	2

[a] Includes lawyers listing the field exclusively or as one of the two or three major fields of their practice.

is not a true one, however, with respect to the St. Louis Bar organizations, and apparently there is some inclination for defense attorneys also to join the Lawyers' Association there today, as suggested in our interviews. The corporation lawyers identify with the defendants' bar groups, and the attorneys handling domestic relations and criminal matters identify with the plaintiffs' associations. The remaining specialty divisions explored—probate and trust, and labor—are in the directions expected; that is, lawyers with probate and trust practice tend to side with the defendants' bar groups and lawyers with a labor practice side with the plaintiffs' bar groups, but the differences are not so marked. The survey data also indicate that lawyers representing unions constitute a very small group in the total practice picture.[12]

Although an analysis of the Bar along practice specialty lines gives some valuable clues into significant cleavages in the profession, it also has some distinct limitations. As Table 1.1 indicates, many lawyers do not concentrate all their practice in one field. This means that these

---

[12] A recent article, "The Lawyers of Labor," *Fortune* (March, 1961), 213, estimates that about 500 American attorneys serve unions, either as salaried "house counsel" or as lawyers in private practice who are on a retainer fee. *The 1964 Lawyer Statistical Report, op. cit.,* p. 26, sets the total number of lawyers in the United States in 1963 as 296,069.

attorneys cannot be neatly categorized on this basis.[13] Moreover, some of the specialties are broad, and obscure important distinctions between kinds of practices included within them; for example, some attorneys with a corporate and business practice represent huge corporations, whereas others service partnerships or individual concerns. Likewise, the size of decedents' estates handled by probate lawyers varies greatly. Other important distinctions can be made on the basis of the complexity of the tasks performed for a client: one lawyer may handle small routine matters for a corporation, whereas other lawyers may provide business concerns with complex advice involving a thorough knowledge of taxation and finance.

Perhaps the best index of the kinds of clients a lawyer services, and the complexity of the legal work he handles, is the organizational setting in which he practices law. The arrangements run the gamut from the solo practitioner (who has his own office or shares an office and common overhead expenses with other attorneys) to the array of partners and associates of the larger law firms. Lawyers we interviewed often cast the distinction between the members of the Bar and Lawyers' Associations in these terms. Moreover, such differences are particularly significant for a social analysis of the Bar in light of Carlin's finding in New York that the size of the firm was the "single most significant indicator of status" in the legal profession.[14]

Another factor generally related to social status is income. Although the practice of law ranks as one of the three most lucrative professions in our society,[15] there is a considerable disparity in earnings among lawyers.[16] Moreover, such income differentials have been identified as an important source of cleavage in the Bar.[17]

---

[13] Our survey data show, however, that lawyers tend to combine certain practice specialties such as corporate and probate and trust, and plaintiffs' and domestic relations.

[14] Carlin, Current Research in the Sociology of the Legal Profession, op. cit., p. 21.

[15] The Statistical Abstract of the United States, 1965 (Washington, D.C.: Bureau of the Census, U.S. Department of Commerce, 1965), p. 230, lists the median income of dentists, lawyers and physicians as over $10,000 a year. No other professional, technical or kindred occupation reaches that level.

[16] Ibid., p. 229, categorizes attorney's salaries in seven work levels in terms of duties and responsibilities. The average salaries of the seven levels range from $7248 to $24,288. Maurice Liebenburg in "Income of Lawyers in the Postwar Period," Survey of Current Business, XXXVI (December, 1956), 26 f., finds that in 1954 the medium income of lawyers in the United States was $7833, but one-third received incomes below $5000 and one-fifth over $15,000.

[17] Carlin in Current Research in the Sociology of the Legal Profession, op. cit., pp. 11 ff., and Ladinsky in his Journal of Legal Education article, loc. cit., 135 ff.

We gathered information on organizational setting for the practice of law and income in our sample survey to determine whether differences in these matters were relevant to Bar and Lawyers' Association memberships in both Kansas City and St. Louis. We asked each respondent to select, from among nine alternatives, the kind of practice arrangement in which he had spent most of his time since being admitted to practice.[18] The questionnaire also requested information on average yearly net income during the period of the last three years. Replies to these inquiries are categorized by bar association in Table 1.2.

Table 1.2 indicates the differences in the practice arrangements of members of the rival bar associations in both communities. The disparities are greatest at the opposite ends of the private practice spectrum, that is, between solo attorneys and those in large firms. The former dominate the plaintiffs' associations and the latter (both partners and associates) identify with the defendants' bar groups. The differences in size of firm are most evident when partnerships reach the size of six or more. In fact, the smaller firms, those with two to five partners, are represented fairly equally in the respective bar associations. Lawyers not in private practice, that is, those working for corporations or government agencies, also fail to identify clearly with either bar group, and whatever preferences do exist for the former group differ between the two cities.

Income differentials are relevant for the Kansas City bar group divisions, although they are not quite as pronounced as those relating to size of firm. The attorneys with the more affluent practices tend to be concentrated in the Lawyers' Association. Twice as many of them as Bar Association members earn $20,000 a year or more and fewer have net incomes below $10,000. The same situation does not apply, however, in the St. Louis area. The distribution of incomes below $10,000, $10,000 to $20,000, and above $20,000 are almost identical between members

---

analyze income as a factor in the stratification of the Bars of New York City and Detroit, respectively. Henderson and Sinclair in their study, *Judicial Selection in Texas: An Exploratory Study*, University of Houston Studies in Social Science (Houston: Public Affairs Research Center, 1964), Vol. 1, at p. 17, identify the disparity in incomes of lawyers in Texas as a source of cleavage in the urban Bar there.

[18] We elicited similar information on the practice arrangement of each respondent during the past year, but there was almost no variation between the two kinds of data. This accords with the findings of Carlin in *Current Research in the Sociology of the Legal Profession, op. cit.*, pp. 16 ff., and Ladinsky, in his *Journal of Legal Education* article, *loc. cit.*, 132 ff., that lawyers' career histories show that they tend to remain in the same general social strata of the Bar in which they begin the practice of law.

TABLE 1.2
LAW PRACTICE ARRANGEMENT AND INCOME OF MEMBERS OF MAJOR BAR ORGANIZATIONS IN KANSAS CITY AND ST. LOUIS AREAS (Percent)

Characteristic	(Plaintiffs') Kansas City Bar Association (N = 137)	(Defendants') Lawyers' Association of Kansas City (N = 178)	(Plaintiffs') Lawyers' Association of St. Louis (N = 157)	(Defendants') St. Louis Bar Association (N = 260)
Arrangement				
Solo practice	36	14	47	16
Two man partnership	14	11	12	7
Partnership 3–5	12	11	17	14
Partnership 6–9	4	9	4	10
Partnership 10–19	1	12	1	6
Partnership 20 or more	0	8	0	3
Salaried employee— law firm[a]	9	17	6	20
Salaried employee— corporation	12	9	7	12
Salaried employee— government	5	2	4	4
Not ascertained	7	7	2	8
Total	100	100	100	100
Income				
Less than $5,000	7	1	6	4
$5,000–$9,999	22	17	20	22
$10,000–$14,999	26	25	22	21
$15,000–$19,999	24	14	15	17
$20,000–$29,999	14	24	21	14
$30,000–$49,999	5	13	12	15
$50,000 and above	0	3	2	3
Not ascertained	2	3	2	4
Total	100	100	100	100

[a] Generally referred to in Missouri as associates.

of the two associations there. Thus practice arrangement is a more important factor than income for bar association identification in both metropolitan communities.

We explored two other factors pertaining to social status—partisan affiliation and education—to determine whether they have any relevance for the associational cleavages in the Metropolitan Bar. Some of our interviewees, particularly on the plaintiffs' side of the Bar, saw the differences in the bar groups in partisan terms, and linked Republicanism to what they termed a "silk stocking" practice (i.e., a high status practice). Few persons commented on law school ties in our interviews, but students of the sociology of the legal profession have found this to be an important factor differentiating elements of the Bar.[19] Data on these matters, elicited in our questionnaire,[20] are categorized by bar group in Table 1.3.

This table indicates that there are far more Republicans in the Lawyers' Association of Kansas City and the St. Louis Bar Association than there are in the rival bar groups in which Democrats predominate. The fact that half or more of the members of the former organizations identify with the Republican party is significant in a state as Democratic as Missouri has been in recent years.[21] The data also show that the number of political independents in any of the groups is negligible, indicating that at least in these two metropolitan areas lawyers are party identifiers.[22]

The education data demonstrate that differences in kinds of law schools attended, which lawyers and sociologists have considered important, are also very relevant for the Bar divisions. The contrasts are greatest in the Kansas City area where almost one half of the members of the Lawyers' Association there attended law school outside the state, about 24 percent of them at one of the five prestigious "national" schools of Chicago, Columbia, Harvard, Michigan, and Yale.[23] On the other

---

[19] Carlin, *Current Research in the Sociology of the Legal Profession, op. cit.*, pp. 25 ff.; Ladinsky, *American Sociological Review, loc. cit.*, 49 ff.; David Riesman, "Law and Sociology: Recruitment, Training, and Colleagueship" in William M. Evan (ed.) *Law and Sociology: Exploratory Essays* (The Free Press of Glencoe, 1962), p. 12 f.

[20] In eliciting information on party identification, we patterned our approach after that utilized by the Survey Research Center at the University of Michigan.

[21] A state-wide survey conducted in the Spring of 1965 by the Public Opinion Survey Unit at the University of Missouri showed that 60 percent of Missourians identify with the Democratic party, compared to 26 percent who are Republicans. The large urban centers of the state are somewhat more Democratic: in Jackson County, the percentage ratio is 64 to 20, and in the St. Louis area (St. Louis City and St. Louis County combined), it is 62 to 24.

[22] The above survey also revealed that about 10 percent of persons living in the two large urban areas in Missouri, as well as the state as a whole, consider themselves Independents. The Survey Research Center's 1964 study showed an identical figure for the national population. See Hugh Bone, *American Politics and the Party System*, 3rd ed. (New York: McGraw-Hill, 1965), p. 480.

[23] We realize there is no completely satisfactory criteria by which to evaluate law schools. We decided on these five on the basis of general reputation. Moreover, it is an objective fact that the latter four law schools, as of 1954 at least, had the largest law libraries in the nation. Albert P. Blaustein and Charles O. Porter, *The American Lawyer* (Chicago: University of Chicago Press, 1954), p. 206.

TABLE 1.3

PARTISAN AFFILATION AND LEGAL EDUCATION OF MEMBERS
OF MAJOR BAR ORGANIZATIONS IN KANSAS CITY
AND ST. LOUIS AREAS (Percent)

Characteristics	(Plaintiffs') Kansas City Bar Association (N = 137)	(Defendants') Lawyers' Association of Kansas City (N = 178)	(Plaintiffs') Lawyers' Association of St. Louis (N = 157)	(Defendants') St. Louis Bar Association (N = 260)
Party Affiliation				
Republican	19	41	24	44
Independent Republican	6	8	8	10
Democrat	63	41	54	35
Independent Democrat	6	3	9	7
Independents	3	2	3	2
Not ascertained	3	5	2	2
Total	100	100	100	100
Law School				
Instate				
University of Missouri	29	24	4	9
Washington University	4	2	31	41
St. Louis University	2	1	39	21
Kansas City	44	19	0	0
Other instate schools	0	0	12	1
Outstate				
Prestige law schools[a]	5	24	2	16
Other outstate schools	14	24	5	7
Not ascertained	2	6	7	5
Total	100	100	100	100

[a] Chicago, Columbia, Harvard, Michigan, and Yale.

hand, nearly one half of the Bar Association members got their legal education at a distinctly local law school, the University of Kansas City,[24] which is today an approved law school with a mixed program (i.e., both night and day classes)[25] but which, until the mid-1930's, was a

---

[24] Recently this law school, along with the University itself, was absorbed into the University of Missouri system. It is now known as the University of Missouri Law School at Kansas City.

[25] Such law schools are sometimes called "multiple division" law schools and frequently just "night" law schools. In 1963, about 90 percent of the students enrolled in schools not approved by the American Bar Association were attending night classes compared to less than 10 percent in morning classes. See *Law Schools*

"proprietary" law school not sanctioned by the American Bar Association.[26] In the St. Louis area the differences are not as great, but more Bar Association members there also go out of state for their legal education, particularly to the prestigious national schools. Also, there are important distinctions between St. Louis lawyers who were educated in local schools. The Bar Association attorneys are more likely to have gone to Washington University, a full-time school, and Lawyers' Association members to St. Louis University, a Catholic school with a mixed program,[27] or to one of the unapproved proprietary night law schools which were formerly located in the St. Louis area.[28]

Thus our study of the memberships of the rival bar associations in both Kansas City and St. Louis indicates that they generally vary in such factors as practice specialty, income, party affiliation, practice arrangement, and legal education, with the latter two factors showing the most pronounced differences. This is significant, since size of firm and kind of law school attended are the important indicators of social status in the legal profession.[29] Moreover, a separate analysis of the backgrounds of the officers of the four associations over the period of the last twenty-five years[30] shows that the leaders of the rebel bar groups are even more likely to possess distinct status characteristics than the rank-and-file members of their organizations; for example, 39 percent of the officers of the Kansas City Lawyers' Association attended one of the five prestige law schools compared with 24 percent of its general membership. Similarly, 67 percent of the leaders of the Lawyers' Associa-

---

and Bar Admission Requirements in the United States in the *U.S. Review of Legal Education* (Chicago: American Bar Association, Section of Legal Education and Admissions to the Bar, 1963), p. 19.

[26] Proprietary law schools were generally founded as private profit-making institutions, but today many are incorporated not for profit. They have no University affiliation. See Carlin, *Lawyers on Their Own, op. cit.,* p. 26. The Kansas City School of Law was not approved by the American Bar Association until it became affiliated with the University of Kansas City.

[27] Carlin includes Catholic and proprietary schools with "mixed" programs in the same category in his analysis of law schools, *ibid.,* p. 25.

[28] Today all the law schools in Missouri are approved by the ABA, but in the depression period a number of unapproved schools operated in St. Louis, including Benton College of Law, City College of Law and Finance and Missouri Institute of Accounting, Law and Law Department.

[29] See footnotes 14 and 19, *supra.* Of course, the two factors are interrelated. The processes of self-selection and firm recruitment result in graduates of prestige law schools joining law firms. See Ladinsky, *American Sociological Review, loc. cit.,* 49; Blaustein and Porter, *op. cit.,* p. 197; Smigel, *op. cit.,* pp. 39 ff.

[30] A yearly publication by Martindale-Hubbel, Inc., contains certain basic data on lawyers in all states. Volume II has the information on Missouri attorneys.

tion of St. Louis have been single practitioners, whereas only 47 percent of the members of that group practice law by themselves. The analysis also showed that the officialdoms of the rival bar groups were distinct, since lawyers serve in official positions in only one of the two associations in their community.[31] The way in which these Bar leaders rally the support of their respective members in the election of lawyer members of the nominating commissions is discussed in the next section.

The Campaigns for Lawyer Seats on the Nominating Commissions

As with elections generally, the contests for lawyer seats on the judicial nominating commissions in Missouri are shaped by three major factors. The first is the set of legal rules that provides the framework under which the elections are conducted. The second is what Key calls the "standards of campaign etiquette,"[32] that is, what the particular political culture feels is and is not proper in the realm of politics. In this case, of course, the standards are set not by the society at large but by a special segment of it: the legal profession itself. Finally, there is the nature of the constituency (in this case, the members of the Bar), who collectively form the electorate for these contests. Campaigns aimed at this target must necessarily take into account the nature of the various divisions of the profession, just as political leaders analyze the various groupings in the general electorate. These three factors constitute the "givens" of the electoral situation, and thus dictate the nature of the strategies employed in the contests for the lawyer seats on the nominating commissions.

The legal rules for the elections[33] provide that lawyer candidates for both the circuit and appellate commissions must be nominated by petition. Since only 20 signatures are necessary,[34] there is the possibility of having several candidates for a position. However, the nature of the Bar rivalries has become so institutionalized that, at least since the period of the early 1950's, there have been only two candidates in each election, one representing the Bar Association and one the Lawyers' Association, in both Kansas City and St. Louis. Each group has evolved

---

[31] Of the 138 individuals we identified as officers in the two bar groups of Kansas City, only 3 held office in both; a similar number of officers of the two associations in St. Louis contained only 2 individuals who had served as officers in both organizations.

[32] V. O. Key, Jr., *Politics, Parties and Pressor Groups* (New York: Thomas Y. Crowell Co., 1964), p. 463.

[33] *Constitution of the State of Missouri*, 1945, Art. V, Sec. 29 (d) and Supreme Court Rule 10.

[34] In appellate commission contests, at least 10 of the signatures must be attorneys residing in a different judicial circuit than the nominee. Supreme Court Rule 10.10.

a practice of nominating its candidate in a caucus, usually attended by officers of the association and other Bar "actives" outside the formal power structure. These meetings are not official because, as one interviewee explained, "Lawyers are an independent group and would resent any formal endorsement of either side." Nevertheless, word goes out about the man who will represent each group in the election, and organizational loyalty is sufficient to prevent other nominations that would split the vote of members of the association. It is particularly important that this eventuality be avoided, since it may lead to the opposition group's candidate receiving the necessary majority vote on the first ballot or force a run-off election[35] with its attendant uncertainties.

The selection of a nominee is governed by certain general principles of "availability." As in our general party system, each association starts with certain "hard-core" supporters. One group can count generally on the loyalty of solo practitioners, educated in local law schools with a plaintiffs' practice or one involving domestic relations or criminal matters. The other draws its followers primarily from the ranks of attorneys from the larger firms, many of whom have been educated at outstate, prestige law schools who specialize in corporate or defense work. But, as discussed in the next section, the system is a highly competitive one, and each group must be concerned with attracting the support of those in the middle of the Bar spectrum, that is, the attorneys who are not committed to either group. The concern with the "vital center" of the profession is revealed in the tendency of three of the four bar associations to draw their candidates particularly from lawyers in the smaller firms.[36]

The closeness of the contests puts a premium on selecting a candidate who not only avoids the negative feature of having an "extremist" kind of practice but also possesses positive availability qualities. It is especially important that he be widely known in the profession. There is the danger that a group's leaders will become myopic and assume that a man well-known in their legal circles will have a wide acquaintanceship in the Bar at large. This is a particular hazard for defendants' organizations, which may fail to take into account that "office" lawyers, who seldom appear in court, may have only a fairly close-knit group of lawyer friends and that their contacts with many members of the profession may be nonexistent or may occur only through the highly impersonal medium of a telephone conversation at which clients' affairs are discussed. Some observers of a recent circuit commission contest

---

[35] Supreme Court Rule 10.14.
[36] The exception is the Lawyers' Association of St. Louis which tends to nominate lawyers in solo practice.

felt that this was a strategic error that contributed to the defeat of the defendants' candidate in that election.

The groups often select trial attorneys as their candidates because lawyers with this kind of a practice have a wide acquaintanceship in the profession involving "face-to-face" contact with a number of attorneys. Lawyers also look favorably on such candidacies because they feel that trial attorneys with extensive courtroom experience may be in the best position to evaluate the merits of prospective judges and that, therefore, they should sit on the nominating commissions. At the same time, the best trial attorneys are often those who are the toughest fighters in the courtroom, and there is the risk that if such a person is selected, his candidacy will not be favored by attorneys whom he not only has bested but, more importantly, has "worked over" or belittled in court.[37] Thus a premium is placed on selecting a person who is both a trial attorney—and a gentleman.

Other factors affect how well-known an attorney is in the profession. He should have been in the practice long enough to have come in contact with a number of attorneys. For that reason, young lawyers are generally excluded as candidates, as are attorneys with a specialized practice that puts them in contact with only a relatively few members of the profession. It is helpful if an attorney has been active in bar association work in which he has been exposed to a wide range of his fellow lawyers. This is particularly important in appellate commission races in which attorneys living outside the two major cities have the franchise. Attorneys active in the Missouri Bar Association are more likely to be known to the "outstate" lawyers, as are attorneys with appellate court practices that put them into courtroom contact with lawyers in all parts of the appellate court jurisdiction.

As availability factors affect the kinds of candidates that are nominated, so Bar folkways shape the character of the campaign for the commission posts. There is a strong tradition that the position shall seek the man: all the candidates we interviewed stressed the fact that others had come and asked them to make the race. Many said they agreed to do so only on the understanding that they would not have to do any campaigning. Part of the reluctance to do so is based on a concern with the time a personal campaign takes from the individual's law practice. Beyond this, there is something repugnant to some lawyers about "politicking" for a position they feel should be decided on the basis of legal ability. This is particularly true of persons on

---

[37] Henderson and Sinclair, *op. cit.*, p. 16, note the same courtroom animosities among Texas lawyers.

the defendants' side of the Bar. Plaintiffs' attorneys are less sensitive about pushing themselves forward, perhaps because they are more used to hustling for legal work than are firm lawyers with a more stable clientele.[38]

In the early days of the Plan some candidates enjoyed such popularity and stature in the profession that no concerted campaign was necessary to ensure their election to the commission. However, the increasing specialization in the law, as well as the sheer growth in the number of lawyers practicing in both communities, tends to circumscribe legal acquaintanceships; this means it is difficult for any individual to be so widely known as to be in that erstwhile position. The realities of Metropolitan Bar politics today require that the candidate's supporters, if not himself, take to the legal "hustings." Usually this involves solicitation of votes through personal contacts, telephone conversations and, particularly in appellate commission races, communication by letter with fellow members of the Bar. One appellate commission candidate on the defendants' side complained, however, that his opponent in a recent race had almost beaten him by throwing cocktail and beer parties to gain support and that if he had it to do over again he would wage a vigorous campaign. Thus the aggressive tactics of the plaintiffs' group may be bringing about some important changes in the traditional rules of campaign etiquette.

Since the two sides draw their support from different elements of the profession, their campaign techniques differ. Over the years, the defendants' side has possessed certain electoral advantages. One is that, traditionally, more leaders of the Bar have come from this side of the legal constituency. This fact has led the defendants to use "endorsements" as a campaign device. (The word is passed that certain pillars of the Bar are supporting a particular candidate with the idea that this will swing the votes of some of the doubtful lawyers.) Another lies in the concentration of their hard-core support in the large law offices where it can be tapped with a minimum of effort.[39] Senior partners

---

[38] Plaintiffs' lawyers' business is generally on a "one shot" basis, that is, individuals who come to see them just once in connection with a personal injury. (See Carlin, *Lawyers on Their Own, op. cit.,* Chapter 3, for a discussion of methods of getting this business through the use of "brokers" or "middlemen" such as policemen, ambulance drivers, and the like.) In contrast, corporate and defendants' attorneys generally do their legal business on a long-term basis, often through "retainer" fees whereby clients pay to have time reserved for their affairs.

[39] For an analysis of the way in which shop size in the printing industry affects the internal politics of the two party system of the International Typographical Union, see Seymour Lipset, Martin Trow and James Coleman, *Union Democracy* (Free Press of Glencoe, 1956), Chapters 8 and 9.

of law firms often act as precinct captains in the campaigns. As one explained, "I'm the Bar Association's representative in our office, and it is my job to line up the support of the other senior as well as junior members of the firm." The ecology of the law offices is also such that the firms themselves are fairly well concentrated geographically in the heart of the central city business district, and this also minimizes campaign "leg-work."

In contrast to this situation the electoral support of the plaintiffs' groups lies with the isolated single practitioner or small firm lawyer, which means that precinct captains cannot be called upon to "deliver" the vote. Moreover, the offices are frequently scattered geographically, not only in the downtown area but also in the outlying neighborhoods where more solo attorneys and small firms are now locating. Thus a special effort is required to marshal their votes through such devices as dividing up buildings by floors among campaign workers or utilizing telephone campaigns based upon divisions of the Bar directory. The endorsement device is not utilized by the plaintiffs' lawyers because they lack the leaders with the traditional standing in the profession, and also because such a "silk stocking" device runs counter to the "democratic" philosophy of some members of the "little man's" segment of the profession.

Both sides use the campaign technique of lining up the support of "fellow travelers," that is, members of the Bar who are engaged in other pursuits besides the private practice of law but who are generally sympathetic to their respective causes. Thus the plaintiffs' lawyers contact government attorneys involved in such matters as workmen's compensation, and those on the legal staffs of labor unions, as potential allies. The defendants' associations look to lawyers working in claims departments of insurance companies and to house counsel of corporations for support in the elections. As one defense attorney put it, "There are twenty lawyers on the legal staff of Monsanto Chemical who represent potential allies for us." Defense-firm clients such as industrial corporations, banks, and public utilities, who employ lawyers in nonlegal work, are also frequently asked to solicit their support for the defendants' candidate. Lawyers operating on the periphery of the profession are less likely than private practitioners to be interested in Bar activities[40] from which basic loyalties arise, and hence both sides make special

---

[40] An analysis of the respondents from both communities who do not belong to either the Bar Association or the Lawyers' Association in their area shows that a considerable number of them are employed by the government or by private corporations.

efforts to get out their vote in the lawyer elections. The results of these elections over the years, together with the "stakes" or "payoffs" involved in them, are discussed in the next section.

The "Stakes" or "Payoffs" of Lawyer Elections for the Commissions

Although normally both groups field candidates for the lawyer elections, on occasion there is no contest when some candidate runs unopposed for a seat on the commission. This does not appear to result from any prior negotiation between the rival organizations. What seems to be more prevalent is for a group, seeking to win the "middle" segment of the Bar, to put up a candidate who turns out to be acceptable to the other side. This may occur because the latter group feels it has no real chance of defeating the candidate, and so, to avoid the chance of antagonizing him, enters no nominee against him. Or they may feel that he really is neutral in the plaintiffs'-defendants' rivalry and go along with his candidacy on that basis. Moreover, there are some attorneys who, even though they clearly have a plaintiffs' or defendants' practice, acquire a reputation for fair-mindedness and hence are acceptable to the other side. This is most likely to happen if such a lawyer goes out of his way to cultivate friendships and socialize with his courtroom opposition. The "eras of good feeling" in Bar politics are rare, however, as we were able to uncover only three unopposed candidacies since the elections began a quarter of a century ago.

The results generally reveal the presence of a competitive situation in both communities. In Kansas City, of the six contested races for the circuit commission, which occurred during our period of study, the Lawyers' Association candidate emerged victorious on four occasions and the Bar Association man won twice. In St. Louis the scales were tipped slightly in the opposite direction: the Lawyers' Association nominee won six times as compared with five victories for the Bar Association. (Deaths and resignations of commissioners in the St. Louis community have necessitated holding more elections there than has been true in Kansas City.) Our investigation of the appellate commission elections indicates, however, that the defendants' groups do somewhat better at this level than they do for circuit commission races. They have won two of the three clear-cut contests in Kansas City, and three of the four in the St. Louis Court of Appeals district.

The relatively few elections that occur under the Plan make it difficult to assess definite trends, but the plaintiffs' group has been winning more in recent elections. Some attorneys attribute this to NACCA and MACCA, which serve as important organizational ralliers of the plaintiff's

lawyers. These interest groups have thus provided the single practitioners and the small firm lawyers with a leadership and *esprit de corps*
they formerly lacked. Moreover, the high professional quality of the
activities of these organizations, together with the rise in size of judgments awarded in personal injury cases, have made plaintiffs' work more
respectable and more lucrative that it used to be.[41] All these factors
have contributed to strengthening the cause of the plaintiffs' lawyers.

There are also some indications that the legal rules for the elections
are working at the present time in favor of the plaintiffs' bar associations.
Under these rules lawyers serving on the commissions, as well as those
voting in the elections, must not only practice law in the court's jurisdiction but also must reside there.[42] Thus attorneys living in suburban
areas outside Jackson County and St. Louis City are disenfranchised
as candidates or voters in circuit court elections, and if they live across
state lines, they are similarly affected in appellate commission races.
All four bar groups are handicapped by these legal provisions, but our
survey data show that the defendants' organizations are affected more
because a greater proportion of their members live outside the jurisdictions of the circuit court in both metropolitan communities and, in the
Kansas City area, beyond the appellate court jurisdiction as well.[43]

Despite these developments favoring the plaintiff's organizations, the
defendants continue to do well in races for the appellate commission.[44]
The suburbanization process affects them less at that level, particularly
in the St. Louis area where few lawyers live outside the state. As previously suggested, attorneys active in Missouri Bar Association activities
with outstate reputations and acquaintanceships tend to make strong
candidates, and these persons have tended over the years to be more
associated with the defendants' than the plaintiffs' bar associations. Moreover, the type of law business of some of the larger firms is such that
the courts of appeals and Supreme Court arenas (the judges of whom
are nominated by the appellate commission) are far more important
to their clients' economic interests than are the circuit courts.[45] Hence

---

[41] A number of defendants' lawyers in the Kansas City area recently have begun
to also handle some plaintiffs' cases as well. This development has not yet occurred
to any significant extent in St. Louis. See Chapters 3 and 4 *infra*.

[42] *Constitution of the State of Missouri*, 1945, Art. V, Sec. 29 (d) and Supreme
Court Rule 10.14.

[43] Almost one-fifth of the membership of the Lawyers' Association of Kansas City
resides outside the state according to our survey data.

[44] A recent Kansas City Appellate Commission race, however, was won by the
plaintiffs' group.

[45] Carlin, *Current Research in the Sociology of the Legal Profession*, op. cit., at

they tend to place more emphasis on, and work harder in, the elections to the appellate nominating body than to the circuit one. It is the latter consideration that constitutes the "payoff" for the participants in the elections of lawyer members of the commission. The ultimate "stakes" in these contests are the judges that go on the circuit benches in Kansas City and St. Louis and the appellate courts of the entire state. Both sides seek to influence that decision by insuring that "their" kind of lawyers sit on the commissions that nominate the candidates from whom the governor makes his selection. Although some attorneys are interested in judgeships personally[46] and work to get commission members selected whom they think will favor their candidacies, most of them are concerned with "policy payoffs," not patronage (i.e., they want to get persons on the Bench who will be sympathetic, or at least not hostile, to their clients' interests).

As the developer and applier of rules of law, the judge shapes the outcome of litigation. This is particularly true in appellate cases and nonjury cases at the lower court level but, even when there is a jury that "finds the facts," the man on the bench has an important role to play in the lawsuit. The manner in which he interprets the "rules of the game" under which the trial proceedings are conducted often helps to tip the scales of justice in one direction or another; for example, the plaintiffs' lawyers seek to have the rules of evidence liberally construed so they can get the maximum evidence introduced into the lawsuit; defendants' lawyers hope that much of the evidence on which the plaintiff bases his case will be excluded by the court.

The struggle proceeds throughout the course of the lawsuit with important decisions made all along the way which affect the economic interests of the parties to the litigation. After the plaintiff's case is presented, will the judge grant the defendant's motion for a directed verdict in his favor or will he let the case go to the jury? After the arguments are heard what instructions will the judge give the jury? And after the jury has finally reached a verdict and assessed damages will the judge let the amount of the judgment stand or will he reduce it? The

---

p. 11 states that firm lawyers in New York City spend more time in appellate courts, while individual practitioners come in contact mainly with lower courts. Our survey data on appearances before circuit and appellate courts in Missouri indicate that the circuit courts are more important to members of the plaintiffs' bar associations and the appellate courts, to lawyers belonging to the defendants' bar groups.

[46] Our survey data show that about 10 percent of the attorneys practicing in both Kansas City and St. Louis have let their names come before one of the nominating commissions, for consideration as a judge.

discretion a judge has in decisions of this nature (a trial judge can, of course, be reversed on appeal, but the overwhelming proportion of cases end in the lower court)[47] makes the kind of person he is and the way he looks at such matters of vital concern to the parties to the litigation.

The "stakes" in the lawyer elections are most important to trial attorneys, particularly plaintiffs' and defendants' lawyers (i.e., those involved in personal injury litigation) because these cases constitute such a considerable share of the court docket, particularly at the trial court level.[48] However, attorneys who do little or no trial work must necessarily consider the kinds of judges who sit on the Bench, since conceivably their clients' affairs may become involved in litigation, even if they personally do not handle the case in court. Beyond this it would appear that the contests for the lawyers' seats on the commission entail other considerations besides the concrete stakes of judgeships. The elections also serve as an outlet for basic rivalries between the social divisions of the Bar previously discussed. The fact that the plaintiffs' and defendants' groups also contest for positions in the integrated state bar association,[49] in which the stakes are far less concrete than judgeships, would seem to bear out the supposition that frequently matters of prestige, rather than substance, are involved.[50]

The rivalry between the two bar groups is fed by the ideologies which each has developed to support its cause. Many lawyers we interviewed described the nature of the clash as one between "liberals" and "conservatives." (This is interesting since, as a group, lawyers often tend to resist generalizations and what they deem to be stereotyped thinking.) One defense attorney expressed it more precisely as "a battle between

---

[47] The Report of the Judicial Conference of Missouri for the period beginning June 16, 1966 and ending June 15, 1967 indicates that the Supreme Court and three intermediate Courts of Appeal handled 1527 cases, while the trial courts of the state disposed of 63,866 cases.

[48] For the first time, the 1966–1967 Report of the Judicial Conference showed the number of personal injury cases handled by the trial courts. (No similar information on appellate litigation was provided.) Of the total of 54,021 civil cases disposed of that year, 12,696 (or 22 percent) were personal injury ones. Of the total number of 13,297 civil cases that went to trial, 3858 (or 29 percent) involved personal injury litigation.

[49] The Missouri Bar was integrated by court order in 1944. For a general study of the subject, see Dayton McKean, *The Integrated Bar* (Boston: Houghton-Mifflin, 1963).

[50] It is only recently that the plaintiffs' lawyers have succeeded in having one of their group elected to the Presidency of the Missouri Bar Association. Although the President can conceivably affect the kinds of activities the Association carries on, most of our interviewees felt that this factor was not nearly so important to the plaintiffs' lawyers as the feeling that one of their men had "made it."

property interests and those who want to acquire property interests, but have not yet done so." Essentially, then, one side represents the "haves" and the other represents the "have nots." This is particularly true in personal injury litigation in which the injured party, often a person of modest means, is trying to collect damages from a corporation or insurance company.

In the process of representing their clients attorneys often are guilty of what Parsons calls the "sentimental exaggeration of substantive claims of clients."[51] As indicated by the above statement, defense and corporation attorneys are inclined to wax eloquent over the rights of property. One attorney we interviewed pointed out that one of the older members of his firm simply could not conceive of a legitimate plaintiff's claim, that all were simply attempts to get "something for nothing" by blackmailing established institutions into settling claims rather than bearing the cost and inconvenience of litigation. In contrast the plaintiffs' lawyer thinks of himself as protecting "the working man" or "little guy" against the "vested interests," particularly unscrupulous insurance companies and claims adjusters whom he feels try to get injured persons to settle claims out of court at far below their real value. He is more inclined to emphasize "human" rights than those of property. Thus both types of lawyer see the legal world through what might be termed "client-colored" glasses.

Many attorneys go further and view with hostility not only opposition parties but opposing counsel as well. The disparate styles of practice of the two major divisions of the Bar, and the fact that they have so little contact in the profession with each other,[52] lead them to regard each other with what one author calls "mutually derogating images."[53] Plaintiffs' lawyers are inclined to think of defendants' and corporation lawyers as "blue-bloods," or as individuals "without a heart" or "cold-blooded with a banker's icy stare," as one of our avid interviewees expressed it. They also criticize the defendants bar organizations as "exclusive clubs run by cliques," which restrict their memberships in contrast to their own "democratic" groups that accept everyone for membership who applies. Plaintiffs' lawyers are particularly scornful of corporation lawyers as "office" or "banker's attorneys" who "never try a law suit," an interesting twist on the business executive's contempt for anyone who has "never met a payroll."

---

[51] See his, "A Sociologist Looks at the Legal Profession" in a work edited by him entitled, *Essays in Sociological Theory* (Free Press of Glencoe, 1954), p. 377.
[52] Carlin, *Current Research in the Sociology of the Legal Profession, op. cit.,* at p. 19 discusses the lack of professional and social contact between the various strata of the New York Bar. The same general situation prevails in the two metropolitan communities in Missouri.
[53] Smigel, *op. cit.,* p. 173.

Defendants' and corporation lawyers are less inclined to condemn their opposition in social class terms, but many display a kind of patronizing attitude toward those who "have never quite made it in the profession." Moreover, they are openly contemptuous of lawyers who run "divorce mills" and, even more, of "ambulance chasers" (that is, attorneys who solicit clients through means that run counter to the canons of the profession).[54] Many accuse the plaintiffs' lawyers of exploiting their clients with contingent-fee arrangements.[55] Also there is some tendency for defendants' and corporation lawyers to categorize attorneys on the basis of the lawyers with whom they have practiced over the years; this brand of guilt by association means that professional sins of practitioners are often visited on their partners or associates.

All of these factors undoubtedly contribute to the greater interest that plaintiffs' lawyers take in the lawyer elections. As suggested previously, the concrete stakes of the kinds of judges who go on the court are very important to them in their trial practices. Beyond this, they feel what Carlin calls the "pinch of the status structure"[56] more keenly than other groups in the Bar. Frequently men of considerable ability and ambition, with lucrative practices, they are strongly motivated to compete in electoral contests with those they feel deny them their rightful place in the profession.

The analysis of lawyer elections under the Plan indicates that a competitive "two party system"[57] has emerged in both Kansas City and

---

[54] Missouri Supreme Court Rule 4.28 prohibits the stirring up of litigation directly or through agents. For a discussion of the problem of enforcing compliance with such canons of legal ethics, and the way in which the stratification of the Bar affects attitudes towards them, see Carlin, *Lawyers' Ethics: A Survey of the New York City Bar, op. cit.*, and Kenneth Reichstein, "Ambulance Chasing and the Legal Profession," *Social Problems*, 13 (Summer, 1965), 3–17.

[55] Under such arrangements, a lawyer receives a certain percentage (usually one-third in Missouri) of the judgment awarded his client; if none is awarded, he receives no fee.

[56] Carlin, *Lawyers on Their Own, op. cit.*, p. 182.

[57] It should be noted that the bar groups meet the criteria of parties and not mere "factions," since they are durable, visible, have not been dependent for their existence upon individual personalities or cliques, and represent important economic and social divisions in the Bar which are supported by conflicting ideologies. See V. O. Key Jr., *Southern Politics in State and Nation* (New York: Alfred A. Knopf, 1949) and William N. Chambers, *Political Parties in a New Nation: The American Experience* (New York: Oxford University Press, 1963), pp. 17–33.

The electoral results also meets the tests of a two-party system as defined in various categorizations of state parties on the basis of competitiveness. See Austin Ranney and Willmore Kendall, "The American Party Systems," *The American Politi-*

St. Louis. Rival bar organizations, representing distinct social status groups in the profession, nominate candidates and pursue techniques and strategies that are adapted to meet the campaign norms and electoral divisions of the lawyer constituency. The stakes of these elections for lawyers relate both to the perceived policy "payoffs" in terms of judges' rulings that affect their clients' economic interests and to symbolic "payoffs" for the contending bar groups involving matters of prestige and ideology.

These contests between bar groups over the selection of judges involve not only the legal profession but also broader societal interests. For one of the key conclusions to be drawn from this chapter is that lawyers' perspectives on judicial selection are shaped, to a great degree, by the kinds of clients they serve. Attorneys want certain kinds of judges on the bench who will interpret rules in a particular way because such matters affect their individual law practices. Generally, however, the matters that advance an attorney's own personal professional interests also advance the interests of persons and organizations that he represents. In other words, in judicial selection, as in the handling of legal affairs generally, attorneys act as spokesmen of the social and economic interests they represent. Thus the presence of plaintiffs' and defendants' lawyers on the nominating commissions (the analysis indicates that, over the years, there has been a fairly even distribution of both groups) ensures that the interests of injured parties of the lower classes, as well as those of wealthy corporations, will be represented when candidates are considered for the bench. The concluding section of this chapter examines the social and economic interests that are represented through the lay members of the circuit and appellate commissions.

THE APPOINTMENT OF LAY MEMBERS
TO THE NOMINATING COMMISSIONS

The decision to include lay persons with lawyers and judges on the nominating commissions was based, at least in part, on matters of political strategy. An obvious point of attack for those who opposed the Plan was to label it a device of lawyers to take judicial selection away from the voters and to vest it in the legal community alone. Placing

---

cal Science Review, XLVIII (1954), 477–485; Joseph A. Schlesinger, "A Two-Dimensional Scheme for Classifying the States According to Degree of Inter-Party Competition," Ibid., XLIX (1955), 1120–1128; and Richard Hofferbert, "A Classification of American State Parties," Journal of Politics (August, 1964), 550–567.

lay persons on the commissions serves to blunt such criticism and thus presumably makes the Plan more acceptable to members of the general public who are required to vote it into effect. Beyond this, some students of judicial selection genuinely believe that representatives of the public will be able to bring perspectives to bear on the selection of judges that lawyers as a special group in society cannot offer. A discussion of the conceptions that lay commissions have of such perspectives, as well as the way they view their role in choosing candidates, is reserved for later chapters dealing with the actual work of the nominating bodies. Here, we concentrate on their actual appointment by the governor.

The only legal qualification for a lay member of a nominating commission is that of residence. Those serving on the circuit courts of Jackson County and St. Louis City must live within the jurisdiction of these courts, while the three laymen on the Appellate Nominating Commission must reside within the boundaries of the Courts of Appeals of Kansas City, St. Louis, and Springfield, respectively. Thus the governor has broad discretion in determining whom he shall select as lay representatives on these bodies. Nevertheless, despite some variations in the thirty-five lay appointments that have been made to the nominating commissions, certain patterns have emerged in such appointments over the years which indicate that governors have developed informal qualifications or principles of "availability" for lay appointees of the nominating commissions.[58]

One obvious characteristic of these appointees is their occupational background: overwhelmingly they come from the business community. The great majority of the lay persons who have served on the nominating commissions have been owners of local businesses or managers and executives of regional and national concerns. Moreover, many of them come from financial institutions that have the most business before the courts, such as banks, insurance companies, realty firms and public utilities. A few professional persons and newspaper editors have been ap-

---

[58] Over the period of our study, 20 lay members were appointed to the circuit nominating commissions of Jackson County and St. Louis City and 15 to the appellate nominating commissions. We have fairly complete data on the appointees of the past ten years, many of whom we personally interviewed. The information on some of the earlier appointees, a number of whom are now deceased, is more sketchy, since we were dependent upon newspaper items for data on them. (The Missouri "bluebook" carries only the names and no detailed information on such persons.) For this reason, we are unable to analyze the backgrounds of the lay appointees in the commissions in the detail that is possible for other parties involved in judicial selection; therefore, we have discussed their appointments in terms of general tendencies and patterns.

pointed, and only one person with a labor background has ever served on any of the commissions during the period under study.[59]

Another pattern evident in the appointments is that of choosing persons with close ties to their local communities. Many of the lay appointees were born there (often of prominent families), others came to the community as young men and followed their careers in the immediate environment. At the time of their appointments most of them could be characterized as pillars of the local community, persons active in civic improvement projects or in charitable ventures. (Many of their names appear as chairmen of committees on metropolitan growth, commissioners of land clearance authorities and library boards, while others concentrate on Demolay,[60] Boy Scouts, and governing boards of universities.) They also tend to be active in social organizations such as the Shrine or Rotary, and some are involved in prominent social clubs in their local community.

The political backgrounds of the appointees also reveal certain commonalities. With few exceptions, the lay commissioners have been of the same party as the governor. However, relatively few have been involved in what Milbrath calls the "gladiatorial activities" of politics,[61] and only three have sought or held public or party office—one served in the legislature and two ran unsuccessfully for public office.[62] A more prevalent type of political participation for the gladiators is that of working for individual candidates, particularly for the governorship or in fund-raising ventures. Thus some have served as campaign managers in gubernatorial races, others as treasurers in such campaigns, and one held prominent positions in the financial operations of the national Democratic party; but, for the most part, governors avoid persons who are openly active in the political arena, primarily because this activity runs counter to the aura of nonpartisanship that surrounds the Plan.

A final dimension of availability for lay members of the commissions

---

[59] The individual, the president of a local union, was appointed to fill the unexpired term of a member of the St. Louis Circuit Commission who died during his term of office. The labor leader served for only one year.

[60] One member of the Kansas City Circuit Commission was the founder of that organization and was active in its work for many years.

[61] Included as examples of such activities are holding or seeking public or party office, soliciting political funds, attending caucuses or strategy meetings or contributing time in a political campaign. These are to be contrasted with "spectator" activities such as voting or initiating political discussions. See Lester W. Milbrath, *Political Participation* (Chicago: Rand McNally and Company, 1965), pp. 16 ff.

[62] All these were appointments of Governor Smith who is generally considered to have been more "political" than the other governors. The offices unsuccessfully sought were those of mayor and comptroller of St. Louis.

is a natural one: some visibility to the governor who appointed them. In many cases the governor selects close personal friends to the commission. This has been particularly true of appointments to the appellate nominating body, since the broad jurisdictions of the Courts of Appeals districts permits Missouri governors with outstate backgrounds (this has been the dominant trend among recent chief executives of the state) to choose lay persons whom they know personally from such areas. Many of the persons from the metropolitan communities have also been personal friends of the governor, but others come to his attention primarily through intermediaries. In other words, the chief executive looks to political friends or, in some cases, to lawyers in Kansas City and St. Louis for suggestions as to who would make good lay appointees to the commissions. In any event, the appointee frequently never hears of his appointment until he receives direct word from the governor's office about it. Since the position is one of honor and involves what appears (at first blush, at least) to be relatively little time, the tendency is for persons to accept the appointment. Some, however, later resign presumably because of pressures of the position, a matter that will be explored in detail in the chapters dealing with the work of the nominating commissions.

Our interview data indicate the considerations behind lay appointments to the commissions which lead governors to choose individuals with the kinds of backgrounds described above. Although the lay appointees are supposed to represent the general public, this constituency is far too amorphous and uninterested in the judiciary to be politically meaningful to the chief executive. Instead, he is sensitive to the particular elements in society that constitute the "attentive publics"[63] of the courts; these include, besides lawyers, the press and other civic groups who serve as watchdogs of the judiciary generally, and the Nonpartisan Plan in particular. This helps to explain why the governor tends to choose public-spirited individuals whose civic and charitable activities rate so highly with newspaper editors and others who originally promoted and who have continued to support the Plan over the years. Other attentive publics of the judiciary are the economic interests that are involved in frequent litigation. Thus a disproportionate number of the lay appointees come from the financial community and, in particular, from those concerns that have the most business before the courts, such as insurance companies, banks, real estate firms, and public utilities.

---

[63] This is the term used by Gabriel Almond in his study, *The American People and Foreign Policy* (New York: Harcourt Brace and Company, 1950), to describe the groups in the general public who are most interested and informed in foreign policy matters.

Another reason underlies the selection of individuals from the latter groups as appointees: they are more knowledgeable about potential judicial candidates than are other lay persons. As Chapters 3 to 5 indicate, it is difficult at best for laymen to judge the qualifications of lawyers for the bench, but those involved in frequent litigation become most familiar with the members of the legal community. Even if they do not know particular judicial candidates, they have contacts among lawyers (particularly those who represent their own companies and those they have observed in court) to whom they can turn for advice or decisions involving recruitment and selection. This same concern for familiarity with lawyers or a community sometimes leads governors to select laymen who have fathers or other relatives who are attorneys. It also helps to explain why persons with deep roots in their own communities are chosen as lay members. The governor wants people on the commission who know the local situation and who are able to protect his interests in seeing that lawyers well-regarded in their own areas are nominated for the bench.

The appointment of individuals who are personal friends of the governor, and especially those who have been his political supporters, indicates a natural desire of chief executives to have persons on the commissions whom they can trust. Such appointees can also act as a means of intelligence concerning the attitudes of the governor toward various candidates for the bench. We were unable to obtain any reliable evidence to prove that governors as a general practice convey their wishes in appointments to lay commissioners either directly or through intermediaries, although there is little question that this has occurred on certain occasions;[64] in any event, such communications are unnecessary if the member is well-acquainted enough with the governor to know what his attitudes are likely to be on given individuals. (If a lay commission member is a close friend of the governor, or if he is knowledgeable about state politics in general, the chances are that he has some insight into whom the governor personally likes or dislikes, or who his political friends or enemies are.) Thus a layman who is a loyal friend of the governor is in a position to protect the latter's interests in seeing that at least some of the nominees are acceptable to him. As we shall see later, whether this development in fact occurs is a feature of the conceptions that individual governors and lay members have of their roles in judicial selection, as well as how much influence they

---

[64] Many of our interviewers familiar with various appointments claimed that this happened quite frequently. However, given the general expectations and Plan protocol that the lay members will act independently of the governor, it is seldom that these parties themselves will admit that such a practice has occurred.

have on other members of the commission, but the appointment of close friends of the chief executive at least creates the potential for such an occurrence.

Our analysis of the selection of the selectors thus indicates that both the lawyer and lay members of the Nominating Commissions come to these bodies as a result of processes that are political in nature. In the case of the lawyers they emerge as victors in two-party contests between the liberal and conservative sectors of the legal community; the appointment of the lay members by the governor also reflects the presence of social, economic and political, as well as personal friendship factors underlying their selection. These processes, in turn, produce individuals with certain backgrounds and perspectives. The lawyer members represent distinct elements of the profession and are sensitive to the plaintiffs-defendants rivalry among attorneys; the laymen, most often business leaders with close ties to their local communities, some of whom are also close friends of the governor with considerable knowledge of the state political system, bring these considerations to their deliberations in choosing candidates for the bench. The way these perspectives, as well as those of the judicial members of the commissions, join and interact in the operation of the Nominating Commissions is discussed in Chapters 3 to 5. However, it is necessary first to explore another dimension of the total process: the recruitment mechanism through which names of certain candidates are placed before the nominating bodies for consideration as judges.

2

THE RECRUITMENT PROCESS

In analyzing the recruitment of lawyers for the bench as a progressive, winnowing process, it is helpful to separate the factors that eliminate the various candidates at different stages of the procedure. One of Seligman's major "blocks to free recruitment" under the Nonpartisan Court Plan is a legal one: all candidates must reside within the jurisdiction of the court on which they can serve. For appellate judgeships this is not a major obstacle but, as the immediate discussion of circuit judges indicates, it does constitute an effective barrier for many lawyers practicing in metropolitan Kansas City or St. Louis who might otherwise be eligible to sit on the trial courts in those two areas.

A second major factor in recruitment is the decisions that lawyers themselves make concerning attempts to seek a judgeship. Essentially these are complex decisions that involve assessment of how life on the bench will compare with that of the attorney in private or government practice; what personal sacrifices are involved in becoming a judge; and whether one is qualified for the bench. Beyond an attorney's own desires in the matter there is the practical question of how the various participants in the selection process will react to his candidacy.

Finally, recruitment is not a matter that depends solely upon affirmative action of lawyer prospects themselves. To a considerable degree it involves initiatives taken by other individuals, both those who are directly connected with judicial selection under the Plan, and those who are not. In other words, a process has developed over the years that goes beyond the formal procedure whereby lawyers submit their names for consideration by the commissioners; instead, informal recruitment mechanisms have evolved which reflect norms of the legal community concerning what is and is not proper behavior in the selection process.

This chapter explores these various aspects of the recruitment of

49

judges under the Plan. It is clear that many of the considerations discussed here—particularly those involving the deterrents and attractions
of a judicial career—apply to the recruitment of judges under any selection system. Despite many similarities, the recruitment of circuit and
appellate judges differ somewhat, especially with respect to the kinds
of lawyers who seek positions on the two kinds of benches. Therefore
the chapter deals with these two groups separately.

THE RECRUITMENT OF CIRCUIT JUDGES[1]

Legal Requirements and the Elimination of Candidates

It will be recalled from the previous chapter that lawyers serving on
the circuit nominating commissions, as well as those voting in such
elections, must reside in Jackson County or St. Louis City. A similar
constitutional provision[2] requires that all judges of the circuit courts
there be residents of the two jurisdictions. Thus the fact that a number
of lawyers are suburbanites means that many of them are ineligible
to sit on these circuit benches. Although we have no data to determine
the effect this requirement has had over the twenty-five-year history
of the Plan, its present-day impact on the recruitment of circuit judges
can be determined by analyzing the residence situation of lawyers included in our 1964 sample survey.

Since recruitment to two separate circuit courts is involved, we divided
the respondents by the two urban communities. The results show that
of the 369 lawyers who have their main practice in Jackson County,
79 (or about 21 percent) live beyond the county's boundaries, and hence
are ineligible for the circuit bench. In the St. Louis area, among the
371 respondents who have their main practice in the city, 67 percent
reside in surrounding areas, most of them in suburban St. Louis County.
Thus the pool of political candidates for the St. Louis circuit bench
is much more seriously affected by the residency requirement than the
one in Jackson County.

In considering the effect of the requirement on the recruitment pro-

---

[1] In addition to circuit courts, judges of the probate courts in both communities,
as well as the Court of Criminal Corrections in St. Louis City, are selected under
the provisions of the Plan. However, the judge of the latter court was "frozen"
in office when the Plan took effect, and only three appointments to the probate
courts were made over our period of study.

[2] *Constitution of the State of Missouri*, 1945, Art. V, Sec. 25.

TABLE 2.1

EFFECT OF RESIDENCE REQUIREMENT ON ELIGIBILITY FOR JACKSON
COUNTY AND ST. LOUIS CITY CIRCUIT JUDGESHIPS—
BY SELECTED FIELDS OF PRACTICE

Field of Practice[a]	Jackson County			St. Louis City		
	Eligible	Ineligible	N[b]	Eligible	Ineligible	N
Plaintiffs'	82%	18%	82	31%	69%	80
Criminal	94	6	16	38	62	21
Domestic relations	85	15	41	43	57	37
Defendants'	70	30	63	32	68	63
Corporation	80	20	154	26	74	178
Probate and trust	83	17	108	34	66	142

[a] Includes lawyers listing the field exclusively, or as one of the two or three major fields of their practice.
[b] Number of cases.

cess, it is important to determine not only its consequences in terms of the number of lawyers affected but also its differential impact on attorneys with different legal and social backgrounds. It will be recalled from the previous chapter that a significant division within the Bar on the matter of judgeships exists between plaintiffs' and defendants' lawyers, and that lawyers with other practice specialties tend to ally themselves with the two core groups; criminal and domestic relations attorneys ally themselves with the plaintiffs' lawyers; and corporate and, to a less marked degree, probate and trust lawyers ally themselves with the defendants' lawyers.[3] Table 2.1 shows the extent to which the residency requirement advantages or disadvantages the two sides in terms of having lawyers with their practice specialties eligible for the circuit bench.

The table indicates that the residence requirement has a limited effect on the eligibility for Jackson County judgeships of lawyers in any of the six fields of practice examined, although more attorneys in the defendants' and allied specialties live outside the court's jurisdictions than those with a plaintiffs', criminal, and domestic relations practice. In St. Louis City, attorneys in all fields are seriously affected by the requirement, and it is interesting to note that the courtroom antagonists (the

[3] Labor lawyers constitute a very small group and, therefore, they have been eliminated from the analysis.

plaintiffs' and defendants' lawyers) suffer equally by the requirement. However, proportionately fewer of the allies of the plaintiffs' live outside the city, particularly those with a domestic relations practice, whereas corporation attorneys are most effected by the residency requirement.

Beyond the plaintiffs'-defendants' dichotomy, the previous chapter indicated that the most significant division in the Bar clustered around differences among lawyers on matters of practice arrangement and legal education, the same characteristics which constitute the best indicators of social status in the legal profession. Since such matters, in turn, are indirectly related to clientele (the legal affairs of the most affluent and highest status institutions and individuals in the society are handled by attorneys who thereby attain the highest standing among their fellow lawyers), they also bear on the question of the representation of broad social interests on the bench through the legal profession. The effect of the residency requirement on lawyers with varying practice arrangements and kinds of legal education is shown in Table 2.2.

Table 2.2 indicates that upper status lawyers are more likely than

TABLE 2.2

EFFECT OF RESIDENCE REQUIREMENT ON ELIGIBILITY FOR JACKSON COUNTY AND ST. LOUIS CITY CIRCUIT JUDGESHIPS —BY PRACTICE ARRANGEMENT AND LEGAL EDUCATION

	Jackson County			St. Louis City		
Practice Assignment	Eligible	Ineligible	N	Eligible	Ineligible	N
Solo	89%	11%	91	43%	57%	93
Firm, 2 to 5 partners	75	25	77	31	69	81
Firm, 6 or more partners	70	30	61	28	72	50
Employee—law firm	75	25	48	23	77	61
Employee—corporation	71	29	45	27	73	45
Employee—government	89	11	18	50	50	16
Law School						
Instate						
Night[a]	82%	18%	124	48%	52%	128
Full-time[b]	78	22	109	42	58	121
Outstate						
Prestige[c]	74	26	53	27	73	45
Other	74	26	72	12	88	26

[a] Schools offering night class only, or night and morning classes.
[b] Schools offering morning classes only.
[c] Chicago, Columbia, Harvard, Michigan, and Yale.

those of lesser status to be affected by the residency requirement. Proportionately more partners and associates of law firms, as well as attorneys employed by corporations, live outside the circuit court's jurisdictions in both urban communities than do solo practioners, or those relatively few respondents in our sample who work for government agencies. The residency situation of lawyers who attended different kinds of law schools shows a similar pattern: those most disadvantaged by the requirement attended law school outside the state, whereas those least affected went to local night law schiols. Despite these differences the situation of the upper status lawyers in Jackson County is not serious, since about three-fourths of them live in the court's jurisdiction anyway. However, the pool of St. Louis firm and corporation lawyers (as well as those who attended outstate law schools) who are eligible for the city bench is confined to about one-fourth of their total membership. Thus three-fourths are eliminated from the recruitment process by reason of the residency requirement alone.

Two other factors that bear closely on the recruitment of judges are age and party affiliation. As the subsequent analysis indicates, attorneys take into account the particular stage of their legal career when they feel it is desirable and feasible that they should seek a position on the bench; moreover, the persons involved in screening potential judges also consider age as one of the crucial items in a lawyer's candidacy. Despite the claims of nonpartisanship made for the Plan, all the parties to the recruitment and selection process are highly sensitive to the party politics of the various aspirants for the bench.

Table 2.3 shows clearly that the residence requirement narrows the pool of young lawyers who are eligible to sit on the circuit bench, particularly in the St. Louis area. The subsequent discussion indicates that the elimination of attorneys under 35 is not crucial for recruitment purposes, since informal qualifications of experience mean that lawyers in this age group are seldom considered seriously for judgeships.[4] However, those from 35 to 44 constitute prime prospects for the bench, as do those in the succeeding age bracket of lawyers under 55 years of age. In contrast the data indicate that the requirement has a limited effect on partisan advantage. In the St. Louis community both parties are similarly handicapped in terms of the eligibility of their followers

---

[4] Of the 58 appointees under the Plan, only 2 of them were under 35 years of age and both of them were 34. There is a legal provision that circuit judges be 30 years old (*Constitution of the State of Missouri*, 1945, Art. V, Sec. 25), but given the age factor in lawyers' candidacies, this requirement has no real effect on the recruitment process in the two urban communities.

TABLE 2.3

EFFECT OF RESIDENCE REQUIREMENT ON ELIGIBILITY FOR JACKSON
COUNTY AND ST. LOUIS CITY CIRCUIT JUDGESHIPS
—BY AGE AND PARTY AFFILIATION

	Jackson County			St. Louis City		
	Eligible	Ineligible	N	Eligible	Ineligible	N
Age						
Under 35	71%	29%	76	26%	74%	78
35 to 44	71	29	124	25	75	107
45 to 54	88	12	78	30	70	76
55 and over	88	12	90	47	53	111
Party Affiliation[a]						
Republican	70%	30%	147	33%	67%	173
Democrat	83	17	199	32	68	181

[a] Independent Republicans and Independent Democrats are small categories and
have been included with regular party identifiers in the table. Political Independents
are eliminated from the analysis because they constitute so few respondents.

for circuit judgeships; in Jackson County, the Republicans are harder
hit by the residency qualification than the Democrats, but they nevertheless have a considerable pool of candidates from which to draw members
for service on the bench.

The preceding analysis points up the joint effect of legal requirements
and residential patterns on the recruitment of circuit judges, particularly
in the St. Louis area. The ecological facts of life in metropolitan Missouri
are such that a disproportionate number of young attorneys, as well
as those educated outstate and practicing in firms or with corporations,
live in suburbia and thus are eliminated from the recruitment net for
circuit judges.

Decisions of Lawyers Concerning Circuit Judgeships

Our sample indicates that the gross impact of the residency requirement
makes about 45 percent of the lawyers practicing in Jackson County
and St. Louis City ineligible for circuit judgeships. Nevertheless, a considerable pool of eligible candidates remains: more than 400 such persons
were included in our sample. The next step in our analysis involves
separating those eligible attorneys into those who have, and have not,
sought judgeships over the years, together with the respective reasons

underlying the opposite decisions made on the issue by the two groups. In keeping with the model of recruitment as a progressive, sifting and winnowing process, we shall first concentrate on these attorneys who indicated in our survey that their names had never been before a nominating commission for consideration as a circuit judge.[5] This is by far the more numerous of the two groups, constituting about 89 percent of the eligible lawyers in the two urban communities.

Reasons Why Lawyers Do Not Seek Circuit Judgeships

Attorneys who have never sought judgeships were asked to indicate their reasons for not doing so.[6] Although the responses vary considerably, they can be divided into three broad categories. The first set of reasons relates to a personal desire to remain in private practice, rather than to go on the bench, that is, a preference for the role of a lawyer in society rather than that of a judge. The second series of reasons is given by attorneys who would like to go on the bench but who feel that financially they cannot afford to do so or that they are not qualified for the bench by reason of age or the particular kind of legal experience they have had. Finally, there are those attorneys who want to go on the bench and feel qualified to do so but who believe that the nature of the selection process utilized under the Nonpartisan Court Plan is such that they have no real chance of being chosen. A subanalysis of the data by type of respondent further indicates that attorneys practicing law in a particular legal and social milieu tend to give certain reasons for not seeking a judgeship, while lawyers with different backgrounds emphasize other rationales for deciding not to become candidates for the bench.

There is, however, one major reason for not seeking a judgeship which lawyers in all groups in the Bar advance about equally: the fact that they do not feel that they would enjoy judicial work as much as they enjoy the practice of law. About one-fifth of the Bar are what might be termed "advocates," that is, they prefer to battle for their clients' interests rather than to play an impartial role in the judicial process. As one respondent stated: "The practice of law is an adversary proceed-

---

[5] The specific question read as follows: "Since the Nonpartisan Court Plan was established in Missouri in 1940, has your name ever been placed before a nominating commission for consideration as a judge?"
[6] We asked attorneys whom we personally interviewed in our study who had never sought a judgeship their reasons for the decision, and then utilized the most prevalent answers as suggested responses in our questionnaire. An "other" category was also provided for respondents to indicate reasons besides those we suggested.

ing; being a judge is nothing greater than a baseball referee—there can be no advocacy." Some lawyers frankly say they are emotionally unsuited for a judgeship because they do not possess what lawyers call "judicial temperament," by which they mean the ability to be willing and able to listen to both sides of the case. Thus many attorneys in their thinking counterpoise the roles of advocate and judge and do not seek to go on the bench because they either prefer, or feel they are better suited for, the advocate's role in the judicial process.

Beyond the issue of the disparate functions performed by attorneys and judges in litigation some attorneys do not want to become judges because they feel that what might be termed the "world of the judge" is considerably different than that of an attorney, and that one must make a considerable social adjustment when he ascends to the bench. As a wary respondent put it, "I do not wish to have the restrictions on participation in political and other activities, association with other lawyers, and other limitations which propriety would seem to require of a judge." Thus some attorneys regard entering the world of a judge as tantamount to withdrawing to a religious cloister. Interestingly enough, this is an attitude that some judges assume when they go on the bench.[7] If this analogy is too severe, the one of passing from carefree bachelorhood to the regimen of married life is contained in one young attorney's statement: "At the age of 35 I value my independence of coming and going when I please. Later in life (45–50), I will probably feel differently about the matter."

One of the reasons frequently advanced for not seeking judgeships by lawyers we personally interviewed in our study was that of the financial sacrifice necessary to go on the bench. However, in the sample survey, only about 9 percent of the respondents who did not seek a judgeship cited this as a reason for not doing so. As might be anticipated, the proportion of lawyers that is deterred by financial considerations rises with income. Among lawyers who earn more than the current salary of a circuit judge, 21 percent of those who earn between 20,000 to 30,000 dollars a year[8] and 32 percent of those who net more than 30,000

---

[7] Although the "world of the judge" lies beyond the focus of our study, personal interviews with members of the judiciary indicated a variety of conceptions as to the proper relationship of judges with members of the Bar. Some, immediately on ascending to the bench, terminate all social relationships with former attorney friends because they are concerned that fraternizing with lawyers leaves one vulnerable to criticisms of favoritism. Other judges see no reason to socially ostracize themselves, and feel that such isolation tends to result in too much of an "ivory tower" concept of the law, and too little understanding of the thinking and attitudes of members of the Bar.

[8] The present salary of Jackson County and St. Louis City Circuit judges is actually 19,000 dollars.

dollars yearly say that they have not sought a judgeship because of financial reasons. However, attorneys in their fifties or over within these salary brackets are less likely to be deterred by pecuniary matters than are lawyers under 50 with comparable earnings. As one of them stated, "My financial needs being now less, I would like to be a judge." Thus lawyers with the financial obligations of a growing family behind them are more willing to take a cut in earnings to go on the bench. Another aspect of the financial situation of a judgeship that troubles many attorneys, however, is the fact that on current salaries a judge cannot build up a nest egg, yet present retirement benefits are restricted to one-third of his final salary.

About one-third of the responses lawyers give for not seeking a judgeship relate to deficiencies in practice experience that attorneys feel are needed to qualify a person for the bench. Sometimes these qualifications are self-imposed; that is, they relate to the attorney's own definition of the kind of experience that is needed for the bench. In other instances they are a feature of what he thinks other persons (particularly those who are influential in the selection process) require of potential candidates. In either case young attorneys are inclined to take themselves out of contention because they feel that a certain number of years in practice is required before one becomes a judge. However, they differ on the particular period that is required; the minimum experience appears to be ten years, but some speak in much longer terms. One 36-year-old attorney suggested that a "judge should be more seasoned with age and experience. At age 50 I should be better able to answer this question" (why he had not sought a judgeship). At the other end of the age spectrum attorneys over 60 tend to feel they are too old to go on the bench.

A considerable number of lawyers disqualify themselves for a judgeship because of the specialized nature of their practice. "House counsel" for corporations, as well as many lawyers working for government agencies, feel that since they are no longer in private practice, they should not, or will not, be seriously considered for a judgeship. Moreover, many persons who are in private practice nevertheless think that they are not prime prospects for the bench because their practice is limited to specialties such as taxation and patent law. Some attorneys tend to create boundaries based on the level of courts before which they practice most: those who spend their time before the federal courts often feel that this disqualifies them for the state bench. Finally, some impose a trial experience qualification on judgeships. Attorneys who have tried relatively few cases before the circuit court are often inclined to feel they are not prepared to become a trial judge. Some go further and identify a torts practice as the one that is most desirable for such a judge.

Finally, there remain lawyers who would like to go on the bench, and feel qualified to do so, but eliminate themselves from contention because they feel that the selection process itself is in some way stacked against their candidacies. In Lippman's terms they carry certain "stereo-types"[9] or pictures around in their heads of how the process works and these conceptions (whether or not they actually accord with reality) pattern their behavior. Certain lawyers feel that they have no real chance of being nominated by the circuit commission for a judgeship; others see the ultimate appointment power of the governor as the real stumbling block to their selection, and some regard both steps in the selection process as insuperable obstacles to their being chosen as a judge.[10]

Table 2.4 indicates how various groups in the Bar perceive the nomination process as affecting their candidacies. In terms of the Bar rivalries analyzed in Chapter 1 lawyers in the plaintiffs' coalition are somewhat more inclined than those on the defendants' side of the profession to feel that they are disadvantaged by the commission. The differences are most pronounced between attorneys at the top and bottom social strata of the profession: solo practitioners and those who attended night law school tend to feel that "bluebloods," large firm attorneys, and those educated in prestige law schools are in a favored position, a sentiment that the latter group apparently feels has some merit. Relatively few of them ascribe their failure to seek a circuit judgeship to an unfavorable commission attitude toward their candidacies.

Both in our personal interviews and in comments on some question-naires in our survey we encountered allegations that despite the claims of nonpartisanship for the Plan it is actually a "self-perpetuating Demo-cratic political system" and that Democratic governors are not likely to appoint Republicans to the Bench.[11] Charges were also made that one has to be active in party politics to be seriously considered by the governor for a judgeship. However, analysis of the data in our survey shows that with respect to lawyers as a group party affiliation has a

---

[9] He first used this term in his classic study, *Public Opinion* (New York: Harcourt Brace & Co., 1922). Eulau and his colleagues, Buchanan, Ferguson, and Wahlke, in their selection, "Career Perspectives of American State Legislators," in Marvick, *op. cit.*, p. 220, point out that ". . . politicians are particularly skilled in reality-test-ing. They are likely, therefore, to be especially sensitive to those political conditions that either facilitate or obstruct their careers."

[10] Of the 172 respondents who said their candidacies were deterred by the assessment of their chances with either the nominating commission or the governor, 55 indicated a concern with both.

[11] Actually, since 1953, six Republicans have been appointed to the circuit courts of Jackson County and St. Louis City by three Democratic governors.

TABLE 2.4

ATTITUDES OF VARIOUS CATEGORIES OF LAWYERS
TOWARD THEIR CHANCES OF BEING NOMINATED
AS CIRCUIT JUDGE

Characteristic	Deterred[a] (%)	N
Bar Association		
Plaintiffs'[b]	30	133
Defendants'[c]	23	175
Fields of Practice		
Plaintiffs'	40	75
Domestic relations	30	43
Criminal	26	23
Defendants'	28	58
Corporation and business	22	145
Probate and trust	24	121
Law Practice Arrangement[d]		
Solo	33	100
Firm, 2 to 5	22	72
Firm, 6 or more	10	50
Legal Education		
Instate, night	33	110
Instate, full time	22	144
Outstate, other	20	50
Outstate, prestige	10	41

[a] Percentage of category who said they had not sought
judgeship because they did not feel they had a good chance
of being nominated.
[b] Kansas City Bar Association and Lawyers' Association
of St. Louis.
[c] Lawyers' Association of Kansas City and St. Louis Bar
Association.
[d] Associates, corporation, and government lawyers are not
included in the analysis since they tend to eliminate themselves on age and practice specialty qualifications.

limited effect on assessments of their chances of being chosen a judge
by the governor. About 24 percent of the Republican respondents, compared to 19 percent of the Democrats, give this as a reason for not
seeking a judgeship. The level of party involvement also has no appreciable consequence for the calculations of Democratic lawyers as far
as gubernatorial appointment is concerned; those who have not been

actively engaged in party affairs are no more likely than party activists to be deterred from candidacy because of this factor.[12] The one group that is affected by perceptions concerning the effect of party participation on judicial possibilities are those lawyers who have been involved in the work of the minority party: about twice as many of them (37 percent compared to 17 percent of their less-involved Republican colleagues) say they have not sought a judgeship because they did not think they could be appointed to the bench. Thus a negative, "kiss of death" conception of party politics is the major one affecting decisions not to try to become a circuit judge.

The analysis shows that a variety of reasons deter lawyers from seeking judgeships. Of course, these factors are not mutually exclusive, and more than one factor prevents some attorneys from becoming candidates. Those who feel that limited practice specialties disqualify them from serious consideration are often inclined also to believe that the selection process operates against their chances. Moreover, different reasons affect lawyers' thinking about a judgeship at different stages of their legal careers and, taken together, they may result in a permanent bar from candidacy. Age and financial factors are frequently linked in this fashion, as indicated by the comment of one respondent: "I have practiced about 14 years. At first, it would have involved no financial sacrifice, but I was too inexperienced to be considered; now I feel the financial long-range prospects through development of my practice offer a better future." This sentiment is in accord with the observation made by one of the interviewees that to get the best lawyers on the bench, you had to get them while they were still willing to "live poor."

Reasons Why Lawyers Want to Become Judges

Although casual comments appear in the literature concerning the attractions of a judicial career, or what David Riesman has called "the pull of the robe,"[13] we have no studies that actually directly involve the

---

[12] In devising an index of party activity, we assigned one point to each act of participation beyond voting, including attending political rallies; working for parties or candidates by getting people registered to vote, canvassing, passing out literature, poll watching, et cetera; making speeches for candidates; contributing money to a party or candidates and serving as a campaign manager. Two points were assigned for holding a party office at the city and county level, and three points for serving in a state or national party office. A total point count was computed for each respondent; those scoring three points or higher were considered as being "active" in party affairs, and those with two points or less, as "inactives."

[13] He uses the phrase in his article, "Some Observations on Law and Psychology,"

question of why lawyers desire to go on the bench rather than remain in the private practice of law. In our personal interviews we asked open-ended questions concerning the reasons underlying the inter-viewee's interest in a judgeship. We then utilized the answers we gained in these interviews to develop a list of choices from which affected lawyers (those in our sample survey who said their names had been before nominating commissions) could indicate their reasons for wanting to become a judge. (An "other" category was also provided for them to write in reasons besides those specifically mentioned.) We followed a similar procedure with judges to whom we sent comparable question-naires. We thus sought to gain both subjective insights into motivations behind "the pull of the robe" from the open-ended personal inter-views, as well as some measure of the relative importance of the various reasons for seeking judgeships from the closed-end questionnaires. Ad-mittedly, the latter purpose is limited somewhat by the fact that the respondents concerned number about 80 persons (55 lawyers from the survey who indicated that they had sought judgeships, and about 25 circuit judges appointed under the Plan from whom we elicited the necessary information).[14] Nevertheless, it is possible to get some general idea of the weights lawyers attach to the various reasons underlying the attractions of a judgeship.[15]

There is a variety of reasons why lawyers want to become judges, and in many instances more than one reason prompts an attorney to seek a judgeship. Although it is not possible to completely categorize motivations along the lines of altruism versus self-interest,[16] some of the reasons emphasize more idealistic considerations, whereas others involve matters of primary concern to the individual career of a lawyer.

It will be recalled from the preceding section that some lawyers clearly prefer the role of the advocate to that of the "referee" in the judicial process. Many of the candidates for the bench volunteered the infor-

---

The University of Chicago Law Review, 19 (1951), 35. John P. Dawson discusses attractions of a judgeship in his selection, "The Functions of the Judge," which appears in a work edited by Harold J. Berman, entitled, *Talks on American Law* (New York: Vintage Books, Random House, 1961), pp. 27 ff.

[14] Since the inception of the Plan, 34 judges have been appointed to the circuit courts of the two communities, but because of deaths, retirements, and the like, we were unable to obtain completed questionnaires from 9 of them.

[15] Of course, with the limited number of persons involved, we were unable to do a subanalysis of the data by type of respondent, as we did in the preceding section dealing with reasons why lawyers did not attempt to become judges.

[16] Eulau et al., in Marvick, *op. cit.,* at p. 242, divide their categories of motivations for seeking a legislative career into "(a) goals that may be called altruistic or contributive, and (b) goals that are essentially selfish and exploitative."

mation that they had the opposite reaction; that is, they definitely wanted to be an adjudicator, rather than a combatant, in the legal encounter. One said he liked the "fair play connected with the position"; another said that although many persons might not believe it, his main reason for going onto the bench involved matters of "conscience." "Sometimes in a lawsuit," he explained, "when the other attorney pushes you fairly hard, you go fairly far on your own and later you ask yourself whether you have conducted yourself completely as you should from a moral standpoint." One judge respondent pointed out that as a practicing lawyer you can't pick your clients and you have to represent your client's point of view whether you personally agree with it or not. He suggested that because of this situation, "Any thinking person would prefer to be in a judge's position because there you are only trying to arrive at justice and not substantiate a particular side of the case."

About one-fourth of the respondents said they wanted to go on the bench because of service to the community. Different lawyers emphasize particular aspects of this service. Some put it in its broadest societal perspective of "helping to solve community problems by making laws more meaningful" or of helping to settle the "major controversies in a society, most of which end up in the courtroom." Others view the service function more in strictly legal terms, such as improving the administration of justice by clearing up a backlog of cases, or mitigating the problems of the practicing attorney. Professional conceptions are also involved, since some attorneys feel that, if called on, it is the duty of a lawyer to become a judge. As one respondent suggested, "A judgeship represents more or less the ultimate for one trained in the Law. After a lawyer has had substantial experience he can bring that experience and background to bear on rendering service to society." It is also interesting that attorneys who stress idealistic reasons for judicial candidacies are inclined to think that all attorneys want to become judges, thus projecting their own ambitions on the Bar as a whole. This tendency is particularly true of those attorneys who have been successful in their efforts and now occupy positions on the bench.

Despite the concern of some studies analyzing the motivations of candidates that persons tend "to cloak their decisions in impersonal rationalizations,"[17] we found many attorneys couched their reasons for seeking a judgeship in terms of their individual careers. About one in five attributed a desire for a judgeship to frustrations and aggravations of what some call the "rat race" of private practice. Particularly prominent

---

[17] See Frank Sorauf's study, *Party and Representation: Legislative Politics in Pennsylvania* (New York: Atherton Press, 1963), p. 100.

was the complaint that after court hours a judge can enjoy his leisure time, but practicing attorneys have to bring work home at night and even on weekends. One former trial attorney remembered vividly the Sunday nights he devoted to preparing cases on the next week's court docket, and the fact that in many instances they never came to trial at that time because of postponement or settlement. Others emphasized the harassment of clients who called at all hours of the night or the frustrations of being forced to become bill collectors for unappreciative "deadbeats" who failed to pay up even after they received sizable court judgments as a result of their attorney's efforts. One judge confided that he had never become accustomed to the pressures of private practice, and that although judges had some pressures on them also in terms of case loads, they could not compare with those to which practicing attorneys are subjected. One of his colleagues echoed the sentiment by remarking that he went on the bench, "to add ten years to my life."

Although some studies of reasons why persons seek public office have failed to indentify honor and prestige as a major motivation,[18] about one-fifth of the candidates and judges said this factor was involved in their decision to attempt to go on the bench. As some students of the subject have observed, prestige is a relative matter; that is, it concerns the present social status of the candidate compared with the status of the public position sought.[19] Both the 1947 and 1963 studies of the National Opinion Research Center of the prestige ratings given various occupations by the general public show that those of lawyers and county judges are almost identical: in 1947 the latter slightly outranked the former, and the reverse occurred in the more recent study.[20] Thus, as society at large views the situation, there is no real gain in prestige for lawyers who become lower court judges. As previously suggested, however, there are definite differences in social status within the legal

---

[18] Sorauf, for example, did not find these as factors in the motivation of state legislative candidates in Pennsylvania, *ibid.* On the other hand, Robert Rosenzweig did find these motivated Massachusetts candidates for a variety of offices including the Governor's Council, United States House of Representatives, State Senate and State House of Representatives. See his, "The Politician and the Career in Politics," *Midwest Journal of Political Science*, 2 (August, 1957), 166 ff.

[19] Rosenzweig, *ibid.* Also Mitchell, *loc. cit.*, 682 ff.

[20] In the 1947 study, the N.O.R.C. score of a county judge was 87 and the position ranked 13th; that same year, the comparable ratings of a lawyer were 86 and 18th, respectively. In 1963, a lawyer rated 89 in score and 11th among the occupations rated, while the county judge rated 88 and 14th, respectively. See Robert W. Hodge, Paul M. Siegel and Peter H. Rossi, "Occupational Prestige in the United States, 1925–63," *The American Journal of Sociology*, LXX (November, 1964), 290.

profession, and it is entirely possible that attorneys' perceptions of the prestige of a judgeship vary on this basis. Our data indicate that a larger proportion of solo practitioners than firm lawyers seek a judgeship for reasons of prestige, but the differences are not great and there are too few respondents involved to permit any definite conclusions on this point.[21]

About one-fifth of the respondents said that financial reasons were included among those that prompted them to seek a position on the bench. Relatively few of them (about 5 percent) stated that they wanted to become judges because they could earn more money than they made in private practice; more of them were attracted by the fixed salary and retirement benefits which they preferred to the more uncertain income of private practice. When these figures are compared with those presented in the preceding section involving financial considerations, that is, the one lawyer in ten who did not seek a judgeship because he was unwilling to make the pecuniary sacrifice to go on the bench, it appears that the salaries of judges may actually be more of an attraction than a deterrent to judicial candidacies as far as the Bar as a whole is concerned.[22]

How the Recruitment Process Operates

Thus far we have been concentrating on the "whos" and "whys" of recruitment; to round out the analysis, it is necessary to look at the "hows" of the process.[23] In some respects the last two phases of reqruitment are closely related, since some attorneys attribute the reason they became a judicial aspirant to the fact that other persons asked them to be a candidate. However, as Sorauf suggests in his study of legislative candidates in Pennsylvania, "Such an explanation, of course, often begs the question and mistakes the occasion for the cause."[24] Persons do not seek public office just because they are asked but because they

---

[21] Twenty-three percent of the solo lawyers, compared to 15 percent of the firm respondents, said that the honor and prestige connected with a judgeship was one of the reasons they sought the office.

[22] We gathered financial information from circuit judges which showed their average yearly net income for the three years immediately preceding their appointment, and then compared those data with the statutory salary of a judge at the time each went on the bench. The comparison shows that 12 of the 23 respondents from whom we had information took no cut in salary when they became a judge.

[23] Seligman in an article, "A Prefatory Study of Leadership Selection in Oregon," *loc. cit.*, at p. 154, says that the "who" has been stressed to the neglect of the "how" of recruitment.

[24] Sorauf, *op. cit.*, p. 99 f.

have some underlying reasons for wanting the position involved, and the invitation merely provides the opportunity to translate that hope into reality.

Under the formalities of the recruitment process, the nominating commission announces through newspapers and special Bar media that a judicial vacancy is present and invites lawyers to submit names for consideration. However, behind these formalities, a kind of recruitment "politics" has evolved over the years, based on the strategies and expectations of both the recruiters and the recruited as to how the system operates. We gained insight into the informal workings of the process through personal interviews with members of the nominating commissions, lawyers who have been nominated for judgeships over the years, as well as those who have been actually selected as judges.

The recruitment of lawyers for the bench comes from a variety of sources. One is the candidate himself. A few of the respondents said that their candidacy was entirely their own idea. In fact, one admitted that he had been planning his judicial career since he began practice and said he had deliberately cultivated the friendship of persons over the years whom he thought were in a position to further his candidacy. However, the admitted "self-starters" are comparatively few in numbers because of the tradition in American politics (and especially in legal and judicial circles) that the office should seek the man. In fact, some of the lawyers who had not sought a judgeship gave this as their reason: no one had ever asked them. As one of them put it, "No one ever flattered me with any suggestion that I was judicial material;" another said, "I have not had the slightest indication that anyone, other than myself, had any interest in selecting me as a judge." To one respondent, inquiring of a lawyer why he has not been a candidate for a judgeship is "like asking a spinster to subscribe to the reasons why she has never married—truthfully!" Thus many and perhaps most lawyers feel that Bar folkways dictate that you be asked to be a judge, rather than overtly seeking the position.

A considerable number of our interviewees said that they had been asked seek a judgeship by other lawyers. Close personal friends and lawyers in the same social strata of the Bar, with practice specialties and clientele similar to those of the candidate, are most inclined to be the source of such recruitment. In circumstances like these, however, it is sometimes difficult to separate the recruiters from the recruited. A clever attorney, by simply raising the issue of a judicial vacancy, does not find it too difficult to implant the idea of his own candidacy in a fellow lawyer's mind, so that the latter unwittingly plays the role of the recruiter. Moreover, on one occasion, three attorneys went to the nominating commission on behalf of a colleague, only to end up themselves on the panel as the three nominees. (The story has a happy ending, however, since the temporarily forgotten friend later became a judge.)

One of the major recruiting agencies is the nominating commissions themselves. Although not all members share the opinion, many of them feel that they should not be content with merely receiving nominations from others but that they should actively seek out members of the Bar and urge them to become candidates.[25] This is particularly true when members of the commission are not satisfied with the caliber of the lawyers who are referred to them. As one of them remarked, "Of course we encourage lawyers to become candidates. At the time of the most recent appointment, most of the names we originally received for consideration were jokes."

Of the members of the circuit nominating commission, the person who has traditionally been most active in recruiting candidates for judgeships has been the presiding judge of the Court of Appeals who serves as ex-officio chairman of the body. In part, this is attributable to the "activist" attitudes of certain judges who have filled that position for considerable periods of time over the history of the Plan. Beyond this any individual occupying this post is in an excellent position to play this kind of a role, since he generally is a person who has been a member of the local Bar for a long period of time, and who, by virtue of his contacts both while in practice and subsequently as a member of the bench, has had "face-to-face" relationships with many lawyers. This experience means that he knows a wider range of his fellow attorneys than most other persons do; moreover, having seen many of them perform in the courtroom, he has superior information on their capabilities as potential members of the bench.

Many lawyers on the nominating commission also recruit candidates. Again this varies with the "activist-nonactivist" attitudes of individuals. Attorneys who have served on commissions for a considerable period of time[26] are inclined to be more involved in recruitment, since the experience of going through the screening process a number of times naturally gives them a broader knowledge of judicial material than is

---

[25] Supreme Court Rule 10.26 provides for the Commission's tendering nominations (subject to formal action of the Commission) to qualified persons to determine whether such a person will agree to serve if nominated.

[26] Supreme Court Rule 10.04 provides that no commission member may succeed himself, but this bar to service is temporary rather than permanent. Moreover, persons can serve out the unexpired term of another member.

possessed by newly appointed members. With less frequency lay-persons on the commission attempt to recruit candidates. They generally defer to the judgment of the member of the Bar who sit on the commissions. Some of our interviewees indicated that they had been asked to submit their names for consideration by lay commissioners. The commissioners involved, however, definitely fall within the category of "political" lay appointees outlined in the previous chapter and, throughout their terms on the commission, played a more active role than most laymen in the entire recruitment and selection process.

Another source of recruitment of candidates are sitting judges on the circuit bench. They quite naturally tend to have an interest in who their future colleagues will be. Moreover, as judges, they also have unique information on the capabilities of the attorneys who try suits in their courtrooms. Some judges feel no compunctions about advancing names for the commission's consideration, while others feel that for them to do so would be "presumptuous," as one circuit judge asked about the matter suggested. However, even judges with this attitude sometimes become involved in the process, because the members of the commission come to them for advice, in which case most of them feel it is proper and even mandatory for them to suggest candidates.[27]

Another source of recruitment is the governor. Chief executives are generally not actively inclined to seek out candidates (or at least we were unable to get lawyers to say that this occurred), but one of our interviewees candidly stated that the governor of the state had come to him and said that if he could get himself on a panel he would appoint him to the bench. (Unfortunately for the candidate, political circumstances subsequently prevented the governor from making good his promise.)

A major decision for many candidates is whether they should let themselves be recruited for the bench. Although some of the lawyers we interviewed took a cavalier attitude toward their candidacy (that is, they entered their own names for consideration—or took no action to stop others from doing it for them—without giving much thought to the issue), others carefully assessed the implications of their candidacy. If a lawyer has previously not given much thought to going on the bench, he wants to find out what it is like to be a judge. Many attorneys also explore the impact that a try at a judgeship will have on their law practice. Others, who definitely want to become judges, take "sound-

---

[27] Grossman, *op. cit.*, points out at page 39 that while the sitting judges have no official role to play in the selection of federal judges, the views of some of them are solicited or offered in virtually all cases.

ings" to ascertain whether now is the right time to make their move or whether they should wait for a more propitious occasion. To find the answers to these questions the potential candidate must consult a number of persons who possess the information he needs.

An obvious source of insight into the world of the circuit judge are the members of the bench themselves. They are in a position to tell the attorney what the rewards and frustrations of a judgeship are, how it compares with private practice, and the changes that a judgeship makes in a person's total "way of life." Moreover, a visit to a judge can also help to assess how he and his colleagues will react to the lawyer's candidacy; that is, it may give the attorney some indication how he would be regarded as a future colleague by the present members of the bench. One of our interviewees said that when he was assessing his situation he went to see some of the judges, "not to seek their support," but to get "background information." Of course, if the visit to the court also accomplishes the former function, so much the better for the lawyer's candidacy, especially if the judges involved have access to the commission.

The decision to seek a position on the bench raises real problems for the lawyer who is associated with other attorneys in the practice of law.[28] Many feel a sense of duty to colleagues who gave them a start in the law and nursed them through the early difficult years of practice to the point where they are making a real contribution to the law firm. Others, less idealistically inclined, fear the effect that an unsuccessful candidacy will have on future relationships with partners who may well construe an interest in a judgeship as an indication of dissatisfaction with their present legal lot and an eventual intention to leave the firm. Nor is it always possible for the candidate to know exactly how to interpret his partners' response to his broaching of the subject: "We would, of course, be sorry to see you leave the firm, but, if you think you would like to be a judge, we won't stand in your way and will wish you well." Is this a bit of professional gallantry or are his partners really not too distressed at the idea of his possible departure from the firm? In any event, the issue must be faced, since it is far better to inform one's colleagues of the matter than to let them

---

[28] Some lawyers, including solo practitioners, also said that clients, on occasion, view an attorney's decision to seek a position on the bench as an indication that he is deserting them, and doesn't really care what happens to their legal affairs. However, this problem is not nearly so serious as the one involving colleague relationships.

find out for themselves from newspaper accounts of the list of "applicants" the nominating commission is considering for a judicial position.[29]

Finally, lawyers with a deep interest in going on the bench often seek the advice of "knowledgeables" before deciding whether to make a try for a judgeship at a particular time. One interviewee said he had thought about attempting to become a judge in the past, but held off because he was discouraged by a member of the commission who told him this was not a good time to file. Another, who carefully calculated his candidacy from a number of standpoints, said that Judge _____ (who told him that he wanted to see him on the bench) acted as his advisor and helped him to map his strategy. "He suggested that I let my name go before the commission, and that it would not hurt my chances of eventually becoming a judge if I made the panel of three, but was not appointed; in fact, he thought it might even heighten my chances the next time around," the interviewee explained. "But he told me the next time a vacancy occurred I should appoint an emissary to go down and talk to the governor about my chances, because if my name appeared on two panels without my being selected as a judge, I would be a 'dead duck' for future appointments."[30] The interviewee said that the next time he was in Jefferson City he called on the governor and got acquainted with him.[31]

Thus recruitment usually involves candidate calculations, strategies and "touching base" with a number of parties directly and indirectly involved in the process. Attorneys frequently refer to "waiting for the right time" to make their bid for the bench. And waiting for the right time means, in essence, that they try to second-guess what will eventually occur in the selection process described in subsequent chapters. Therefore, although recruitment necessarily precedes selection in time, anticipation of the selection process helps to shape the nature of recruitment.

---

[29] Many attorneys we interviewed were quite resentful of the practice of publishing the names of "applicants," and also felt that this label for describing lawyers who sought to become judges demeaned the selection process, as well as the judiciary itself. Supreme Court Rule 10.27 grants the commission discretion as to whether some, all or none of the names of possible nominees shall be published; it also provides that the Commission itself shall not describe possible nominees as "applicants" or suggest by any other term that they are seeking to be nominated.

[30] Our analysis shows that only 5 of the 55 respondents who sought to go on the bench had their names before the nominating commission more than twice. Moreover, 42 of them made only one such try at the position.

[31] This lawyer later went on the bench, although he was appointed by another governor.

Recruitment and selection are thus closely integrated parts of the total process by which lawyers come to occupy positions on the bench.

Effect of Lawyers' Decisions Concerning Circuit Judgeships on Personnel Recruited for the Bench

We have already analyzed the consequences of the residency requirement in terms of the characteristics of lawyers in the two communities who are ineligible to serve on the circuit bench. With the progressive sifting and winnowing model in mind, there remains the matter of determining how the reasons underlying lawyers' decisions concerning a judgeship, together with recruitment practices themselves, affect the kinds of eligible lawyers that tend to be eliminated at the recruitment stage of the process. Table 2.5, which compares the characteristics of lawyers not seeking to go on the bench with the characteristics of lawyers who are seeking the position,[32] contains the information bearing on this matter.

The table shows that lawyers under 35, associates of law firms and those employed by corporations, and attorneys with limited trial experience are inclined to be removed from candidacy for a circuit judgeship by their own decisions and those of other persons who recruit lawyers for the bench. Also in this category are lawyers earning less than $10,000 a year (many of whom, of course, are younger lawyers) together with Republican attorneys who have not been active in partisan affairs. One interesting fact also shown by the table is that, with the exception of criminal lawyers who constitute a very small segment of the Bar, no group of lawyers with a particular field of specialty is eliminated at this stage of the recruitment process.[33] The same is true of attorneys attending various types of law schools.

With the information on the who's, why's, how's, and effects of recruiting circuit judges in mind, we next discuss a comparable analysis of appellate judges in the state, that is, those of the three intermediate courts of appeals and the supreme court of Missouri. As already suggested, many features of the two recruitment processes are similar, and the discussion that follows points out the major differences between them.

---

[32] Originally we included the circuit judges in this latter group, but decided to eliminate them from the comparative analysis since their characteristics reflect the results of the selection, as well as the recruitment, process.

[33] As suggested previously, the attorneys specializing in criminal law constitute a very small proportion of the Bar. Table 2.5, for example, shows that only 23 respondents had this practice background.

TABLE 2.5

COMPARISON OF CHARACTERISTICS OF ELIGIBLE LAWYERS NOT SEEKING
CIRCUIT JUDGESHIP WITH LAWYERS SEEKING POSITION

Characteristic	Lawyers Not Seeking Judgeship (%)	Lawyers Seeking Judgeship (%)	Total (%)	N
Age				
Under 35	99	1	100	75
35 to 44	87	13	100	116
45 to 54	81	19	100	95
55 and over	85	15	100	133
Field of Specialty[a]				
Plaintiffs'	79	21	100	95
Criminal	100	0	100	23
Domestic relations	81	19	100	53
Defendants'	88	12	100	66
Corporation and business	84	16	100	172
Probate and trust	85	15	100	142
Amount of Experience[b]				
Less than 25 cases	98	2	100	148
25 to 99 cases	82	18	100	101
100 cases or more	77	23	100	140
Practice Arrangement				
Solo	79	21	100	127
Partnership, 2 to 5	86	14	100	84
Partnership, 6 or more	86	14	100	58
Associate	96	4	100	50
Salaried employee—corporation	100	0	100	44
Salaried employee—government	88	12	100	24
Legal Education				
Instate, night	88	12	100	163
Instate, full time	89	11	100	124
Outstate, other than prestige	86	14	100	58
Outstate, prestige	82	18	100	50
Income				
Under $10,000	96	4	100	115
$10,000 to $19,999	83	17	100	170
$20,000 to $29,999	88	12	100	68
Over $30,000	89	11	100	47
Partisan Activity[c]				
Inactive Republican	95	5	100	100
Active Republican	85	15	100	65
Inactive Democrat	90	10	100	126
Active Democrat	76	24	100	102
Independent	100	0	100	11

[a] Includes lawyers listing the field exclusively, or as one of two or three major fields of their practice.
[b] Refers to amount of experience before circuit court.
[c] See footnote 12, *supra*, for the index used to measure the amount of party activity.

71

THE RECRUITMENT OF APPELLATE JUDGES

The "block to free recruitment" of circuit judges created by the residency requirement has no appreciable effect on the process of recruiting lawyers to the appellate bench. The only area of the state in which residency qualifications are any bar at all to judicial aspirants is in Jackson County, where about 14 percent of the practicing attorneys live outside the Kansas City appellate district, primarily in Johnson County, Kansas.[34] The residency situation that created such a problem for the St. Louis City circuit bench is virtually nonexistent as far as eligibility to serve on the St. Louis Court of Appeals is concerned: only about 1 percent of the attorneys practicing in the City live across the state line in Illinois, and hence are disqualified for service on that bench. The fact that the St. Louis suburbs are located in the county and other areas on the Missouri side of the Mississippi River means that they are included in the Appellate Court jurisdiction. Similarly, attorneys practicing in "outstate" Missouri are, with a few exceptions, also eligible to serve on the Court of Appeals serving their respective areas.

Although the pool of eligible candidates for the four appellate benches in the state is much broader than that for the circuit benches in Jackson County and St. Louis City, our survey data indicate that only about one half as many of our lawyer respondents (25 compared with 55) have attempted to go on these courts as have sought positions on the circuit courts in the two metropolitan communities. This undoubtedly results, in part, from the fact that there were fewer appointments to vacancies to the appellate than to the circuit courts during our period of study.[35] But beyond this, many attorneys view their chances of obtaining a circuit judgeship as being much more realistic than their aspirations for a seat on the higher benches of the state.

In fact, our survey data indicate that, in effect, two separate pools of candidates exist for the different levels of courts. Among the 55 lawyer respondents who sought a position on the trial courts of the two metropolitan communities, only three also were candidates for either a Court of Appeals or the State Supreme Court. The obverse is also

---

[34] It will be recalled that 21 percent of this group of attorneys practicing in Jackson County were ineligible for service on the circuit court. The difference between the 21 and 14 figures is attributable to the fact that some of these attorneys live in suburban Missouri counties like Clay which qualifies them for service on the Kansas City Court of Appeals, but not for the Jackson County Circuit Bench.

[35] From 1940 through 1964, 24 appointments under the Plan were made to the appellate courts, compared to 34 to the circuit and probate courts of Jackson County and St. Louis City.

true: only five of the upper court "applicants" permitted themselves to be considered for a trial judgeship in either of the metropolitan communities. Thus the circuit and appellate nominating commissions are involved in screening two distinct groups of lawyers as potential judges.

Comments made by both successful and unsuccessful candidates indicate that the pull of the appellate robe differs somewhat from the attractions of a circuit judgeship. Attorneys seeking service on the upper bench are much more inclined to emphasize the intellectual aspects of their work than are attorneys who are oriented toward the trial bench. Particularly appealing to some attorneys is the opportunity to try their hand at legal writing; others stress the role the appellate judge plays in "molding the law," "developing legal principles," or "making significant contributions to jurisprudence and the administration of justice." Thus the attorney with a scholarly bent and a desire for contemplation finds an appellate judgeship much more appealing than the drama and pressures associated with the trial judge's role of refereeing the spirited combat between opposing counsel, clients, and witnesses in lower court.

A comparison of the characteristics of lawyer respondents who sought to go on one of the appellate benches with those attorneys in our sample who have been candidates for the circuit courts indicates that, generally, the former is a more elite group.[36] For example, they are more apt to have attended a full-time law school and to be associated with a law firm than are "applicants" for the circuit court; moreover, more defendants' attorneys and those specializing in probate and trust work are willing to be considered for an appellate than a circuit judgeship. Lawyers earning more than 30,000 dollars a year are also more inclined to consider an upper court position.

Two other differences appear between the lawyers seeking positions in the two kinds of courts. As a group, the ones who desire to go on the upper bench are older than their colleagues who express an interest in a trial court position. The appellate applicants are also less likely to have been active in partisan affairs than their counterparts involved in the lower level recruitment process.

The recruitment process under the Plan is thus a complex procedure that reflects a variety of forces at work in the particular subculture of society from which members of the judiciary are drawn. Included

---

[36] The small number of cases included in the two subsamples being compared (55 for the circuit, and 25 for the appellate benches) raise serious questions of reliability. We have, therefore, confined our comments to only major differences in characteristics between the two subsamples. Again, no circuit or appellate judges are included in the analysis for the reason set out in footnote 32, *supra*.

are the motivations that cause some attorneys to seek to leave their private practices for the world of the judge; the informal qualifications the legal community has developed to assess the candidacies of aspirants, as well as the folkways that govern how the delicate relationships between the recruiters and recruited shall be handled. For those lawyers who manage to overcome the various obstacles created by the recruitment procedure, there remains the even more complex process that follows: the screening of the candidates by the Nominating Commissions for the circuit and appellate benches.

3

PARTY FACTIONALISM AND

JUDICIAL SELECTION IN

JACKSON COUNTY

Judicial selection under the Missouri Plan is affected by a wide variety of influences. Some are *external* in nature, emanating from the environment in which the nominating commissions and the governor function. These influences include: the structure of the legal profession; the composition and orientation of the principal groups that constitute the clientele of the courts; and the political milieu, which is an amalgam of the state and local political systems. Nominations and appointments are also affected by influences of an *internal* nature, essentially by the orientations and objectives of those who have a formal role in the choice of judges. Thus the internal factors that affect judicial selection include: the role orientations of the nominating commissioners and the governors; the decision-making procedures utilized in the selection process; the strategies of the various participants; and the patterns of interaction among members of the nominating commission, and between nominating commissioners and the governor.

Although there are important similarities in the selection process for all the Plan courts in Missouri, there are also basic differences in the functioning of the Plan from one area of the state to another, and from one court level to another. Three separate nominating commissions are involved in the selection of judges: one each for the Jackson County and St. Louis City circuits; and a third for the appellate courts of the state. This chapter focuses principally on the selection of judges for the Jackson County circuit bench, but also deals with those facets of the selection system that are basically similar for all Missouri Plan courts.

The next two chapters, which discuss the selection of St. Louis City circuit and appellate judges, respectively, emphasize the differences in the operation of the three selection processes. Chapters 4 and 5 also assess the impact that the selection process has on the kinds of attorneys who are nominated and appointed to the circuit and appellate benches.

THE ENVIRONMENT OF THE SELECTION PROCESS

From the discussion in Chapter 1 it will be recalled that there has been long-standing conflict between the plaintiffs' and defendants' segments of the Metropolitan Bar. In the years since 1940, however, several changes in the Jackson County legal profession have converged so as to greatly diminish the impact of the plaintiffs'-defendants' rivalry upon the judicial selection process.

The Ecology of Legal Practice

One of the most significant changes affecting judicial politics has been the emergence of the large, "corporate" law firm. Members of these firms rarely become involved in actual courtroom litigation but, instead, devote most of their time to out-of-court legal matters. Increasingly, young attorneys join such law firms immediately after the completion of law school and undergo an early inculcation of the philosophy that all firm members belong to "one happy team," which devotes its time to "the business," not to politics or even civic matters. Firm members are also discouraged from seeking public office, including the judiciary.

The growth of this segment of the Bar has served to mute the traditional conflict over judicial selection. Most members of the "law corporations" would identify with the defendants' element of the Bar. Yet they do not have a very wide acquaintance within the Bar, are never significantly involved in trial practice, have few contacts within the political community, and are not very interested in or knowledgeable about the judiciary, particularly at the trial court level. The net effect is a withdrawal from the arena of combat of a group of attorneys who could be expected to add strength to the efforts of the defendant's faction.

Other changes in the structure of legal practice in Jackson County have led to a reduction in the strength of the plaintiffs' segment of the bar vis-à-vis judicial selection. An increasing number of solo practitioners and small-firm plaintiffs' attorneys in recent years have begun to divest themselves of some of their trial work. Particularly when large amounts of damages are at stake, plaintiffs' lawyers tend to refer the courtroom phase of litigation to established and successful courtroom lawyers. This development has tended to make some plaintiffs' attorneys less interested in judicial selection.

A further development affecting both segments of the Bar is the trend toward diversification in the practice and clientele of the legal firms that specialize in trial work. This usually occurs when a plaintiff's trial firm, having built a reputation for success in its handling of personal injury litigation, begins to attract business from the corporations who are defendants in such litigation.[1] As a result of the referral practices of solo attorneys discussed above, diversification has also occurred in the business of trial firms that once specialized in representing defendants in personal injury suits. Both trends have resulted in a substantial growth in the significance and case load of the trial firms with a mixed plaintiffs-defense practice. By about 1950 these mixed-practice firms had come to occupy a strategic role in the judicial selection process in Jackson County. Because they represented both plaintiffs and defense clients, they tended toward ideological neutrality. Thus their involvement in judicial politics dampened the conflict between the extremes on the plaintiffs-defense continuum.

The Court's Economic and Social Clientele

In the early 1960's the bulk of litigation in the Jackson County Circuit Court consisted of criminal proceedings, juvenile matters, and personal injury suits. Three of the thirteen divisions of the circuit court dealt exclusively with criminal cases; a fourth judge was permanently assigned to juvenile cases. However, in terms of sheer volume, personal injury litigation accounted for the greatest portion of the business of the circuit bench. Therefore, the parties most frequently affected by circuit court decisions have been the casualty insurance companies, public utilities, and the railroads.

Other businesses have a far more limited stake in circuit court decisions. The banking community centers its attention on the probate division of the circuit court, which handles the appointment of executors

---

[1] Usually, the result is not a complete shift in clientele for the successful trial firm, since it can accommodate the new defense clients without relinquishing its plaintiffs' business. However, a frequent limitation placed upon such law firms by a corporate client is that the law firm agree not to take cases involving plaintiff's suits against the corporation, although the law firm remains free to handle damage suits against other corporations.

and appraisers of estates. Similarly, realtors have a substantial concern only with the relatively few court proceedings which involve appraisal of property values or settlement of zoning disputes.

Most nonbusiness groups also have had a rather narrow interest in the decisions of the circuit bench. The work of the juvenile division elicits the attention of the broadest array of social groups and public institutions. Social service organizations active in the welfare field, members of the social work profession, and both the laity and the clergy of various religious denominations constitute the principal clientele of the juvenile division. Law enforcement agencies are also concerned with the functioning of the juvenile system, especially with the basic orientation that the courts take toward juvenile offenders. Many of these same groups also tend to be attentive to the decisional activity of the criminal divisions of the circuit bench. Interest in both juvenile and criminal matters is likely to be directed largely to the issue of a punitive versus a rehabilitative philosophy of justice.

Labor initially opposed the adoption of the Missouri Plan and still is hostile toward it as a matter of principle. Yet, today, neither union officials nor union attorneys appear to have very much interest in the functioning of the Plan. Some of the litigation of traditional concern to unions now comes before federal administrative agencies and the federal courts rather than the state courts. This trend has diminished labor's stakes in state court litigation. In addition, many labor leaders are reluctant to become involved in a selection process that is considered to be of a "nonpartisan" nature, for fear that their activities would lead to the same "kiss of death" result so frequently associated with labor's efforts to influence nonpartisan elections of councilmen in some of the nation's large cities.[2]

The newspapers in Jackson County are consistently a major part of the court's clientele with respect to the entire range of judicial activity. In the narrowest sense the newspaper's interest in the courts is the same as that of any other potential litigant. Of paramount significance is the possibility of libel suits against the newspapers. In the broadest sense the newspapers have consciously adopted the role of public guardian relative to the functioning of the courts, including the process by which the judges are chosen. In this capacity the metropolitan dailies have given extensive news coverage to all aspects of the Missouri Plan's operation, as well as to the decisions of the courts. Over the years the

---

[2] William H. Form, "Organized Labor's Place in the Community Power Structure," reprinted in Oliver P. Williams and Charles Press, *Democracy in Urban America* (Chicago: Rand McNally & Company, 1961), pp. 328–346.

newspapers have also commented editorially on virtually every facet of the judicial selection process, always with an eye toward preserving the "integrity" of that process, and insuring the selection of "qualified" personnel for both the nominating commission and the bench itself.

Excepting labor, all of the above clientele groups thus have had a considerable interest in the decisions of the circuit court. Yet their role in the judicial selection process has been quite limited. With the exception of social worker activity designed to influence the choice of juvenile judges,[3] none of the clientele groups has taken concerted action either to promote or to oppose candidates for the judiciary. Individual members of these groups may occasionally have had influence in the selection process, but generally it is because they have been personal friends of nominating commissioners or the governor. Moreover, their opinions are generally considered to be expressions of individual rather than group interest.

The failure of the clientele groups to become involved in judicial selection can be attributed primarily to the norms that surround the selection process. There is wide acceptance of the view that lawyers are the only "outsiders" who may legitimately attempt to influence the decisions of the nominating commission. In deference to these views members of the interest groups are chary about taking any action that might be construed as an attempt to control the courts; they depend instead upon other participants in the process for the representation of their interests. As one respondent observes:

The insurance companies, railroads, and banks are very interested in who gets on the bench, but they don't do very much actively to influence the nomination process. They don't have to. Their attorneys go to bat for them, and without being or needing to be asked.[4]

---

[3] Since there is no segment of the Bar that has views parallel to those of the groups interested in juvenile matters, these groups tend to intervene directly in the selection process. However, the clientele of the juvenile division has had virtually no influence over the choice of judges for that division. This is attributable to two factors: (1) participants in the selection process are not very receptive to the views espoused by most of the groups which constitute the clientele of the juvenile division; and (2) vacancies on the juvenile bench are not always filled by the recruitment of new judges but by the transfer to that division of an incumbent judge from another division of the circuit bench.

[4] Throughout the book, all quotations drawn from the personal interviews are presented without any identification of the respondent making the statement. Subsequent quotations, unless otherwise identified, are taken from the personal interview protocols. For a discussion of the numbers and types of respondents interviewed and the interview format employed, see the Appendix.

The Court as Clientele

In a manner of speaking, the court is also part of its own clientele. Individual judges on the circuit bench have a vital interest in the maintenance of an organizational system conducive to their own professional and emotional well-being. Although circuit judges sit in separate, largely autonomous divisions—and never sit collegially on matters of case disposition—other facets of the circuit judges' role lead them to place a high premium on amicable interjudge relations. Most judges associate more intimately with colleagues on the bench than with any other group of individuals. Moreover, each judge has a distinct interest in the capacity for work of newcomers to the bench, since his own case load is partially determined by the dispatch and care with which other judges dispose of their assigned work. Additionally, most judges desire that a minimum level of quality be maintained in the recruiting of new judges, since the appointment of a patently unqualified person to the bench would demean the prestige of the entire bench in the eyes of the Bar and the general public.

The appointment of judges lacking political circumspection may also have serious consequences for the maintenance of the support that the court needs. This support is of two basic types. First, there must be some minimal support from the Bar, the public, and other political-governmental agencies if the court is to continue performing its institutional functions. Second, some minimal measure of support must exist for the judicial career to continue to be personally rewarding in the eyes of the individual judges. Many of the perquisites of judicial office depend on the perceptions of the court that are held by other public officials. Thus the judges depend on the respect and good will of legislators and the governor for salary increases and the improvement of retirement benefits. For a variety of reasons, then, the incumbent judges have a substantial interest in the kinds of persons who are selected to fill new or vacant judgeships.

Incumbent circuit judges have become participants in the judicial selection process in a variety of ways. Many have served as advisers to aspirants for the bench; some have functioned as advisers to the judicial nominating commission. But their most important role has been through their personal involvement in the recruitment of candidates for the bench, and their subsequent efforts to promote the candidacies of those who agree to become applicants for nomination. Of course, not all judges assume such an active role. Some refrain from doing so out of personal inclinations. Although willing to provide assessments of candidates being considered by the nominating commission, these judges feel that any other activity designed to influence judicial selection would be both presumptuous and improper. Other incumbent judges, particularly Republicans, do not often become involved in recruitment, mainly because they feel that they could have little effect upon the outcome of the selection process.

In addition to the circuit judges, the presiding judge of the court of appeals serves as an exponent of the institutional interests of the court system. The fact that he occupies an intermediate position in the state court hierarchy, with his court serving as the next higher forum of appeal for many trial court decisions, leads the presiding judge to have an obvious stake in the quality of the trial bench. Poor circuit judges, whose decisions inspire a large number of appeals, can drastically affect the work load of the court of appeals and can also create difficult problems for the entire state court structure.

The Political Setting

The most important element in the environment of Jackson County judicial selection has been the political system. For this reason partisan political activity has been virtually a prerequisite for judicial office. Specifically, the type of partisan activity and especially the factional affiliation of judicial candidates have been largely determinative factors in the selection of judges for the Jackson County circuit bench.

With the adoption of the Missouri Plan in 1940, judicial selection moved out of the vortex of ward politics in the local political arena and into the orbit of gubernatorial politics at the state level. Yet local political groups continued to have an important voice in judicial selection even after 1940, mainly because they continued to play a decisive role in state-wide primary politics within the Democratic party, the party that controlled the governorship throughout the Missouri Plan era, except for the period from 1941 to 1945.

To understand the exact manner in which local political groups continued to influence judicial selection after the institution of the Missouri Plan, it is necessary to examine briefly the recent political history of Jackson County.

In the decade before 1940 Thomas J. Pendergast had become the overlord or the entire Democratic political machine in Jackson County.[5]

---

[5] The most complete accounts of Pendergast era politics are contained in William M. Reddig, *Tom's Town; Kansas City and the Pendergast Legend* (New York: J. B. Lippincott Company, 1947) and Maurice Milligan, *Missouri Waltz; The Inside Story of the Pendergast Machine by the Man Who Smashed It* (New York: Charles Scribner's Son's, 1948).

He assumed this preeminence after about thirty years of bitter rivalry among a number of political factions, including the Pendergast "Goats" and Shannon faction "Rabbits,"[6] these being the chief rivals for power. Other factional elements that became part of the Pendergast combine included (a) Little Tammany, which received this appellation because of its resemblance to the organization of bosses Tweed and Croker of New York; (b) Democracy Incorporated, a faction that before 1930 had attempted to play the role of mediator between the Pendergast and Shannon forces; and (c) a faction that had the nucleus of its political strength in eastern Jackson County.

Before 1930 the control that each of these factions had over patronage was generally commensurate with its strength at the ballot box. At that time the selection of judges and other court personnel was almost entirely the result of the patronage politics of the local ward and precinct organizations. This arrangement continued in the period of Pendergast hegemony. Not only were most judicial offices parceled out to different factional elements within the Democratic party but certain court positions, including judgeships, were regarded as the permanent property of specific factions.

This system of allocation came to an abrupt end with the adoption of the Missouri Plan for judicial selection and the nearly simultaneous political disintegration that occurred in Jackson County following the imprisonment of Pendergast for income tax evasion in May 1939. In the following year the Pendergast machine was swamped by reform forces in the municipal elections. Never again was there a unified party apparatus possessing the political potency once displayed by the Pendergast organization.

With the dissolution of the Pendergast combine and the reversion of Democratic party politics to multifactionalism, each of the separate party groups that had been subordinated to Pendergast leadership during the 1930's assumed autonomous status.[7] New factional leaders emerged

---

[6] Reddig suggests that these terms first gained currency when the Irish followers of Pendergast, many of whom kept goats, lived in the lower class section of the West Bluff area of the city. The Shannon followers lived over the hill, adjacent to a wooded valley replete with rabbits and other small game. In one particularly heated election campaign, a Shannon orator is said to have referred to the Pendergast followers as Goats, because of their numerous pets. Jim Pendergast is reputed to have accepted the label gladly, since to him the animals symbolized love of freedom and disregard for status distinctions. On their way to a party convention, Pendergast is said to have shouted to his delegation: "When we come over the hill like goats, they'll run like rabbits." Reddig, op. cit., p. 34.

[7] The most thorough treatment of Democratic factional politics in the period after 1940 is Howard D. Neighbor, Reform; Metamorphosis of Nonpartisan Politics in

from time to time, as the old chieftains died, were imprisoned, or fell before the challenge of younger and more crafty politicians, but the factional structure remained basically the same throughout the Missouri Plan era.

Collectively, these factions—the Democratic party "regulars"—fared most poorly in Kansas City municipal elections. With the exception of the 1959–1963 period, when the "regulars" joined forces to dominate the city council, various reformist elements controlled city politics. Although some reform groups had ambitions for expanding their power beyond the confines of the city, they lacked the organizational base for competing effectively in the county and state political arenas, which continued to be dominated by the old-line Democratic factions.

The outcome of county and state races within Jackson County thus came to depend on the shape of factional politics at any given time. In its totality the factional structure was exceedingly complex and mercurial, as first one and then another combination of factions came into existence for the purposes of a particular election. Most of the factions were involved in city as well as county and state politics; there were frequently different factional alignments for each of these separate political levels.

Yet there was considerable stability in the factional alignments revolving around the politics of Democratic gubernatorial primaries. In three of the five primaries occurring from 1944 to 1960 the recipient of the Democratic nomination either had no significant opposition in the primary or had the support of all the Democratic factions within Jackson County. The remaining contests pitted the Pendergast organization against a coalition of the other factions, a coalition that was led by the Eastern Jackson County (Sermon) faction and that included many of the reformist political groups from Kansas City.[8] In both contests, the candidate backed by the Pendergast faction was victorious.

Because of their importance in gubernatorial politics, the machine or regular Democratic factions in Jackson County thus continued to have relevance for the selection of judges. At a minimum the factions served as reference points by which aspirants for the bench could be designated in terms of their political acceptability to the governor. Nomi-

---

Kansas City, Missouri, with an Analysis of the 1959 Election (Kansas City, Missouri: Community Studies, Inc., 1962).

[8] The eastern Jackson County faction assumed a much greater prominence in county and state politics after 1940. Operating under the aegis of the Eastern Jackson County Democratic Club, the faction was led by Roger Sermon, whose power was enhanced considerably by virtue of his close association with U.S. Senator, later President, Harry S. Truman.

nees who were identified with a political faction that stood in opposition to the governor at some critical juncture had almost no chance of being appointed to the bench, whether or not they had ever participated personally in a campaign against the governor.

During some gubernatorial administrations the regular Democratic factions had far more than this minimum role in the selection process. Especially during the period from 1945 to 1956, leaders of the major political factions were frequently consulted by Missouri governors about appointments to the Jackson County circuit bench. Directly, this constituted a somewhat limited role for the factional leaders, since they were restricted to commenting upon the political acceptability of panels of nominees already submitted to the governor. Indirectly, however, the consultative role of the factional leaders had a far greater significance. Prospective candidates for the circuit bench, bearing in mind the governor's inclination to rely on the advice of certain factional leaders, could be deterred or encouraged in their quest for office, depending on their relationship to the factional leaders who had the ear of the governor. Thus the recruitment process came to be affected by the nature of factional politics. Moreover, some members of the judicial nominating commission were solicitous of the views of certain factional leaders. For these reasons the faction leaders' consultative role with the governor and nominating commissioners tended to have reverberations throughout the entire judical selection process, affecting nominations and appointments.

Of course not all factional affiliations have been helpful to aspirants for judicial office. Identification with some "North End" political elements has usually been an outright barrier to selection under the Missouri Plan.[9] Even a close association with the Pendergast faction would not have been a commanding advantage in the period after the mid-fifties. By this time all of the North End factions, including the Pendergast organization, had diminished in political strength. Thus governors elected in the late fifties and sixties did not depend on the "regular" Democrats to the extent that former Democratic governors had. Yet all the governors chosen down to 1960 had depended, at earlier stages of their political careers, on the Pendergast, Shannon, or Eastern Jackson

---

[9] The North End was the original base of Pendergast political strength in Kansas City. An area of about six wards located in the northwestern corner of the city, it contained large numbers of Negroes and immigrants. By the 1940's the Italians had begun to supplant the Irish as the dominant group in several North End wards, and political leadership came to be drawn increasingly from the ranks of the Italians.

County organizations, and thus continued to have close relations with the leaders of those factions.

The other factions were not in such a strategic position. They not only lacked decisive strength at the ballot box but many of them, and all of their leaders, had emerged only after the disintegration of the pre-1940 Pendergast combine. Thus governors chosen in the late fifties and afterward owed the small faction leaders nothing and associated with them very little.

Political groups other than the Democratic organization "regulars" have also played important roles in judicial selection in Jackson County. Lawyers associated with reformist group politics have been active in state-level politics, and have worked either as individuals or as part of a reformist political coalition on behalf of gubernatorial candidates. Thus identification with the reformist or antimachine faction within Jackson County politics has often had a decisive effect upon a candidate's chances for appointment to the bench.[10] In some periods a reformist affiliation has been helpful; in others, it has been enough to preclude nomination or appointment to the bench.

Involvement in factional politics of either the machine or antimachine variety has not been the only route to the Jackson County circuit bench. Throughout the period since 1940 judicial appointments *have* gone to lawyers who have lacked close ties with any of the factions. Generally, these lawyers have been supporters of the governor appointing them, and usually have worked for him during one of the election campaigns that was critical to the governor's success in moving up the political career ladder. By the 1960's there was clearly evident a trend toward the selection of judges who had been political "independents" from a factional or organizational standpoint. This trend coincided with the relative decline in strength of the Jackson County party organizations in the state political arena.

One consequence of this trend favoring political independents is that there are often significant changes from one gubernatorial term to the next in the make-up of the lawyer group having the highest "eligibility" for appointment to the circuit bench. These changes are traceable primarily to the proclivity that governors have for appointing persons with

---

[10] The antimachine or reform groups are never referred to as factions by Jackson County politicians; there the designation "faction" is reserved for the Democratic regulars. Any precise usage requires that the reform groups be classified as factions, even though the scope of their political activities has generally been more limited than that of the "machine" political organizations. For a definition of faction, see footnote 57, Chapter 1, *supra*.

whom they have had close personal or political relations. Since the web of personal-political relationships of one governor is likely to differ somewhat from that of the preceding governor, there is a concomitant shift in the group of individuals with the greatest entree to the governor and thus the greatest chance to receive judicial appointments.

Gubernatorial politics has thus had a decisive effect on the chances of individual attorneys to be chosen for positions on the Jackson County circuit bench. Generally, the governor's predilection for appointing political supporters tends to place the whole category of political lawyers in a preferential position in the judicial selection process.

Although the emphasis given to political experience is largely attributable to the governor's orientations, members of the judicial nominating commission also contribute to this politicization of the selection process. The nominating commissioners are inclined to assign importance to the candidates' previous political experience for several reasons. They do so, in part, because they know the governor will prefer nominees who have had political experience. Because of the governor's preference on this matter, it becomes almost a certainty that one of the nominating commissioners will advance the cause of a candidate who has political connections with the governor. In response, other nominating commissioners will often rally behind other candidates whom they believe to be equally close to the governor politically. There is another much simpler reason for the commission's perferring to nominate political lawyers. The commissioners, particularly the lay commissioners, are much more likely to be acquainted with politlcal lawyers than of their nonpolitical colleagues, given the public visibility of the former.

Thus, partly because of the governor's orientation and partly because of the orientations of the judicial nominating commissioners, there is a politicization of the entire nominating process, as indicated by the disproportionate numbers of applicants, nominees, and appointees who have backgrounds of activity in partisan and public affairs.

To a large extent Jackson County judicial selection under the Missouri Plan has been affected by the political legacy of the Pendergast era. Not only did the Pendergast faction dominate the local politics of Jackson County and Kansas City for a decade but it was the only metropolitan-based political organization to assume a significant role of any longevity in state politics. One consequence was that long after the Pendergast group had ceased to hold controlling power at either the local or state levels the selection of judges could turn on the question of where a candidate stood in the array of Pendergast versus anti-Pendergast political forces. Thus, although the Pendergast machine lost its political omnipotence before the adoption of the Missouri Plan, it retained its political relevance for most of the period of the Plan's operation.

ROLE ORIENTATIONS OF PARTICIPANTS IN THE SELECTION PROCESS

The milieu of Bar, clientele, and state politics described in the preceding section sets the broad limits within which the judicial nominating commission and the governor perform the function of choosing judges for the circuit bench. Yet within these general confines each nomination and appointment is affected by highly particularistic forces.

The selection process is a preeminently personalistic one. Especially at the nominating stage, it has involved intense campaigns by competing groups working on behalf of a wide array of candidates. Something of the flavor of this process is revealed in the following editorial comments by the Kansas City *Star:*

The hardest test of a judicial commissioner comes in his ability to withstand the heat. As soon as a vacancy occurs in the court the campaigns start. Friends of candidates solicit long lists of supporters for their men. Telephones jangle day and night. Close personal or political friends of the commissioners are urged to telephone recommendations and to bear down on them. The bush is beaten for every possible influence.[11]

Thus the nature of any given campaign depends on a host of factors, including the make-up of the nominating commission, the occupant of the governorship, and the various influences that lead specific lawyers to become candidates at a given moment in time.

Yet, aside from the environmental forces that impinge on the commission, there are other factors that tend to introduce important regularities into the nominating process and thus to limit the influence of the idiosyncratic factors surrounding specific nominations. Of primary importance in this respect are the role orientations of the participants in the selection process—the nominating commissioners and the governor. The structure of roles within the judicial nominating commission is considered first.[12]

---

[11] Kansas City *Star*, August 16, 1947.

[12] In utilizing the concept of *role* for this study, there is no intention of advancing yet another definition which would purport to be useful for all kinds of political or social inquiry. There probably has already been too great a proliferation of such definitions, without any concomitant increase in conceptual clarity. On this point, see William A. Rushing, "The Role Concept: Assumptions and Their Methodological Implications," *Sociology and Social Research*, 49 (October 1964), pp. 46–57. For this study of Missouri Plan judicial selection, role is conceptualized as involving both normative components (expectations of those interacting with the occupant

Role of Lay Commissioners

From a political standpoint a critical role on the nominating commission is played by the gubernatorially appointed lay nominating commissioners. Many lay members have been quite active in party politics and can thus serve as points of access for those who wish to urge that consideration be given to candidates bearing political credentials. Moreover, lay commissioners are widely viewed as spokesmen for the governor's interests in the nominating process, particularly if the lay members have been appointed by a governor still in office.

Lawyers criticize several aspects of the lay member's role in the nominating process. The most fundamental objection is that lay members lack experience and insight that would permit them to make sound evaluations of the capabilities of candidates for the judiciary. Lawyer critics also contend that most lay people do not even make an honest attempt to arrive at any independent judgment of the abilities of aspirants for nomination. Instead, they are said to turn to others for advice about the judicial candidates and, in the process, become mere pawns of those who wish to influence the selection of judges.

Most objectionable, say the lawyers, is the tendency for the laymen to turn to the governor, or to political associates of the governor, for cues to which candidates they should support for nomination. Only slightly less reprehensible, in the estimate of attorneys, is the fact that the lay commissioners tend to defer to the wishes of the presiding judge. They do so, according to their critics, because of the lay commissioner's presumption that the presiding judge will have come to know the legal abilities of most contenders, since they will have tried cases in his court. Quite clearly, this objection is directed not so much at the lay members

---

of a position with respect to his behavior, as well as the occupant's own expectations) and behavioral components. Operationally, this inquiry attempts to gain an understanding of both these dimensions by focusing on (a) the perceptions of each participant in the formal selection process of the kind of behavior which he felt was expected of him, and his expectations with regard to the behavior of other formal participants; (b) the views held by those who were not formal participants as to the behavior which they expected of the formal participants; and (c) the statements of all the above as to what each participant actually did when it came to specific decisions affecting judicial selection. By considering all these factors in conjunction it was possible to arrive at reasonably accurate portrayals of the role orientations of those who were involved in judicial selection. Admittedly, the approach utilized is not as methodologically rigorous as might be desirable. But when the process studied stretches years into the past, and when the bulk of the evidence is of a retrospective nature, any effort to be more precise would simply promise more than could be delivered.

as against the inflation of the role played by the presiding judge in the decision process. Somewhat less objectionable, in the view of the lawyers, is the tendency for lay commissioners to seek advice from lawyers whom they employ as counsel for their businesses or from lawyers whom they know socially.

The foregoing assessment of the role of the lay nominating commissioner is disputed by most of those who have participated in the formal selection process. Lawyer nominating commissioners, although agreeing that some lay commissioners have at times deferred to the views of the lawyer commissioners and the presiding judge, nonetheless aver that the lay members play an important and largely autonomous role in the nomination of judges. One lawyer commissioner observed: "A conscientious layman will go out and get information from both lawyers and laymen on the persons being considered for a judgeship. In fact, the lay commissioner can get more objective information from the lawyers than can the lawyer members of the nominating commission."

The courts of appeals judges, speaking from a slightly different perspective in their capacity as chairmen of the nominating commission, emphasize a different function performed by the lay commissioners. One judge stated:

At the beginning of the nominating commission's deliberations, the laymen are usually very quiet. They just sit and listen as the lawyers discuss the merits of the various candidates. But toward the end of the deliberations the laymen become influential, particularly because they are able to mediate the differences between the lawyers on the basis of who they feel has made the stronger case.

This mediating function appears to be especially important in instances where the lawyer members of the commission share the same general orientation but simply disagree in their assessments of the candidates. In instances where there is an ideological schism between the lawyer commissioners, particularly where one represents the plaintiffs' and the other, the defense's point of view, there would be virtually no possibility that the lay members could mediate the differences between the lawyer commissioners.

The lay nominating commissioners stress still other dimensions of their own role. One lay commissioner maintained the following:

The lay commissioner has a more objective viewpoint. He is not affected by personalities the way the lawyers are. That is, the layman has the advantage of not having known the candidates previously, and can therefore investigate them objectively.

In his own view, then, the layman is not affected by the professional rivalries, petty animosites, and largely superficial biases that frequently distort the assessments lawyers make of one another.

The extent to which the lay commissioner can avoid the evaluative astigmatism that reputedly afflicts the attorney clearly depends on the degree of his sophistication about the legal profession. Throughout the history of the Plan few laymen have been astute enough to contend with the lawyers on anywhere near equal terms in the assessment of the legal ability and judicial potential of candidates for the bench. The laymen who have done so have employed a variant of the approach described by one lay nominating commissioner:

If you are a layman you evaluate the judicial qualifications of the various candidates by discussing them with lawyers, and with lawyers that you know well, so you can assess what they say.

The weakness of the Missouri Plan is that the (Nominating) Commission may be swayed by efforts on behalf of certain individuals, rather than by the merits of the candidates. For that reason, I question the wisdom of some of the lay appointments made to the nominating commission. Some of these men never really stand up for anything. And you need men on the commission who are vigorous, who will resist pressure, particularly since some of the greatest pressure that the lay member is subjected to comes from his closest lawyer friends.

If a layman knows enough lawyers, and will talk with different kinds, he can size up the qualifications of the candidates pretty well. So, I didn't follow the lead of the lawyers on the nominating commission, but instead sought the advice of attorneys that I knew personally.

Not many commissioners have had either the contacts or the energy to conduct this kind of intensive investigation of the prospective nominees. Some laymen admit that their unfamiliarity with the legal and judicial professions is a handicap for which they can compensate only partially through consultation with lawyer acquaintances. One lay commissioner remarked:

All I can find out about a candidate from talking to lawyer friends is whether the candidate is honest and socially acceptable. I can't learn anything that would allow me to judge the candidates' qualifications for a judicial position, so I usually rely heavily upon the lawyer members of the commission and the presiding judge.

Consultations about judicial candidates are not always instigated by the lay commissioners themselves. Both the candidates and the campaigners for the candidates approach the lay commissioners in an effort to enlist their support. Lawyer friends or social acquaintances of the laymen and lawyers in the firms that handle the legal business of the laymen provide major avenues of access by which various segments of the legal community present their views on the contenders for nomination.

Lay commissioners also become the targets for political leaders who wish to influence the selection process or for political lawyers who are known to be close to the governor. Lay members who have been intimately involved in state and local politics (who are politically *aucourant*) have little need to inquire of others about the political acceptability of the various judicial candidates. They already know. Of course they are generally willing to listen to the views of others who presume to speak for the political community about candidate acceptability.

However, for most of the period of the Missouri Plan's operation in Jackson County, the lay nominating commissioners were not simply respondents to political pressures but were highly political in their orientations to the nominating process. The feature of their political outlook that had the greatest significance for the nominating process was their allegiances and antipathies toward the various factions within Democratic party politics.

The Lawyer Commissioners

According to the rhetoric of Missouri Plan advocates, the lawyer nominating commissioner occupies (or, at least, should occupy) the central role in the process of judicial selection. The lawyer commissioner is expected to serve as a representative of the entire Bar, bringing to bear on the choice of judicial personnel an informed, professional judgment and evaluating candidates according to the legal profession's criteria for determining the characteristics of "good" judges. This lawyer participation in judicial nominations is presumed to be the chief advantage of the Missouri Plan over the elective or appointive methods of recruiting judicial personnel.

This "ideal" role postulated for the lawyer nominating commissioner has departed from reality in several important respects. First, it rests on the assumption that the lawyer commissioners and the presiding judge, who constitute a majority of the commission, will have similar perspectives toward the nominating process. In fact, the presiding judge, even though he too is a lawyer, frequently has different impressions of candidates for nomination, and often emphasizes different indicators of potential judicial ability than do the lawyer commissioners. In Jackson County, however, the greatest divergence between lawyer commissioner and presiding judge orientations has been the differential emphasis placed on the political background of candidates for nomination. For most Plan nominations the presiding judge attached far greater importance to the partisan political activities of aspirants for the bench than did most of the lawyer nominating commissioners.

A second source of dissention within the lawyer-judge segment of the nominating commission has its origins in the ideological friction that may exist between the two lawyer nominating commissioners. In approximately two-thirds of the nominations occurring between 1940 and 1964 there were distinct lacunae between the viewpoints of the two lawyer members of the nominating commission. In these instances one lawyer member invariably had a corporate or corporate-defense practice and had won his position on the nominating commission principally through support of the corporate-defense oriented membership of the Kansas City Lawyers' Association. The second lawyer member, for most of these nominations, had a predominantly plaintiffs' practice and had been supported in his bid for a commission seat largely by the plaintiffs'-leaning membership of the Kansas City Bar Association.

One consequence of the resulting ideological stalemate was a considerable reduction in the chances for nomination of candidates coming from either extreme of the plaintiffs-defense continuum of legal practice. This narrowing of the zone of candidate acceptability also affected the lawyer sources which commission members relied on for the evaluation of candidates. Attorneys who had a predominantly plaintiffs' or defense practice were rarely consulted, since one or another of the lawyer commissioners could be expected to oppose the kinds of candidates that would be recommended by such attorneys. Instead, communication between nominating commissioners and the Bar tended to be directed toward the middle of the legal practice continuum, particularly toward attorneys affiliated with mixed plaintiffs'-defense trail firms.

Neutralization of the plaintiffs'-defense issue had the additional consequence of accentuating the political dimension of the selection process. The issue of the candidate's field of legal practice was a prime concern only to the lawyer nominating commissioners. Given its low saliency for other commission members and given an ideological stand-off between the lawyer commissioners, neither lawyer commissioner could hope to use the plaintiffs'-defense issue as a ground for seeking allies among the remaining commissioners. The result was a shift in the focus of nominating decisions away from the issue of *legal* background, with is limited appeal, and toward the issue of *political* background which had some salience for virtually all members of the nominating commission.

For this reason the role of the lawyer commissioners in the nominating process came to be determined largely by their political orientations. Commissioners drawn from the plaintiffs' segment of the Bar had generally been affiliated politically with one of the major Democratic factions in Jackson County politics. Some of them had participated in the anti-Pendergast political movements of the late 1930's and afterward, yet they had no special animus toward other Democratic factions. By contrast most of the lawyer commissioners drawn from the corporate-defense segment of the bar were Republicans who had never been very active in partisan politics, not even in reform or anti-Pendergast politics at the local level.

The manner in which political issues affected nominations depended substantially, then, on the degree of congruence between the political viewpoints of the lawyer commissioners and those of the lay commissioners and the presiding judge. For much of the period between 1940 and 1964 there was far greater commonality of political outlook between the plaintiffs'-leaning lawyer commissioners and the lay-presiding judge segment of the commission than between the latter and the corporate-defense lawyer commissioners. The plaintiffs' lawyer commissioners tended to come from the same political milieu, to hold many of the same values, and to have knowledge of the same political terrain as did most of the lay commissioners and the presiding judges. The corporate-defense lawyer commissioners thus were at a relative disadvantage when nominating decisions turned on issues of a partisan political nature.

Of course no lawyer commissioner is likely to have a purely political role orientation. The extent to which a given commissioner's role is predominantly political is determined mainly by his own background and personal inclinations. It is also affected by the orientations of the other commission members, especially those of the presiding judge.

The Presiding Judge

The presiding judge of the Kansas City Court of Appeals almost always has had a prime influence in judicial nominations and, at times, has virtually dominated the nominating process. Yet this influence does not stem from any powers associated with the judge's formal position as chairman of the nominating commission, since some chairmen have done little more than function as presiding officers over the meetings of the nominating commission. Instead, the influence of the presiding judge rests upon other bases, including the skills that he displays in the bargaining process associated with the making of nominations. These skills, however, are of distinctly secondary importance, for they are only the means for the translation of potential into actual influence. That potential influence is determined largely by the presiding judge's ability to function as a spokesman for the various "communities" or groups that interact within the judicial selection process.

At a minimum the presiding judge serves as a knowledgeable representative of the judicial institution itself—a role that none of the other nominating commissioners can assume. In this capacity the presiding judge can expect some modicum of deference, particularly from the lay commissioners, since they are likely to accept his views about the various judicial candidates as being at least partial reflections of his concern for the maintenance of a "quality" bench.

The presiding judge also is attuned to the array of interests that have paramount significance for the Bar. He is a lawyer himself; moreover, his experience on the Court of Appeals entitles him to speak about the legal ability and "temperament" of the lawyers who have tried cases before him. If the presiding judge and the lawyer commissioners differ in their assessments of a given candidate, the lay members of the commission will often accept the judge's views, on the grounds that he has acquired a more impartial, reliable estimate of the legal abilities of the candidates than has the practicing attorney.

However, the presiding judge's circle of acquaintanceship in the Bar tends to narrow progressively the longer he is on the Court of Appeals bench. Because of the nature of appeals court litigation, the presiding judge comes into contact with very few lawyers, and these are rarely of the type who become candidates for the circuit bench. Many candidates for judical nomination will also have entered the practice of law after the time when the presiding judge went on the appellate bench. To maintain their credibility as informed appraisers of the practicing Bar's capabilities, most presiding judges therefore acquire information about likely judicial candidates from state or federal trial judges who have frequent contact with the practicing lawyers.

Finally, the presiding judge may function in a political role. The coin of this particular realm—the coin that is indispensable in the commission members' interactions with respect to the political dimension of the nominating process—is the coin of political knowledge. To be fully effective in dealing with the political dimension, a nominating commissioner must have an intimate knowledge of local and state politics. He must understand the mosaic of political cliques and factions in Jackson County, their interrelations, and the changes in the patterns of these relationships over time; he must understand the political pedigrees of the entire range of contenders for judicial nomination, including their past associations with the governor or political figures close to the governor, and extending even to the political associations of their fathers, grandfathers, or other relatives; and he must understand the political inclinations and temperament—the political style—of the governor in office at a particular time.

Few Court of Appeals' judges have detailed knowledge of all these facets of the political terrain. Even to acquire the minimum information essential for performance of a political role, the presiding judge must overcome the handicap of the isolation imposed by the appellate judgeship. The norms of Missouri Plan "nonpartisanship" are also a liability, militating against the judges' assuming active, participant roles in partisan politics. Because of these constraints, some appellate judges assume very limited judicial roles, deriving their chief professional satisfaction from the researching and writing of case opinions.

Most Kansas City Court of Appeals judges have been unwilling to accept such restricted political roles. Largely for reasons of temperament, they remain curious about politics after they go on the bench. Although they may not be active in partisan councils, they continue to be deeply interested spectators of the political world, using their judicial status as a basis for entree to governors, public officials, and party figures at various levels. The result has been that politically knowledgeable appellate judges held the presiding judgeship and thus were chairmen of the circuit nominating commission for approximately seventy percent of the judicial nominations made in the Jackson County circuit during the 1940–1964 period.

The overall role of the presiding judge in the nominating process is thus affected by his proficiency in each of the separate role dimensions discussed here. The ability that he displays in these different role orientations depends, to some degree, on the nature of his own personal background and experiences. Judges who, before going on the bench, had their major legal and political experience outside Jackson County rarely acquire sufficient information about the Bar, politics, and politicians to permit them to deal effectively with these aspects of the nominating process. Other appellate judges have attained high levels of proficiency in all three role orientations, and thus have served as effective spokesmen for the judicial, legal, and political worlds. Through such a combination of roles they acquire the capability of exerting a pervasive influence over judicial nominations.

These judges cannot dictate nominations, but must usually compromise with fellow commissioners for their own preferences to be accepted by the nominating commission. Yet the more forceful and persuasive of the presiding judges have left their own distinctively personal imprint on every panel chosen when they were chairmen of the nominating commission. As one lawyer observed: "The whole selection process is marked by lobbying, and by an intense power struggle, where personal relations are very important. And it's a process where the presiding judge of the court of appeals is a very important man, so that his likes and dislikes are crucial." Thus the personality, the values, and inevitably the prejudices and biases of such a presiding judge become critical factors in the choice of judicial nominees.

Of all the judges who have served as chairmen of the Jackson County nominating commission, one has most clearly epitomized the role of the "strong" presiding judge. A member of the circuit bench describes the role of this particular presiding judge as follows:

He is a master politician, and he has maneuvered beautifully to control the selection of nominees for the circuit bench. And, in a way, he has created his own dynasty as a result. He himself had no strong factional affiliation, but he knows the factional affiliation of almost everyone. He also has some deep political prejudices of which he himself is largely unaware. Prior to going on the bench he had no reputation for political acumen. But he has an uncanny political sense, and he has played the game of political chess more skillfully than anybody else. For one thing, he always has had more information, more "intelligence," than anybody else involved in the process. For another, he could very effectively bridge the political and legal worlds.

Often referred to as the "autocrat" of the commission, this presiding judge was credited with being especially persuasive when it came to narrowing down the "finalists" to the panel of nominees sent to the governor.

Friendship, past associations, and family pedigree were among the major benchmarks that he used in deciding whom he would support for nomination to the circuit bench. Concern for these qualities was tempered by the high emphasis that he placed on political partisanship. Yet, except for his animus against Republicans, he appeared to have no antipathy toward any particular political groups or factions.

Out of his strong personal and political convictions, this presiding judge fashioned his definition of the qualities that were needed for a circuit judgeship. Although his own legal practice had been of a corporate and mixed plaintiffs'-defense nature, he appears to have attached little importance to the practice backgrounds of judicial candidates, but instead emphasized the extent of a candidate's trial experience, his integrity, and his capacity for judicial temperament once on the bench. Despite his strong partisanship, he occasionally opposed candidates who had insufficient experience in legal practice, but rather had been primarily political jobholders.

This judge is said to have been "close to every governor of the state over a period of many years." Reputedly, he was able to use the insights gained from these associations and from his general knowledge of state politics as bases for strategy within the nominating commission.

In order to keep the process of nomination within controllable bounds, he never sought, or welcomed, advice from sources outside the nominating commission itself. Within the commission this judge gained his most solid and consistent support from the lay nominating commissioners. He knew them intimately—their strengths and weaknesses, their prejudices and interests—and he couched his appeals to them in terms that were most appropriate for the commissioner, in view of the situation at hand. This was done in such a skillful manner that it hardly ever aroused resentment; usually, it elicited gratitude. This particular judge was also a keen enough student of power relations to know when it was a provident time to stop the search for consensus and to insist on the capitulation of an obstinate minority.

The impressions that most Jackson County lawyers have of the presiding judge's role, as well as the resentment of some toward the scope of that role, largely reflect their reactions to the behavior of the judge described above. Yet some other presiding judges, although not members of the nominating commission for nearly so long, have had an influence only slightly less potent. Of course, much depends on their sagacity. As one nominee observed: "The presiding judge is extremely influential, to the extent at least that he can almost always name at least one of the three on the panel of nominees. And of course, you only need to name one, if he's the right guy."

The influence of the presiding judge, or any other member of the nominating commission, is contingent on the pattern of role orientations existing within the commission. Moreover, any given decision of the nominating commission is affected not only by the discrete combination of role orientations within the commission but by the specific relationship existing between the commission and the environment.

In legal theory the governor is part of this "environment," participating only in the appointment stage by selecting one person from a list of three names submitted to him by the nominating commission for each judicial vacancy; but the mere fact that the governor picks the judges has ramifications for the entire selection process, particularly as it affects lawyer "availability" for judicial recruitment. In practice even the governor's direct participation in the selection process is not limited to the appointment phase, but extends back into the nominating process in such a way as to make the governor a full-fledged participant in virtually all facets of judicial selection.

Role of the Governor

Eighteen of the nineteen Missouri Plan appointments to the Jackson County Circuit Court during the period from 1940 to 1964 were made by Democratic governors. The remaining appointment occurred during the administration of Republican Forrest C. Donnell, who served as governor from 1941 to 1944. In discussing the role that the governor has played in judicial selection, attention is therefore limited to the orientations of Democratic governors, as these have been shaped by the milieu of state politics, particularly Democratic party politics.

The absence of strong, cohesive state-wide party organizations has led to a form of "friends and neighbors" politics in Missouri.[13] When coupled with the state's "low-pressure" interest group politics,[14] the result has been a style of gubernatorial politics best described as cronyistic. Politicians usually rise to the top of the state political structure in Missouri—and thus to the governorship—through a tedious process of advancement via a number of lesser public offices. By the time they have reached the top, Missouri governors have become obligated to a host of political supporters and friends; usually they have also incurred a considerable number of political enmities.

These features of state politics should permit the governor a wide range of discretion in the selection of appointive officials. The breadth of his potential discretion has been even further widened by the fact that the Missouri governorship has been a political dead end in recent history. Until 1964 Missouri governors could not immediately succeed themselves in office. Although they could serve multiple nonconsecutive terms in the governorship, only one did so. Neither has the governorship very often been a steppingstone to national political office. Thus the structure of Missouri politics has allowed Missouri governors to be relatively free of many kinds of political obligations present in other state political systems, including the necessity of giving primacy to partisan considerations in making gubernatorial appointments.

Yet Missouri politics has not produced governors who were inclined to utilize the full range of discretion permitted by the system. Missouri governors have assumed highly partisan orientations, especially in their appointments to public office. Moreover, the politics of gubernatorial appointments has been essentially the politics of rewarding friends or supporters who assisted the governor at one stage or another in his advancement to the state's highest office. Only rarely have other objectives become involved in the governor's selection of public office personnel. During the period covered by this study few Missouri governors had significant legislative programs. Occasionally they did become committed to a particular policy program which they deemed important

---

[13] V. O. Key, Jr., *Southern Politics in State and Nation* (New York: Alfred A. Knopf, 1949), p. 110, and *passim*.

[14] Nicholas A. Masters, Robert H. Salisbury, and Thomas H. Eliot, *State Politics and the Public Schools; An Exploratory Analysis* (New York: Alfred A. Knopf, 1964), particularly Chapter 11, "Missouri: Low Pressure Politics," pp. 12–98.

enough to justify the use of patronage resources in return for legislative or other support critical to its acceptance. However, most gubernatorial appointments served no policy objectives, but were dispensed to friends and political associates, generally to those who had supported the governor in the past.

Another common feature of the orientation of most recent Missouri governors has been their commitment to the values of the state's rural Democracy. While each depended for nomination and election on the support of individuals and political organizations within the metropolitan areas, all the Democratic governors have reflected the basic political conservatism of the state's nonmetropolitan areas.[15] They also have shared the outlook toward the Missouri Plan prevalent among most outstate politicians and lawyers.

During their terms of office all the Democratic governors serving in the years from 1945 to 1960 were basically antipathetic toward the Plan.[16] Governor Phil Donnelly remained a bitter opponent of the Plan throughout his two four-year terms in office. It was not until after he left the governorship that Donnelly came to embrace the philosophy of the Plan, and to favor it over the older partisan method of judicial selection. Forrest Smith, who was governor from 1949 to 1952, never did become a supporter of the Plan, although he reluctantly admitted that there had been an improvement in the quality of the bench as a result of the Plan. Governor James T. Blair is reputed to have remained an active opponent of the Plan throughout his term of office (1957 to 1960) and to have desired a return to the system of partisan elections used prior to 1940. The last governor to serve during the period studied, John Dalton, did not openly express opposition to the Plan, but was known to consider it to be unsatisfactory in several fundamental respects.

Thus the governors who participated in the selection of nearly all Missouri Plan judges chosen before 1965 displayed basically similar political styles and had essentially the same attitudes toward the Missouri Plan. Yet there were also important differences in the roles and perspectives of Missouri governors during the period from 1940 to 1964.

Of greatest significance for the selection of Jackson County circuit judges are the differences in the relationships that various Democratic

---

[15] Harry Lazer observes that the urban political machines had long cooperated with the rural forces dominating state politics, in return for control of their own political bailiwick. See his *The American Political System in Transition* (New York: Thomas Y. Crowell Company, 1967).

[16] Sidney Schulman, "Judicial Selection," in John Honnold, editor, *The Life of the Law; Readings on the Growth of Legal Institutions* (New York: The Free Press of Glencoe, 1964), p. 251.

governors have had with the party factions in the county. Governors Dalton and Blair were not dependent politically upon the support of the Jackson County factions for nomination or election to the governorship, although James T. Blair had been closely associated with various factional leaders earlier in his career and continued those relationships after he became governor. Governor Forrest Smith had received the support of all the old-line Democratic factions in the 1948 primary, thus enabling him to carry the county despite opposition from a candidate backed by the reform groups. Until he encountered political difficulties because of his reputed connections with North End politicians and underworld figures, Governor Smith took his cues regarding judicial selection from leaders of the Democratic "regular" factions.

Factional cleavages impinged most heavily on gubernatorial politics and thus on Jackson County judicial selection during the incumbency of Democratic Governor Phil Donnelly. In both 1944 and 1952 Donnelly's candidacy for the Democratic gubernatorial nomination led to a rupture in the Jackson County party structure. In the earlier contest Donnelly received the support of both the Pendergast and Shannon factions. The remainder of the "machine" factions were arrayed against him as were the antimachine, reform Democrats. The reform groups urged opposition to Donnelly primarily on the grounds that his election would lead to a reestablishment of machine-controlled politics in the county and state. Much the same factional line-up occurred in the 1952 gubernatorial primary. This time Donnelly's organizational support in Jackson County came entirely from the Pendergast faction. These events had their most dramatic consequence for judicial selection in Donnelly's second term of office, when a protracted conflict between the Governor and the Jackson County nominating commission developed primarily because of the manner in which factional political considerations were injected into judicial nominations.

The Jackson County dimension of Missouri gubernatorial politics was thus predominantly faction-oriented for most of the 1940 to 1964 period. The manner in which factional politics affected judicial selection was principally a result of another feature of the judicial selection process: the fusion of the nominating and appointing phases of selection in Jackson County.

This fusion of the nominating and appointing dimensions of selection was a consequence of the injection of gubernatorial preferences into the nominating stage. Whether these preferences were injected through direct involvement by the governor in the nominating process or by application by the nominators of the appointing authority's standards, the result was a compression of the entire selection process into the nominating stage. To the extent that this occurred, the appointment of judges constituted nothing more than a *pro forma* ratification of choices already made.

The fusion of the nominating and appointing functions has affected the selection of most judges chosen for the Jackson County circuit bench. Yet the extent of fusion and the manner in which it has occurred have varied from one gubernatorial administration to another. The principal sources of that variation have been the perspectives that different governors have taken toward the selection process and their varying conceptions of the proper relationship between the nominating commission and the governor.

The types of strategy involved in decisions affecting judicial selection have thus centered around the role that the governor has had in the selection process. In this sense the following account of judicial selection "games" is largely an extension of the analysis of the governor's role.

NOMINATING AND APPOINTING GAMES

It is expressed in various ways. A political lawyer says: "The panels of nominees sent to the governor are stacked. There is one strong political candidate that everybody knows will be selected by the governor and two others who are just window dressing." Another attorney elaborates a bit more fully:

The nominating commission loads the panels so that there's only one whom the governor will pick.

Somebody close to the situation will know that a particular lawyer has been opposed to the governor some years ago, or that the lawyer and the governor have had a falling out. The commission knows that this lawyer won't be named by the governor, so they nominate him. Then, they put on a Republican lawyer, knowing that he won't be named by the governor either. Then they put on another Democrat that they know is politically acceptable to the governor. That man will get the appointment.

Better than nine-tenths of those interviewed who professed knowledge of the matter—and that included lawyers, politicians, nominating commissioners, and judges—expressed the opinion that panels had been "stacked" by the nominating commission in the manner suggested by the lawyers quoted above.

Lawyers from every major practice specialty, including lawyers nominated for the circuit bench, assert that panel-stacking has been a common occurrence. One nominee spoke of his suspicions about the particular panel to which he was named:

I knew as soon as the panel was named who would be appointed. There was even talk of the same sort in the newspaper and among the lawyers. But the capstone came at a meeting of one of the bar associations right after the panel had been announced. Everyone was going around shaking hands with this particular nominee, even though he hadn't yet been chosen by the governor.

Participants in the nominating process also testify to the existence of panel-stacking. Speaking of the general pattern of decisions made by the commission, one nominating commissioner observes:

A good many times, if you're acquainted with the political background of the candidates and their ties with the governor, you know who will be picked. I'm including the members of the nominating commission when I say that. If the commissioners are politically aware, they know who has the inside track.

Of course, not all nominating commissioners may be politically "aware," at least with respect to every panel nominated. Speaking of a specific nomination, the commissioner quoted above noted:

Not everybody on the commission checks things out as thoroughly as they should. The presiding judge and I were the only ones on the nominating commission who knew of the close relationship between that nominee and the governor at the time the panel was selected.

Even if the commissioners are politically aware, it is often difficult to stop the nomination of a candidate who is a political favorite of the governor. This difficulty is largely attributable to the decision-making procedures utilized by the nominating commission. These procedures have generally facilitated the stacking of panels.

Nominating Procedures

Although there have been some variations over the years, the procedures utilized by the Jackson County nominating commission have usually followed the same basic pattern.[17] When a circuit judicial vacancy occurs, the nominating commission publicly announces that it is ready to receive the names of persons who should be considered for the vacancy. Recommendations from lawyers, businessmen, and others flow

---

[17] The Missouri Constitution [Article V, Section 29(d)] specifies only that the nominating commission "may act only by the concurrence of a majority of its members," and under "such rules as the Supreme Court shall promulgate." Until 1954, the Supreme Court Rules contained no provisions relative to the nominating process. In a revision of its Rules in 1954, the Court set forth certain requirements relating to the calling of nominating commission meetings, the selection of a temporary chairman if needed, and empowered the commission to consider for nomination persons other than those whose names are submitted by individuals outside the commission. Nothing in the revised Rules stipulated the balloting procedures to be employed by the commission.

into the commission, as well as "applications" filed directly by lawyers who wish their own names to be considered. The commission then determines which of the persons whose names are before it would be "available" for a judgeship in the event they were nominated for it. This determination usually has been made by means of a questionnaire sent to each of the persons under consideration, requesting certain personal and professional information, as well as an indication of availability.

If, reviewing the list of interested candidates, the nominating commission members are dissatisfied with either the caliber of the candidates or the range of choice open to them, they may attempt to generate additional candidacies. During some periods the commission has simply announced again that it is open to recommendations as to persons who might be considered for nomination. At other times commissioners have taken a more direct role by themselves seeking out candidates and persuading them to allow their names to be considered by the nominating commission. There usually follows a period during which commission members will consult others outside the commission as to the abilities of the various candidates under consideration.

Then the nominating commission meets for the purpose of paring the list, which may contain as many as 50 or 60 names. The process has often been quite informal, with commission members discussing each of the names on the list, and eliminating those who, by mutual agreement, are not deemed qualified for consideration. One lawyer nominating commissioner stated: "The great majority of the persons suggested are laughable and are quickly eliminated from further consideration. This quick narrowing-down process will usually leave from 10 to 20 names for more serious consideration." At times this initial pruning has been accomplished entirely by the lawyer commissioners and the presiding judge, with the lay commissioners deferring to their judgment.

Other nominating commissioners have proceeded, in a more formal way, to narrow the original list of candidates. Often this entails the casting of a ballot by each commissioner, who votes for the five, sometimes ten, candidates that he feels should be given further consideration. A composite list is then made from these choices, and the commission concentrates its attention on that particular grouping.

A variety of procedures have then been employed to reduce the candidates to the number that are to be nominated for the vacancy or vacancies to be filled. The types of technique utilized in the six-year period served by one nominating commissioner were described by him as follows:

In reducing the list to the three persons to be submitted to the Governor, no standard procedure is followed. Sometimes the commissioners rank the entire list of names according to their preferences, using a preferential ballot type of procedure. At other times the commissioners each vote for three persons of their choice.

Whatever the balloting system, the commission generally proceeds by dropping from consideration those who receive the lowest number of votes until such time as all the nominees have been selected. Frequently a secret ballot is used in these final stages.

The group of nominees that results from the final stage of balloting often comprises only a tentative panel. After the preferences of the commissioners are determined, attention frequently will be given to the partisan balance of the panel. The rule of thumb has been to nominate two lawyers having the same partisan affiliation as the governor and a third from the other major party.

One other factor that has a bearing on all of the above procedures is that of the continuity in the pool of candidates considered by the nominating commission. As long as the membership of the nominating commission remains stable, the commission tends to maintain something of a core roster of candidates who will automatically be considered whenever a vacancy occurs. Candidates who finish near the top in the selection of one panel will most likely in a perferential position when the nominating commission considers the selection of nominees for the next vacancy.

Except for very limited periods, the entire nominating process has been colored by the commission's efforts to attain unanimity on its choice of panels to be sent to the governor. At the preliminary stages when the commission is narrowing down the list of candidates under consideration, the rule of unanimity is generally not observed. If any member of the nominating commission has strong feelings that a particular candidate should be kept in the running, the other members of the commission generally defer to his wishes, but commission members strive for consensus on the nominees that are to be submitted to the governor for his consideration.

Unanimity is sought for a number of reasons, the most critical being the feeling among the commissioners that dissent would undercut the legitimacy of the nominating process, particularly in the eyes of members of the Bar. In one sense the commitment to unanimity is merely a product of tradition. Members of the nominating commission point to the fact that past commissions, with certain glaring exceptions, have always followed a rule of consensus. The exceptions, particularly the divided nominating commission involved in a deadlock with Governor Donnelly, are pointed to as examples of the dysfunctionality of dissensus within the commission.

There have been numerous occasions on which the consensus about the final panel of nominees was strictly *pro forma* in nature. Some members of the nominating commission have frequently been opposed to one of the nominees placed on the panel sent to the governor, but have decided to concur in the views of the majority because of their feeling that expression of their views through a formal dissent would not be in the best interests of the commission.

Employment of the rule of unanimity has had several important consequences for the nominating process. It has the effect of equalizing power within the commission. Insistence on unanimity has also been an important weapon in the process of bargaining over nominations. Individual nominating commissioners, or minority blocs within the commission, have occasionally utilized the threat of a minority report to advance the cause of candidates not favored by a majority of the commission. Yet majority blocs have not often capitulated in such circumstances. They, too, have been able to invoke the principle of consensus as a way to secure the minority's acquiescence.

Other features of the nominating process have more directly facilitated the stacking of panels. Of principal importance has been the latent nature of political considerations in the nominating process. Rarely has the political dimension of nominations been a topic for direct, open discussion in the commission's deliberations. Thus efforts to block nominations on political grounds must consist of *sub-rosa* lobbying among individual commissioners or must take the form of arguments presented to the commission about the legal abilities of the candidates in question. Frequently neither tack is successful, as one lay nominating commissioner indicates in the following account:

We were able to decide rather quickly on two nominees. The problem came with the third nominee. The presiding judge and one of the lawyer commissioners were backing the same man for the third spot on the panel. The other lawyer commissioner and I were somewhat reluctant about this particular candidate. The other lay commissioner wouldn't take a position on the matter. It was sort of a sticky situation because our only real objection was that this man (being considered for the third nomination) had a political tinge to his candidacy. Both of us who were holding out had a high respect for the presiding judge, and neither one of us wanted to come out and say why we opposed the man backed by the presiding judge, namely, because of his political taint. This candidate was also an honest and able lawyer. Therefore, we wouldn't be on very sound grounds to oppose him for lacking professional qualifications. The upshot was that we finally agreed to go along, and so this man's name was put on the panel as the third nominee. Once that was done, I was certain that the third nominee would be appointed by the governor.

The political "taint" referred to by the lay commissioner resulted from the "fact that the governor was using pressure to get this man named to the panel."

On other occasions members of the nominating commission have not felt such constraints when faced with the issue of a gubernatorially favored candidate. Even a minority of the commission can sometimes block such a candidate, given the reluctance of commission members to make nominations on a simple majority basis. Similarly, a majority can sabotage the candidacy of an attorney favored by the governor without departing from consensus-based decision making. If they remain cohesive and are willing to wait out the other side, they can force the minority to abandon its candidate and join in the search for a compromise nominee that will be acceptable to all commissioners. An instance of this kind is described in the following comments of a lay nominating commissioner:

> There was a deadlock in the commission when we selected that panel. Two commissioners were for . . . [this particular candidate], and they didn't want to see anybody else nominated who would interfere with their candidate's chances to be appointed. Two other commissioners were opposed to this man. This situation dragged on for two or three weeks. I saw that we were deadlocked, principally because we had agreed that we wanted to get a man that all five of the nominating commissioners could endorse. We didn't want a minority report with respect to the panel nominated.

Another member of the nominating commission indicates the grounds for objection to this candidate:

> The governor called up . . . [a member of the circuit bench] about getting . . . [this lawyer] placed on the panel of nominees. The governor didn't dare call me about it, but he was willing to call this judge, thinking that he would relay the message to me. I told the circuit judge that we weren't going to nominate the man, and I told him why.

The candidate in question confirms the contention that he was favored by the governor and explains his failure to be nominated as follows:

> I obtained a promise from the governor that if I could get my name on a panel, then he would select me for a circuit judgeship. But word of this got out and that ruined my chances to be nominated. The reason was, of course, that my nomination would have made for a very embarrassing situation for the other nominees. They would have resented the fact that their presence on the panel would be superfluous since it would be known in advance whom the governor was going to select.

The stalemate was eventually broken when the two commissioners opposing this candidate joined with the lay commissioner "caught in the middle" to back a compromise candidate, one that was reluctantly accepted by the minority faction in the commission. Ironically, the compromise candidate had such a close personal (though not political) relationship with the governor that his appointment was a foregone conclusion. Only two members of the commission majority appear to have been aware of this fact at the time the nominations were made.

A further characteristic of the nominating process that tends to facilitate the stacking of panels is the commission's practice of selecting panels with a partisan balance. This has amounted to a kind of token bipartisanism, since members of the nominating commission generally have named Republicans to the panels with the expectation that the governor would not appoint them to the bench. Through adherence to such a token bipartisanism, the nominating commission could claim to be fulfilling its obligations to the nonpartisan principles of the Missouri Plan, and could thus shift to the governor the onus for the failure to achieve nonpartisanship in practice. In addition, panel-stacking has been simplified considerably by the inclusion of Republican nominees on panels where there is virtually no possibility that a Republican will be appointed.

Rigging, Loading, and Wiring of Panels

The term "panel-stacking" has been used in a generic sense to indicate any form of panel selection wherein the nominating commission, through the choice of a particular combination of nominees, seeks to preempt the appointing function, or where the commission accedes to the governor's express wishes by nominating the person he desires to appoint. There are actually three principal variants of the panel-stacking game: rigging, loading, and wiring. Panel-rigging is the selection of a combination of nominees so that the governor will, in effect, have no choice. The classical "rigging" game formula is the one presented earlier: nominate one political friend of the governor, one political enemy, and one from the other party (unless the governor has given some indication that he would consider appointment of a minority party lawyer, in which case another political enemy can be substituted). Thus the distinguishing feature of this game is the inclusion on the panel of one, but only one, nominee whom the governor is known to favor for political or personal reasons.

A more flagrant form of panel-stacking occurs when the commission presents a combination of candidates so that the governor is forced to appoint someone he does not want, but someone that he will accept as the lesser of evils. This is known as panel-loading in the argot of Jackson County lawyers. The most blatant instance of panel-loading in the history of the Missouri Plan occurred when a panel of three Republican nominees for the St. Louis Court of Appeals was presented to a Democratic governor known to be adamantly opposed to the idea that he should appoint any Republican to the bench. Only slightly less blatant instances have occurred in the selection of Jackson County circuit judges, as we shall see in a subsequent discussion of the two-year hiatus between Governor Donnelly and the nominating commission.

The third variant of panel-stacking is what is called "wiring" the panel. This term is used to designate commission compliance with the expressed wishes of the governor as to whom he would like to appoint to the bench. Thus, in panel-wiring, the governor makes his perferences known to one or more members of the nominating commission, either directly or through an intermediary. The commission then names a panel containing the name of the lawyer preferred by the governor, plus two other nominees chosen on a "what difference does it make" basis.

Political lawyers feel that the governor's influence over nominations tends to be channeled through the lay nominating commissioners principally, the presiding judge secondarily, and rarely if ever through the lawyer nominating commissioners. The governor is considered to have access particularly through the lay members that he has appointed to the nominating commission, but is reputed often to have entree even to those lay commissioners appointed by preceding governors. Frequently the governor will use indirect means to convey his wishes to the nominating commission. One such means is described by a Democratic attorney who condemns the role that Missouri governors have had in the nominating process:

The lawyers here believed that the Missouri Plan would remove politics from the selection of judges. Instead we got a nominating commission amenable to all kinds of pressures. Some of those pressures are from the governor. The governor will contact a political friend here in Kansas City and have his friend contact a nominating commissioner, telling the commissioner that the governor would like to have a certain individual put on the panel. This has been true in some periods more than in others. One of the lay nominating commissioners, who was a prominent business man, told me that the pressure which the governor put on the nominating commission was terrific.

Some political lawyers are not so much incensed by gubernatorial influence over nominations as they are by its occasional brazenness. One attorney lamented:

Governors manipulate the nominating commissioners in such a way as to get the persons they want to appoint named to panels. Past governors have done this, but at least they went through the motions of taking some time after receiving the nominations before announcing their appointments. In many instances they even invited the nominees down to Jefferson City for an interview. But some recent governors haven't even gone through the motions. In the case of the last judge selected, the governor announced his appointment almost as soon as he had received the names of the nominees.

Lawyer reactions to such gubernatorial behavior appear to have led to an increasing cynicism about the Missouri Plan. According to one circuit judge, suspicion about panel-wiring had become so widespread by the early 1960's that it basically altered the conceptions that many lawyers had of the nature of judicial selection under the Plan. This judge said:

There is probably greater dissatisfaction with the Missouri Plan among Jackson County lawyers today than there has ever been before. It is mainly because of what happened on the last appointment to the circuit bench. The word was out that the governor had made it clear that he would appoint_____if his name were placed on the panel by the nominating commission. Since that did come to pass, lawyers here are now convinced that every appointment is set up. There is an especial bitterness among the lawyers who felt that this kind of thing had never happened before. Of course, it had happened before. But the present governor was simply not very discreet, so more people became aware of what was happening.

Although none of the nominating commissioners interviewed admitted to having served as an agent of the governor in the nominating process, the members of the nominating commission did agree that governors occasionally had been able to influence the selection of nominees. A lay commissioner stated:

You always get a lot of pressures in a position like that, when you're on the nominating commission. People come to you asking you to back a certain man. Some of those who do that are people that are close to the governor.

A lawyer commissioner felt that gubernatorial efforts to influence nominations were even more clear-cut. He observed:

One of the weaknesses of the Missouri Plan is the disposition of some governors to try to get the commission to submit names, and one name in particular, that they want to select for the bench. The governor who was in office during the first part of my term on the commission did that, and he did it by working through the presiding judge. Later on, the same kind of outlook was taken by the next governor. Not only were these two governors guilty of this sort of thing, but at least one earlier governor was also.

Logrolling Among Commissioners

In addition to the three variations of panel-stacking, members of the nominating commission have engaged in another type of decision-making, which is referred to, in the vernacular of the lawyers, as "horse-trading," "vote-swapping," or logrolling. As the name implies, this is a bargaining game wherein the commission selects its nominees on the basis of agreements between individuals or groups of commissioners for the reciprocal support of each other's candidates.

Logrolling may, in some circumstances, be the sole basis of decision-making within the commission. At other times logrolling is merely one of several games being played simultaneously within the nominating commission. In situations where one or more nominating commissioners is secretly pursuing a stacking strategy, the remainder of the commission may be engaged in logrolling. Even if the entire nominating commission is involved in rigging a panel, the members also may be engaged in a secondary logrolling game that has as its purpose the selection of the specific lawyer to be favored out of all those who are politically close to the governor. Bargaining may also focus on selection of the other nominees to be placed on a stacked panel. Even though the second and third nominees on such a panel are not expected to be appointed by the governor, nominating commissioners often vie for the opportunity to designate such "window dressing" nominees. They do so because it affords them the opportunity to discharge obligations to personal friends who have asked their assistance in getting a judicial appointment. Finally, logrolling becomes an element in panel-stacking games for the simple reason that the nominating commissioners usually interact over a period in which several panels are chosen. Agreements among commissioners for the support of each other's candidates may therefore not be limited to the nominees chosen for a single panel, but may entail understandings of support that can be consummated only with the selection of several panels.

It is conceivable, of course, that members of the commission may be playing all four nominating games simultaneously. For this to occur some commissioners must have information that is not available to the other participants. No member of the commission would be content, knowingly, to pursue a logrolling strategy when others were rigging a panel with a candidate to whom he objected, or to play a panel-loading game when others were wiring a panel. On the other hand, logrolling can sometimes be an effective strategy against attempts to stack a panel.

Of the three forms of panel-stacking, the rigging and loading games would appear to have occurred with far greater frequency than panel-wiring in the Jackson County Circuit. Least frequent, as a sole basis for decision strategy, has been logrolling, although this strategy often does occur as a game within one of the other nominating games.

Although it is legitimate and useful to distinguish between the rigging, loading, and wiring variants of panel-stacking, these nominating games have virtually the same implications for the overall nature of the judicial selection process. In all these games gubernatorial politics assumes a position of dominance in judicial selection, with a resulting fusion of the nominating and appointing functions.

This fusion of the nominating and appointing functions has one other important implication for judicial selection. To the extent that the nominating commission engages in panel-stacking, the only really meaningful choice made by the commissioners is in their selection of the one nominee in whose favor the panel has been stacked. The other nominees are only panel-fillers or "window dressing." Their prime quality is their political disqualification—that is, they must be politically unacceptable to the governor. None of their other qualifications is very germane, although commission members may seek "filler" nominees with characteristics such that they will make the panel "look good." Thus the commission may place in nomination a lawyer with a reputation for great legal ability, knowing full well that he will not be chosen by the governor. They may nominate minority-party lawyers and thus, through "token bipartisanism," appear to follow the principles of nonpartisanship laid down by the Missouri Plan. Finally, they may choose "filler" nominees who are close personal friends of one or more nominating commissioners.

It should be pointed out, however, that the panel-stacking games discussed here do not always succeed. Governors occasionally refuse to go along with the commission's attempts to load panels and commissioners sometimes rebuff gubernatorial attempts to rig the list of candidates. These features of the nomination and appointment process are discussed more fully in the following section.

THE DECISION-MAKING PROCESS: 1941 TO 1963

Fifteen judges were chosen for the Jackson County bench during the period covered by this study.[18] Each nomination and appointment reflected a variety of factors: the role orientations of individual members of the nominating commission in office at that particular time; the extent to which the orientations of the various commissioners converged or conflicted; the alliances that developed among the five commission members; and the relationship of the commission to the governor, including the specific panel "game" (rigging, loading, etc.) that prevailed for a particular appointment. Identification of the factors relevant to these judicial appointments is based on information obtained through personal interviews. The types of persons interviewed and the interview agenda utilized are discussed in the Appendix.

---

[18] The description of the process of judicial selection in Jackson County covers events which occurred prior to mid-1963, when personal interviewing in the area was completed. Thus, the analysis of the decision-making process does not include appointments to the Jackson County Circuit bench which were made by Governor Dalton in December of 1963 and August of 1964.

Instead of attempting to detail all of the factors relating to each separate nomination and appointment, this analysis traces the general pattern of decision-making from the years 1941 to 1963; it also analyzes in detail specific incidents to illustrate the complex relationships that can develop between participants and events during the course of the nomination and appointment process.

Over the years the most important factors in the process of choosing members of the Jackson County trial bench have been political in nature. Of particular significance have been the factional ties and party affiliations of the candidates seeking a judgeship. These considerations have tended to dominate the thinking not only of the governor but also of the nominating commissioners, who have used these political criteria for gauging the chief executive's probable reaction to the various nominees.[19] For this reason appointments made under the Missouri Plan are categorized in terms of the general political orientations of the various nominating commissioners and governors.

The period from 1941 to 1943 can be generally characterized as one dominated by the reformist elements that wrested political control from the Pendergast and other factions in the late 1930's and early 1940's. Both lay members of the nominating commission (one Democrat and one Republican) reflected this type of general orientation toward politics, as did the two lawyer members of the nominating body. This congruence in political views was evident in the two panels nominated during this period, for neither contained nominees who were active in factional politics in Jackson County. More important was the partisan affiliation of the nominees, since a Republican, Forrest Donnell, occupied the governor's office. Reportedly, both panels (the first contained two Republicans and one Democrat and the second reversed this mix) were stacked in favor of the Republican nominees. Whether this actually occurred, Donnell did name Republicans to both posts, a practice he followed in his appointments to the other Plan courts in the state.

As a result of changes in the composition of the commission, another general pattern of relationships prevailed during the period from 1944 to 1949. Lawyer and lay commissioners with less animus toward the Democratic factions in Jackson County were added to the commission. Beyond this the two Democratic governors who served during this period, Phil M. Donnelly and Forrest Smith, came to office with the support of the Pendergast faction in Jackson County. The end result of the convergence of political orientations was the appointment of three

---

[19] Carl J. Friedrich discusses a similar phenomenon, which he calls the "Law of Anticipated Reactions." See his "Public Policy and the Nature of Administrative Responsibility," *Public Policy*, Vol. I (Cambridge: Harvard University Press, 1940), pp. 3–24.

Democratic lawyers to the bench: one had been formerly affiliated with the Pendergast organization, a second received the political support of the organization, and a third had been active politically in the reformist element in Jackson County politics. Thus the Pendergast tie became an important element again in the judicial politics of the area.

This state of affairs was not to persist for long. A lawyer, active in the citizens group that defeated Pendergast in the 1940 Kansas City municipal election, was added to the commission in 1951 along with a lay member who, at one time, had crossed political swords with the Pendergast oganization. These changes in its make-up produced a cleavage in the commission for the remainder of the term of Governor Smith. Moreover, Governor Smith, who was the prototype of the professional politician with deep party and personal loyalties, selected all Democrats for his last four appointments to the bench, two of whom were close personal friends of his. This course of events set the stage for the explosive situation that developed during the second administration of Governor Phil Donnelly. Known as "the Donnelly incident," it became a *cause célèbre* of Plan supporters and critics. For this reason, and also because it illustrates graphically the close relationships that can exist between Bar and partisan politics, the incident is analyzed in some detail in the following case study.

The Donnelly Incident

In the 1952 general election Phil Donnelly, who had served as governor from 1945 to 1948, succeeded in winning an unprecedented second term in the Missouri governorship. The Pendergast organization had been the only major faction in Jackson County to support Donnelly's candidacy in the Democratic primary. From the first, then, the Governor faced a judicial nominating commission that was hostile to the one political faction with which he was on good terms. Included was Clarence Chilcott, the lawyer member already referred to, who had been active in the citizens group that defeated Pendergast in the 1940 Kansas City election. The first plaintiffs' lawyer to serve on the commission, Chilcott was an admitted opponent of the Missouri Plan.

Besides Chilcott, the two Democratic lay members of the commission were also opposed to the Pendergast organization. John P. Mullane, an honorary Missouri "colonel," was appointed to the nominating commission during the Smith administration.[20] Mullane had once been accused by Pendergast faction leaders of using his position as a Kansas

---

[20] It is a Missouri political custom for governors to appoint persons active in civic and political affairs to their staff as honorary "colonels" in recognition of their services.

City election commissioner to aid a rival political organization. The other lay member, Frank S. Land, active in local civic affairs and the national founder of the Order of the Demolay, had not been intimately involved in factional politics, but was also considered to be anti-Pendergast in his proclivities.

The other two commissioners were not involved in Jackson County politics, but their backgrounds and role orientations also contributed to the impending deadlock between governor and commission. Charles Blackmar, a corporate attorney and Republican long active in national politics, felt that the nominating commission should work toward achieving a more equitable partisan balance on the circuit bench, and that the quality of the bench should be improved. Nick Cave, presiding judge of the Kansas City Court of Appeals and ex-officio chairman of the nominating commission, was a Democrat from out-state Missouri with comparatively little knowledge of Jackson County politics.

The first Jackson County circuit court vacancies to occur after Donnelly began his second term of office were for three new positions created by action of the 1953 session of the state legislature. Before that Republican lawyer commissioner Blackmar had intimated that unless there were a change in the partisan attitude of the nominating commission—particularly with respect to the nomination of Republicans—the proposed legislation for adding new circuit judgeships in Jackson County might not receive sufficient support for passage. There was also speculation that prospects for a separate bill raising judicial salaries might also be jeopardized unless the nominating commission had a change of heart about nominating Republicans for the circuit bench.

Nonetheless, the state legislature enacted both the judicial pay raise and the legislation expanding the Jackson County circuit bench from 10 to 13 divisions. The Kansas City *Times* speculated:

A great deal of pressure is expected to be applied on members of the . . . judicial commission to include among the nominees several Republican lawyers. Republican leaders may attempt to persuade the commission to submit one panel of three Republican nominees to assure that party of one appointment.[21]

After a month of intermittent deliberations, during which more than 50 attorneys were considered, a divided nominating commission sent three three-men panels of nominees to the Governor in early October of 1953. The lengthy time taken by the commission in reaching its decision was attributed to disagreement among the commissioners about two facets of the nominations. A minority of the nominating commission,

---

[21] May 21, 1953.

consisting of Blackmar and Presiding Judge Cave, objected to what it construed to be the majority's injection of political considerations into the nominating process. The same minority of commissioners also held out for the selection of "outstanding members of the Bar," arguing that some of the more eminent attorneys might now be interested in a judgeship, in view of the legislature's recent enactment of the measure boosting judicial salaries. However, Blackmar and Cave were unable to gain acceptance for either point of view.

The panels selected by the three-man majority—lawyer commissioner Chilcott and lay commissioners Mullane and Land—were arranged along factional and partisan lines. One panel consisted entirely of Republicans. Another contained the names of three Democratic nominees identified with the Democratic Coalition, a league of Democratic factions that had worked against Governor Donnelly in his bid for a second gubernatorial nomination. The third panel consisted of one "independent" Democrat and two Democrats associated with the Pendergast faction, the faction that had been the mainstay of Donnelly's Jackson County strength in the 1952 primary. Within a week Donnelly returned the panels to the nominating commission, expressing dissatisfaction with the politically inspired make-up of the panels, and indicating his refusal to make appointments from those panels.

In a letter to the nominating commission the Governor stated his reasons for declining to act:

Careful study and consideration of the nominations submitted to me by the . . . circuit Judicial Commission for the three vacancies now existing . . . leads to the conclusion that in the selection of such nominees consideration was given not only to the party affiliation of the nominees, but even to the intra-party affiliation of those selected.

The selection of nominees on such a basis violates the spirit and principle and completely thwarts the intent of the non-partisan court plan as voted and approved by the citizens of this state.

The Governor concluded by urging that the "commission reconsider its action and submit . . . nominations selected in accord with the purpose and intent of the nonpartisan court plan of Missouri."[22]

The nominating commission refused to accede to the Governor's request that it reconsider the nominations and in November 1953 once again sent the same panels of nominees to the governor. In a letter accompanying the resubmitted panels the commission chairman re-

---

[22] Letter from Gov. Phil M. Donnelly to The Honorable Nick T. Cave, chairman, 16th Circuit Judicial Commission, Kansas City, Missouri, dated September 17, 1954. All further quotations from Donnelly are taken from this letter.

marked that a majority of the commission was of the opinion that it lacked constitutional authority to reconsider its previous decisions.

Once again the Governor refused to make appointments from these lists, and returned the panels to the nominating commission. In so doing, Governor Donnelly replied explicitly to the commission's contention that it was without authority to reconsider its original nominations. The Governor contended that the commission "might" reconsider its previous action and submit new panels for the vacancies existing so long as those vacancies continued to exist. The Governor's recommendation to that effect was dispatched to the nominating commission on February 5, 1954.

For about eight months the deadlock continued, despite the introduction of a new element into the situation. In July 1954 the Missouri Supreme Court cut much of the ground from under the nominating commission's contention that it was powerless to reconsider its original nominations.[23]

---

[23] The Supreme Court's action consisted of the addition of a new section to its Rule 10 which detailed the procedure that the nominating commission was to utilize in withdrawing nominations once they had been submitted to the governor. The section of the new rule most germane to the deadlock between the Jackson County nominating commission and the Governor read as follows: "Whenever there are existing at the same time two or more vacancies in the same court, and the commission has nominated and submitted to the Governor lists of three persons for each of such vacancies, the commission, in its sole discretion may, if it desires to do so, before the Governor acts by making an appointment, withdraw the lists of nominations, change the names of any such persons nominated from one list to another and re-submit them as so changed, and may substitute a new name for any of those previously nominated when a name has been withdrawn for cause."

In one respect the new Supreme Court rule substantially accorded with the position taken by the Jackson county nominating commission on the issue of whether the nominations submitted to the Governor could be withdrawn and completely different ones substituted in their place. The new Supreme Court rule limited the commission's authority to substitute new nominees, and said on this point: "After any commission has nominated and submitted to the Governor the names of three persons, for appointment . . . any name or names may be withdrawn for cause deemed by such commission to be of a substantial nature affecting the nominee's qualifications and showing he is not a fit and proper person to hold the office, and another name or names may be substituted therefor at any time before the Governor acts by making an appointment to fill such vacancy. Nothing herein contained shall be deemed to impose (or to recognize) any obligation whatsoever upon any commission to reconsider or withdraw any nomination, whether or not the Governor shall have requested reconsideration thereof, or shall have purported to reject such nominations. If any nominee dies or requests in writing that his name be withdrawn the commission shall nominate another person to replace him." Section 10.29, Supreme Court Rules, Revised Statutes of the State of Missouri (Jefferson City: Committee on Legislative Research, 1960), p. 4906.

Late the next month (August 22, 1954) the nominating commission for the second time resubmitted to the Governor the original panels chosen in October 1953. Dropping the argument that it lacked "authority" to reconsider the panels, the chairman of the nominating commission nonetheless reported:

After full and frank discussion covering all facts and circumstances in connection with the nominations which have heretofore been submitted, a majority of the commission finds no good and legal cause or reason to certify panels other than those which have heretofore been submitted.[24]

Approximately a month later the Governor sent to the nominating commission a thirteen-page typewritten letter which reiterated all the reasons which he had already given for not making appointments from the panels in question. In addition, the Governor's response gave heavy emphasis to some revelations that had been made earlier in the year by the Kansas City *Times*.

In a story dated March 17, 1954, a *Times* staff member reported that lawyer commissioner Clarence Chilcott had acknowledged having entered into an agreement with G.O.P. legislators about the make-up of the three disputed panels. Chilcott reportedly admitted that he had agreed to the naming of one panel consisting entirely of Republican lawyers, and said that he had done so to expedite passage of the legislation creating three new divisions of the Jackson County circuit court. Chilcott claimed that he had been under considerable pressure from Republican state legislators and that his agreement with the legislators was essential to ensure passage of the judicial salary increase legislation, as well as the bill to add new judges.

Chilcott's version of what had transpired was confirmed by lay nominating commissioner Mullane. Under the circumstances, said Mullane, the commission had no choice but to name one Republican panel.[25] Neither Mullane nor Chilcott offered an explanation of why the second and third panels had been allotted to the two major factional groupings within the Democratic party. Apparently, that was not part of any deal with the legislature.

Chilcott, long known as an opponent of the Missouri Plan, denied that the nominations made were in any way the result of his antipathy toward the Plan. Although readily confessing his opposition to the Plan in principle, Chilcott commented that "since I'm a member of the commission it is my duty to make the plan work."[26]

[24] Letter from Judge Nick T. Cave, chairman of 16th circuit nominating commission to Governor Phil M. Donnelly, dated August 23, 1954.
[25] Kansas City *Times*, March, 17, 1954.
[26] *Ibid.*

These disclosures gave Governor Donnelly all the ammunition he needed in his lengthy, ringing denunciation of the nominating commission. After citing with approval the dissenting votes of the presiding judge and lawyer commissioner Blackmar, the Governor again expressed his displeasure with the "political" character of the panels sent to him. Then, lambasting the alleged agreement between Chilcott and the Republican legislators, the Governor suggested that the three majority commissioners resign their seats on the commission in order to resolve the impasse between the commission and the Governor.

The Governor's suggestion for ending the deadlock fell on completely deaf ears. The nominating commission convened again in October 1954, with the Governor's lengthy rebuke before them for official consideration. The majority voted to stand by their original nominations, and indicated their intention to continue serving on the commission. Then, on November 4, 1954, the majority voted to resubmit the original panels to the Governor once more. There the matter stood for a little more than a year.

A means to resolve the impasse between the Governor and the nominating commission did not occur until November 1955, when Jackson County lawyers balloted to elect a full-term commissioner for the position occupied by Chilcott. Because he had been filling out the unexpired portion of a term left vacant by the death of his predecessor, Chilcott was eligible to succeed himself. He filed for reelection, stating that his candidacy was designed to preserve the independence of the judicial nominating commission and thus the integrity of the Missouri Plan.

Chilcott's sole opponent in the race was David R. Hardy, a 38-year-old attorney with a large trial practice in which he handled cases for both plaintiffs and defendants. Hardy billed his candidacy as an effort to save the Nonpartisan Court Plan, and specifically pledged that he would work for a solution of the conflict between the Governor and the nominating commission. For the first time in the Plan's history the contest for a lawyer commissionership turned into a full-fledged political campaign, with each side issuing a series of brochures stating the case for its candidate.

In an election in which more than 90 percent of the eligible lawyers cast ballots Hardy emerged with a two-to-one margin of victory and was sworn into office on January 5, 1956. On his motion at a commission meeting about two weeks later, the original panels selected by the nominating commission were rearranged and sent on to the Governor for his approval. In announcing the decision of the commission its chairman noted the following:

We are returning to the governor the same names as required by Supreme Court Rule 10, since there have been no names voluntarily withdrawn or withdrawn for cause. However, the commission under the authority of the same rule, transposed a few names from one panel to another.[27]

The new panel alignment greatly increased the Governor's range of choice among party and factional representatives. The old arrangement had presented one panel of Republicans, another consisting of one "independent" and two Pendergast Democrats, and a third containing the names of three Democratic Coalition Democrats. The result of the re-shuffling was one panel containing the names of a Republican, the independent Democrat, and a Pendergast Democrat; a second panel consisting of one Republican, one Pendergast Democrat, and a Democratic Coalition lawyer; and a third panel containing the names of a Republican and two lawyers identified with the Democratic Coalition.[28]

Governor Donnelly expressed his disappointment that the nominating commission had not given him a new slate of names to consider. He then proceeded to make appointments from the revised lists of nominees, naming two Republicans and a Pendergast Democrat. The Governor's decision confounded most of his critics, who had assumed that his earlier recalcitrance had been a protest against his inability to select more than one Pendergast faction affiliate. Also, his choice of two Republicans was puzzling: most interviewees attributed it to sheer spite; others felt it was a consequence of Donnelly's "lame duck" status at the time the appointments were finally made in February 1956; and still others ascribed his action to the fact that the Pendergast organization had declined in power between 1953 and 1956.

The hiatus in Jackson County judicial selection, which lasted from late 1953 until February of 1956, reveals in somewhat exaggerated fashion several of the basic dimensions of the selection process for the Jackson County circuit bench. It clearly exemplifies the manner in which political considerations affected nominations and appointments. The impasse also demonstrates the crucial nature of relationships between the nominating commission and the Governor, as these are affected by the kinds of decision strategies present in the selection process. The "loading" of panels to force gubernatorial appointment of specific persons favored by the commission had occurred before, but the fact that three simultaneous appointments were involved increased the opportunities for panel-stacking and made its usage more obvious.

The 1953-1956 deadlock also illustrates the effect of influence patterns

[27] *Kansas City Times,* January 20, 1956.
[28] Shortly after these panels were sent to the Governor, the Republican attorney included on the second panel withdrew his name, and the nominating commission submitted that of another Republican.

within the commission upon the selection process. To a considerable extent the types of nomination made were a result of the presiding judge's inability to assume the kind of leadership role that had been played by most other presiding judges in the Jackson County circuit nominating process. In the opinion of most observers the judge serving as chairman of the nominating commission in 1953 lacked the range of political knowledge and insight that might have permitted him to deter the majority of the nominating commission from proceeding in such a blatantly political manner. This resulted largely from his lack of familiarity with Jackson County politics.

Appointments in the Period 1956 to 1963

After the Donnelly incident the Pendergast organization was never again a major factor in appointments to the Jackson County circuit bench. However, the political backgrounds of the candidates continued to have relevance for the nomination and selection process. During the administration of James Blair two vacancies occurred. In both instances the nominating commission is reported to have stacked the panels in favor of persons well-known in Jackson County Democratic circles. One was a former county chairman and the other a law partner of another such chairman. In each case Governor Blair, an avid Democrat, reputedly appointed the favored candidate, primarily because the other nominees were politically unacceptable to him. Thus, following on the heels of the bitter dispute centering around the events of 1953 to 1956, the commission and governor selected for the circuit bench lawyers who had been more prominently involved in partisan politics than had any appointees prior to that time.

   The final appointment included in this analysis occurred early in the administration of Governor John Dalton. The panel of nominees chosen by the commission consisted of two Democrats and a Republican. The Republican was generally believed to have little chance for appointment, particularly since this was the first Missouri Plan vacancy to occur following Governor Dalton's assumption of office. Both of the other nominees had been active in Democratic politics, although neither was identified with any of the Democratic "regular" factions. Appointment went to the Democratic attorney who had been a personal friend and political associate of the Governor. According to those who were personally interviewed, members of the Jackson County Bar generally believed this selection to have been "wired" by the Governor. Whether it was or not, the political affiliations of the lawyers nominated for this vacancy, as well as later vacancies in the Dalton administration, tended to reflect the new governor's relative independence from the old-line Democratic factions in Jackson County politics, and his closeness to lawyers who were political independents from an organizational standpoint.

An overview of the appointments to the Jackson County trail bench from 1941 to 1963 reveals that the most important factors in the selection process were political rather than professional in nature. There was some tendency for plaintiffs' attorneys to receive more nominations when their most vocal representative, Clarence Chilcott, was on the commission than when less avid lawyers represented that segment of the profession, or when both lawyer members came from a defense-corporate practice. However, the presence on the commission of lawyer members from both sides of the Bar, plus the importance in the nominating process of attorneys and firms with a mixed negligence practice, generally served to screen out attorneys with an exclusive plaintiffs' or defendants' practice.[29]

The politicization of the selection process is attributable, in turn, to the nature of Jackson County politics, especially to the centrality of factionalism and its effects upon state gubernatorial politics. The resultant political considerations became the dominant element within the nominating and appointing games that characterized most of the selection process. To be sure, other considerations were involved in the selection of nominees and judges. Candidates for the bench won nomination because they were personal friends of nominating commissioners, or had been active in certain fraternal lodges or veterans' organizations to which nominating commissioners belonged. But these kinds of considerations were not often sufficient to insure appointment to the bench. Other qualities, especially political qualities, were a prerequisite for appointment. Usually another prerequisite was that the candidate had to be in the favored position in whatever panel-stacking strategy was being pursued at the time a given judicial vacancy was filled. The determination of which candidate would fill that favored spot was usually a product of the kinds of power relationships existing within the nominating commission. Generally, the decision-making process in the commission was one in which voting blocs of varying size negotiated the panel arrangements that would produce the intended results in terms

---

[29] Our survey data on nominees shows that during the period from 1942 to 1963 only two nominees listed personal injury litigation as their exclusive field of practice. Both represented the defense side in such litigation, and were nominated when the corporate-defense segment of the Bar controlled both lawyer commissionerships on the nominating commission.

of judicial appointments. For much of the Plan period the presiding judge of the court of appeals served as leader and chief strategist for the majority voting blocs or for the entire commission.

The nature of the process by which the circuit judiciary is chosen under the Missouri Plan is therefore contingent on a large number of factors. An important change in any one of the major components of the selection system for Jackson County would presumably lead to different kinds of judges being elevated to the circuit bench there. Certainly, a differently constituted selection system across the state in St. Louis has led to a bench that differs in many respects from the one that the Missouri Plan has produced in Jackson County.

4

⟨⟨⟨⟩⟩⟩

THE PLURALISTIC NATURE OF

JUDICIAL SELECTION IN THE

ST. LOUIS CIRCUIT

The selection of judges for the St. Louis City circuit bench has been a far more open process than the selection of Jackson County circuit judges. Compared with Jackson County, a much wider range of interests has had access to the nominating process in St. Louis. The structure of nominating commissioner roles and the mode of decision making predominating in the St. Louis commission have also contributed to a system of judicial selection in which there have been relatively few impediments to the candidacies of any significant group of lawyers. Many of these differences are traceable to the characteristics of the milieu in which the St. Louis selection process has occurred.

THE ENVIRONMENT OF THE SELECTION PROCESS

As was the case for Jackson County, the adoption of the Missouri Plan effected a transfer of judicial selection from the realm of St. Louis ward and precinct politics to the domain of state gubernatorial politics. Thus the political factors of greatest relevance to judicial selection have been determined largely by the manner in which the local political system has impinged upon state electoral politics, especially the politics of gubernatorial primary elections.

A St. Louis circuit judge has generalized as follows about the broader consequences of this change for the process of judicial selection:

For former influentials like ward and precinct leaders, adoption of the Missouri Plan substituted state senators, state committeemen, city committee chairmen, and lawyers, who have become the new influentials.

In order to assess the validity of that assertion some attention must be given to the general features of St. Louis politics in the period covered by this study. Of primary concern is the politics of the Democratic party, since all but one of the appointments made to the St. Louis circuit bench were by Democratic governors.

The Political Milieu

Although the detailed complexion of St. Louis politics has varied somewhat during this time, its general characteristics have remained basically the same throughout the period from 1940 to 1963. The principal feature of Democratic party politics in those years has been a rather basic and continuing political fragmentation, marked by the absence of any stable, powerful factions.

At the very beginning of the Missouri Plan era, there appeared to be some prospect that St. Louis would be dominated by a Pendergast-style political machine. Under the leadership of Bernard Dickmann, the Democrats, starting in 1932, succeeded in supplanting the Republicans as the majority party in city elections. Throughout the 1930's the Dickmann organization continued to consolidate the party's strength and, by 1940, the Dickmann-led forces had become potent enough to inject themselves into the state political arena. Their ability to do so resulted partly from the collapse of Pendergast power on the other side of the State in Kansas City.

When it came time for the primary election in 1940, the St. Louis political machine was able to get its candidate chosen as the Democratic nominee for governor, but 1940 was not a particularly auspicious time for a new Democratic political force to be entering state politics. Forrest Donnell, head of the state G.O.P. ticket, won the governorship and thus brought to an end an eight-year period of Democratic control of that office. The Dickmann organization had little time to ponder this defeat, since in 1941 they had to face a rejuvenated Republican organization in the St. Louis municipal elections. The Democratic machine suffered its second major setback in those elections and Dickmann, who headed the ticket, lost the mayoralty contest to Republican William Bee Decker. There ensued an eight-year period of Republican dominance in St. Louis city politics.

After the 1941 election disaster St. Louis Democratic politics reverted to its former feudalistic base, with each ward becoming a virtual kingdom ruled by its own separate and largely autonomous political potentate.[1] This situation persisted even after the city returned to the Democratic fold in 1949.

Certain formal structural features of St. Louis government have been a contributory factor in this continuing fragmentation of St. Louis politics. St. Louis has been characterized by one student of its politics as having a bifurcated local governmental structure.[2] Although St. Louis is a charter city, unlike most municipalities it is not part of any county. The specifically "city" offices include a mayor, a comptroller, and the President of the Board of Aldermen (all elected at large) plus an alderman elected from each of the city's wards. As of 1960 about 10,000 municipal employees worked under the administrative direction of the mayor, with all but a very few serving under civil service regulations. But some other essentially "municipal" offices are under state rather than local control. Thus the governor appoints the Board of Police Commissioners, which supervises and sets policy for the city police department. The governor also chooses a St. Louis Board of Election Commissioners.

In addition to the city offices, state law creates other offices charged with the performance of functions that are carried out by county units of government elsewhere in Missouri. Although elected by the voters of the city, these officials (such as the sheriff, collector of revenue, and the magistrates) operate independently of the city administration, and do not come under the provisions of the city charter. Many of the jobs existing in this part of the governmental structure are not subject to civil service regulations. Together with such other independent government entities as the Board of Education, the "county" type offices provide virtually the only source of patronage existing within the city. It is to these offices, therefore, that the party professionals have given their attention, since patronage has continued to be the lifeblood of the local party organizations. Moreover, since they depend upon effective ward organizations for their continuance in office, members of the Board of Aldermen have allied with the "county" officeholder groups, and together have constituted the dominant element within the party organization.

Associated with this bifurcation of the governmental structure has been a deep cleavage running across the entire political community. Interest groups, political actives and elites, and socio-economic groups

[1] The account of St. Louis politics in the 1930's and early 1940's is based largely upon John H. Fenton, *Politics in the Border States*, (New Orleans: The Hauser Press, 1957), pp. 139, 140.

[2] Robert H. Salisbury, "St. Louis Politics: Relationships Among Interests, Parties, and Government," *Western Political Quarterly*, 13 (1960), pp. 498–507.

have been affected by this cleavage. Each of these segments of the political community has tended to be divided in terms of political orientation. Some members of each segment have been oriented primarily to the patronage-style politics surrounding the county office component of local government; other members have been oriented toward the policy-focused municipal office component. These cleavages result in the diffusion of political interests that might otherwise have greater impact upon gubernatorial and state politics.

The absence of any cohesive Democratic organization meant that St. Louis' hegemony in state politics was very short-lived. Although no aspirant for the Democratic gubernatorial nomination could afford to alienate all the St. Louis ward bosses, his chances for success have not rested entirely upon his ability to attract the support of one, or even a handful, of political overlords. It is true that coalitions of ward leaders have been formed frequently, yet these have tended to be kaleidoscopic in nature, varying from election to election, with no particular combination having the permanence or strength to affect gubernatorial politics decisively.

Both the general political system and that part of it relevant to judicial selection have thus been characterized by a constantly changing universe of interests and groups, none of which has held commanding political power. One result is that the political dimension of judicial selection has been basically pluralistic in nature. In a loosely structured political environment no political groups are entirely screened out of the process whereby judges are chosen. Although some political groups have been more influential than others, this influence has been intermittent, and partially subject to the influences that emanate from the total environment in which the choice of judge is made. In addition to the political milieu, a significant part of that environment is the legal ecology.

The Legal Ecology

The picture of the legal profession drawn by lawyers interviewed in St. Louis is that of a Bar containing numerous solo practitioners and few large law firms. There are also relatively few St. Louis lawyers or law firms that have a mixed plaintiffs-defense personal injury practice. As one attorney remarked: "The lines here are pretty clearly drawn. Usually you have lawyers handling an entirely plaintiffs' business or an entirely defendants' business." St. Louis lawyers also say the Bar is divided evenly along partisan lines.

These perceptions of the St. Louis legal profession are confirmed by the information contained in responses to the mail questionnaire sent to Missouri attorneys. Compared with Jackson County attorneys, more

St. Louis lawyers are engaged in solo practice, and a lesser proportion are members of large law firms, as is indicated by the data in Table 4.1. More St. Louis attorneys have specialized practices limited to a single field of law; moreover, slightly fewer St. Louis than Jackson County lawyers engage in a personal injury practice representing plaintiffs and defendants equally. The St. Louis Bar appears in one respect to be less polarized along plaintiffs'-defense lines. Considerably fewer St. Louis respondents are members of the National Association of Claimants' and Compensation Attorneys, and membership in that organization provides one of the best indicators of the militancy of the plaintiffs' segment of the Bar.[3]

The survey data also indicate that the Bar in St. Louis is divided almost evenly along partisan lines, with 48 percent claiming Democratic party affiliation, and 47 percent identifying themselves as Republicans. The comparable figures for Jackson County are 57 percent and 36 percent, respectively. (About 3 percent of the attorneys in both areas claim to be political independents, with the remainder indicating no party preference.) Table 4.1 also reveals that although Republicans in Jackson County tend to be concentrated disproportionately in the larger law firms as compared with their Democratic colleagues, both Republicans and Democrats in St. Louis are more evenly distributed over all practice arrangements.

Republican attorneys in Jackson County and St. Louis are similarly distributed over the various fields of legal practice, both groups tending to concentrate disproportionately in the general corporate, probate, and trust fields. However, St. Louis Republicans are better represented in most fields of practice than are Republicans in Jackson County; for example, of all the attorneys that are involved in personal injury litigation in Jackson County, only one-third are Republicans. In St. Louis slightly more than one-half of all persons engaged in one form of personal injury practice or another are identified with the G.O.P.

St. Louis Democratic lawyers are also less active in partisan affairs than are their Democratic colleagues across the state in Jackson County. Although Republicans in both areas have approximately equal levels of involvement in partisan politics, Republican attorneys in St. Louis

---

[3] Forty-six percent of the mail questionnaire St. Louis respondents had limited their practice to a single field within the year preceding the survey, as opposed to 38 percent in Jackson County. At the same time, only 7 percent of the St. Louis lawyers engaged in a personal injury practice representing plaintiffs and defendants equally, while the comparable figure for Jackson County was 9 percent. Of the 133 lawyer respondents living in St. Louis, only 2 percent were members of the National Association of Claimants and Compensation Attorneys, while about 11 percent of the 291 Jackson County lawyers were NACCA members.

TABLE 4.1

LAW PRACTICE ARRANGEMENT, BY PARTY AFFILIATION, FOR ATTORNEYS RESIDING IN JACKSON COUNTY AND ST. LOUIS (PERCENT)

Practice Arrangement	Jackson County			St. Louis City		
	Total[a] (N = 291)	Democrats (N = 165)	Republicans (N = 104)	Democrats (N = 64)	Republicans (N = 63)	Total[a] (N = 133)
Solo	25	32	15	36	35	36
Two-man partnership	10	11	8	6	5	5
Three to nine lawyers	16	18	16	19	25	22
Large firms or corporation[b]	31	25	41	20	21	20
Government agencies[c]	7	6	6	17	0	9
Not ascertained, more than one arrangement	11	8	14	2	14	8
Total	100	100	100	100	100	100

[a] Includes attorneys identifying themselves as independents and those for whom no party identification was ascertained.
[b] Includes members of firms with ten or more lawyers and salaried employees of law firms and corporations.
[c] Includes salaried employees of local, state, and national governmental agencies.

have been more active in partisan affairs than have St. Louis Democratic lawyers.[4] Finally, St. Louis attorneys, whether Republicans or Democrats, have been more active in seeking and holding nonlegal public office than have attorneys of either partisan persuasion in Jackson County.[5] These features of the St. Louis legal ecology complement the fragmented political system and thus contribute to the diversity of the environment surrounding judicial selection. The Bar in St. Louis is more fragmented than the Jackson County Bar in terms of the size of law firms in the two areas. Not only is the St. Louis Bar characterized by

[4] The differentials in partisan involvement are revealed in the data below:

Points on Index of Party Activity	Jackson County Lawyers		St. Louis City Lawyers	
	Democrats (N = 165)	Republicans (N = 104)	Democrats (N = 64)	Republicans (N = 63)
1 point	11%	16%	28%	17%
2–3 points	36	30	27	33
4–6 points	21	20	17	21
7 or more	7	7	5	5
None, no answer	25	27	23	24
Mean	2.55	2.40	2.17	2.52

[5] A comparison of scores on the Index of candidacy for nonlegal public office for Democratic and Republican attorneys is as follows:

Points on Index	Jackson County Lawyers		St. Louis City Lawyers	
	Democrats (N = 165)	Republicans (N = 104)	Democrats (N = 64)	Republicans (N = 63)
1 point	5%	5%	6%	6%
2 points	7	6	17	18
3 or more	5	5	6	6
None, no answer	83	84	71	70
Mean	0.43	0.35	0.62	0.64

The Index of candidacy for nonlegal public office is computed by allotting two points for each of the following types of offices held, and one point for each of the offices sought unsuccessfully: elective or appointive city, county, state, or federal offices, excluding those offices classified as "legal" in nature. Categorized as legal offices are: city attorney or counselor's office; county prosecutor or counselor's office; legal staff members of state or national agency; justice of the peace or magistrate; law school faculty member; law clerk; circuit or appellate court judge; membership on state Board of Law Examiners; and special assistant to the attorney general.

a more even partisan balance in virtually every field of practice but, as a group, Republican attorneys are more active politically than their Democratic colleagues. These aspects of the legal ecology thus reinforce the pluralistic tendencies emanating from the political milieu. The pluralistic nature of the environment is also partially attributable to the role that the court's clientele has taken in the selection process.

The Court's Clientele.

Although lawyers have had a preponderant influence over the nominating process in both judicial circuits, the impact of nonlawyer groups on judicial nominations has been of far greater significance in St. Louis than in Jackson County. In the latter circuit, businessmen rarely have participated directly or openly in the nominating process, largely for fear that the "interests" would be accused of attempting to control the courts. Even covert involvement of economic groups appears to have been quite limited in Jackson County. Elements of the business and corporate community in St. Louis do not seem to have been deterred from either kind of involvement in judicial nominations.

Although organized labor has shown little interest in judicial selection in either Jackson County or St. Louis,[6] some segments of the St. Louis business world have been involved in the nominating process in a variety of ways. Their most frequent activity, and also their least important, has been the writing of letters of endorsement for attorneys whom they would like to see nominated for judicial office. Such letters are frequently dispatched on behalf of candidates who have solicited business support, but they are also sent in support of candidates whom businessmen have sponsored on their own initiative. These letters come mainly from insurance company, railroad, and banking executives.

A much more important form of business participation in the nominating process has consisted of personal "lobbying" of nominating commissioners, particularly the lay commissioners, who have been prominent in St. Louis business circles. In addition to conveying their views about prospective nominees, individuals within the business community also provide feedback as to their evaluation of past nominations. One lay commissioner observed: "Some of my business friends weren't happy

---

[6] Nicholas M. Blassie, an officer in a St. Louis local of the Meat Cutter's Union, served as a lay member of the nominating commission for slightly over a year, filling out the unexpired term of a lay commissioner who died in office. During Blassie's tenure on the commission (November 14, 1951 through December 31, 1952), no vacancies occurred on the circuit bench and Blassie therefore did not participate in the selection of a single panel.

with some of the nominations that were made while I was on the commission, and chastised me for them."

Business involvement in the selection of St. Louis circuit judges has been even more important at the appointment stage. The extent of business influence has fluctuated from one gubernatorial administration to another and, generally, has varied inversely with the closeness of relations between the governor and organizational political leaders. Yet the business community, year in and year out, has continued to have an important voice in the overall selection process.

Unlike their counterparts in Jackson County, incumbent circuit judges in St. Louis appear rarely to have become involved in the selection process. Moreover, the St. Louis judges interviewed for this study expressed no real interest in becoming involved in the choice of their future colleagues, implying that the selection process was not even salient for them.

The basis for this difference in the behavior of the two circuit benches is not entirely clear. The Jackson County circuit bench seems to have been highly sensitive to a number of issues having political implications, especially issues growing out of public dissatisfaction with the dispensation of justice in criminal and juvenile cases. To cope with these problems, the court through *en banc* decisions effected changes in specific judicial assignments or in the general procedures through which judges were assigned to particular divisions of the court. These experiences may partially account for the greater interest that Jackson County judges have had in the recruitment of new colleagues, for they may have sensitized the judges to the need for recruiting to the court lawyers whose behavior would not reflect adversely on the bench.

On balance, the participation of business groups in the selection of St. Louis City circuit judges has meant that the involvement of the court's clientele has contributed to the greater openness of the selection process there, as compared with the situation in the Jackson County circuit. The exact manner in which this participation has affected nominations and appointments will be discussed in greater detail in the remaining sections of this chapter.

ROLE ORIENTATIONS OF PARTICIPANTS
IN THE SELECTION PROCESS

Perhaps the best single indicator of the difference in the selection process of the two Missouri Plan circuits is the nature of candidate campaigns for judicial office. Campaigning for nomination and appointment have been of very limited significance in Jackson County, largely because of a relatively closed selection process in which factional politics and the strategies pursued by nominating commissioners have been the dominant factors.

Campaigning for judicial office has been far more vigorous in St. Louis. Candidates and their supporters initiate letter-writing campaigns, and importune friends and associates—whether lawyers, businessmen, or politicians—to press for their selection by the nominating commission or the governor. As a result, members of the St. Louis nominating commission complain far more than do Jackson County commissioners about the kinds of "pressures" exerted on behalf of contenders for judicial office. Yet, in one sense, both the nominating commissioners and the governor have "invited" these pressures, since they have assumed orientations that have made such campaigning worthwhile.

The role orientations of the different types of nominating commissioners generally have been far more diffuse in St. Louis than in Jackson County. For that reason, there has been the potential for a much larger number of factors to become relevant to selection decisions than was the case in the Jackson County circuit. In terms of the interrelationships among members of the nominating commission, the relative lack of specificity in role orientations has produced greater flexibility and has enlarged the array of probable voting combinations among nominating commissioners. With respect to commission relations with the governor, the looseness of the role structure within the nominating commission has led to greater diversity in the types of strategies or games characterizing the selection process.

The Lawyer Commissioners

Ten of the fourteen panels of nominees selected for the St. Louis circuit bench through the summer of 1963 were chosen by nominating commissions on which both the plaintiffs' and corporate-defense segments of the Bar had at least nominal representation. The first two exceptions were in the period from 1941 to 1948, when only two vacancies on the circuit bench were filled, and when both lawyer nominating commissioners came from the corporate-defense, or Olive Street, side of the Bar. Two other panels (chosen in mid-1956) were selected when both lawyer nominating commissioners were nominally representatives of the plaintiffs', or Chestnut Street portion of the Bar.[7]

---

[7] Most St. Louis lawyers use these terms to distinguish between the higher and lower status attorneys who practice in the downtown area. Rental and property values are considerably higher on Olive Street and attorneys who have their offices

The term "nominal" is used to designate the orientation of these lawyer nominating commissioners despite the fact that there is a uniform relationship between a commissioner's practice background and the sources of his support in races for lawyer commissionerships. Candidates sponsored by the St. Louis Lawyers' Association invariably had essentially plaintiff's practice backgrounds; candidates supported by the St. Louis Bar Association had corporate or corporate-defense practices. Yet the plaintiffs'-corporate split in the lawyer segment of the commission appears never to have been a very important factor in nominating decisions until the 1960's. Before that time the lawyer commissioners appear to have had basically similar orientations toward the nominating process, despite their divergent practice backgrounds. This similarity in outlook apparently extended to the use of common standards for evaluating candidates for nomination.

In general, the lawyer commissioners drawn from the plaintiffs' side of the Bar appear to have represented the values of the corporate-defense segment of the Bar much more consistently than they did the viewpoint of the lawyers responsible for their election to the commission. Regarding one such lawyer commissioner, a fellow lawyer commissioner drawn from the Olive Street segment of the Bar said: "He and I were quite close. I was apprehensive when he first came on the nominating commission. Although he wasn't a trial lawyer, he had done office work for one of the biggest ambulance chasers in St. Louis. Strangely enough, he was never corrupted by his experience in that firm, and was never influenced by his past, by the fact that he'd been a plaintiffs' man earlier in his career." A defendants' attorney also gave unstinting praise to this particular lawyer commissioner, saying: "He was very high class, and certainly didn't have the outlook of a plaintiffs' lawyer." In fact, most of the lawyers interviewed who professed to know anything about this commissioner classified him in the corporate-defense wing of the Bar. In terms of the support that elected him to the commission, this was a misperception. In terms of the role that this commissioner actually played in the nominating process, this classification would appear to be quite accurate. Not only this commissioner but the other plaintiffs' backed lawyer commissioners serving before 1960 are widely reputed to have shared the values of their corporate-defense-oriented fellow lawyer commissioners and of the similarly oriented presiding judges who served as chairmen of the nominating commission.

Changes in commission membership in the 1960's appear to have led

---

there tend to have corporate or defense practices. Chestnut Street, with its lower property values and greater proximity to the courthouse, is the principal location for plaintiffs' and criminal practice attorneys.

to a polarization of views within the lawyer-judge segment of the nominating commission. It is difficult to say whether this development is attributable to a generally increased militancy on the part of the plaintiffs' lawyers in St. Louis. Alternatively, it may have been because the lawyer commissioner chosen through support of the Chestnut Street lawyers merely happened, by chance, to have a greater affinity for the plaintiffs' point of view. Whatever the reason, some nominating commissioners view with alarm the prospect of an increased power for the plaintiffs' groups. According to one commissioner:

The division within the Bar between the plaintiffs' and defendants' groups hasn't affected judicial selection up to now. But there is a growing trend. The Lawyers' Association is made up mostly of damage suit lawyers, and most of the Lawyers' Association people belong to NACCA. All that they're interested in is a big verdict in suits for plaintiffs.

The last time that a lawyer member of the nominating commission was chosen, the Lawyers' Association backed their man to the hilt, and they whipped the Bar Association candidate hands down. Later, when a panel of nominees was selected the new nominating commissioner went right down the line for Lawyers' Association lawyers. There will be another lawyer vacancy on the nominating commission before long. If the damage suit crowd wins that, they will control the nominating commission, and we will get some very bad judges.

Yet for most of the period of the Missouri Plan's operation in St. Louis there was little difference in the orientation of the lawyer commissioners with regard to the practice background of applicants for judicial nomination. Unlike the Jackson County commission, the St. Louis body never did exclude from consideration even those attorneys on the extremes of the Bar's ideological continuum, namely, the lawyers with a principally defense or plaintiffs'-oriented personal injury practice. However, the fact that there was no absolute barrier to the nomination of lawyers with plaintiffs' or defense backgrounds does not mean that all types of lawyers had equal chances to be nominated. Over the years the St. Louis nominating commission displayed a rather systematic bias in favor of candidates with a corporate or corporate-defense background. This bias is at least partially attributable to the common ideological orientation of the lawyers and presiding judges serving on the commission prior to the 1960's.

In several respects the role orientations of St. Louis lawyer commissioners were affected more significantly by political factors than by the plaintiffs-defense issue. Indeed, the muting of the plaintiffs'-defense issue resulted partially from the impact of political considerations upon the nominating process.

It will be recalled that in Jackson County the partisan orientations of the nominating commissioners had an extremely important bearing upon the judicial selection process. There, most nominating commissioners identified with the Democratic party, and the feature of their political orientation having the greatest bearing upon judicial nominations was their factional allegiances and antipathies. In St. Louis, where political factions have had only slight impact in terms of gubernatorial politics, the factional affiliations of nominating commissioners have had practically no relevance for judicial nominations. What has been relevant is the presence on the nominating commission of lawyer commissioners identified with the Republican party. Although there were only three Republicans among the eight lawyer nominating commissioners participating in the selection of panels from 1941 through 1963, their participation stretched over almost all of this period. Thus at least one of the lawyer commissioners was a Republican in eleven of the fourteen panel selections made by the nominating commission. For four of these eleven panel selections, both lawyer nominating commissioners were Republicans.

The presence of Republican lawyers on the nominating commission has been a factor contributing to the pluralism of the judicial selection process in the St. Louis circuit. In conjunction with influences stemming from the political and Bar environments, the fact that both political parties had representation on the commission led to a broadening of the array of candidates that could be given serious consideration for judicial nomination. Thus in St. Louis the nomination of Republican attorneys for judicial positions did not always constitute the kind of token bipartisanship present in Jackson County nominating politics. The St. Louis nominating commission not only gave serious attention to Republican prospects for the bench but, occasionally, set up panels in such a way as to maximize the prospects that the Republicans would be appointed.

The partisan allegiances of these Republican lawyer commissioners also affected their general role orientations, principally by increasing the dimensionality of their roles. One consequence was that lawyer commissioners with different practice backgrounds, but with the same political party affiliations, could interact on the basis of their partisan attachments, thus submerging differences that might arise from their incompatible legal ideologies. This appears to constitute at least a partial explanation for the fact that one of the plaintiffs' lawyer commissioners discussed above had an outlook that was basically similar to his corporate-oriented lawyer colleagues on the nominating commission. For one-half of the nominations in which he participated, both he and his lawyer colleague on the commission were Republicans.

The presence of Republican attorneys on the nominating commission would have been of negligible importance except for one other characteristic of the lawyer commissioners' partisan orientations. All three Republican lawyer commissioners had been active in G.O.P. politics at one time or another during their careers. Two of the three had been elected to the St. Louis circuit bench in the pre-Missouri Plan era, but had been defeated in the Democratic electoral landslides of the mid-thirties. The third, the plaintiffs-backed lawyer commissioner, had been active in county-level Republican politics in outstate Missouri early in his career, and then moderately active in city G.O.P. politics after moving to St. Louis.

By contrast, only one Democratic lawyer nominating commissioner had been significantly involved in party activities. Interestingly enough, he was from the silk-stocking, Olive Street segment of the bar, and thus was exposed to the same kind of role strains that affected the plaintiffs-oriented Republican who was a lawyer member of the commission at a later period. All of the other Democratic attorneys serving on the nominating commission apparently had never been active in partisan affairs.

The partisan orientations of the lawyer nominating commissioners thus had two principal effects: first, they constituted cross-cutting cleavages which tended to produce more diffuse role orientations, and thus greater possibilities for cooperation between the lawyer commissioners from different ideological wings of the Bar; and, second, the differences in the intensity of partisan identifications among lawyer commissioners made it possible for Republican attorneys to be given serious consideration for judicial nomination and not to be used only for the symbolic "window-dressing" purposes so prevalent in Jackson County nominations. Before any further conclusions can be drawn about these effects, it is necessary to examine the role orientations of the lay nominating commissioners and the presiding judge.

The Lay Commissioners

The lay members of the St. Louis circuit nominating commission have been markedly less political in their orientations to the nominating process than the lay commissioners in Jackson County. The St. Louis lay commissioners also have played a much less significant role in judicial nominations than have the lay members of the Jackson County commission.

Instead of representing partisan political interests, the largest number of lay nominating commissioners have been spokesmen for the values of the business community. Drawn entirely from banking, commerce, and industrial firms, they have generally shared the values of the corporate lawyers serving on the nominating commission, and have usually deferred to the lawyer commissioners and the presiding judge for assessment of the legal abilities of judicial candidates. In addition, these lay commissioners occasionally have turned for advice to the legal counsel employed by their own business firms.

Lay commissioners of this type had rarely been active in partisan politics prior to their selection as members of the nominating commission, but were chosen because of their prominence in St. Louis business circles. Their "apolitical" backgrounds were reflected in their perspectives toward judicial nominations, for they did not look with any particular favor upon candidates who had been politically active. They appear to have paid no attention to gubernatorial preferences regarding nominations, and had neither direct nor indirect contact with the governor about the composition of panels of nominees. Some lay commissioners with this orientation readily admitted that they had always considered politics to be "dirty" and that they had opposed the nomination of candidates with strong political backgrounds.

This group of apolitical commissioners has had considerable influence in judicial nominations since they held at least one lay commissionership when thirteen of the fourteen panels of nominees were selected in the 1941 to 1963 period. In two of these selections, the apoliticals occupied both lay positions.

In addition to the dominant apolitical group, there were two other types of lay commissioners as defined by the nature of their political orientation. First there were the political "Brahmins," men drawn from the top-level or near top-level segments of the St. Louis economic elite. These commissioners had been active politically, mostly as political financiers, but had little contact with the ward-based organizational politics of St. Louis. They were, then, from the "silk-stocking" segment of the political world, had close relations with the governor (and could thus be presumed to provide a point of access for his views about nominations), and effectively bridged the worlds of state politics and local business. However, the significance of the political Brahmins in judicial selection was quite limited in the period studied because of the simple fact that only two of the lay commissioners were of this type. They each participated in the selection of one panel of nominees, and their fellow lay commissioners were in each instance drawn from the "apolitical" group.

The third type of lay commissioner, accounting for three of the commissioners serving in the period, may be labeled the "organizational politicos." They had far more significance than the political Brahmins, but considerably less than the apoliticals, particularly in the decade prior to 1963. Their lesser significance is not completely attributable to the frequency of their participation in the selection process, since the politicos took part in the choosing of ten of the panels of nominees picked by the commission. However, only once did the politicos hold both lay commission seats. In the other nine nominations they were teamed with apolitical lay colleagues.

The "organization politicos" appear to have had both the necessary political contacts and the inclination to inject partisan considerations into the nominating process. All had been active in local and state politics. One had been a state legislator; another had held local appointive public positions, and was reputedly the political ally and protégé of a veteran state legislator who is alleged to have been responsible for the lay member's appointment to the nominating commission. However, none of these lay commissioners was in the top echelon of the Democratic party leadership.

Their fellow nominating commissioners verify that these particular lay commissioners consistently gave support to Democratic attorneys who had a base of support in St. Louis organizational politics. On occasion, they were known to suggest to fellow commissioners that certain candidates had already been cleared with the governor and thus were assured of appointment if the commission would but nominate them. However, except for a brief period from 1949 to 1951, the politicos appear to have had great difficulty in establishing alliances with others on the commission, and thus, for the most part, were relatively uninfluential in commission decision-making.

The Presiding Judge

Lawyers interviewed for this study generally agree that the presiding judge of the St. Louis Court of Appeals has had at a minimum a somewhat greater influence than any other single member of the nominating commission. Estimates of the extent of that influence range from the opinion that he is "first among equals" to the remark that he "can always see that he gets one or two of his preferences on the panel." Most members of the nominating commission discount the latter estimate of the presiding judge's influence, saying that he has played an essentially "neutral" or administrative role in the selection of nominees.

The presiding judges of the St. Louis Court of Appeals have been knowledgeable about, and sensitive to, the political dimensions of the judicial selection process. Yet they do not appear to have had the degree of political information possessed by their counterparts in Jackson County, nor to have been able to use their political knowledge for influencing the selection process to the same extent that the presiding judges have in Jackson County.

Although most of the presiding judges have been strong political partisans, only one who served as nominating commission chairman had been involved in ward-level, organizational politics, and he was involved in the selection of only one panel of nominees. Yet the presiding judges have not been unfavorably disposed toward candidates with political backgrounds. As one presiding judge remarked: "I never have felt that a man's having a strong political background should be held against him. It's in the American tradition for lawyers to be in politics and we shouldn't penalize those who have been in politics by refusing to consider them for judicial appointments."

As contrasted with the Kansas City presiding judges, the St. Louis judges have frequently solicited the views of persons outside the commission, asking them for appraisals of the abilities of candidates. They have consulted colleagues on the appellate bench and, especially in the case of the younger applicants with whom they are unacquainted, they have asked members of the circuit bench for recommendations about those candidates. They have also sounded out the opinions of lawyers, primarily those who are close personal friends.

Over the years the lawyers most often consulted by the presiding judges have been from the corporate and corporate-defense segments of the Bar. This has been true chiefly because most of the presiding judges have come from corporate or corporate-defense practice backgrounds. Naturally, they formed their closest associations with lawyers of similar practice orientations. Thus the presiding judges not only have consulted with the corporate-defense attorneys about candidates being considered for judicial nomination but also have shared most of the values of these attorneys. However, they have not been unalterably opposed to the nomination of plaintiffs' attorneys for the bench, and occasionally have voted for the inclusion of plaintiffs' attorneys on panels of nominees.

The presiding judges serving as chairmen of the nominating commission for most of the 1941–1963 period have therefore been much more closely identified with the Olive Street than the Chestnut Street segment of the St. Louis Bar. Also they have held in greater esteem both the values and the nominating commission representatives of the St. Louis Bar Association, as contrasted with those of the Lawyers' Association.

The role orientation of the presiding judge, together with the roles assumed by other members of the nominating commission, has largely determined the outcome of the St. Louis nominating process and, occasionally, of the appointment process as well. Yet the nominating and appointing phases of judicial selection in the St. Louis City circuit have not been fused nearly so much as they have been in the Jackson County circuit. Still, the nature of gubernatorial politics and the roles of specific governors in judicial selection have had an important effect upon nominating commission decisions, even when there has been a distinct separation between the nomination and appointment dimensions of the selection process.

The Governor

As a result of the political milieu discussed earlier, Democratic governors generally have dealt with a wide array of St. Louis political groupings on their way to nomination and election, but, by the same token, Democratic governors have rarely been beholden to one or a few ward-based political organizations, since none has been powerful enough to exert a dominant influence over election outcomes. Moreover, as contrasted with Jackson County (Kansas City), the St. Louis political factions existing after 1940 had never held preeminence in state politics. Therefore Democratic governors generally have not been indebted to organizational politicians for past support rendered at critical junctures during the governor's climb up the ladder of state offices leading to the governorship. One consequence has been that Missouri governors have had considerable latitude in their dealings with individual St. Louis political leaders. The fragmentation of St. Louis politics has had the additional effect of reducing the importance for the governor of organizational politics per se. His political reference group could thus be broadened to include elements of the St. Louis economic community (particularly those involved in funding political campaigns) and independent political actives (especially those who might have worked on the governor's behalf in one or another of his election campaigns). To a greater extent than in his dealings with Kansas City, the governor also is apt to consider relations with St. Louis from the standpoint of their impact upon future political transactions. In this regard governors have taken into account the effect that their relationships with St. Louis political leaders might have upon the passage of their state legislative programs.

The process of judicial selection in St. Louis has faithfully mirrored the major characteristics of gubernatorial politics sketched above. In its political dimension, judicial selection is the politics of jobs. Especially in the appointment phase, judicial selection consists of the myriad activities of politically oriented people, who are supporting candidates for judicial office primarily because of personal or political loyalties and friendships. As in Jackson County, the group of candidates least likely to receive judicial appointments are those who have opposed the governor in past elections, or those who have been identified with political organizations that have opposed the governor. Yet the more amorphous and diverse nature of political groupings, and the relatively lower salience of organizational politics, means that relatively fewer persons in St. Louis will be *persona non grata* to the governor because of their identification with specific political groups.

Most appointees to the St. Louis circuit bench have been party activists. Generally, if the governor is presented with a choice between a political independent or nominal partisan adherent and someone who has been active in party affairs, he will select the party activist. Some appointees have had only a moderate involvement in politics, but generally they have received potent support from others who have been intimately involved in partisan activities. In a few cases partisan considerations have been irrelevant, and judgeships have been bestowed on close personal or family friends of the governor.

Despite the fact that most judges have been politically active, and that many have had support from influentials in organizational politics, extensive participation in ward politics has not been the primary route to the St. Louis circuit bench. Only two of the judges appointed down through 1963 had been intimately involved in organizational politics. Both were Democrats; one was a ward committeeman, and the other was president of a ward-based Democratic organization. St. Louis lawyers contend that in both these instances the judgeships were essentially rewards given to those who had been long and faithful supporters of the party organization. Yet, some background in ward politics has frequently facilitated a candidate's efforts to secure a judgeship. The kinds of contacts and associations resulting from involvement in that level of politics often give judicial candidates entree to the types of political leaders who can be of assistance to them in the appointment stage of the selection process.

With few exceptions, leaders of the ward organizations have had relatively little influence on the governor's appointment decisions. Support from ward politicians would not necessarily jeopardize a candidate's chances for appointment. Yet ward-level support is not often critical, for two reasons. The first is a general factor already discussed: the St. Louis ward organizations are not highly salient in the eyes of the governor. A second factor is that, given a multiplicity of ward leaders who have approximately equal political strength, all the candidates competing for a judgeship can usually rally support from one or more ward politicians, and thus can neutralize the impact that these politicians can have on judicial appointments.[8] There have been a few instances where competition for appointment has involved a clear-cut contest between candidates supported by ward politicians, on the one hand, and candidates supported by political leaders such as state legislators and chairmen of the city Democratic committee, on the other. In these contests the ward-leader candidate has invariably lost.

Neither has the St. Louis city administration had a very important role in judicial selection. On occasion, the mayor has communicated to the governor his endorsement of nominees for the circuit bench. Such endorsements have generally been for nominees who have held positions in the structure of municipal government, most frequently in the city counselor's office. Mayoral support appears to have had little weight with the governor, and to have been motivated largely by the mayor's feelings of loyalty toward employees of the city government. Besides, very few attorneys with a background primarily in city offices have become candidates for the bench. Moreover, down through 1963, only one nominee with this kind of background had been able to secure a judicial appointment, and he succeeded largely because he had the support of several state legislators.

This failure of city officeholders to become more potent candidates for judgeships suggests that the bifurcation of the local governmental structure that was discussed earlier has important consequences for judicial selection. The isolation of "city office" politics from state politics seems to present almost insuperable difficulties for those judicial candidates with a background essentially in municipal government.

Although ward leaders and political figures in city government have had little impact upon judicial selection, other elements of St. Louis politics have had an important role in the choice of circuit judges. Among these are individuals who have worked on behalf of the governor in primary or general election campaigns. Often these individuals have had no connection whatever with ward organizations, but have been what might be termed "free-lance" party actives. Most prominently involved have been political lawyers, as well as businessmen, particularly those who have served as financial contributors to gubernatorial election campaigns.

Others who have been influential in judicial selection include political leaders with whom the governor must deal in order to accomplish his

---

[8] Another factor that may have relevance was stressed by a member of the St. Louis City Democratic Committee. He said: "I don't think that the ward committeemen have been too influential as far as appointments to the bench are concerned. Most of the nominees for judgeships have come from wards where the Democratic party has been weak."

ROLE ORIENTATIONS OF PARTICIPANTS IN THE SELECTION PROCESS   143

objectives during his term of office. This group consists primarily of state legislators, and those who are deemed to have influence with state legislators.

State legislators from St. Louis had a decisive influence in three of the circuit court appointments made down through 1963, and had a lesser but still important role in the selection of two other judges. Legislators are reputed to have been involved in efforts to influence the governor's choice in virtually all of the remaining appointments. One lawyer respondent attested to the ubiquity of legislator activity, saying that "there isn't a public office vacancy for which most legislators don't have at least one, two, or three candidates."

The influence of state legislators in judicial selection derives principally from their power in the legislative process. State senators or representatives who hold key positions of formal or informal leadership in their respective houses are often able to have a decisive influence over gubernatorial legislative programs, either through outright defeat, delay, or serious modification of the governor's proposals. Legislator influence originating from this source, therefore, tends to be most relevant for judicial selection in circumstances where there may still be doubt about the passage of legislation which the governor considers crucial.

The legislators who have had the most consistent and potent effect upon judicial appointments usually have been those who have attained considerable legislative seniority. To achieve the necessary longevity in office, they must have had a solid base of political support. Thus most have been leaders of some important political group within the Democratic party, or have been close allies of one or more ward leaders. One state senator is reported to have had influence with every Democratic governor since 1944. He has served continuously in the Missouri Senate since 1912, and has been undisputed political boss of a flophouse and Negro district in downtown St. Louis. Among political lawyers this particular state senator is widely credited with influence over judicial selection throughout the entire period of the Missouri Plan's operation. Some contend that his influence has been evident in almost every appointment, but there is general agreement that he has been more involved in some selections than others. In all probability his influence on judicial appointments has been overrated. As one political lawyer remarked: "He is the greatest man of mystery I know. He gets credit publicly for lots of things that he probably never had anything to do with, or never even thought about. Many people say that he is the man that's behind nearly everything. I doubt it, but I don't really know."

One other type of political influence over St. Louis judicial appointments may be traced to the fragmentation of political power there. As compared with Jackson County, where this was never mentioned as a factor, judicial selection in St. Louis is said, time and again, to have been the result of "outstate" political forces. In the eyes of many lawyers, the outstate influence has been pervasive. It is said that many judges have formerly lived outstate; indeed, some are accused of having moved to St. Louis solely in order to seek a circuit judgeship. These same lawyers express the belief that politicians from outstate often have more voice in the selection of St. Louis judges than do the political leaders from St. Louis itself.

This theme of "outstate influence" is so recurrent in the conversation of lawyers and politicians as to be tantamount to a kind of political paranoia. However, there is little evidence to support the contention that outstate "political" forces have actually been an important factor in nominations and appointments to the St. Louis circuit bench. There has been a tendency for lawyers who have been associated politically with the governor while living outstate to become candidates for the judiciary when they later move their residences and law practices to St. Louis. The fact is that all the Democratic governors serving during the Missouri Plan period have hailed from outstate, and have retained an essentially rural Missouri orientation while in office. This partially explains the presumed advantage of St. Louis circuit bench candidates who themselves had been politically active outstate before moving to St. Louis. Yet at least part of their advantage is attributable to the fact that St. Louis political organizations did not usually have commanding influence with Missouri governors, who thus have had a fairly wide range of discretion in the choice of political elements to which they could give their attention.

Of course, most of the political relationships discussed in this section have varied somewhat from one gubernatorial administration to another. One Democratic governor is generally said to have had close relations with ward-level political organizations and, specifically in the area of judicial politics, to have deferred to the ward politicians' views with respect to judicial appointments. Other Democratic governors have been almost totally unconcerned with the views of the organization politicians. One governor is said to have been "on the outs with nearly every leading political figure" in St. Louis. The same governor is alleged to have remarked that he didn't much care what St. Louis politicians thought, since only a handful of wards in the city had given him consistent support in his various bids for statewide public office. Between these two extremes are other governors who have had fairly close relations with some St. Louis party organizations, but who have not been too dependent even upon them.

In general, then, the fragmentation of Democratic politics in St. Louis has been reflected in the process of judicial selection, primarily through its effects upon gubernatorial politics and its consequences for the governor's role in the selection of judges. However, the St. Louis nominating commission has responded to influences besides those emanating from the governorship, as the following analysis demonstrates.

THE SELECTION PROCESS: 1941 TO 1963

The diversity and diffuseness of role orientations within the St. Louis nominating commission have contributed toward a highly fluid pattern of interrelationships among commission members. Before 1960 there were no very deep or stable cleavages within the nominating commission. Nor were there voting blocs of any great potency or duration. The resulting fragmentation of power within the nominating commission was essentially a product of the shifting patterns of interaction among the frequently varying role types on the commission.

For most of the period before 1960 there did exist within the commission a fairly persistent nucleus of potential power. This consisted of the two-man combination of the presiding judge, who generally had a corporate-defense orientation, and the lawyer commissioner drawn from the Olive Street or corporate-defense portion of the bar. (This combination was present on the nominating commission when eleven of the fourteen panels of nominees were chosen.) But despite their presence on the nominating commission, the influence of the commissioners with a corporate-defense orientation was never sufficient to permit them clearly to dominate the nominating process. The second lawyer member of the nominating commission was frequently a "swing" man, voting on some occasions with the defendants-oriented group and, at other times, joining forces with politically oriented lay commissioners. In addition, the Republican partisan affiliation of either the lawyer commissioners or the presiding judge, as well as the tendency of most presiding judges to be inclined toward candidates with political backgrounds, created still other bases for interaction among nominating commissioners. Overlaying all of these factors was the further tendency of individual nominating commissioners to support the candidacies of lawyers with whom they had close personal or professional relations.

As a consequence, nominating decisions in the St. Louis circuit have generally been the result of a highly complex and unstable bargaining process among commission members. There have been times at which the bargaining transactions have involved interactions between groups of nominating commissioners, but generally the bargaining has been individual in nature. Each commissioner tends to have his own list of favorites whom he promotes for nomination to the bench. If he remains a member of the commission long enough and is persistent and skillful in his support, he can usually succeed in getting many of his favorites placed in nomination.

Most St. Louis lawyers and judges conceive of the St. Louis commission's selection of judicial nominees in bargaining process terms. Nominating commissioners are said to engage in a "bit of horsetrading," swapping votes back and forth for each other's favorites. One circuit judge implied much the same thing when he remarked that a candidate only needs the solid support of one lawyer member of the St. Louis commission in order eventually to be placed on a panel of nominees.

Consonant with the individualistic nature of the bargaining process has been the utilization of majority rule for the choices of nominees. Commissioners participating in judicial selection at all points throughout the 1941–1963 period agree with the statement of one commissioner that "it has been difficult to get any unanimous agreement and is often necessary to drop down to three votes to select persons for a panel." Actually, the nominating commission rarely has sought unanimity in its nominations. Generally the commission has balloted for each panel position only until some candidate has secured a majority of the votes.

The fact that decision-making has been characterized by individual bargaining does not necessarily imply that the bargaining process has been either clandestine or conspiratorial. Nominating commissioners stoutly deny engaging in behind-the-scenes maneuvers to predetermine nominations, but some commissioners admit to having discussed candidate selection with other commission members prior to commission meetings. At times these conversations have dealt with the question of the strategy to be pursued in order to enlist support for a candidate favored by one or another of the nominating commissioners. Such contacts appear to have occurred infrequently and to have been incidental to the principal form of bargaining which has occurred in the nominating process.

One of the principal features of that bargaining process has been the acceptance of what might be termed the rule of reciprocity. Following this norm, a commissioner will be inclined to "go along" with the nomination of a candidate who receives strong and consistent support from one or more members of the commission, even if he has some reservations about the candidate being supported. He will often acquiesce even if he has a candidate of his own that he would strongly prefer,

THE SELECTION PROCESS: 1941 TO 1963   147

since he realizes that other commissioners will be inclined to reciprocate during future nominating transactions.

This form of bargaining behavior is possible only when there is a basic consensus within the commission, as well as mutual trust and tolerance among commission members. Also, such individual bargaining can occur only when the nominating commissioners are confident that there is parity among commission members in terms of the opportunity for each to secure nomination of his favored candidates, and where no voting bloc or combination exists that might be capable of foreclosing consideration of candidates sponsored by any particular member of the commission.

St. Louis lawyers not only see the nominating process in bargaining terms but also subscribe to the belief that nominations are "stacked." Despite differences of opinion about the extent of such panel-stacking, there is widespread agreement that the commission, on at least some occasions, has consciously employed a strategy of selecting a particular combination of nominees for the purpose of manipulating the outcome of the appointment process.

Many attorneys feel that in some instances these nominations have been "wired," that is, that persons chosen for inclusion on the panel of nominees have been selected at the behest of the governor himself. However, in the two clearest instances of nominations that went to personal or family friends of the governor, there is no evidence that would indicate that the governor actually sought to influence the nominating process. In one such instance the commission made its choice in the face of widespread rumors that the panel was being "fixed" for a personal favorite of the governor, who was certain to be appointed no matter who else was named to the panel. A member of the nominating commission said about this selection:

There was a rumor that this panel was fixed, but it wasn't. The governor didn't contact anyone on the commission about this nomination.

The members of the commission were cognizant of the rumors that the panel was wired. But we took the position that this was our best candidate, and that he shouldn't be penalized by rumors of that sort.

The ability of the commission to operate on the basis of such a rationale is facilitated by the fact that they never discuss the political dimensions of the selection process in their meetings. One commissioner made this comment about the decision-making process:

I had always thought before I went on the nominating commission that there might be all kinds of skulduggery engaged in at the nominating commission sessions.

But to my surprise I found that those meetings are beyond and above reproach. They're like church sessions. There is no discussion of a candidate's politics, religion, or any other thing of that sort. It's just a matter of a man's qualifications, just a discussion of his merits.

The practice of excluding political factors from overt consideration has several consequences for the nominating process. As was the case in Jackson County, submergence of the political dimension makes it more difficult to counter the stacking of panels or the nomination of persons who are certain to be appointed because of their close personal relationships with the governor. These latent political issues must be dealt with either through negotiations outside commission meetings or through the independent action of several commissioners who happen to share the same orientations toward the nominating process, and who have equally complete and reliable information about the political and personal backgrounds of the various contenders for nomination. For most of the 1941–1963 period in St. Louis there were no cohesive working coalitions that could negotiate outside commission meetings in order to block nomination of candidates who would be prohibitive favorites of the governor. Given the number of apoliticals among the commission membership, there was also little prospect that such nominations could be blocked through concerted action by a majority within the commission meetings.

The disinclination to deal with political issues in an open manner thus had different consequences in Jackson County and St. Louis. In Jackson County, where commissioners were politically alert and where fairly cohesive blocs existed within the commission, relegation of political issues to the latent level only served to facilitate the stacking of panels. In St. Louis the refusal to deal with political considerations as manifest issues made it more difficult to forestall the nomination of politically favored candidates. It could have facilitated the stacking of panels in St. Louis also but the voting blocs essential for such a stacking strategy did not often exist.

Although circumstances militated against panel-stacking becoming the dominant mode of decision making in St. Louis, panels have been stacked on a few occasions. One of the most complicated instances of panel-stacking is alleged to have occurred in the nomination of a Negro attorney for the circuit bench in 1956. A commissioner participating in the selection of that panel contends that most members of the nominating commission felt, at the time the panel of nominees was selected and sent to the governor, that the Negro attorney would not be appointed. Another nominee had been more active in Democratic politics, presumably would have greater political support, and thus was assumed to have been a heavy favorite to secure the appointment. Members of the Bar appear to have reached the same conclusions about the Negro attorney's chances. One attorney said: "No one gave him even an outside chance. All the lawyers I knew expressed the opinion that he had been put on the panel just as window dressing."

Yet, at least some members of the nominating commission appear to have considered the possibility of another outcome. One respondent remarked:

Some members of the nominating commission approached me prior to the naming of this panel and asked me what I thought the governor would do if he received a panel containing the name of a Negro. I told them that, knowing Governor Donnelly, if he thought the commission was trying to put him on the spot by sending down the name of a Negro, he would respond by appointing the Negro. And this is precisely what he did.

This is probably a much too simplistic explanation of the Negro attorney's appointment by the governor, since he had impressive political support, and since his creditable performance in a public legal position had previously come to the governor's attention. The explanation offered above is revealing, however, in terms of the kinds of strategic considerations that are sometimes taken into account by members of the nominating commission.

Two other instances of panel-stacking occurred during the second administration of Governor Phil Donnelly. One of these panels is reputed to have been selected following protestations to the Governor about his practice of naming only Democrats to the bench. Said an attorney: "Donnelly had been contacted by certain people who suggested to him that he should get away from the practice of always naming Democrats to judgeships. The governor is said to have told them that if they would get a couple of good Republicans on the next panel, that he would appoint one." The very next panel sent to the governor not only contained the name of a "good" Republican, but of a nominal Democrat, and of a second Republican who was in ill-health, as well as politically objectionable to the governor. The Governor chose the Republican on whose behalf the panel had been stacked.

The second instance appears to have been an even more transparent case of panel-stacking. This occurred at a time when the nominating commission had two circuit court vacancies to fill. For one of these vacancies the commission selected a panel of three Democratic nominees. For the second panel they chose two Republicans and one Democrat. The lawyer receiving the appointment from the second panel had long been prominent in St. Louis Republican politics, and had been appointed by Governor Donnelly to legal and policy-making positions at the state level. In addition to the nominal Democrat, this panel also included the Republican attorney discussed in the preceding paragraph, the one who was politically objectionable to the Governor.

Neither panel-stacking nor the selection of the governor's personal friends has constituted the principal mode of decision-making in the St. Louis circuit. Generally, the nominating commission has functioned simply as a conduit through which the varied political forces have flowed. Lawyers who feel that they have the political resources necessary for securing gubernatorial appointment naturally have tended to become the most active candidates for judical nomination. Usually their success in winning placement on a panel of nominees has been largely independent of their political strengths or weaknesses.

Therefore politicization of the nominating process in St. Louis has not been primarily a product of a commission-imposed structuring of nominee selection. In Jackson County, nominations were frequently the result of a process in which nominating commissioners were craftily piecing together panels with political motives, and for political effect. The politicization of the nominating process in St. Louis has had different origins, being attributable principally to influences stemming from the environment in which the nominating commission functioned. Thus in St. Louis the political considerations generated by gubernatorial involvement in the choice of judges tended to structure the entire selection process, leading certain kinds of lawyers to become more frequent and active candidates for nomination than others. With the exception of its solicitude for Republican aspirants, the St. Louis nominating commission afforded relatively equal access to contenders of every political coloration. It neither restricted nor amplified the chances of any specific political groups, thus allowing the political dimensions of judicial selection to pass undistorted through the nominating stage.

JUDICIAL SELECTION SYSTEMS AND THE CIRCUIT JUDICIARY

As a result of differences in process variables and environmental factors, the judicial selection systems of the two Missouri Plan circuits have functioned somewhat differently. The consequence, according to the preceding analysis, has been the creation of differentials in access to the bench of each circuit, so that some types of lawyers have had better opportunities to receive judicial nominations and appointments than have others. In general, access was found to be more open and the selection process more pluralistic in the St. Louis circuit than in the Jackson County circuit.

If these (and earlier) generalizations about the selection process are valid, they should be reflected in variations in the characteristics of nominees and appointees for the two circuit benches. Although the data utilized in the ensuing comparative analysis do not include information on all nominees and appointees to the two circuit benches since 1940, they are sufficiently complete to provide a gross test for many of the propositions advanced above.[9]

The data in Table 4.2 provide a general confirmation for several of the earlier conclusions about the effect of legal practice orientations on chances for judicial nomination and appointment. The effects on nominations are considered first. In both circuits the proportion of nominees having general corporate or mixed plaintiffs'-defense practices is higher than the proportion of attorneys having such practice specialities in the Bar generally. Of particular interest is the relatively high percentage of Jackson County nominees with a mixed personal injury practice. These data are in accord with the earlier finding that the plaintiffs-defense stalemate on the Jackson County nominating commission, to-

---

[9] The data on nominees and appointees are incomplete, particularly with respect to the nominees. Questionnaire responses were received from 9 of the 15 judges appointed to the Jackson County circuit and probate benches prior to 1963. Four of the remaining six were deceased at the time of the survey. The data are more complete for the St. Louis City circuit judges, with responses being received from 11 of the 14 judges appointed through mid-1963. One of the remaining judges was deceased at the time of the mail survey and two other judges failed to respond.

Responses were received from 10 of the 20 persons who were nominated, but not appointed, to the Jackson County circuit and probate benches. Two of these respondents were nominated twice, so the ten responses represent 12 of the 30 nominations made during the period covered. Six persons accounting for 7 nominations during this period were appointed to the court later in the period and are therefore classified in the appointee category. No responses were received from 10 nominees, who altogether accounted for 11 nominations.

The response rate was somewhat better for the *nominated only* category in the St. Louis City Circuit. Responses were received from 12 of the 18 persons nominated, but not appointed, to the St. Louis Circuit and probate benches. Because of multiple nominations for three of these 12 respondents, they accounted for 17 of the 28 nominations going to the nominee only category. Four persons nominated for the St. Louis bench were also nominees on later panels from which they were appointed to the bench and account for five of the 28 nominations in the period under consideration.

In both the Jackson County and St. Louis Circuits there were 15 and 14 nominations, respectively, which went to the nominees on each panel who received gubernatorial appointment. Data on all these persons are recorded only in the *Judges* category, even though many had been unsuccessful nominees on panels nominated previously to the one from which they were eventually appointed.

TABLE 4.2

Selected Fields of Legal Practice of Attorneys, Judicial Candidates, Nominees, and Judges in Jackson County and St. Louis City Circuits (Percent)[a]

Fields of Practice[b]	Jackson County					St. Louis City				
	Attorney Sample (N = 291)	Judicial Candidates (N = 32)	All Nominees (N = 19)	Nominated Only (N = 10)	Judges (N = 9)	Attorney Sample (N = 133)	Judicial Candidates (N = 15)	All Nominees (N = 23)	Nominated Only (N = 12)	Judges (N = 11)
Corporate, general	42	53	53	50	56	37	40	48	59	36
Defendants'	15	12	16	10	22	16	13	30	25	36
Criminal	5	3	5	0	11	6	7	13	0	27
Plaintiffs'	23	34	21	20	22	20	20	22	25	18
Mixed plaintiffs-defense	9	6	32	30	33	7	0	13	0	27

[a] The categories used for comparison in Table 4.2 through 4.6 are defined as follows: the *attorney sample* refers to the mail questionnaire respondents residing in the two circuit court jurisdictions; *Judicial Candidates* are those mail questionnaire respondents in each circuit who indicated that their names had been considered by the nominating commission for one or more Missouri Plan judicial vacancies; the category *all nominees* consists of all persons nominated for the circuit bench, including those appointed to the bench, who returned mail questionnaires similar to those used in the lawyer survey; the category *nominated only* consists of those nominated but never appointed to the bench; and the category *Judges* consists of those nominees actually appointed to the circuit bench. Data for the last three categories eliminate multiple nominations, so that information on a given individual is recorded only once no matter how many times he was nominated. Data on judges who had been nominated to panels prior to the one from which they were appointed are also recorded only once.

[b] Includes lawyers listing field exclusively, or as one of the two or three major fields of practice since admission to legal practice.

gether with the importance of mixed practice firms in the legal ecology, led nominating commissioners to support candidates with a mixed personal injury practice. The tendency to give preferential treatment to such candidates also existed in St. Louis, but to a lesser degree.

In Jackson County the proportion of attorneys having defense, plaintiffs' or criminal practice orientations was approximately the same in the Bar generally and among the nominees for the circuit bench. However, in the St. Louis circuit in addition to the disproportionately large numbers of nominees having general corporate or mixed personal injury practices, the proportion of nominees with a defense or criminal practice was high compared to the proportion of all attorneys having a major portion of their practices in these fields. Part of this difference—that with respect to defense attorneys—is in accord with an earlier finding of a pro-defense bias within the St. Louis circuit nominating commission.

Another test of the extent to which various practice specialities have been favored in the nominating process consists of a comparison of the kinds of attorneys who have been candidates for judicial nomination and the kinds actually nominated.[10] Such a comparison, also presented in Table 4.2, reveals that the relationships between candidate and nominee characteristics are generally the same as those for the attorney and nominee comparison.

Whichever comparison is used, the data reported in Table 4.2 indicate that nominee characteristics in both circuits are not representative of the practice specialties of either the rank-and-file Bar or of the attorneys who have actually been candidates for nomination. Moreover, the total deviation is approximately equal for both circuits, although different practice groups are relatively favored in its two circuits. Therefore, these data suggest that, along the dimension of fields of practice specialization, the nominating process in the St. Louis circuit has been no more "open" than has that in the Jackson County circuit.

The data on practice specialization presented in Table 4.3 reveal, however, that attorneys with law practices limited to a single field were seriously disadvantaged in the selection process for the Jackson County circuit bench. These attorneys were only slightly disadvantaged in the

---

[10] Fifty-five lawyer respondents to the mail questionnaire indicated that they had been considered for nomination to the Missouri Plan bench by the judicial nominating commissions. By comparison of these returns with known characteristics of those actually nominated for the bench, it was determined that eight of the 55 respondents had actually received nomination. These eight respondents were omitted from the *judicial candidate* category in order to obtain a sharper differentiation between the characteristics of those who became active candidates but failed to receive nomination, and those who were in fact nominated.

TABLE 4.3

EXTENT OF LEGAL PRACTICE SPECIALIZATION IN SELECTED FIELDS,
JACKSON COUNTY AND ST. LOUIS CITY CIRCUITS (PERCENT)[a]

	Attorney Sample[b]	Judicial Candidates	All Nominees	Nominated Only	Judges
Jackson County	29	28	15	20	11
St. Louis City	35	40	30	25	36

[a] Figures recorded are percentages of those in each category whose practice had been limited to a single one of the following fields of practice since admission to the Bar: general corporate, personal injury primarily for the defense, criminal, personal injury principally for the plaintiff, and personal injury about equally for the plaintiffs and the defense.

[b] N's for this and other categories, by circuit, are the same as those appearing in Table 4.2.

St. Louis circuit nominating process, and not at all disadvantaged in the appointment process. Furthermore, a closer analysis of the data indicates that attorneys specializing in all but one of the major practice fields were nominated and appointed to the St. Louis circuit bench, the exception being that none was nominated who had specialized in a corporate practice. In Jackson County only those specializing in corporate or defense fields were nominated; only one attorney with a practice limited to a single field was appointed to the Jackson County circuit bench, and he was a defense attorney. From this standpoint, then, the selection process in St. Louis was more open, and provided greater access to the bench for attorneys with highly specialized practices than did the selection process in Jackson County.

The law practice arrangements of individuals considered for the circuit bench do not appear, in themselves, to be important factors in the selection process. Instead, the relationship between law practice arrangement and success in competition for circuit judicial nominations and appointments is largely attributable to the tendency for practice arrangements to coincide with other characteristics such as the extent and nature of political party activity; the type and extent of legal practice specialization; and the individual's "availability" for judicial office, which is affected by his age, income level, and relationships with colleagues.

The data in Table 4.4 indicate that attorneys from middle-sized firms have relative advantages in both the nominating and appointing process for the Jackson County circuit bench. Lawyers from two-man partner-

TABLE 4.4

LAW PRACTICE ARRANGEMENTS OF ATTORNEYS, JUDICIAL CANDIDATES, NOMINEES AND JUDGES IN THE JACKSON COUNTY AND ST. LOUIS CITY CIRCUITS (PERCENT)

Practice arrangement	Jackson County					St. Louis City				
	Attorney Sample (N = 291)	Judicial Candidates (N = 32)	All Nominees (N = 19)	Nominated Only (N = 10)	Judges (N = 9)	Attorney Sample (N = 133)	Judicial Candidates (N = 15)	All Nominees (N = 23)	Nominated Only (N = 12)	Judges (N = 11)
Solo	25	47	16	10	22	36	60	13	17	9
Two-man partnership	10	6	21	30	11	5	13	17	17	18
Three to nine lawyers	16	22	37	20	56	22	13	17	33	0
Large firm or Corp.	31	12	11	20	0	20	7	22	8	37
Government agency	7	6	10	10	11	9	7	17	8	27
Not ascertained/ more than one arrangement	11	7	5	10	0	8	0	14	17	9

ships are favored at the nominating stage but not in the appointment phase, while the reverse is true for solo practitioners. The overall advantages of those from middle-sized firms indicates both the propensity of such firms to have mixed personal injury practices and the fact that attorneys from such firms are relatively active in party politics. Similarly, the relative advantage of solo practitioners in the competition for judicial appointments reflects the extent to which attorneys from solo practices have been politically active in Jackson County politics.[11]

Table 4.4 reveals that attorneys employed by government agencies and those coming from two-man partnerships have been favored as nominees for the St. Louis circuit bench. Salaried employees of government agencies also are in a favored position in the appointment process, as are those from large firms.[12] The relative overall advantage of lawyers working for government agencies is primarily a consequence of the greater political visibility that accrues to attorneys who hold public office. The relatively high success of large firm attorneys in competing for appointments to the St. Louis circuit bench has resulted from gubernatorial decisions that turned largely on nonpolitical issues, when the governor chose close personal friends for the bench or responded to influences exerted by those who were promoting defense-oriented nominees.

As was observed in the analysis of the selection systems of the two circuits, partisan affiliation has been a factor of major importance in the nominating and appointing processes. In both circuits approximately 70 percent of all Missouri Plan nominations have gone to Democratic attorneys. Of the judges named to the Jackson County and St. Louis circuit benches, 73 and 71 percent, respectively, have been Democrats. Yet these similarities in the partisan identifications of nominees and judges obscure some important differences in the role of partisan considerations in judicial selection for the two circuits. As was suggested in the earlier analysis, the Jackson County nominating process has been more highly politicized and more partisan than has the nominating phase

---

[11] The mean scores on the Index of Party Activity for attorneys residing in Jackson County, by type of practice arrangement, are as follows:

Practice Arrangement	Score
Solo	2.8
Two-man partnership	2.2
Three to nine lawyers	3.0
Large firm or Corp.	2.1
Government agency	1.6

[12] All judges appointed to the St. Louis City circuit bench from a large firm or corporate practice were salaried employees. None were law firm partners.

of judicial selection in the St. Louis circuit. Thus the nomination of Republicans for the Jackson County circuit bench usually has amounted to a mere token bipartisanism, and frequently has been an integral part of the panel-stacking strategy pursued by the nominating commission. Consonant with this interpretation is the fact that two of the four Republican appointments to the Jackson County circuit bench came during the administration of Republican Governor Forrest C. Donnell. The remaining two Republican appointments were products of Democratic Governor Phil Donnelly's pique over the nominating commission's panel-loading tactics in the 1953–1956 impasse between the Governor and the commission. By contrast three of the four Republican appointments to the St. Louis circuit bench occurred during Democratic administrations. Although two of those three resulted from loaded panels, they were panels loaded on behalf of the Republicans, in contrast to the situation in Jackson County.

Other effects of the role of political factors in circuit judicial selection are revealed in the data presented in Table 4.5. In both circuits, candidates and nominees for the bench and the judges appointed to the bench have been far more active in partisan politics than has the rank and file membership of the Bar. There are no substantial differences in the level of partisan activity of those nominated to the two circuit benches, but those appointed to the Jackson County bench had been more active in partisan politics before appointment than had the judges chosen for the St. Louis city circuit bench. This supports the earlier observation that partisan political considerations have had relatively greater influence upon judicial selection in the Jackson County circuit.

The data in Table 4.5 also provide collateral support for the conclusion that panel-stacking has tended to occur with greater frequency in the Jackson County than in the St. Louis City circuit. In the Jackson County circuit the mean party activity index score of those nominated (but not appointed) to the circuit bench was 2.6, compared to 5.2 for those who became judges. The mean party index score of nominees to the St. Louis bench was also 2.6, but for the judges the figure was 4.2. The greater differential between the levels of party activity of unsuccessful nominees and nominees appointed to judgeships in the Jackson County circuit is consistent with the proposition that the Jackson County nominating commission more frequently engaged in panel-stacking. Specifically, these data provide some confirmation for the conclusion that the Jackson County nominating commission frequently "dressed up" panels with the names of lawyers who were chosen primarily because they had not been active enough politically to receive gubernatorial appointment. Of course, these data do not reflect the extent to which

TABLE 4.5

EXTENT OF PARTISAN ACTIVITY OF JUDICIAL CANDIDATES, NOMINEES, AND JUDGES OF THE JACKSON COUNTY AND ST. LOUIS CITY CIRCUITS (PERCENT)

Party Activity Index Score[a]	Jackson County					St. Louis City				
	Attorney Sample (N = 291)	Judicial Candidates (N = 32)	All Nominees (N = 19)	Nominated Only (N = 10)	Judges (N = 9)	Attorney Sample (N = 133)	Judicial Candidates (N = 15)	All Nominees (N = 23)	Nominated Only (N = 12)	Judges (N = 11)
No points	27	3	11	20	0	27	7	17	25	9
1–2 points	32	19	26	30	22	33	20	9	8	9
3–4 points	26	56	32	40	22	24	47	52	67	36
5–8 points	12	13	26	10	45	14	26	22	0	46
9 or more points	3	9	5	0	11	2	0	0	0	0
Mean score	2.5	3.9	3.7	2.6	5.2	2.2	3.4	3.4	2.6	4.2

[a] See footnote 12, Chapter 2, for a discussion of the construction of the party activity index.

panel-stacking in the Jackson County circuit involved the selection of candidates whose factional affiliations were unpalatable to the governor. According to the earlier analysis of the nominating process, such factionally-based political manipulation was the most frequent form of panel-stacking occurring in the Jackson County circuit.

Finally, Table 4.6 presents data that reinforce the hypothesis that a public office background has tended to facilitate candidate chances for judicial appointment to a greater extent in the St. Louis than in the Jackson County circuit.[13] There are no appreciable differences in the public legal office backgrounds of nominees and appointees in the two circuits, but a higher proportion of appointees to the St. Louis bench have sought or held nonlegal public offices than have appointees to the Jackson County bench. Moreover, St. Louis judges generally have been more intensively involved in nonlegal public office politics prior to their judicial appointments than have Jackson County judges.

The greater importance of public office politics in St. Louis judicial selection is largely attributable to differences in the political context of the selection process in the two Plan circuits. In both areas attorneys from public office backgrounds are more likely to become candidates for judicial office than are typical members of the Bar; they generally have a greater diversity of experience, and are better known to the nominating commissioners as a result of the public nature of their official duties. However, at the appointment stage of judicial selection, other features of public office experience become more salient. In Jackson County such experience has usually been of secondary importance as a means for acquiring the political credentials essential for gubernatorial appointment. There, the factional ties of judicial aspirants have been the primary determinants of their acceptability to the governor. Operating in a more loosely structured political environment, St. Louis lawyers with public office backgrounds have frequently enjoyed superior entree to the governor. The nature of their official duties often has brought them into contact with the governor, or failing that, the nature of their jobs usually insures that the governor will have come to know something about them. In addition, the political activities of those who hold public office lead them to become involved in gubernatorial elections, and to have frequent contact with both local and state political leaders, including state legislators. These political associations have often proved decisive in the competition for judicial office in the St. Louis circuit.

---

[13] The Index of Public Legal Office is calculated by scoring one point for each legal office held. The legal offices used for the index are listed in footnote 5 of this chapter.

TABLE 4.6
Extent of Public Office Holding of Judicial Candidates, Nominees and Judges, Jackson County and St. Louis City Circuits (Percent)

Public Legal Office Index Score	Jackson County				St. Louis City			
	Judicial Candidates (N = 32)	All Nominees (N = 19)	Nominated Only (N = 10)	Judges (N = 9)	Judicial Candidates (N = 15)	All Nominees (N = 23)	Nominated Only (N = 12)	Judges (N = 11)
No points	47	21	20	22	47	30	42	18
1–2 points	50	63	70	56	53	61	58	64
3–4 points	3	11	10	11	0	9	0	18
5 or more points	0	5	0	11	0	0	0	0
Mean Score	0.8	1.4	1.1	1.8	0.9	1.2	0.8	1.5
Nonlegal Public Office Index Score								
No points	72	37	30	45	47	48	75	18
1–2 points	19	47	60	33	33	34	17	55
3–4 points	6	16	10	22	20	9	8	9
5 or more points	3	0	0	0	0	9	0	18
Mean Score	0.7	1.3	1.2	1.3	1.3	1.4	0.6	2.4

Although many of the variations in nominee and appointee characteristics for the two circuits are relatively small, the differences reported in this section are all consistent with the conclusions drawn from the earlier analysis of the selection process in the Jackson County and St. Louis circuits. These data thus provide further support for the observation that the judicial selection process tends to be shaped by the particular mixture of influences that emanate from the environment and by the effect of these influences on the interactions that constitute the formal selection procedure.

5

THE APPELLATE JUDICIARY:

SELECTION THROUGH

COOPTATION

The staunchest advocates of the Missouri Plan feel that the high quality of the state's appellate benches constitutes decisive proof for their contention that the Plan has had beneficial effects. The most outspoken critics of the Plan also believe that the quality of the appellate judiciary is the determinative issue for judging the merits of nonpartisan judicial selection. To the critics, however, the kinds of persons chosen for the courts of appeals and the Supreme Court exemplify much of what is wrong with the Plan. For many of those interviewed in the study, then, the appellate judiciary, particularly the Supreme Court, becomes the principal focus of ideological conflict about the Missouri Plan.

Among lawyers, this polarization of views about the state's appellate courts substantially reflects the plaintiffs-defense schism existing within the Missouri Bar. This ideological cleavage also coincides largely with the division within the legal fraternity between the lawyers who have been influential in appellate judicial selection and those who have not. The Missouri Plan's strongest supporters have tended to dominate the selection of appellate judges; those less sanguine about the Plan, and certainly the critics of the Plan, have had virtually no impact on the nomination and appointment of appeals court and Supreme Court judges, although they have been influential in circuit court selection. Partially because of the greater impact that they have had on trial court selection, the plaintiffs' segment of the Bar is more satisfied with the Missouri Plan circuit benches than with the appellate judiciary, while the reverse is true for the corporate-defense segment of the Bar.

Behind these divergent opinions about the respective merits of the appellate and trial court benches lie substantial differences in the factors that affect the choice of judges for these two types of courts. These differences are manifested in a variety of ways: in the sorts of individuals who become involved in efforts to influence judicial selection; in the orientations of those who participate formally in the selection process; and in the kinds of considerations that weigh most heavily in the assessment of judicial candidates. Before discussing these more specific ways in which the appellate selection process differs from circuit judicial selection, it is necessary to examine the broad environment in which the choice of appellate judges occurs.

THE ENVIRONMENT

Indeed, one feature that most clearly distinguishes appellate from circuit judicial recruitment is the high degree of congruence between environmental factors and the formal process through which appellate judges are selected. The first section of this chapter therefore examines the political milieu and the legal-judicial context in which the choice of appellate judges takes place. Later portions of the chapter analyze the decision-making process in appellate selection, and relate that process to the more important environmental influences that impinge upon selection. Throughout there is also an effort systematically to compare the selection process for the Missouri Plan circuit and appellate courts.

The Political Milieu

The political environments relevant to circuit and appellate judicial selection, although similar in some respects, are fundamentally different in others. The political forces affecting trial court judicial selection have been determined largely by the manner in which state and local (metropolitan) political structures have intersected. The political forces relevant to appellate judicial selection, especially the selection of Supreme Court judges, have originated almost exclusively from the realm of "outstate" Missouri politics.

The outstate political milieu can be defined with considerable accuracy as that which remains of Missouri politics after one subtracts the organizational politics of metropolitan St. Louis and Kansas City. The residue is the politics of the state's rural Democracy—or at least it has been that for most of the period under consideration in this study.

Several aspects of the outstate political environment have been discussed in earlier chapters, including the personalistic, "friends and neighbors" character of gubernatorial politics. In terms of its import for appellate judicial selection, this particular facet of state politics must be placed within the context of the larger "political culture."[1] In recent decades the distinguishing feature of that political culture[2] has been a fundamental economic and political conservatism, one reflecting a traditionalistic orientation that has had as its basic premise a low expenditure, low governmental services philosophy. Although that orientation has been most strongly entrenched in rural Missouri, it has constituted the guiding political principle for the entire state political system by virtue of the fact that outstate political elements have dominated state politics in the period dealt with in this study. The result, in terms of the policy outputs of state government, has been a *status quo* orientation toward virtually all political issues, and a public expenditure policy which has been rigidly incrementalist in nature.

Although Missouri's political conservatism has largely reflected the norms of the outstate political culture, the dominance of that culture in state politics has been partially attributable to the orientation of the metropolitan segment of the state's population, and to the fragmentation within that segment produced by its division between two widely separated metropolitan areas. St. Louis, on the eastern border of the state, is an aristocratic, eastern-oriented city whose residents are facetiously said to venture no farther west than their own suburbs. Kansas City, on the western border of the state, is strikingly different. A city that bears many marks of its relatively recent frontier status, Kansas City is said to be the beginning of the American West, and to have its major orientation toward the western hinterland that provided the agricultural commodities that were once its economic lifeblood. Thus, as Missouri lore expresses it, St. Louis faces east, Kansas City faces west, and the

---

[1] Political culture refers to the basic orientation of both political leaders and citizens toward politics. Specifically, it refers to attitudes on such matters as the proper ends or purposes of political activity; how the political process works; what benefits individuals may expect to receive from it; as well as the part they should play in the process. One work on the subject is Lucian Pye and Sidney Verba, *Political Culture and Political Development* (Princeton: Princeton University Press, 1965).

[2] Daniel Elazar in his provocative study entitled, *American Federalism: A View from the States* (New York: Thomas Y. Crowell Co., 1966), has distinguished three basic political subcultures operating in the United States, the individualistic, the moralistic and the traditional. The first conceives the primary purpose of politics to be individual self-advancement; the second holds it to be the achievement of the good commonwealth; while the third emphasizes the preservation of the existing social order. He classifies metropolitan Missouri as individualistic, and outstate areas as traditional in political orientation.

rural folks have controlled everything in between—which means virtually the entire state.

Even discounting the poetic license involved in this imagery, there is considerable substance to the contention that neither metropolitan area has ever been vitally interested in politics at Jefferson City, the state capital. Except for one period during the Pendergast era, no metropolitan-based political group has ever approached dominant status in Democratic state party councils. Even during the Pendergast period the balance of state-wide political power continued to rest in the hands of a variety of outstate political groups, including the Bourbon Democrats, agricultural leaders, the banking and financial community, and the plantocracy of the state's delta region.[3]

The state's conservatism has also been a consequence of the orientation of the major interest groups involved in state politics. Whether from the metropolitan or nonmetropolitan areas, most of the political interest groups have had as their central purpose the *prevention* of certain kinds of governmental activity at the state level. Even organized labor, which has its greatest strength in the St. Louis and Kansas City areas, does not challenge the conservatism of the state government. Indeed, aside from the bread-and-butter issues of direct concern to union leaders and members, organized labor takes little interest in state politics. When it does, it is usually found working in league with the conservative, hold-the-line elements within the Democratic party. The reason, as Salisbury observes, is the following:

No one seeks to depart from existing conditions in any dramatic, drastic, or rapid way, but rather to preserve things as they are, as far as possible. In this sense, labor groups are as conservative as business groups in the state, differing only in the specific objects of their conservative desire.[4]

The few groups that do seek an enlargement of governmental activity pursue their goals in the same spirit, contenting themselves with minor

---

Cf. Fenton, *Politics in the Border States* (New Orleans: The Hauser Press, 1957), p. 136. Fenton states that Pendergast was able to "dictate the selection of Democratic nominees for state-wide offices during the thirties." While there is no denying that Pendergast had a very strong influence in Democratic party councils during that period, it is erroneous to conclude that he had unlimited discretion in selecting party slates. Rather than supplanting the outstate political elite, Pendergast sought an accommodation with it. Instead of challenging the norms of the outstate political culture, he accepted those norms, largely because he felt that his own objectives (which were primarily patronage oriented) could most readily be achieved under the cloak of respectability provided by a continuation of the traditionalistic political order.

Nicholas Masters, Robert H. Salisbury, and Thomas H. Eliot, *State Politics and the Public Schools* (New York: Alfred A. Knopf, 1964), pp. 38–39.

adjustments in the system, and with a gradualist approach to the expansion of governmental resources.

Aside from its effects on policy outputs, the dominant outstate political culture has also had an important bearing upon the process by which party and governmental officials are recruited. Given a state Democratic party which has not been characterized by any important, lasting factions, recruitment to the top state-level public offices, particularly the governorship, has occurred through an essentially cooptative process. Thus the selection of state officials proceeds through informal negotiations among the leaders of the Democratic party until consensus eventually develops as to the specific candidates who will receive leadership support.[5] In order to gain such support for the governorship, aspiring politicians usually have had to serve apprenticeships in a variety of lesser public offices. By service in such offices, gubernatorial aspirants have come to know the state's political leaders, and to demonstrate their acceptability in light of the norms of outstate politics.

Although the positions that gubernatorial aspirants take on specific political issues are important determinants of their political acceptability, the critical factor is their position on the more fundamental question of the role that government should assume in the total economic and social system. Therefore, the prime attribute of those who are acceptable is that they should not have displayed any tendency to challenge the status quo, that is, to depart from the accustomed way of doing things. In short, they must be "safe" and must have persuaded other political leaders that they can be depended on not to use the instrumentality of government in such a way as to alter the state's basic social and economic order.

Throughout most of the Plan era, Missouri political folklore has proposed the existence of a dominant, cohesive elite within the state's political system. That elite has been referred to colloquially as "the establishment" and is reputed to have been centered around banking and financial interests, particularly around the Central Missouri Trust Company of Jefferson City.

Although we cannot dispute the influence that Central Missouri Trust has had in state politics, in one sense the scope of that influence has been greatly exaggerated. This financial institution has been primarily concerned with policy relating to the deposit of "idle" state funds. In the process of attempting to influence decisions affecting the placement of such deposits in various banks throughout the state, Central Missouri

<hr>

[5] Fenton, op. cit., pp. 142, 148. Warren Hearnes, who became governor after the period covered by this study, broke this tradition by challenging the leadership instead of waiting his "turn" for the governorship.

ust has become involved in state politics generally. As a result, it
s been one of the principal political job brokers in state-level politics
much of the period since 1940.

Yet Central Missouri Trust has been only one of several groups in
.ssouri who, together, have served as recruitment "gatekeepers" in
: state political system. The chief reason why Central Missouri Trust
ne to symbolize the entire "establishment" in the eyes of so many
.ssourians was that it had greater visibility than most other members
the political elite, mainly because its major interests related to one
rly narrow policy question. Central Missouri Trust could also serve
a symbol of the state's entire political elite because the positions that
took on political candidates and issues largely reflected the views
other "establishment" members. This resulted principally from the
:t that officers of the Central Missouri Trust Company subscribed
the same basic political philosophy as other members of the political
te. Frequently Company officials also consulted with other political
ders of the state's rural Democracy before taking a stand on matters
state-wide importance.

Although Central Missouri Trust officers and other political leaders
ve had a dominant role in recruitment for state-wide public offices,
ey have not constituted any tightly knit political cabal intent on ma-
pulating the political process solely for their own purposes.[6] The leader-
ip process has been far more informal and more casual than that.
iestions of a substantive political nature, or of political candidacies,
ve often produced disagreements within the leadership element. A
y to the nature of the political system lies in the process by which
ch disagreements have been resolved. The usual approach has been
e of mutual accommodation, of settling disputes through a search
r consensus, rather than through a bargaining process among indi-
luals or groups within the leadership ranks.

The extent to which outstate political leaders have acted in concert
sults primarily from the fact they have been products of the same
litical culture. That culture not only has placed an emphasis on con-
rvatism with respect to the issues of politics but also has stressed
atters of political style. Thus the norms of outstate politics facilitate
e development of a public officialdom which has, as its most important
iality, a kind of political blandness, a disinclination to "rock the boat"
 to stir up political demands through programmatic or ideological
proaches to politics. These stylistic norms of the Missouri political
lture have had their most significant effects in the area of gubernatorial

Iasters, Salisbury, and Eliot, *op. cit.*, pp. 36–37.

politics, in terms of both the kinds of individuals recruited for the go
ernorship and the role that the governors have played in the state
political process. The specific ways in which these facets of state politi
have influenced the governor's role in appellate judicial selection a
examined later, after the legal-judicial environment of appellate selectic
is discussed.

The Legal Practice Context

One respect in which circuit and appellate judicial selection stand i
sharpest contrast is in the much greater intensity of interest displaye
by those who become involved in the choice of the appellate judiciar
Even among the formal participants, the governor, for example, conside
appeals court and Supreme Court judgeships to be the most prestigio
positions included within the scope of his appointive powers. Not on
the governor, but the remaining participants in the formal selectic
process, and other groups concerned with the state judiciary, perceiv
that far more important stakes are involved in appellate than in circu
judicial selection. Many business firms, and their legal counsel, consid
a sympathetic appellate bench to be crucial to the protection of the
interests. They find some degree of plaintiffs' attorney influence in circu
judicial selection tolerable only because the appellate courts can h
relied on to counter "excesses" resulting from the selection of plaintiff
oriented trial court judges. Also, largely because they are members
collegial courts, the appellate judges themselves have had a far great
interest in judicial recruitment than have their counterparts in the tri
courts. Finally, the corporate and defense segments of the state B;
have generally viewed the appellate judicial forum as more crucial fi
their clients' interests than the trial court arena. As a result they hav
had a perspective toward judicial selection which has been quite simil;
to the point of view held by the incumbent appellate judges and b
business and other elements of the courts' clientele. The consequenc
has been a convergence of interests within the legal-judicial environmer
surrounding appellate judicial selection.

Such a convergence of interests has occurred despite the fact th;
the characteristics of the entire state Bar do not differ appreciably fro:
those of the lawyers residing in the metropolitan Missouri Plan circuit
As can be seen from Table 5.1, the proportion of attorneys specializin
in each of the major fields of legal practice is nearly identical for a
Missouri lawyers and for that portion of the Bar living in the St. Lou
City and Jackson County circuits. The percentage of attorneys engage
in a plaintiffs' or a defense personal injury practice is the same in bot

TABLE 5.1

MAJOR FIELDS OF PRACTICE OF MISSOURI
ATTORNEYS—BY PLACE OF RESIDENCE

Fields of Practice[a]	St. Louis City and Jackson County (N = 424)	St. Louis County (N = 374)	Outstate (N = 348)	Entire State (N = 1146)
Corporate, general	35	47	20	34
Probate, trust	31	37	36	35
Plaintiffs'	19	17	22	19
Defendants'	12	11	13	12
Plaintiffs'-defense	5	2	13	6
Real property	12	10	22	14

[a] Those listing field exclusively or as one of two or three major fields of practice in the year preceeding the survey.

the metropolitan Plan circuits and in the remainder of the state, and in each area the plaintiffs' practitioners outnumber those representing the defense. However, personal injury litigation of all types constitutes a major source of income for a considerably greater portion of the outstate Missouri Bar, than for those residing in the remainder of the state.

Thus the ecology of legal practice in the state does not account for the greater influence that corporate and defense attorneys have had in appellate as compared to circuit judicial selection. The differential in their influence between the two court levels appears, instead, to be largely attributable to the fact that the corporate-defense segment of the Bar has been far more interested in the appellate than in the circuit benches. Also, because of the greater prestige attached to the position, the corporate-defense attorneys have generally been able to advance more potent candidates for appellate lawyer commissionerships than they have for lawyer seats on the circuit nominating commission. Perhaps of equal importance in accounting for the success of the corporate and defense attorneys in appellate selection is the fact that the plaintiffs' wing of the Bar has until quite recently directed most of its efforts toward influencing recruitment to the trial courts.

The pattern of lawyer influence in appellate judicial selection has also been affected by the nature of state-wide Bar politics. Until the mid-1960's, most leadership positions in the Missouri Bar Association were held by attorneys with corporate or defense legal practices. Because of their prominence in state Bar circles, such attorneys have had a much broader acquaintanceship with lawyers from all parts of the state than have attorneys with a plaintiffs' practice.

The Clientele of the Appellate Courts

In most respects the orientation toward appellate judicial selection taken by the corporation and defense element of the state's Bar is identical with the point of view held by the principal litigants before the appellate courts. Aside from the state's Attorney General's office, which is the single most active litigant in the appellate courts, the groups that have the largest number of cases before these courts are the railroads, the insurance companies, and the public utilities. The presumed role that these litigants have had in Missouri Plan judicial selection has been the basis for some of the sharpest criticism leveled against the Plan.

The respondents interviewed for this study agree that the business concerns most heavily involved in appellate court litigation have consistently attempted to influence the decisions of both the nominating commission and the governor in order to insure the recruitment of judges that would be sympathetic to their interests. A few respondents contend that these sorts of litigants have had a dominant role in appellate selection. One such respondent, who commented primarily on the selection of Supreme Court judges, offered the following assessment of the role that business interests have had in appellate judicial selection:

Under the Plan, the Supreme Court of the state is chosen by the lobbies. That's due to a number of things. First, there is the general apathy which affects the kinds of attorneys who become members of the appellate nominating commission. Most of the attorneys who receive ballots for the appellate commissioner elections throw them in the waste basket. But other attorneys are quite interested, and the result is that the nominating commissionerships go to the lawyers who represent the interests—the insurance companies, the utilities, the banks, and the railroads.

Then you have to look at the kind of men who are chosen as lay commissioners. Those whom the governor consults in selecting the lay commissioners are the heavy contributors to the governor's election campaigns. So they also represent the interests.

When it comes to the appointments made under the Plan, both the political organizations and the lobbies put the heat on the governor. Frequently they will get together on a candidate. But the lobbies dominate.

So, through the whole process, in a variety of ways, these groups are important. Mind you, they don't always get involved directly. They can depend upon their legal representatives to get behind a good candidate and back him for a judicial position. Nor do they even allow themselves to realize what they're doing. All they have to do is to convince themselves that only certain kinds of men would be good for the bench. In their own minds, these people have only one objective: the selection of highly qualified people for the judiciary.

So, under the Missouri Plan, the political bosses have been cut out. But the real question now is how to get a court that is favorable to big business. What I mean is, that this is the major concern of those who are involved in the selection of Supreme Court and appeals court judges under the Plan.

In the view of this respondent, the conservatism of the appellate courts is traceable directly to the effects of the Missouri Plan, and to the fact that the conservative economic interests that constitute the most potent element within the courts' clientele tend to dominate the selection process.

A majority of attorneys in the state probably would not agree that the "lobbies" have dominated the entire appellate selection process. Most of those interviewed for the study, including the lawyer respondents, do concede that several appointments to the appellate courts can be attributed to the influence of business groups such as the railroads, the public utilities, or banking and financial concerns. Almost all of the respondents defend the propriety of this involvement by the business community in the selection of the state's appellate judiciary. Business firms are recognized as having an especially vital and legitimate interest in the selection of Supreme Court judges because of the importance that Supreme Court decisions have for the economy of the state. For the most part, business efforts to influence the choice of Supreme Court justices, as well as courts of appeals judges, are reputed to have been of an indirect nature, with businessmen depending on their attorneys for the representation of the firms' interests.

The one business concern generally credited with having been most influential in the selection of Missouri Plan appellate judges is the Central Missouri Trust Company, a banking and financial institution whose general role in Missouri politics was discussed earlier. Officers of this banking firm have long held important positions in state Democratic party councils, partly as a result of their role as political financiers for gubernatorial and other state-wide election campaigns.

The basis of Central Missouri Trust Company influence in the politics of appellate judicial selection is the closeness of its relationship with recent Democratic governors. Largely as a result of its ability to influence gubernatorial decisions relating to Missouri Plan court appointments, the firm has also been drawn into the politics surrounding the selection of the panels of nominees that are submitted to the governor by the appellate nominating commission.

The chief issue posed by the widespread allegations concerning the role of Central Missouri Trust is not whether it has had influence in appellate judicial selection; there is no question but that its influence has been rather extensive. Instead, the principal issues relate to the nature of the company's involvement, the motives behind it, and its consequences for the kinds of judges chosen for the appellate bench.

From the standpoint of its own economic interests Central Missouri Trust has never been vitally concerned with the decisions of the state judiciary, or with the kinds of judges who go on the bench. The Company has relatively little litigation before the state courts, and the chances are quite remote that there would ever be litigation involving the issue that has provided the *raison d'être* for its activity within the state political arena. That interest, it will be recalled, is in the decisions relating to time deposits of state funds in banks and financial institutions. Decisions as to the placement of such deposits are vested by law in the offices of the governor and the state treasurer, both elective positions that have been occupied by Democrats during the past two decades. Therefore, in order to influence decisions affecting state deposits, the Central Missouri Trust Company has had to become involved in state and Democratic party politics to the extent necessary for the establishment of access to the governor and the treasurer.

In its efforts to control the outcome of primary and general elections for the governorship and treasurership, the Company has necessarily entered into alliances with politicians throughout the state, incurring obligations to many of them. Often, these political allies expect Central Missouri Trust to reciprocate by assisting them in the accomplishment of their own political objectives. One respondent discusses the significance that these relationships have had for judicial selection:

It is just a case that because they (Central Missouri Trust) are involved in politics in so many ways, they get to know a large number of people. And because they know these people, sometimes pretty intimately, they're willing to do favors for them, to put in a word for them in order to help them get something they want. So if some man has come to know the people at Central Missouri Trust through his past activities in politics, and that man someday wants to be a judge of the Supreme Court of the state, it's only natural that those whom he's befriended in the past, would now help him to get the judgeship he wants.

Not only the aspirants for judicial office but also those who wish to advance the cause of some particular candidate for a judgeship have attempted to use their entree to Central Missouri Trust as a means for influencing court appointments.

The involvement of Central Missouri Trust in appellate judicial selection therefore exemplifies the Company's more general role as a political job-broker in state politics. However, this does not mean that all aspirants for judicial positions have had an equal chance of securing Central Missouri Trust Company support. Officers of the company who have been most intimately involved in judicial politics have themselves had an orientation to judicial selection that is in basic agreement with the viewpoint of the corporate-defense segment of the Missouri Bar. Moreover, the kinds of politicians with whom Central Missouri Trust has had the most intimate relations—and, therefore, those whom they would most often support for judicial appointment—have themselves been predominately conservative in their political and economic outlook.

Of course, Central Missouri Trust Company is not the only business concern that has been influential in the selection of judges for the appellate bench. Representatives of the railroads and public utilities firms are also credited with having had a decisive influence over several appointments to the appellate courts, particularly the Supreme Court. Their influence, however, is reputed to have been far more intermittent than that of Central Missouri Trust.

Other than business firms, no other portions of the courts' nonlawyer clientele appear to have had an important role in the selection of appellate-level judges. Labor unions, which have a relatively important stake in some kinds of state court litigation, have publicly stated their opposition to the Plan. They have never made any concerted effort to influence the nomination or appointment of appellate judges, although on one occasion organized labor did mount a perfunctory, unsuccessful campaign to defeat three Supreme Court justices who were running for new terms of office under the Plan's retention provisions. Except in that one instance, which is discussed in Chapter 6, Missouri labor leaders have maintained a hands-off stance toward the appellate bench, apparently because of the conviction that entrance into this particular legal-political thicket would do them more harm than good.

Litigant influence on appellate judicial selection has thus been exercised principally by the business and corporate elements of the courts' clientele. Although such influence has consistently been a factor in the selection of the appellate judiciary, the business clientele of the courts cannot be said to have dictated appellate court appointments. Business groups have had a decisive role in some appointments, while in others they have been only peripherally involved. Business thus constitutes only one of several interests affecting the selection of appellate judges in a system described by one respondent as "multipartisan, rather than nonpartisan, a system involving a host of interests of a conservative nature." Among the most conservative of those interests have been the interests of the judiciary itself.

The Courts' Institutional Interests

Because they are members of collegial decision-making bodies, members of the state's appellate courts have a far greater interest than the circuit judges in the kinds of persons who are recruited for membership on their respective benches. Supreme Court judges also have much more effective access to the judicial selection process than do judges on the trial bench, since one of their own number (the Chief Justice of the Supreme Court) serves as chairman of the appellate nominating commission. Circuit judges, on the other hand, have no formal representation in the selection process, since the chairmanship of the circuit nominating commission is held by the presiding judge of the court of appeals.

Through the Chief Justice, members of the Supreme Court can secure representation for their views as to the kinds of persons they would prefer to see elevated to membership on the state's appellate benches. To the extent that their views affect the outcome of the selection process, judicial recruitment becomes a form of cooptation in which judges already on the bench seek to have vacancies filled by men who share their own philosophies and values.

According to those personally interviewed for this study, the basic value disposition of the Missouri Supreme Court membership since 1940 has been a commitment to political and economic conservatism. Both the critics and supporters of the Court rank it among the most conservative of the nation's highest state tribunals. The Court's defenders, who view its conservatism as a virtue, argue that a judgment as to the state Court's ideological bent should not be based upon a comparison with the U.S. Supreme Court, because that court hears cases involving basic social and philosophical issues whereas the Missouri Supreme Court does not. Those critical of the Missouri Court's conservatism feel that it is legitimate to compare the two benches, and point to the number of times the state tribunal has been reversed by the U.S. Court in cases involving civil liberties, labor relations, and employer liability under the Federal Employer's Liability Act. Labor lawyers are especially critical of the Missouri Supreme Court on a wide range of issues relating to organized labor.

Defenders and critics of the Missouri Supreme Court agree that it is more conservative than most other state courts of last resort, particularly in the area of personal injury litigation, where the Missouri Court utilizes the doctrine of appellate *remittitur*. Under this doctrine, appellate courts may reduce the amount of damages awarded to the plaintiff by a trial court in personal injury suits, ostensibly for the purpose of maintaining uniformity across the state in terms of the amount of damages awarded for specific types of injuries. Plaintiffs' personal injury lawyers are especially critical of the use made of this doctrine, contending that it reflects judicial bias in personal injury litigation at the appellate court level.[7] One attorney stated:

---

[7] Supporters of the Plan are quick to point out that the *remittitur* is not a product of the Plan, but was already in use when the Missouri Supreme Court was an elective body.

Our circuit judges have been able to discard any prejudices that they may have picked up in private practice, for there is no particular bias at the trial court level. But at the appellate level we have some very conservative judges, on both political and economic questions. You only have to look at their opinions to see that.

Aside from the conservative reputation that the appellate courts have in specific types of cases, the Supreme Court, in particular, is widely reputed to exhibit the general stylistic conservatism and *status quo* orientation typical of the outstate political culture. This orientation is said to be reflected in both the decision-making activity of the Court and the perspectives that its members take toward judicial recruitment. According to one attorney, the prevailing attitude toward the Court's decision functions is epitomized by the injunction: "Let's be careful now, people are beginning to talk." The watchword with respect to recruitment, according to this source, is: "We mustn't get any wild people here."

Supreme Court members themselves confirm the degree to which the justices have tended to stress conformity to the mores of traditionalistic politics in their orientation toward judicial recruitment. One member of the Court characterizes the general process whereby new justices are chosen:

Men are picked for membership on the Supreme Court because they share the views of the men already on the Court. The members of the Court wouldn't seek out someone who they thought would disagree. They would frown on non-comformity.

When asked in what specific ways a man would brand himself as a nonconformist, this judge responded:

By being "wild." For example, by being a pro-labor attorney. Moreover, I imagine that anyone who had expressed opinions or attitudes against the prevailing judicial position would not be appointed to the Missouri Supreme Court.

The chief objective of the Supreme Court membership has been the maintenance of a "respectable" appellate bench. For that reason, even the most able lawyers or lower court jurists are conceded to have had virtually no chance for appointment to the Supreme Court bench if they had earned the reputation of being "controversial" or "outspoken" on public issues. The desire for "respectability" has also militated against the selection for appellate court membership of attorneys with an exclusively plaintiffs-oriented practice.

Members of the Supreme Court bench also tend to frown upon applicants who are "strong-willed," and who might therefore be "contentious." In the words of one respondent: "The judges on the Supreme Court are a 'happy family.' They don't want colleagues who will dissent from

their opinions, who will cause disagreement and trouble." A member
of the Supreme Court confirms the existence of this kind of attitude
in his comments about a particular nominee for the Supreme Court
bench:

Just between you and me, it's a good thing that . . . didn't receive the appointment. He would not have fit very well on the Supreme Court, because he would
have tried to dominate the Court. He would have been a fly in the ointment down
here.

The most reliable source of candidates having orientations acceptable
to the sitting judges is that segment of the bench and Bar that has
already established its position on the values most salient to members
of the Court, that is, attorneys and judges who have had the opportunity
to display their judicial abilities as well as their legal philosophies
through the writing of case opinions. Supreme Court commissioners,
court of appeals judges and commissioners, and trial judges and attorneys who have served on special assignment in some appellate judicial
capacity are the prime candidates. Aside from the fact that such candidates are "known" quantities in terms of their judicial orientations, their
participation in the appellate judicial process has also provided a means
by which they can be judged on the basis of their judicial "craftsmanship"
and their willingness to work. As one Supreme Court justice remarked:

Very often, the men chosen for membership on the Supreme Court have demonstrated that they can and will do work either because they've been circuit judges
or else because they've been commissioners of the Supreme Court.

I don't mean to say that the members of the Court are opposed to a lawyer's
being chosen for membership on the Supreme Court bench. But if such a man
is chosen, both he and the nominating commission are running a certain risk. With
the case of a commissioner or a circuit judge there is some record that you can
go by, so that you can make a judgment as to the kind of judicial ability a
man has. But with the case of a lawyer who has never served in a judicial capacity
nobody knows whether he'll turn out to be a good judge or not. Many good
lawyers—very fine lawyers—don't make good judges.

While circuit judges don't ordinarily write case opinions, some are assigned to
the appellate courts on special assignments where they do have that opportunity.
If anyone wants to know what kind of judges they will make, all he has to do is
to pick up the record and look at the kinds of opinions they have written.

Of all the candidates who have had judicial experience of this sort,
those who are best known to members of the Supreme Court are the
"statutory judges", called Supreme Court commissioners. The tendency
for these commissioners to become candidates for Supreme Court judgeships and the frequency with which they have been nominated and
appointed to such judgeships have led to widespread criticism of "in-

breeding" on the Supreme Court and of the Court's efforts at "self-per-
petuation." One attorney characterized the practice of elevating Supreme
Court commissioners to full membership on the Court as follows:

This amounts to a situation where a closed group is able to perpetuate itself in
office. Members of the Supreme Court have had a chance to observe the commissioners rather closely for a long time. They know that the commissioners are safe;
they won't rock the boat, or do anything to detract from the dignity of the Court—
meaning the conservatism of the Court.

The first commissionerships were established more than a half-century
ago as a temporary means of providing the Supreme Court with additional personnel so that it could dispose of the backlog of cases then
pending. This temporary expedient turned into a permanent feature
of the court system, and the Supreme Court now has standing authoriza-
tion to appoint six commissioners, subject only to the requirement that
an equal number of appointments go to Democrats and Republicans.
The appointments are made for four-year terms and are renewable at
the discretion of the Court.

In most respects, the commissioner's role in the Supreme Court decision-making process is indistinguishable from that of the Supreme Court
justice. Although the commissioners do not have the power to vote on
the disposition of cases and do not participate in hearings on extraordi-
nary writs or writs of original jurisdiction addressed to the Supreme
Court, they are, in all other respects, an integral part of the decision-making process. Like the judges, they are assigned to one of the two divisions
of the Court. They participate in case hearings and in the initial vote
taken on the disposition of cases, and are included in the general rotation
scheme through which cases are assigned for the writing of opinions.
However, if they vote in the minority on the initial "straw vote" taken
in a case, any dissenting opinion that a commissioner writes must be
endorsed by a judge of the Court before it will appear in the printed
record.

Although commissioners are selected in the name of the entire Supreme Court, in practice they tend to be chosen by the Supreme Court
justices of the division in which the vacant commissionership exists.
The process of selection generally takes place entirely behind the scenes,
with the Court usually announcing the appointment of a new commissioner simultaneously with its announcement of the existence of a vacancy. This approach is motivated by the Court's desire to prevent competition for the commissionerships, and by its desire to retain complete
control over the selection process. For that reason the Court does not
invite applications for commissionerships, nor does it often solicit
recommendations.

The Court is reputed occasionally to have given an especially promising but untried prospect a "trial run" by appointing him as a special commissioner or judge of the Court. If he acquits himself well in that capacity, the prospect then will be offered a permanent commissionership when one becomes available. The result is that the process of recruiting court commissioners is virtually continuous. Attorneys and lower court judges are under constant surveillance by members of the Court for the purpose of determining who among them would be best qualified for a commissionership.

The Court searches for several kinds of traits in those who are appointed as commissioners. They prefer men who have had judicial experience, particularly experience in writing appellate decisions. They also seek men who have the capacity and willingness to handle the work load associated with appointment to a commissionership. Occasionally, the Court has also sought for commissionerships men whose political and public office experience would be useful in securing legislative approval of measures relating to the judiciary's interests, such as judicial salary and retirement benefits. When persons of this kind are appointed as Supreme Court commissioners, in addition to performing the duties specified earlier, they function as "lobbyists" for the Supreme Court and the state judiciary.

The Court also is concerned with the kind of reputation that prospective commissioners have in legal circles. On one occasion a metropolitan newspaper carried a story quoting a St. Louis political boss and plaintiffs' attorney to the effect that "his man" was about to be appointed as a Supreme Court commissioner. One respondent described the result as follows:

When the Supreme Court judges saw that newspaper item they decided they couldn't go through with the appointment, so they backed off. They felt they couldn't afford to pick a man who had the reputation of being close to that particular political lawyer. It wasn't that the politician involved was a bad lawyer, but he had a certain kind of reputation which made it undesirable for someone associated with him to be named as a commissioner of the Supreme Court.

Although the prestige and salary associated with the position make it attractive to many persons, a commissionership is valued chiefly because it can become a steppingstone toward a Supreme Court judgeship. Frequently this prospect has been stated explicitly by Supreme Court members in their negotiations with candidates. Thus the possibility that the position will lead to "full membership" on the Court often becomes a decisive factor in a candidate's decision to accept a commissionership.

Court commissioners receive salaries equal to those of the Supreme

Court judges, but nonetheless look upon the judgeship as being more prestigious, partly because the commissioners lack the power to vote in the decision-making process. Supreme Court justices also have more secure positions, possessing what amounts to life-time tenure, while the commissioners serve at the pleasure of the Court and have their appointments renewed only if their work has been satisfactory. For these reasons most commissioners persistently seek advancement to judgeship status.

The ambition of the commissioners for advancement therefore coincides with the desire of the Supreme Court justices to have Court vacancies filled by those who share their own values. Because they have worked so closely together on cases involving the entire range of issues that come before the Court, the Supreme Court justices are thoroughly acquainted with the judicial philosophies of the various commissioners. In addition, they need not be concerned with how the commissioners will perform as Supreme Court justices, since they have already seen them perform in that role.

The elevation of Court commissioners to full court membership has been the dominant mode of judicial cooptation, and also the most criticized. Especially critical are attorneys in private practice, who feel that they cannot compete on equal terms for Supreme Court judgeships with commissioner candidates. In response to these criticisms, justices of the Court stress the desirability for new members of the Court to have judicial experience that would prepare them for a role on the Court. Moreover, the Supreme Court justices realize that it would be extremely difficult for them to recruit able commissioners unless the possibility existed for their later advancement to judgeships on the Supreme Court bench.

Judicial selection through cooptation is not limited to the selection of Supreme Court justices, but also characterizes the choice of courts of appeals judges. There, too, cooptation occurs most frequently through the elevation of court of appeals commissioners to judgeships. Since the work load of the Supreme Court judges depends significantly on the kinds of persons appointed to the courts of appeals benches, Supreme Court members are chiefly concerned with the quality and ideological propensities of candidates for the appellate bench. They are much less concerned with their personality characteristics, since the Supreme Court justices do not work closely with appeals court judges as they do with their own colleagues.

At both levels of the appellate court system, the court commissioners occupy roles that are in some respects basically antithetical to the avowed principles of the Missouri Plan. Appellate judges are themselves selected on a "nonpartisan" basis through relatively open procedures that are frequently marked by spirited competition. Appellate court commissioners are not even chosen under provisions of the Missouri Plan, but on a partisan basis, through a virtually closed process in which appointments are determined solely by the preferences of the appellate judges.

Before they can be advanced to judgeship status the commissioners admittedly must run the same gauntlet as all other candidates under the Missouri Plan selection process. Yet they start that process with important advantages which they owe to the anomalous method by which they became court commissioners in the first place.

PARTICIPANTS AND DECISION-MAKING IN APPELLATE SELECTION

The appellate nominating commission is larger than the circuit commission (seven members as compared to five), and its members come from widely scattered points throughout the entire state. This diversity in the geographical origins of the commission membership results from the requirement that one lay commissioner and one lawyer commissioner come from each of the state's three appellate court districts; its chief consequence is that appellate commission members are rarely as intimately acquainted with each other as are members of the circuit commission. Interaction among appellate nominating commissioners also tends to be less frequent, and more formal than interaction among circuit nominating commissioners. Face-to-face contacts of appellate commissioners are limited mostly to the meetings at which the commission selects panels of nominees.

These structural features of the appellate selection system lessen the impact of the commissioners' interpersonal relations upon nominating decisions. Each commissioners' behavior is therefore largely determined by his general role orientation, rather than by influence patterns within the commission. Generally, selection decisions for the appellate courts have revolved around two principal clusters of interests: the legal-judicial, which is reflected in the role orientations of the lawyer nominating commissioners and the Chief Justice, and the political, which is largely represented by the governor and the lay nominating commissioners. Nominations and appointments are essentially the products of the manner in which the role behaviors of these participants intersect. Therefore, the decision-making process at the appellate level must be examined in conjunction with the discussion of the roles played by the various participants.

The Lawyer Nominating Commissioners

For reasons that were discussed in Chapter 1, the lawyer members of the appellate nominating commission have generally come from the ranks of the higher status, corporate and defense attorneys of the Bar. In the view of both the lawyer commissioners and the element of the Bar for which they speak, one of the central issues in the selection of appellate court judges is the practice background of prospective candidates.

Most appellate lawyer commissioners do not feel that attorneys with an exclusively plaintiffs' orientation should be given consideration for appellate court judgeships. Their basic attitude is reflected in the views that one appellate lawyer commissioner expressed about the plaintiffs' element of the Bar:

NACCA is made up of a group of fellows who are primarily personal injury lawyers. They're allied with certain doctors. I never knew too much about them. Their philosophy and mine is so totally different that I never had anything in common with them.

But they're primarily made up of lawyers who promote damage suits. We don't need lawyers to promote damage suits. The litigants are bad enough at promoting them. They'll promote plenty, without the lawyers getting in on it too.

Lawyer members of the commission have no such reservations about candidates with a defense practice. One appellate judge, commenting on his own selection, recalled that one of the lawyer commissioners was especially interested in the kind of practice that he had. "When he found out that I had represented casualty insurance companies, he became pretty enthusiastic about my candidacy," reported the judge.

Their preferences with respect to the types of attorneys who should be recruited to the appeals bench are consistent with the lawyer commissioners' views as to the kinds of interests that deserve representation in the selection process. One lawyer commissioner observed: "The members of the business community are the ones that should be heard in the matter of judicial selection. That's because businessmen have only one interest, that of getting good judges on the bench."

These attitudes are also reflected in the fact that the appellate lawyer commissioners turn to lawyers similar to themselves for assessments of candidates with whom they are unacquainted. They also rely to some extent upon their fellow lawyer commissioners for the evaluation of candidates that are unknown to them. The fact that the lawyer commissioners are drawn from all three appeals court districts in the state means that almost all candidates for judgeships will be known by one or another lawyer member of the nominating commission. Lawyer commissioners will thus tend to defer to the assessments of the other lawyer members of the commission who reside in the same region of the state as the candidates, especially if they do not know the candidates very well. This leads to a degree of geographical specialization in the functioning of the commission, particularly with respect to selections for the three courts of appeals.

The extent to which the lawyer commissioners' preferences determine the outcome of the appellate judicial selection process depends on the degree to which their views coincide with those of the Chief Justice of the Missouri Supreme Court. If the three lawyer commissioners and the chief justice agree, they can dominate the nominating process, since together they have a majority of the votes on the nominating commission.

In most respects the lawyer commissioners and the chief justice bring the same perspectives to the nominating process. However, there is one issue that creates the potential for a rift between them: whether court commissioners should be elevated to the courts of appeals and Supreme Court benches. The lawyer commissioners are not opposed to this practice in principle, but they also represent a constituency that wishes to keep open the possibility that such court appointments will go to practicing attorneys who have had no judicial experience.

If the issue of elevating court commissioners does not divide them, the lawyers and the chief justice are usually able to exert a decisive influence in the selection of most nominees to the appellate bench. However, the extent of their control over nominations is partially dependent on the role that the chief justice plays in the nominating process.

The Chief Justice

The influence of the chief justice on appellate judicial selection has varied slightly depending on the incumbent of that office, but he has generally been much less influential than the presiding judges of the courts of appeals in circuit selection. Certainly none of the chief justices of the Supreme Court has ever had the dominant influence in appellate judicial selection that has been exercised by the presiding judge of the Kansas City Court of Appeals in the choice of Jackson County circuit judges.

Several features of the appellate nominating process help account for the more restricted role of the chief justice. By custom, the chief justiceship of the Supreme Court is rotated among the membership of the Court every seventeen months. After holding the position for that period, a member of the Court must normally wait until the remaining six justices have had their terms as chief justice before he will assume the position again. Therefore the frequency of rotation into the chief justiceship, as well as the number of justices involved in that rotation, means that any one member of the Supreme Court can expect to participate in relatively few appellate court nominations. The length of time between his terms as chief justice also means that a specific member of the Supreme Court finds it almost impossible to develop as close relationships with his fellow commissioners as some of the presiding judges of the courts of appeals have established in judicial selection at the circuit level. In addition, the size of the appellate nominating commission and the infrequent contact among its members not only tend to reduce the importance of interpersonal relations as a factor in decision-making, but also make it difficult for the Chief Justice to create the kinds of coalitions which the presiding judges have used to influence the circuit selection process.

These limitations on the scope of the chief justice's influence in judicial selection have meant that most occupants of that position have assumed a role oriented principally to the representation of the appellate courts' institutional interests. Since these interests coincide, for the most part, with the interests of the lawyer nominating commissioners, the chief justice can still have a modicum of influence over nominating decisions, but the influence derives from the chief justice's role as interpreter of the courts' needs rather than from his personal influence with his fellow commissioners.

Indeed, in their capacity as commission chairmen, chief justices have usually functioned merely as presiding officers over commission deliberations. Most have scrupulously avoided even the appearance of attempting to dominate commission decisions. One member of the appellate nominating commission commented:

Only once while I was on the nominating commission did the chief justice openly express his opinions about a candidate. During my term five different Supreme Court justices served as chairmen of the commission. If they ever exerted any influence over the commission's decisions it wasn't apparent from what took place in the meetings. Each one was careful not to express any preference or criticism of the candidates being considered. The one exception occurred when a chief justice came to the name of one candidate—a professional candidate, he called him—and the judge remarked that he didn't think that this man was the right caliber for the court. So he put the man's materials in the stack of rejects.

However, not all chief justices have been quite this reticent in commission deliberations. A few have participated rather freely in the commission discussions in which the various candidates are evaluated, using as their rationale for involvement the position taken by one member of the Supreme Court:

I think the chief justice should speak out if he knows that a candidate is either very bad or very good. After all, the Supreme Court judges have had an opportunity to see these men, and they know from having watched them try cases or from having reviewed their decisions whether they will be capable appellate judges.

The question of whether a man will be a good judge or not is something that can be determined only if you've had personal contact with the individual. Some men just don't have a legal mind and will not make good judges.

The lawyer nominating commissioners are especially apt to have confidence in the views of the chief justice, particularly when he is evaluating candidates with whom they are unacquainted. Since many candidates for appellate judgeships are likely to have practiced before the Supreme Court or to have had their work as judges reviewed by the Court, the chief justice is usually better acquainted with a wider array of the candidates than is any other single member of the nominating commission.

Relationships between the chief justice and the lawyer nominating commissioners have generally been amicable, but that has not always been true of relationships between the chief justice and the lay commissioners. When political considerations do not intrude, the lay members are inclined to accept the chief justice's evaluation of the contenders for nomination. As one respondent observed:

The chief justice stresses that it would not be good for the court or the State if the appointment were to go to a man who would be a dissident or disruptive influence. He reminds the members of the nominating commission that they can't afford to select the kind of man who would slow up the work of the Court. This line of argument appeals especially to the lay members of the commission. They are impressed by the picture which the chief justice paints of the Supreme Court's being a "happy family."

However, the lay nominating commissioners' orientation toward the nominating process frequently leads them to spurn the advice of the chief justice. If the lay commissioners become committed to a candidate for political reasons (especially candidates backed by the governor), they are not very likely to defer to the views of the chief justice even if he presents the strongest of arguments against the candidate in question.

Of course, the chief justice is not always hostile to politically potent candidates, even those who are known to have the support of the governor. Some chief justices—though a distinct minority—have been highly political in their own orientations toward judicial selection. Of one such judge, it has been said:

Judge_____ was entirely a creature of Tom Pendergast. After he became a member of the Supreme Court bench he began to work night and day to fill the courts with Pendergast people. At the same time, he was using his position on the Supreme Court as a base from which to run the state's politics. He continued to do that after the Missouri Plan was adopted, and was always in the thick of high-level state politics, promoting certain candidates for the governorship and other state-wide offices. Until the day he died, he kept a hand in state politics, and did a fair job of influencing what went on.

In his more usual role as spokesman for the interests of the appellate judiciary, the chief justice is not guided solely by his own views, since he also represents the outlook of his appellate bench colleagues. He speaks particularly for the views of other Supreme Court members, since the close interaction between them leads the chief justice to become aware of his colleagues' preferences with regard to the kinds of candidates acceptable for membership on the bench. In addition, the chief justice generally sounds out the opinions of his colleagues with reference to the candidates being considered for specific vacancies, primarily to discern whether any of the candidates would be unacceptable in their eyes. The chief justice also frequently asks his fellow justices for recommendations of persons whom they would like to have considered for nomination.

The interests of the chief justice, the lawyer commissioners, and certain clientele groups of the appellate courts have thus converged in such a way as to produce a common orientation toward the judicial selection process. Of paramount importance to this group have been the professional standing and the ideological orientation of candidates for the appellate bench, for their chief objective has been cooptation to the bench of individuals who have values similar to their own. Although they have also supported candidates with backgrounds of extensive participation in partisan politics, such candidates have had to be acceptable on ideological and professional grounds.

Arrayed against this group have been other participants in the selection process who have given first priority to political considerations. The lay nominating commissioners, the governor, and the governor's confidants within the state political elite have constituted a second community of interest with respect to judicial selection. Although spokesmen for this group comprise a minority of those involved in the formal nominating process, their general role in judicial selection insures that their preferences with respect to judicial candidates will not be systematically ignored by the nominating commission. For one thing, the governor's desire to confer appellate judicial appointments on close political associates and supporters induces lawyers with backgrounds of extensive partisan activity to become candidates for the appellate bench. Since many of these candidates can secure the support of the lay nominating commissioners, all they need for nomination is the vote of one additional person from among the remaining members of the nominating commission. One or more political candidates have usually been able to garner such support from a lawyer nominating commissioner or from the chief justice. Thus there has rarely been a complete polarization of views within the nominating commission.

The Lay Commissioners

There are sharply divergent views on some aspects of the role that the lay commissioners have had in the selection of the appellate judiciary. In the estimate of most persons interviewed the lay commissioners do not have any competence for judging what is generally deemed to be the principal qualification for the appellate judiciary: knowledge of the law. Yet some respondents, including a few lawyer commissioners, feel that the lay members of the nominating commission provide a different and valuable perspective in the process of appellate judicial selection. Their principal contribution, according to this view, is their knack for judging men, for understanding that brilliant lawyers do not always make the best judges, since brilliance must be accompanied by "common sense" as well as a capacity for organizing work, and getting it done.

The evidence suggests that although most lay commissioners have depended almost exclusively on the other members of the nominating commission for assessments of the judicial caliber of candidates, not all of them have done so. Some lay members have relied on sources of information outside the commission for their evaluation of judicial candidates but usually they depend on lawyer acquaintances whose practices are concentrated in the corporate and defense fields.

However, most lay members have given highest priority to the political dimension of the selection process, and some are reputed to have been guided solely by political considerations. One lawyer nominating commissioner observed:

Starting with Governor Forrest Smith and coming down to the present, the governor has acted politically in picking lay members. The lay members also act politically in the selection process.

A member of the Supreme Court expresses much the same view, saying that "some of the laymen are more concerned with politics than anything else, and some of them will do whatever the governor wants them to do when it comes to the selection of panels of nominees." Despite some variation in the inclinations of individual lay commissioners, it is generally conceded that they provide the major channel through which political influences are injected into the appellate nominating process.

Of all the members of the nominating body, the lay commissioners are most concerned with the political experience of prospective nominees, principally because they themselves usually have been quite active politically, and naturally view candidates with similar experiences in a favorable light. Moreover, they have few other bases on which they can judge candidates, since they rarely have first-hand knowledge of the legal abilities of those being considered for nomination. They do have expertise in the political arena, and can bring their knowledge of state politics, and of the participants in state politics, to bear upon the assessment of judicial candidates.

For these reasons the governor and other political leaders have a far greater potential for influencing the decisions of the lay commissioners than they do those of the remaining members of the nominating commission. The governor usually has entree even to those lay commissioners who have been appointed in preceding gubernatorial administrations, since many of them have moved in the same political circles as has the governor.

The Governor

The governor desires to use appointments to all judgeships as rewards to political supporters and associates. He may grudgingly accept the circuit nominating commission's tendency to manipulate nominations so as to preclude the appointment of gubernatorial favorites to that bench, but he looks with much less equanimity upon similar efforts by the appellate nominating commission. The governor uses a variety of political resources and techniques in an effort to prevent the commission from estopping his use of appellate court appointments as rewards for political friends. One of the techniques most frequently employed for that purpose has been gubernatorial involvement in the nominating process.

Instances of gubernatorial involvement in the appellate nominating process are alleged to have occurred during at least half of the period since the Missouri Plan's adoption in 1940. Two governors, who together served a total of twelve years, are reputed never to have intervened in the nominating phase of selection, either directly or indirectly. One was Forrest Donnell, the only Republican to become governor during the Missouri Plan era; the other was Phil Donnelly. A member of Governor Donnelly's administration, who was frequently consulted by Donnelly on such matters as judicial appointments, remarked:

Donnelly never tried to influence the nominating commission. He was the kind of man who thought it was unethical to pressure the commission. He was also the kind of man who resented the pressures that were put on him to appoint a particular person to a given position.

Other governors serving in the period prior to 1964 had no such inhibitions about attempting to get their own favorites placed on panels of nominees. Only their tactics and their degree of success appear to have varied. One governor is reputed to have resorted to a very simple expedient for influencing the selection process: he merely let it be known that he preferred a certain person for a judicial vacancy and that he would appoint him if he happened to be nominated. Of this governor, one respondent stated:

> Prior to the time that panel was even selected, the governor indicated that he would appoint Judge _____ if he were named to the panel. (He) was nominated and then very quickly appointed by the governor. But . . . [this particular governor] did that all the time. I don't think that he ever made an appointment but that it wasn't known beforehand whom he would appoint if that individual happened to get nominated.

Other governors have taken a different approach to influencing the nominating process, working through intermediaries who relay the governor's wishes to members of the nominating commission, or contacting lay nominating commissioners directly to enlist support for their candidates.

The orientation that a particular governor takes toward the nominating process sometimes shifts as a result of his experiences with the nominating commission. One governor, who appears to have made no attempt to affect the composition of panels chosen during the very first part of his administration, soon decided that such intervention was essential in order to protect himself against the commission's panel-loading tactics. An observer remarked:

> The governor felt that one of the first panels chosen by the appellate nominating commission during his term of office had been manipulated so as to force him to appoint the man most favored by the commission itself. The governor resented that very much. He didn't want to be pushed around, to be handed a panel that was rigged in favor of a certain man. Of course, it was generally known that the governor wanted to name either one of two different lawyers that he favored for that vacancy. But he took no part at all in the preliminaries of the nomination, and neither of the people he favored was placed on the panel of nominees.
>
> As a result of what happened on that nomination, the governor decided that, when future court vacancies arose, he would push to get someone on the panel that he did like. He came to the conclusion that it was to his advantage to get into the act very soon, rather than to sit back and hope that a man he wanted would be named to a panel by the appellate nominating commission.

Another governor is reputed to have made efforts systematically to control nominations from the very begining of his administration. He is said frequently to have contacted political cronies about their willingness to be appointed to the appellate bench, assuring them that if they were willing, he would see to it that their names were placed on the panel of nominees.

Much of the controversy and political intrigue surrounding appellate judicial selection has revolved around nominating commission-gubernatorial relations. Some members of the nominating commission take umbrage if there is the slightest sign that the governor is attempting to intrude into their domain; some governors have resented anything that smacks of a nominating commission effort to euchre them into merely rubber-stamping the commission's first choice for a judicial vacancy.

Resentment over the governor's attempts to influence panel composition usually is confined to the chief justice and the lawyer members of the nominating commission. They rarely make this an explicit issue in deliberations over panel selection, but when gubernatorial interference does become an overt issue, it usually is dealt with on other than political grounds. A lay commissioner comments on one such instance:

One of the candidates for this vacancy was a political and personal friend of the governor, and was the governor's choice for the judgeship to be filled. The governor hadn't put any pressure on me with respect to this candidate, but he had let it be known that this man was his choice.

As soon as the nominating commission met to draw up the panel, the chief justice announced that this particular candidate was the governor's choice. From the beginning, it was clear that this man didn't have a chance. The chief justice, in particular, spoke out against him, pointing out his lack of qualifications for the appellate bench. One of the lawyer commissioners was also strenuous in his opposition to him. While I wasn't especially for or against this candidate, I would have gone along with his nomination, but he was eliminated almost from the start.

In addition to arguments about the judicial potential of this gubernatorially favored candidate, the lawyer commissioners and the chief justice also justified their rejection of the candidate on the basis of the kind of campaign he had waged in order to secure the nomination. A member of the nominating commission commented:

He had a tremendous number of letters of endorsement—five or six times as many as anyone else. Rather than helping him, that only hurt the candidate. If a man was all that good to have so many letters of recommendations, why wasn't he already on the Missouri Supreme Court, or on the U.S. Supreme Court?

In other instances, the nominating commission's refusal to nominate a candidate backed by the governor has presented greater difficulties of justification. On one occasion a spokesman for the lay members asked the lawyer commissioners and the chief justice point blank if they would mind specifying their grounds for opposing a particular candidate. The answer given was that the candidate in question was an able one, but that there were other candidates of greater ability. It was clear that the major reason for the commission's rejection of the candidate was resentment of the governor's attempts to have the panel "wired" for his choice.

The same kind of petulance that is occasionally displayed in the nominating commission's treatment of gubernatorially favored candidates has sometimes also characterized the governor's behavior in making appointments to the bench. Chapter 3 has discussed one such instance at the circuit court level, that is, Governor Phil Donnelly's selection of two Republicans for the Jackson County circuit bench in retaliation for the nominating commission's having "loaded" the panels of nominees submitted to the governor. Similar responses by the governor have occurred in his selection of judges for the appellate level benches. A political advisor to one governor indicates that this was a principal motivation behind the governor's selection of a court of appeals judge:

The nominating commission played politics in picking that panel. They picked a Republican who was in poor health, and a young man without very much experience, who was a Democrat. The third man was also a Democrat and was one of the most able circuit judges in the entire state. (This third nominee) had also been politically close to the governor for a number of years. The reason that the appointment went to the young fellow without much experience was that the governor didn't like the way the commission had set up the panel. He felt that the commission had stacked the panel in favor of the Democratic circuit judge.

A further factor in this particular selection was the governor's resentment of the nominating commission's refusal to nominate the candidate whom he had supported for the judgeship.

Gubernatorial retaliation against the nominating commission's panel-loading tactics has also been evident in appointments to the Supreme Court bench. In response to what he considered to be the nominating commission's efforts to stack appellate court panels, one governor is reputed to have responded in the manner described by one respondent:

About this time, the appellate judicial nominating commission was so shamefully loading panels that the Governor would roar every time he received one from them. One time the panel that he got from the nominating commission was not only loaded, but was so bad, that he made his appointment with an eye to only one thing: affronting the chief justice and the nominating commission in the hope that he could put a stop to their tactic of loading panels.

Usually, however, the tensions produced by commission efforts to load panels, and by gubernatorial activities designed to influence nominations, have been taken in stride by all the participants in the selection process. This was true even when the appellate nominating commission named an all-Republican panel of nominees for a St. Louis Court of Appeals vacancy in 1950. The governor at the time was Forrest Smith, a Democrat with a highly partisan orientation to the judicial selection process. Governor Smith is reputed to have given some consideration to sending this panel back to the nominating commission, but finally decided against that course of action.

In at least one other instance, the governor and the appellate nominating commission are reputed to have struck a bargain regarding selections to the Missouri Supreme Court bench. In return for his compliance with the nominating commission's panel-loading game involving a Supreme Court vacancy, the governor is said to have been assured that his preference for the next vacancy would be placed on the panel of nominees by the nominating commission. However, such instances of collusion between the governor and the nominating commission seem to have been quite rare. Generally, the appellate judicial selection process has been characterized by neither panel-loading (lawyer commissioner-chief justice dominance) nor by panel wiring (lay commissioner-governor dominance).

The lawyer commissioners and the chief justice have a majority of the votes on the nominating commission and can control nominations if they remain cohesive. Their preferred strategy is one of judicial co-optation—of selecting candidates who, through their performance in certain judicial capacities, have already demonstrated that their values are acceptable in the eyes of the Supreme Court and of that wing of the Bar which has controlled the lawyer commissionerships. Toward this end, they have frequently backed court commissioners and court of appeals judges for appellate court vacancies. Such candidates therefore have little difficulty in securing the support necessary for nomination, but they frequently have great difficulty in the competition for gubernatorial appointment. The reasons for this are twofold. First, at least half of the court commissioners are Republicans. The probability of their receiving appointment to the Missouri Plan bench has been quite low throughout most of the Plan's existence. The second factor militating against their being chosen by the governor is the fact that most of the Democratic commissioners and judges who are nominated for the appellate bench have neither the political backgrounds nor the sources of political support that are generally prerequisites for gubernatorial appointment. Thus, the candidates who are most preferred from the standpoint of a pure cooptation strategy are quite vulnerable to competition from nominees with better political credentials.

If the lawyer commissioners and the chief justice were single-minded enough in purpose, and were willing to face the consequences, they could still pursue a strategy of pure cooptation. However, such a tactic would arouse resentment among the rank and file of the Bar, who are already critical of the placement of so many court commissioners and judges on panels of nominees for the appellate benches. The lawyer commissioners, in particular, are not inclined to pursue such a course of action, since it would discredit them in the eyes of their constituency: the Bar.

A pure cooptation strategy also very likely would endanger the Missouri Plan itself. Most Missouri governors serving since 1940 have been basically unsympathetic toward the Plan, but because they have recognized the support the Plan enjoys within the state, they generally have avoided actions that could be construed as efforts to "wreck" it. In part, the governor's willingness to reach an accommodation with the pro-Plan interests has been based on the fact that the "nonpartisan" judicial selection process has functioned so as to permit him to name political cronies to the bench. If that possibility were completely foreclosed through the nominating commission's systematic adherence to a panel-loading strategy, the basis for gubernatorial compromise with the pro-Plan interests would largely disappear. Moreover, the utilization of such a strategy would provide the governor and other politicians with a powerful argument in favor of repealing the Plan, since they could plausibly charge that the Court Plan had become the instrument of a self-perpetuating group.

These kinds of considerations have generally led the lawyer commissioners and the chief justice to seek an accommodation with the kinds of interests that pivot around state and gubernatorial politics. The lawyer commissioner-chief justice contingent still prefers candidates with prior judicial experience, especially those who have demonstrated their ideological acceptability. Yet they are willing to accept other types of candidates whether or not they have had judicial experience, so long as they are the kinds of lawyers who would be expected to have values congruent with those of the incumbent judges. Interaction between the political and legal-judicial communities involved in selection therefore transforms the process into one of modified cooptation in which partisan political considerations weigh quite heavily.

The kinds of political considerations involved in appellate judicial selection are reflective of the governor's outstate political orientation. With the exception of Republican Forrest C. Donnell of St. Louis, the Missouri governors serving during the Plan period have been Democrats from outstate Missouri. They have not only subscribed to the basic political values of rural Missouri, but their closest political associations have been with politicians who are also from the outstate area. This feature of the governor's political orientation largely accounts for the fact that a high proportion of the "political" candidates for the appellate judiciary have come from outstate rather than metropolitan Missouri.

The governor's outstate orientation has also been evident in the appointments made to the appellate courts, particularly the Missouri Supreme Court. Of the ten Supreme Court vacancies filled from 1941 through 1964, eight went to nominees from the outstate area, with one each of the remaining appointments going to Kansas City and St. Louis attorneys. In the case of eight of these ten vacancies, the governor could have chosen nominees from the metropolitan areas, for the panels submitted to him had contained the names of one or more nominees from either St. Louis or Kansas City.

The selections made for the two court of appeals districts containing the St. Louis and Kansas City metropolitan areas have been less affected by outstate political considerations. The principal reason for this is that the governor has had relatively little choice in the matter. For the four vacancies occurring on the St. Louis Court of Appeals bench, eleven of the twelve nominees submitted to the governor were from metropolitan St. Louis, and all four appointments went to attorneys from that area. The governor had a slightly greater option in choosing from among the nominees for the five Kansas City Court of Appeals vacancies, for only seven of the fifteen nominees were from Kansas City. Yet, even here, the option to choose outstate nominees was not always a meaningful one. Four of the eight outstate nominees for the Kansas City Court of Appeals bench were from the opposite political party to the governor in office, and none of the governors involved ever crossed party lines in making appointments under the Missouri Plan. Two of the four remaining outstate nominees received appointment to the bench, and the other three Kansas City Court of Appeals judgeships went to Kansas City nominees. The selection process for the Springfield Court of Appeals district cannot even be said to have entailed an outstate versus metropolitan dimension, since this district is predominantly rural, and "outstate" political considerations have thus characterized the entire selection process for the district.

Another feature of the governor's rural Missouri outlook is his adherence to the conservative economic and political philosophy of that part of the state. Moreover, four of the five governors serving in the period from 1940 to 1964 were lawyers. As did most outstate attorneys, they had a general practice representing a wide range of clients, but ideologically the governors identified with the views of the corporate and defense segment of their clientele. Thus they tended to have much the same perspective toward judicial selection as the members of the Supreme Court and the lawyer commissioners of the appellate nominating commission. Included in this common viewpoint was an animus toward the selection for the appellate bench of lawyers having a basically plaintiffs-oriented practice. Yet the governors were not hostile to lawyers whose practices entailed some personal injury work on behalf of plaintiffs, for most of their political favorites were outstate lawyers who usually handled plaintiffs' litigation as part of a widely varied general practice.

The tensions between the governor and those who promote a cooptative system of judicial recruitment thus have not been products of an essentially ideological disagreement. Mainly, the tensions have resulted from the governor's desire to use appellate court appointments as rewards for political and personal friends. In that respect, the governor's role in appellate judicial selection is basically similar to his role in the selection of circuit judges. Both are outgrowths of the cronyistic nature of Missouri gubernatorial politics.

One other facet of the governor's attitude toward the Missouri Plan has also been relevant to the appellate selection process. With the exception of the Republican governor serving from 1941 to 1944, every Missouri governor holding office during the period studied has had to contend with widespread suspicion that he was bent on sabotaging the Missouri Plan; several of them have accordingly made appointments to the appellate benches designed to allay such doubts on the part of the Plan's supporters. As one respondent noted, the governors have adopted the strategy of appointing an occasional "fair-haired boy" of the pro-Plan interests, so that there would be less criticism when the remainder of the appointments were given to political cronies.

APPELLATE AND CIRCUIT SELECTION SYSTEMS

The characteristics of the persons chosen for the circuit and appellate benches reflect both the differences and similarities in the selection processes for the two levels of the Missouri Plan judiciary. Table 5.2 presents data on the legal practice and political backgrounds of the trial and appellate judges, and compares them with similar data for respondents to the lawyer survey who indicated that their names had been considered for nomination by the circuit or appellate nominating commission. Mail

TABLE 5.2

COMPARISON OF SELECTED CHARACTERISTICS OF APPLICANTS
AND APPOINTEES TO MISSOURI PLAN CIRCUIT
AND APPELLATE BENCHES (PERCENT)

	Circuit Courts		Appellate Courts	
	Applicants (N = 55)	Appointees[a] (N = 20)	Applicants (N = 25)	Appointees[a] (N = 16)
Practice Arrangement				
Solo	49	15	32	25
Two-man partnership	7	15	12	32
Three to nine lawyers	20	25	36	25
Large firm and Corp.	15	20	16	12
Government agency	5	20	0	6
Not ascertained/more than one arrangement	4	5	4	0
Selected Fields of Legal Practice				
Corporate, general	49	45	36	50
Defendants'	15	30	28	25
Criminal	0	20	4	6
Plaintiffs'	36	20	16	19
Mixed plaintiffs'-defense	9	30	24	31
Party Activity Index Score				
No points	7	5	16	0
1–2 points	27	15	28	37
3–4 points	46	30	36	19
5–8 points	15	45	12	19
9 or more points	5	5	8	25
Mean score	3.4	4.6	3.1	4.9

[a] The data on appointees is limited to those judges who returned mail questionnaires similar to those used in the lawyer survey. Responses from circuit judges accounted for some 60 percent of all judges appointed to the two Missouri Plan circuit benches; responses were received from two-thirds of all judges appointed to the appellate benches from 1940 through 1964. Most of the remaining judges were deceased at the time of the mail survey.

questionnaire returns from nominees for the appellate benches were insufficient to permit their inclusion in the analysis.[8]

---

[8] Mail questionnaire responses were received from only 2 of the 20 persons nominated (but not appointed) to the three courts of appeals benches. The response rate for those nominated (but not appointed) to the Supreme Court was far higher, with 9 of the 12 persons in this category returning questionnaires. These nine

The data on practice arrangements of applicants for the two benches indicate that a slight majority of candidates for appellate nomination come from medium and large-sized firms, whereas a substantial majority of applicants for the trial bench are from solo practices, two-man partnerships, or are salaried employees of government agencies. However, at the appointment stage these relationships are reversed, with small firm attorneys enjoying a slight advantage in the competition for appellate judgeships. The principal explanation for this lies in the fact that two-thirds of those selected for appellate judgeships are from outstate Missouri and, typical of that region, most have had solo or two-man partnership practice arrangements. Among Supreme Court justices, in particular, there is a sharp outstate-metropolitan dichotomy with respect to past law practice arrangements. Of the Supreme Court justices included in the Table 5.2 data, only two were from metropolitan areas, and both had been associated with large law firms prior to their judicial appointments. The remaining five Supreme Court justices were from outstate Missouri, and all but one had been in either solo or two-man partnership law practices.

Outstate predominance within the appellate judiciary also accounts for the kinds of legal practice specialties represented on the appeals and Supreme Court benches. Given the difference in orientation of those involved in appellate versus circuit judicial selection, attorneys with corporate or defense practices might reasonably expect to be in a more

---

persons accounted for 15 of the 18 nominations (83 percent) that went to nominees who never became judges, since 4 of them were nominated more than once.

An examination of the characteristics of those *nominated only* for the Supreme Court, over the period 1940–1964, reveals: (1) a practice arrangement pattern similar to that of the judges appointed to the Supreme Court, with nominees from outstate Missouri having solo or two-man partnership practices and those from the metropolitan areas coming from medium (3–9 lawyers) or large firms; (2) a heavier concentration (44%) than among the judges' of persons with a defendant's practice background, with none of the nominees having specialized in personal injury litigation "principally for the plaintiff"; but with a percentage equal to the judges having engaged in a mixed plaintiffs-defense practice; and (3) a lower range of scores on the party activity index among the nominees than among those appointed, with over half of the nominees scoring 1–2 points and none scoring nine or more points. The mean party activity index score for the nominees is 3.3.

In general, these data suggest that unsuccessful nominees for the Supreme Court more resembled the kinds of persons preferred by the legal-judicial community than the political community. Consonant with that interpretation is the fact that 6 of these 9 nominees were court commissioners, and a seventh was a court of appeals judge. Three of the commissioners were Republicans and the remainder were relatively inactive Democrats, as was the one Democratic court of appeals judge.

favored position in competing for judicial office at the appellate level. Yet, virtually the same proportion of applicants and appointees to the two benches have specialized in these fields of practice. (A higher proportion of appellate applicants specialized in personal injury litigation for the defense, which is consistent with the more pro-defense orientation of the appellate nominating commission.) Political factors largely explain the relative success at the appellate appointment stage of attorneys whose practices include the representation of plaintiffs. Outstate attorneys are favored by the governor for political reasons, and most of these lawyers have a quite diverse clientele that usually includes plaintiffs litigants.[9] This is evident in the geographic origins of the appellate judges whose practices involved negligence or personal injury litigation, either primarily for the plaintiffs or for the plaintiffs and defense equally. Of the eight judges having such a practice, who returned questionnaires in the judges survey, six were from outside Missouri.

The data on political backgrounds point up both differences and similarities in the selection process for the two court levels. Appellate judges were slightly more active politically before their appointments than were circuit judges. Yet there are significant differences in the distribution of party activity index scores within the two groups. Among trial judges, there is a predominance of those who had been moderately active politically, whereas appellate judges' scores are clustered at both the upper and lower ranges of partisan involvement. In part, this upper level of involvement reflects the fact that more appellate judges were active at the higher levels of party politics, several having served on state central committees. The higher party activity scores of judges as compared to applicants reveals the extent of politicization in the selection process at both court levels, and the premium thus placed on political qualifications for judicial office. The greater spread between the scores of appointees and applicants for the appellate as compared to the circuit bench reinforces the conclusion that appellate judgeships are among the most highly prized positions in state-level job politics. Consistent with this finding is the fact that even those "promoted" to the

---

Among respondents to the lawyer survey, attorneys residing in the outstate area had less highly specialized practices than did the attorneys from metropolitan St. Louis and Jackson County. Only 29 percent of the outstate lawyers had limited their practices to a single one of the major fields of practice (general corporate, probate and trust, personal injury, and real property) in the year preceding the survey, compared to 38 percent of the metropolitan lawyer respondents. Among appointees to the circuit benches, 25 percent had specialized in a single field of practice, while none of the appellate judges had done so. Again, this largely reflects differences in metropolitan versus outstate legal practice.

appellate bench from court commissionerships generally have had considerable political experience. Most court commissioners who fail to secure appellate judgeships have been from the minority party, or apoliticals, or individuals with little previous political involvement.

Although the public office backgrounds of circuit and appellate judges will be explored in the following chapter, one feature of the appellate judges' deserves attention here because of its relevance to the selection process: slightly under one-third of the appointees to the appellate benches had previously served as commissioners on the courts to which they were appointed.[10] Such commissioners constituted the highest proportion of appointees to the St. Louis Court of Appeals, where half of the judges had served in that capacity; by way of contrast, none of the judges chosen for the Kansas City Court of Appeals had such experience prior to their appointments. Four of the ten justices chosen for the Supreme Court had previously been commissioners on that Court.

Much the same situation exists with respect to the nominees for these appellate benches. From 1940 to 1964 a total of 19 panels containing the names of 57 nominees were chosen to fill vacancies on the Kansas City and St. Louis courts of appeals and the Supreme Court. Twenty-one (37 percent) of those nominations went to court commissioners, with the highest proportion occurring in the nominations for the Supreme Court bench, where court commissioners received just under half of all nominations. The bulk of the commissioners named to Supreme Court panels had served in that capacity on the Supreme Court, but 2 of the 14 had been commissioners on the courts of appeals.

In general, these data underscore a point made in the earlier analysis of the selection process. There it was suggested that appellate judicial selection has been most decisively affected by the interaction of two communities of interest: the legal-judicial, which pursues a strategy of cooptation in recruitment; and the political, which stresses partisan political criteria in the choice of judges. The data examined in this section, particularly those on the partisan and court commissioner backgrounds of the appellate judges, indicate that both sets of participants in the selection process have had an influence upon the characteristics of judicial personnel of the upper courts. A fuller examination of these and other characteristics, together with a comparison of the kinds of judges chosen under the Missouri Plan and under other selection systems, are subjects of the next chapter.

---

[10] Appointees to the Springfield Court of Appeals are excluded from this analysis since that court has never utilized commissioners.

PART II

THE CONSEQUENCES

OF THE PLAN

From its inception, the debate over the Nonpartisan Court Plan has turned on the ultimate question of whether it brings better results than alternative means of choosing judges, particularly the system of partisan elections with which it is most often counterpoised.[1] Unfortunately, despite the gallons of ink that have been spilled on the issue over the years by both proponents and opponents of the Plan, these debates generally have shed heat rather than light on the matter. Disputants most frequently talk past each other with their arguments, each totally committed to the soundness of his position. This means that there is virtually no reliable evidence on the subject available for persons who seek an honest assessment of the consequences of the two systems of choosing judges.

The debates are fruitless for two major reasons. First, both sides frequently fail to spell out the criteria they use to make their evaluations, that is, they do not clearly articulate the particular matters they are examining in reaching their judgment. Even more prevalent, however, is the failure to produce any empirical data to support the existence of the consequences they claim flow from the selection system they espouse or attack. Instead, judgments are made on the basis of logical

---

As noted previously, there are three other methods of choosing judges in the United States, including gubernatorial and legislative appointment, as well as popular election using nonpartisan ballots. The particular rivalry between the Plan and elective systems stems from the fact that the Plan was developed by leaders of the Bar initially out of concern for the "evils" they associated with political machine domination of the popular election of judges. Moreover, this latter method of choosing judges is still the one most used by states in the nation, and thus it represents the most promising target for inroads on the Plan's behalf.

assumptions or unsystematic and incomplete observations of how the respective systems, in fact, operate.[2]

There is no ready answer to the question of whether selection under the Plan is better than selection by popular election, since this judgment is essentially a matter of individual preferences and values. However, it is possible to explore the consequences of choosing judges under both systems in Missouri, since the Nonpartisan Court Plan replaced the popular election of appellate judges, as well as circuit judges in Jackson County and St. Louis City, and the judges formerly chosen by the voters were "held over" in office under the provisions of the Plan. Moreover, circuit judges in outstate Missouri, including those in urban St. Louis County, are still popularly elected. Thus a comparative analysis can be used to assess results obtained under both selection systems. The following four chapters of the study are concerned with such a comparison.

In making our analysis, we have attempted to examine a variety of matters involved in assessing the consequences of the two systems. Included are explorations of such subjects as the backgrounds and quality of judges who have been chosen under both methods, as well as their respective patterns of behavior while on the bench. We have also considered the situation that each group of judges faces on being retained in office, as well as their tendencies to remain on the bench or to leave the judiciary for other pursuits.

We employ two distinct methodological approaches in our analysis of the consequences of the Plan. One is to examine objective data on various facets of the issue. Chapter 6 compares the social backgrounds of nonpartisan and elective judges, together with their respective tenures in office. The other approach is to use the subjective evaluations of the bench and the Bar concerning various aspects of judicial selection. Thus Chapter 7 investigates lawyer attitudes toward the operation of the Plan and elective method of choosing judges; it also explores their opinions (and those of judges) as to how to improve the operation of the Plan. Chapter 8 contains the ratings of the performance of the two kinds of judges by lawyers practicing before them, as well as an evaluation of the most important qualities of a judge as seen by practic-

---

[2] One exception to this general statement is an article by Herbert Jacob entitled "The Effect of Institutional Differences in the Recruitment Process: The Case of State Judges," *Journal of Public Law,* 13, (1964), 104–119, in which the author compares the backgrounds of state judges chosen under each of the five selection methods in the United States. Of course, Jacob, unlike most persons writing on the subject, is not attempting to support any particular system of selection; that is, his purposes are scholarly, not advocatory.

ing attorneys and members of the bench themselves. The final chapter in this part, which deals with the "policy outputs" of the state judicial system, utilizes both methodological approaches. Chapter 9 explores the subjective perceptions of attorneys concerning the orientation of judges on the plaintiff-defendant issue with which so much of the state's litigation is concerned; it also contains an objective analysis of the nonunanimous decisions of the state Supreme Court during our period of study.

6

SOCIAL BACKGROUND AND

TENURE OF PLAN AND

ELECTIVE JUDGES

Two important considerations involved in analyzing the consequences of particular judicial selection systems are the kinds of individuals that these systems elevate to the bench and the tenure situation that each group of judges faces, that is, whether they tend to remain in office for a considerable period of time or are replaced at fairly frequent intervals. This chapter compares the records of Plan judges and judges selected in Missouri under partisan elections, along both these dimensions.

Comparative studies employ two major types of analysis. One is that of looking at the present-day situation of two entities being analyzed. For example, this chapter compares the background and tenure of circuit judges in Jackson County and St. Louis, who are selected under the Plan, with judges in St. Louis County and outstate areas, who are popu-larly-elected with the use of partisan ballots. The other basic approach is to examine a common entity and note changes in it that occur over time. In this instance, one can compare the background and tenure of Jackson County and St. Louis circuit judges (as well as all appellate judges in the state) when they were chosen by means of partisan selections prior to 1940, with judges in these areas who have been selected since that date under provisions of the Nonpartisan Court Plan.

Both kinds of analysis possess certain advantages and disadvantages. The first, which compares the situation in various areas of the state, benefits from holding the time element constant as a factor, but suffers from the fact that regions with varying social and economic conditions, as well as possible differences in what has now become known as "political culture,"[1] are being examined. More specifically, this means in our case that differences among the background characteristics of today's judges in the two major cities and other areas of Missouri may be attributed not so much to the disparate judicial selection methods that they use but to variations in matters such as the social and economic setting for the practice of law (with its impact on the attractions of a judgeship), or the informal qualifications that political leaders, lawyers and the voters set in determining who among the members of the Bar shall ascend to, and remain on, the bench.[2] The other basic approach, which examines an entity over successive chronological periods, benefits from holding the entity itself constant but, of course, cannot control for influences that may be introduced as a result of changes brought on by the passage of time. In the instant case, then, it is conceivable that differences in the characteristics and tenure of pre- and post-Plan judges in Jackson County and St. Louis City are not primarily the result of a conversion from partisan elections to the Nonpartisan Court Plan in 1940 but, instead, result from changes in the legal and political environments of those communities that have occurred since that date.

Any study that attempts to utilize these two comparative approaches faces the potential problems raised above. However, it would be a mistake to overemphasize the informal factors affecting the characteristics and tenure of judges, and to minimize the effects of the selection method used, particularly since a recent study by Jacob demonstrates that variations among the characteristics of state judges in the United States are more closely associated with the system employed to choose them than they are with either urban-rural differences among states or the degree

---

[1] As previously noted, political culture refers to the basic orientation of both political leaders and citizens toward politics. Specifically, it refers to attitudes on such matters as the proper ends or purposes of political activity; how the political process works; what benefits individuals may expect to receive from it; as well as the part they should play in the process. Samuel Patterson applies the concept to the United States in "The Political Cultures of the American States," *Journal of Politics* 30 (February, 1968), 187–209.

[2] As discussed in Chapter 5, Daniel Elazar in his recent study, *American Federalism: A View from the States* (New York: Thomas Y. Crowell Co., 1966), suggests that in an individualistic political culture, the primary purpose of politics is individual self-advancement, while in a traditional political culture, it is the preservation of the existing social order. He classifies the political culture of the two major cities in Missouri as individualistic and that of the outstate areas as traditional. These differences in conceptions of the proper purpose of political activity in metropolitan and outstate Missouri could lead persons influential in judicial selection in these respective areas to choose lawyers with different kinds of backgrounds for the bench

of party competition that prevails in a given area.[3] Moreover, it is possible to use both comparative methods simultaneously as a means of achieving greater control over the conditions described above. In the instant case, we have done this by analyzing data on the background characteristics and tenure of judges in various areas of the state in two time periods: the era from 1917 through 1940, and the era from 1941 through 1964. By comparing the situation in the earlier and later period in the two urban communities that changed their judicial selection method between the two eras, with the St. Louis County and outstate areas that did not, one can partially control for both time and area as factors,[4] and thus better determine the effect of the selection system itself on the characteristics and tenure of judges in Missouri.

BACKGROUND CHARACTERISTICS OF MISSOURI JUDGES

In 1933, Rodney Mott, a pioneer in the study of judicial personnel, commented that "In the long heritage of literature on the perennial question of the selection of judges, the practical question, what kinds of judges are actually selected, has been very generally ignored."[5] Mott's own analysis of the background characteristics of state supreme court and federal judges in the United States[6] remained virtually the sole work[7] until a quarter of a century later when, following the publication of Donald Matthews' study of the social backgrounds of various kinds of political decision-makers,[8] students began to investigate the characteristics of federal judges, as well as those serving on the courts of various

---

[3] See Herbert Jacob, "The Effect of Institutional Differences in the Recruitment Process: The Case of State Judges," *Journal of Public Law*, XIII (1964), 104–119.

[4] Of course, it is conceivable that certain changes might be occurring in the legal and political environments of the two major cities, but not in the St. Louis County and outstate areas. However, the fact that St. Louis City and County are both parts of the same metropolitan area tends to minimize that possibility. In any event, there is no way to control for it.

[5] See Rodney L. Mott, Spencer D. Albright and Helen R. Semmerling, "Judicial Personnel," *Annals of the American Academy of Political and Social Science*, 167 (1933), p. 143.

[6] About sixteen separate characteristics were involved, including educational, legal, judicial, and political matters. Mott's study is further discussed in the following chapter.

[7] Todd Hoopes analyzes the social backgrounds of 106 Supreme Court justices in Ohio over the period from 1803 to 1947. See his "An Experiment in the Measurement of Judicial Qualifications in the Supreme Court of Ohio," *Cincinnatti Law Review*, 18 (1949), 417–466.

[8] Donald R. Matthews, *The Social Background of Political Decision-Makers* (Garden City: Doubleday and Company, Inc., 1954).

states of the union.[9] However, with certain limited exceptions, few of these studies purport to be comparative in nature or to focus on the characteristics of judges chosen under different selection methods.[10]

Among the number of judicial background characteristics of interest to us, we chose six for analysis: age, legal education, place of birth, partisan affiliation, prior judicial experience, and political experience. These varied characteristics reflect both professional and political factors that affect the selection process, and also help to identify important career patterns of members of the bench. They also possess the advantage of having been analyzed by other students of the subject, so that comparisons of our findings with those of other states are possible.[11]

Backgrounds of Trial Judges

As discussed in earlier chapters dealing with the recruitment and selection of Plan judges, age is one of the key factors that is taken into account in assessing the *professional* qualifications of a lawyer for a judgeship. It not only affects the thinking of the members of the nominating commissions but also has a prenatal effect on the process because some attorneys eliminate themselves from consideration on the basis

---

[9] Included among such studies are: John R. Schmidhauser, "The Justices of the Supreme Court: A Collective Portrait," *The Midwest Journal of Political Science,* 3 (1959), 1–50; Claude J. Davis, *Judicial Selection in West Virginia,* (Publication No. 25 Morgantown: Bureau of Governmental Research and Service, 1958); Sidney S. Ulmer, "Public Office in the Social Background of Supreme Court Justices," *The American Journal of Economics and Sociology,* 21 (January, 1962), 57–68; Kenneth N. Vines, "The Selection of Judges in Louisiana," in Vines and Jacob, *Studies in Judicial Politics* Vol. VIII, Tulane Studies, Studies in Political Science (New Orleans: Tulane University Press, 1962); Bancroft C. Henderson and T. C. Sinclair, *Judicial Selection in Texas: An Exploratory Study,* University of Houston Studies in Social Science (Houston: Public Affairs Research Center, 1964), Vol. 1, Ch. V; Joel B. Grossman, *Lawyers and Judges: The ABA and the Politics of Judicial Selection* (New York: John Wiley and Sons, 1965), pp. 198–206; and Sheldon Goldman, "Characteristics of Eisenhower and Kennedy Appointees to the Lower Federal Courts," *The Western Political Quarterly,* XVIII (December, 1965) 755–762.

[10] Mott, *op. cit.,* and Henderson and Sinclair, *op. cit.,* analyze the backgrounds of state and federal justices (the latter study is of Texas only), while Jacob, *op. cit.,* specifically treats the question of whether different selection systems (partisan and nonpartisan elections, legislative and gubernatorial appointment, and the Missouri Plan) result in placing on the state bench, judges with different social backgrounds.

[11] Our decision to analyze these characteristics was also prompted by practical considerations. Complete data on these matters were available from Missouri state manual over the long time-span in which we were interested (1916–1964).

age. The factor cuts two ways in that young lawyers are usually considered to be too inexperienced for a judgeship, while attorneys of advanced years are regarded as poor health risks for the demands of the bench. A comparative analysis of the age when judges selected under partisan election system go on the bench indicates whether political leaders and the electorate are as sensitive to this factor as are the members of the legal community who are influential in the selection process under the Plan.

Another key professional factor is the kind of legal education a lawyer receives before he ascends to the bench. In recent years the trend in preparation for the legal profession has been away from studying law in an older attorney's office and toward law school attendance, so that very few persons today enter the practice of law without the benefit of a formal legal education.[12] However, as previously indicated, a variety of law school possibilities are available to aspirants for the Bar. These run the gamut from a "name" or prestigious outstate institution, which draws its student body from all over the nation, to local schools that offer courses at night to persons who pursue their legal studies on a part-time basis. The assumption is frequently made that the former type of law school provides the superior training because of the quality of its faculty and also because its students are able to devote their full attention to the task at hand. Whether the quality of such education does vary is not important for our purposes, so long as persons involved in the selection process *think* it does. Moreover, as previously discussed, the kind of law school attended is a major indicator of social status in the legal profession.

Table 6.1 compares Plan and elective judges with respect to the age at which they went on the bench and the kind of legal education that they received. In the pre-Plan period, Jackson County and St. Louis City circuit judges were more likely to be under 40 years of age when they first came to the bench than was true of their judicial colleagues from outside the two cities. After the Plan was instituted, the number of young attorneys who were appointed to the Jackson County Bench dropped drastically, but the proportion that became circuit judges in St. Louis City showed no appreciable change. The two geographical areas that retained partisan elections during both periods (St. Louis County and the outstate circuits) also showed contrasting age patterns: the representation of young attorneys on the former bench rose dramatically, while that in outstate circuits remained constant. The table also

For example, only 1 percent of our sample of Missouri lawyers did not attend law school.

TABLE 6.1
AGE AND LEGAL EDUCATION OF CIRCUIT JUDGES IN MISSOURI BY GEOGRAPHICAL LOCATION AND PERIOD WHEN SELECTED FOR COURT (PERCENT)[a]

Characteristic	Jackson County (N = 21) 1st Period[b]	Jackson County (N = 19) 2nd Period[c]	St. Louis City (N = 54) 1st Period[b]	St. Louis City (N = 15) 2nd Period[c]	St. Louis County (N = 9) 1st Period[b]	St. Louis County (N = 12) 2nd Period[b]	Outstate (N = 87) 1st Period[b]	Outstate (N = 78) 2nd Period[b]
Age								
Under 40	38	10	24	27	11	50	21	23
40–49	19	42	39	20	67	25	36	35
50–59	19	42	16	53	11	25	21	28
60 and over	19	6	15	0	0	0	11	9
Not Ascertained	5	0	6	0	11	0	11	5
Total	100	100	100	100	100	100	100	100
Legal Education								
Prestige[d]	14	5	9	6	0	8	1	5
Other outstate	14	5	7	0	12	0	13	17
Instate—full-time	5	37	44	47	44	59	38	51
Instate—night	38	42	32	47	44	33	10	8
Law office[e]	29	11	8	0	0	0	38	19
Total	100	100	100	100	100	100	100	100

[a] The first period is 1917–1940. The second is 1941–1964.
[b] Elective judges.
[c] Plan judges.
[d] Chicago, Columbia, Harvard, Michigan, and Yale.
[e] Includes judges who listed no law school education as well as those stating specifically that they read law in an office

shows that while the proportion of attorneys over the age of 60 who became circuit judges declined in Jackson County and St. Louis after the advent of the Plan, few attorneys of that advanced age were ever elected to circuit judgeships in the non-Plan areas of Missouri. Thus the data do not show that any clear relationship exists between the judicial selection method used and the advent of younger or older attorneys to the circuit bench in Missouri. Instead, the important differences between the two groups of judges occur in the middle-age categories. Lawyers in their fifties appear to be advantaged by the Plan while, generally speaking, those in their forties fare better under the partisan election system in Missouri. This latter finding parallels that of studies of other states which use a partisan ballot to elect their judges.[13]

Table 6.1 also indicates that, contrary to much of the mythology that surrounds the Plan, it has not tended to bring to the circuit bench lawyers who received their legal educations at prestigious or other out-state law schools;[14] in fact, considerably fewer individuals of this kind have become circuit judges since the Plan was adopted in Jackson County and St. Louis City than served in this capacity while the elective system was still in effect in these communities. Nor has the Plan resulted in reducing the proportion of judges in these cities who attended part-time night schools; again, whatever trend exists is in the opposite direction. The only significant upgrading in the educational background of judges that has occurred in the two Plan jurisdictions is the tendency for more Jackson County judges in the latter period to have attended instate, full time, schools than to have studied in a law office. However, this appears to be more of a historical trend in the preparation for the law than a result of a particular selection system, since a similar pattern occurs among outstate judges who were chosen by partisan elections throughout both periods analyzed. The fact that virtually no St. Louis City and St. Louis County judges in either period read law in an office also lends evidence to the supposition that the availability of law schools in the immediate area is another key factor in shaping the educational backgrounds of particular groups of judges.

Two background characteristics that reflect *political* factors at work in the judicial selection process are the place of birth and partisan affilia-

---

Davis, Henderson and Sinclair, and Vines, *op. cit.*

Albert Blaustein in his article, "The American Lawyer: A Preliminary Analysis," *The Journal of Legal Education*, 4 (1951–1952), 291–307, notes that while prestigious law schools have furnished more than their share of justices of the United States Supreme Court, their graduates do not tend to populate the benches of lower courts.

TABLE 6.2
BIRTHPLACE AND PARTY AFFILIATION OF CIRCUIT JUDGES IN MISSOURI BY GEOGRAPHICAL LOCATION AND PERIOD WHEN SELECTED FOR COURT (PERCENT)[a]

Characteristic	Jackson County (N = 21) 1st Period[b]	Jackson County (N = 19) 2nd Period[c]	St. Louis City (N = 54) 1st Period[b]	St. Louis City (N = 15) 2nd Period[c]	St. Louis County (N = 9) 1st Period[b]	St. Louis County (N = 12) 2nd Period[b]	Outstate (N = 87) 1st Period[b]	Outstate (N = 78) 2nd Period[b]
Birthplace								
In judicial district	24	42	47	53	33	0	53	54
Outside district	33	32	20	27	33	58	25	26
Outside state	43	26	33	13	34	33	20	14
Not ascertained	0	0	0	7	0	9	2	6
Total	100	100	100	100	100	100	100	100
Party Affiliation								
Republican	33	26	43	26	67	17	36	32
Democrat	67	74	57	74	33	83	64	68
Total	100	100	100	100	100	100	100	100

[a] The first period is 1917 to 1940. The second is 1941 to 1964.
[b] Elective judges.
[c] Plan judges.

tion of the men on the circuit bench. The former bears on what some students of the subject have termed "localism," that is, the informal qualification that candidates for public office, including judgeships, must be born in the area in which they are to serve.[15] The fact that Plan judges are appointed by a state-wide political figure, the governor, creates the possibility that localism will not be as important a factor in Jackson County and St. Louis appointments since 1940 as it was when these communities operated under partisan elections. With respect to partisan considerations, again there is some reason to expect that the institution of the Plan would have an effect on party representation on the circuit bench, particularly since some studies of elective systems have shown that the voting for judges closely parallels that for major party offices which appear on the same ballot,[16] while the Court Plan is widely heralded as serving to minimize partisan factors in the selection process.

Table 6.2 demonstrates, however, that our assumption about the effect of localism on the characteristics of Plan and elective judges did not prove to be true. After the inauguration of the Plan in Jackson County and St. Louis City, more, rather than less, of the circuit judges had their birthplaces in the judicial district in which they serve. This may suggest that the localism factor is introduced into the Plan selection system through the necessity of candidates' being well-known and established in their community in order to be visible and "available" for a judgeship in the minds of the members of the nominating commissions. It may also be, as Jacob has suggested, that the law school tie is important under the Plan,[17] since Table 6.1 also indicates that candidates in the period since 1940 have tended to go to instate institutions, particularly to night schools in their own communities.

Table 6.2 further shows that our general expectation regarding the lessening of partisan factors in the selection of Plan judges, compared to elective judges, is not borne out by the data. Since 1940, the minority Republican party has been less well-represented on the Jackson County and St. Louis City circuit benches than it was during the period when such judges were popularly-elected. However, the table fails to take into account important political developments that have occurred in

---

[15] Jacob, op. cit., develops an index of localism based upon whether a judge was born in the judicial district in which he served and whether he went to law school within the state. Vines, op. cit., applies these criteria (as well as place of childhood residence and schooling) in analyzing the localism of Louisiana judges.
[16] Davis, op. cit., p. 26 in his study of partisan judicial elections in West Virginia, found that judges won by a majority which, on the average, deviated from the party vote for other state political officials by not more than one percent.
[17] Jacob, op. cit., p. 108.

both these communities since the Plan was adopted in 1940. These two cities have become overwhelmingly Democratic since that time,[18] and if voting for judges had paralleled voting for other offices, it is doubtful that few, if any, Republican judges would have been elected to these benches under a system of partisan ballots. Moreover, the St. Louis County situation indicates what has happened in an elective jurisdiction that is not as clearly Democratic as the two cities:[19] Democratic representation on the County circuit bench rose rapidly in the period since 1940 as a result of the growing strength of the party in that area, as well as the practice of Democratic governors of appointing fellow partisans to new judgeships and vacancies on the court.[20] Thus it is erroneous to assume that the Plan has actually disadvantaged the minority Republican party as far as representation in the Jackson County and St. Louis circuit courts is concerned. At the same time, it has not produced the party balance on the bench that some persons, perhaps mistakenly, associate with the nonpartisan emphasis of the Plan.[21]

Students of comparative judicial systems identify the lack of a *career service* as one of the distinctive features of the United States judiciary. Unlike a judge in countries of Europe governed by the Roman law tradition, who enters the judicial service as a young man and is promoted from within,[22] jurists at all levels of our government generally come to the bench from other pursuits. Many come directly from the practice of law. Yet some studies have pointed out that both federal and state judges in the United States have frequently had prior experience in other levels of the judiciary, as well as in law-enforcement positions.[23]

---

[18] Robert F. Karsch in his study, *The Government of Missouri* (Columbia: Lucas Brothers, 1963), p. 21, indicates that in the period from 1944 to 1962, the Democratic party in Jackson County won all races for county offices, while in St. Louis City it carried more than 90 percent of such elections.

[19] *Ibid.*, shows that the Republicans in St. Louis County won more than 60 percent of the elections for county offices during the 1944 to 1962 era.

[20] Of the 10 Democrats who went on the St. Louis County bench in the post-Plan period, 8 were appointed by the Governor and 2 were elected. Of the 8 appointments, 6 came as a result of the creation of new judgeships in the county, and 2 were attributable to vacancies on the bench.

[21] The Plan, of course, does not purport to be bipartisan (that is, to insure an equal representation of parties in the judiciary) but rather nonpartisan (that is, to minimize the importance of party affiliation as a factor in determining who should sit on the bench). Some persons seem to require party balance as proof that nonpartisanship actually does exist.

[22] See Henry J. Abraham, *The Judicial Process* (New York: Oxford University Press, 1962), pp. 31 ff.

[23] Davis, Henderson and Sinclair, Jacob, Schmidhauser, Ulmer, and Vines, *op. cit.*, all make this same point.

These studies also have revealed that a number of our judges have previously served in nonlegal positions (such as legislators),[24] a matter not considered salutary by some students of the subject who view this experience as a potential threat to independent judicial work.[25] This sentiment is generally held by supporters of the Plan who have sought to minimize the influence of political factors in the operation of the courts.[26] Table 6.3 seeks to determine the effect of the Plan on the kinds of public-office careers that circuit judges in Missouri have pursued prior to going on the bench.

The table indicates that the Plan has not brought men to the circuit court in Jackson County and St. Louis with greater judicial experience than the judges who served in these communities in the pre-Plan period. In fact, the trend has been in the opposite direction; that is, the elective judges were more likely to have served in some other judicial capacity prior to their election to the trial court. A closer analysis of such experience indicates that a pool of judicial offices existed in the two major cities in the pre-Plan period which offered aspirants multiple chances at the bench. A candidate who was defeated for a judgeship could seek that post again or could attempt to run for another judicial office. This practice was particularly prevalent in St. Louis City where some members of the circuit bench not only had served in minor court positions (such as city judges) or other comparable posts (such as the court of criminal corrections) but, in some instances, had served in higher positions in the state judicial system, including the courts of appeals as well as the Supreme Court. The same was true, to a lesser extent, in Jackson County. However, the inauguration of the Plan has largely eliminated this pattern of judicial office-holding. Service on a minor court has been regarded by many nominating commission members as a detriment, rather than an asset, for a circuit judgeship: only 1 of 34 Plan circuit judges in the two communities had prior judicial experience on a lower court. (The reasons behind such an attitude include the feeling that persons of genuine legal ability do not find it necessary to take such posts, and that the assembly-line nature of justice that must of necessity be dispensed in tribunals with such crowded

---

[24] Jacob, *op. cit.*, p. 110, finds that judges chosen by governors or legislatures are more likely to have had prior legislative experience than are those who are popularly-elected or selected under the Nonpartisan Court Plan.

[25] Mott et al., *op. cit.*, 147.

[26] For example, Glenn R. Winters, Executive Director of the American Judicature Society, feels that unfortunately, party politics factors dominate the selection of judges under an elective system. See his article, "How Should Judges be Chosen," *Wisconsin Bar Bulletin*, 29 (1956), 7–8, 563–566.

TABLE 6.3

JUDICIAL AND POLITICAL EXPERIENCE OF CIRCUIT JUDGES IN MISSOURI BY GEOGRAPHICAL LOCATION AND PERIOD WHEN SELECTED FOR COURT (PERCENT)[a]

Characteristic	Jackson County		St. Louis City		St. Louis County		Outstate	
	(N = 21) 1st Period[b]	(N = 19) 2nd Period[c]	(N = 54) 1st Period[b]	(N = 15) 2nd Period[c]	(N = 9) 1st Period[b]	(N = 12) 2nd Period[b]	(N = 87) 1st Period[b]	(N = 78) 2nd Period[b]
Judicial Experience								
Minor court[d]	5	5	11	0	0	17	17	4
Court of record[e]	14	5	20	7	11	0	7	10
None	81	90	69	93	89	83	92	86
Political Experience								
Law enforcement	28	48	39	47	67	42	68	86
Legislative	5	0	13	0	11	8	16	17
Other	5	21	2	13	22	8	5	4
None	67	42	48	40	22	58	25	11
Officeholding at Time of Selection								
Judicial office	5	5	9	0	6	17	3	1
Political office	5	5	17	20	11	0	13	7
Total judicial or political	10	10	26	20	17	17	16	8

[a] The first period is 1917 to 1940. The second is 1941 to 1964.

[b] Elective judges.

[c] Plan judges.

[d] Includes justices of the peace, police, city or municipal judges. Magistrates have also been included in the minor court category on the basis of the kind of work they do, even though technically they serve on courts of record in Missouri.

[e] Includes circuit probate courts of common pleas, criminal corrections, courts of appeals and the Supreme Court.

dockets does not prepare one for the more legally-respectable procedures that are associated with the work of courts of record.) Moreover, as discussed later in this chapter, Plan judges are almost never defeated in reelections to office, and thus are not in the market for new judicial posts as often as were elective judges. Furthermore, as we shall see, whatever mobility takes place in the Plan system is an upward one whereby circuit court judges are tapped for higher positions in the judicial hierarchy; no Plan appellate judges have ever served subsequently in lower judicial positions (as was true under the elective system).

Table 6.3 does show, however, that while prior judicial experience of circuit judges in Jackson County and St. Louis declined between the two periods analyzed, the incidence of previous experience in law-enforcement offices has increased since the Plan was instituted. About half of the Plan judges in both cities held such a post before going on the circuit bench. An analysis of these positions indicates that they have been primarily local offices such as circuit attorney, prosecutor or city or county counselor,[27] or assistant state's Attorney General. (The appointment to the last position is often a reward for service in a governor's race, and even when this is not the case, the work of these attorneys in the operation of the state government is such that they frequently become visible to chief executives and hence are likely prospects for a judicial appointment.) However, it is a mistake to attribute an increase in law-enforcement office experience among circuit judges in Missouri to the operation of the Plan alone, since the table also shows that this experience has also become more prevalent among outstate circuit judges. In fact, almost nine out of ten of the latter judges who were elected in the period since 1940 served previously as law-enforcement officials in their area, primarily as prosecuting attorneys. Thus, with respect to Missouri trial judges, although a distinctly separate career judiciary like that operating in countries of Europe does not exist in this state, the lawyers who do ascend to the trial bench have been involved to an increasing extent in law-enforcement work. In other words, a kind of informal apprenticeship has developed whereby the persons who go on the bench will have first served in a governmental capacity that exposes them to (and perhaps motivates them toward) an even higher position involving the public's legal business.

Table 6.3 also shows that this informal career experience of trial judges is, for the most part, legal in nature and that relatively few of them

---

[27] St. Louis City has a circuit attorney who is in charge of the prosecution of felony offenses only. City and county counselors in Missouri handle civil matters for their respective jurisdictions.

have held other political posts. The wishes of Plan supporters that judicial candidates should not be selected from the legislative arena have been respected, but this kind of experience also has not been prevalent among judges selected under the elective system. The same is true of other types of political office, although (somewhat surprisingly) more Plan than elective judges have tended to hold such posts. However, an analysis of the specific kinds of positions that the Nonpartisan Plan judges have occupied indicates that they have been honorific in nature rather than full-time political jobs.

The table makes a final point: although public-office experience is a part of the career ladder of many trial judges in Missouri, they do not usually move from such a post *directly* to a circuit judgeship. This is true even with respect to law-enforcement offices in which so many of the judges have served at some time in their career. Moreover, it applies to elective judges as well as those chosen under the provisions of the Plan. This may suggest that the aura of judicial independence is such that political leaders, as well as members of the Bar themselves, are not inclined to favor as judicial candidates, persons who presently occupy a public office. Another factor that also may contribute to this pattern of public and judicial officeholding (particularly in the outstate areas) is that many young lawyers, just out of law school, serve in a part-time capacity as prosecuting attorney for financial reasons while they develop a private practice. Years later, when they have met the informal judicial qualification of maturity, many of them, perhaps because they enjoyed this experience in law-enforcement work, will make a decision to try for the more lucrative and prestigious position of a judgeship.

Backgrounds of Appellate as Compared to Trial Judges

An analysis of the background characteristics of appellate judges in Missouri does not offer a full range of comparative possibilities because, since 1940, all of the members of the state's upper benches have been chosen under the Plan. It is still possible to make a historical comparison of the pre-Plan appellate judges who were popularly-elected, with those chosen since 1940, but there is no present-day group of judges like those still elected to the St. Louis County and outstate circuits, which can be used to check the effect of chronological (as distinguished from selection method) factors on the background characteristics studied. However, another type of analysis can be employed: the characteristics of the circuit judges in Jackson County and St. Louis City who were selected before and after the institution of the Plan can be compared with similar groups of courts of appeals and Supreme Court jurists to determine whether the inauguration of the Plan in 1940 has had similar or different effects on such characteristics of judges serving at various levels of the state judicial system. Table 6.4 contains data on both circuit and appellate judges for the six background characteristics previously analyzed.

The table indicates that the Plan has had the same general impact on the professional characteristics of appellate judges as it did on those of the trial judges in Jackson County and St. Louis City. Since it was instituted, the tendency at all three levels of the state judiciary has been for judges to be chosen for the bench when they are in their fifties. The table also indicates that no lawyers under forty have been selected for the Supreme Court under the Plan, and that the proportion of persons over the age of sixty has been reduced at all three court levels. As far as educational background is concerned, with the exception of the increase in prestige-school graduates among justices of the state Supreme Court, the trend at all levels has been toward the selection of judges who attended instate law schools, including those offering night classes. On the other hand, judges who read law in an office as preparation for their careers have virtually disappeared from the Missouri bench.

With respect to political factors, the table indicates that the feature of "localism" previously noted among Plan judges in Jackson County and St. Louis City, declines as one ascends the judicial hierarchy. The trend since the adoption of the Plan at the circuit level is toward a birthplace within the judicial district; for the courts of appeals, it is in the direction of a birthplace within Missouri but outside the judicial district; while, for the Supreme Court, it is toward an out-of-state birthplace. However, despite these trends in the two periods studied, Plan judges who serve on the various benches are still primarily Missouri-born. The table further shows that Democratic gains have occurred in the partisan composition of the three levels of courts since the adoption of the Plan, with such gains being most pronounced on the circuit courts. At this level, the majority party enjoys a 3-to-1 ratio in Plan appointments, while it approximates a 2-to-1 ratio for the appellate benches.

Table 6.3 shows with respect to career background that the Plan has had its greatest impact on prior judicial service. As previously discussed, such experience has declined among circuit judges since 1940, but it has risen considerably among judges of the two levels of appellate tribunals: over half of those appointed to the intermediate courts of appeal and 7 of 10 of the Supreme Court appointees under the Plan

TABLE 6.4

BACKGROUND CHARACTERISTICS OF MISSOURI JUDGES IN JURISDICTIONS
ADOPTING THE PLAN BY LEVEL OF COURT
AND PERIOD WHEN SELECTED (PERCENT)

Characteristic	Circuit Courts[a]		Courts of Appeals		Supreme Court	
	(N = 75) Pre-Plan	(N = 34) Post-Plan	(N = 22) Pre-Plan	(N = 14) Post-Plan	(N = 24) Pre-Plan	(N = 10) Post-Plan
Age						
Under 40	28	18	9	7	17	0
40–49	33	32	27	36	25	0
50–59	17	47	14	43	17	90
60 and over	16	3	27	14	16	10
Not ascertained	6	0	23	0	25	0
Total	100	100	100	100	100	100
Legal Education						
Prestige	11	6	0	0	0	20
Other outstate	9	3	32	14	25	20
Instate—full-time	33	41	32	36	33	50
Instate—night	33	44	8	36	0	10
Law office	14	6	28	14	42	0
Total	100	100	100	100	100	100
Birthplace						
In judicial district	40	47	50	43	67	70
Outside judicial district	24	29	9	36	0	0
Outside state	36	21	36	14	21	30
Not ascertained	0	3	5	7	12	0
Total	100	100	100	100	100	100
Party Affiliation						
Republican	40	26	41	36	33	30
Democrat	60	74	59	64	59	70
Not ascertained	0	0	0	0	8	0
Total	100	100	100	100	100	100
Judicial Experience						
Minor court	9	3	0	0	4	0
Court of record	19	6	36	57	50	70
None	72	91	64	50	50	30
Political Experience						
Law enforcement	36	47	64	36	50	80
Legislative	11	0	18	14	13	10
Other	3	18	9	0	8	10
None	53	41	27	64	42	20
Officeholding at Time of Selection						
Judicial office	8	3	18	50	42	50
Political office	13	12	9	0	8	0
Total judicial or political	21	15	27	50	50	50

[a] The Circuit Courts are those of Jackson County and St. Louis City.

have previously served on a court of record. Those with previous law-enforcement experience have become more prevalent on the circuit and Supreme Court benches and less numerous at the intermediate level of the state judiciary. Prior legislative experience has declined among judges of all three courts, even though it was not a prominent feature in the backgrounds of the pre-Plan judges either. The table also indicates that it has become a fairly common practice under the Plan to move lower court judges directly from such positions to an appellate court. At the same time, a similiar movement from other public offices to an appellate judicial post does not occur under the Plan, even though a fairly high percentage of such judges have held law-enforcement positions at one time.

A summary assessment of the impact of the Plan on the Missouri judiciary indicates that it has pushed the age at which lawyers go on the bench upward, and it has also made prior judicial service a more important feature of an appellate judge's experience. Moreover, it has not affected the essentially parochial character of the Missouri bench; judges appointed under the Plan are even more likely than the former elective ones to have been born in the state and to have received their legal education there—many of them in local night law schools. The partisan composition of the state judiciary has not become more balanced; instead, the majority Democratic party has increased its judicial representation, although perhaps not as much as it might have done if the elective system had been retained for the two large city circuits and the state's appellate bench.[28]

TENURE OF MISSOURI JUDGES

Disagreements concerning the nature of the function that judges perform in a political system create conflicting ideas regarding not only their method of selection but also the conditions that should surround their tenure of office. Democratic theory deliberately creates an insecure term for

---

[28] An analysis of the partisan composition of the counties comprising the three courts of appeals jurisdictions revealed that only in the Springfield division are the Republicans dominant politically. As far as the Supreme Court is concerned, an article by Stuart Nagel entitled "Unequal Party Representation on State Supreme Courts," *Journal of the American Judicature Society*, 45 (1961), 62–66, indicates that at the time of his study, the Republican party had a better representation on the Missouri Supreme Court than it did on the highest benches of most of the southern and border states. (The Supreme Courts of the 17 states included in this combined category were dominated by the Democrats by a 92 to 88 percent margin.)

officeholders: they are forced periodically to go before the people in contested elections and to receive a vote of confidence if they are to continue to exercise political power and leadership. However, the judiciary constitutes a somewhat special case: a feeling persists among many persons that its members should enjoy a considerable amount of independence in their work, and that they should not be held directly accountable for their actions to the electorate as are major executive and legislative officials. Moreover, this reasoning suggests that in order to make judicial independence meaningful, security in office must be created to insulate judges against removal because of the unpopularity of their decisions.

This latter sentiment permeated the thinking of the individuals who developed the Nonpartisan Court Plan, and it continues to be the foundation of the secure tenure that Plan judges have enjoyed over the years. However, as the following discussion indicates, a similar (though less explicit) rationale has shaped the tenure conditions associated with partisan judicial elections in the state. The remainder of this chapter is devoted to a comparative analysis of various aspects of the tenure situation of Plan and elective judges in Missouri.

Elections under the Plan

As previously suggested, the founders of the Nonpartisan Court Plan were interested in freeing judicial candidates from the acceptance of financial contributions and political support from party leaders and pressure groups, obligations which they feared might create the potential for favored treatment of those interests by the judges concerned. They also felt that political campaigning not only constituted an undignified activity for a judge but also required an investment of time and energy that might better be devoted to the work of the courts. At the same time, the general ideology of democracy, together with the practical necessity of obtaining the consent of the voters to the Plan, required that the general populace be given some role in determining who would sit on the bench.

As already noted, the procedure that was developed to meet these conditions was a noncompetitive election in which all judges appointed under the Plan (as well as those who were elected to the bench and were held over in office when the new system went into effect) would be required, after a period of judicial service, to go before the people and obtain their consent to retention in office. Such elections would, however, involve no political opponents, and the electorate would merely decide on the basis of the judge's record whether he should remain on the bench. As the Plan operates in Missouri,[29] a judge, after serving for at least a twelve-month period, merely files with the Secretary of State his intention to become a candidate to succeed himself in office. At the next general election after that period, his name (without party designation) appears on a separate judicial ballot with the eligible voters indicating by a "Yes" or "No" notation whether he shall be retained. If a majority of those voting on a judge cast an affirmative ballot, his service continues for another term; if he does not receive such a vote, a vacancy is created for his judgeship and the selection process of the Plan is put into motion to fill it.

As might be expected, this particular feature of the Plan has been severely criticized by some opponents of the Plan who charge that such elections are specious, and actually constitute plebiscites similar to those that usually operate in authoritarian regimes.[30] The typical comment is that "You can't beat someone with no one" or, as one writer has suggested, ". . . in political combat, as in speed contests among horses, the outcome becomes doubtful only after the entry of the second contestant."[31] Critics also accuse the Plan's supporters of inconsistency in their assumptions concerning the capacity of the electorate: if the voters are not able to determine who is capable of serving on the bench, how can they be expected to pass judgment on whether a particular judge should be retained in office?[32] The supporters of the Plan retort that while it is true that most judges will obtain an affirmative vote, the elections make it possible for an incompetent or corrupt judge to be removed from office by the voters. They also argue that while the voters generally do not have the necessary information and capacity to predict which lawyers will make good judges, they are able to evaluate a man's judicial ability on the basis of his actual performance on the bench during a probationary period.[33]

Putting aside the merits of these arguments, there is no question that the system operates to remove two major factors that students of political behavior have identified as influencing how persons vote: partisan affilia-

[*] *Constitution of the State of Missouri*, 1945, Art. V, Sec. 29 (c).

[*] See Frances D. Wormuth and S. Grover Rich, Jr., "Politics, the Bar and the Selection of Judges" *Utah Law Review*, 3 (1953), pp. 459 ff., reprinted in Walter F. Murphy and C. Herman Pritchett, *Courts, Judges and Politics* (New York: Random House, 1961), at pp. 105–111.

[*] See Warren Burnett, "Observations on the Direct-Election Method of Judicial Selection," *Texas Law Review*, 44 (1966), 1099.

[*] See George J. Moran, "Counter Missouri Plan for Selecting Judges," *Florida Bar Journal*, 32 (1958), 471–477.

[*] Winters, *op. cit.*, p. 565.

tion and their reactions to the rival candidates.[34] Moreover, although the third main determinant of voting behavior—the public's assessment of issues (in this case, in the form of decisions of incumbent judges)— remains as a potential factor, both the low level of public information on the subject and the fact that the discussion of such matters lies beyond the "rules of the game" in judicial elections[35] means that this factor is also of minimal importance in helping persons decide how to vote in elections under the Plan.

There are some potential influences present, however, which could serve to fill the vacuum in voting behavior in Plan elections created by the removal of the traditional factors of party, candidates, and issues. One such influence is that of the Bar itself. As previously indicated, the legal profession for a number of years has sought to make its voice heard in judicial elections by means of referenda in which Bar Associations poll their members on the merits of the various candidates, and then pass on the results of such polls to the electorate for its consideration. This device appears to be particularly promising in the context of the Plan elections, since such recommendations do not have to overcome the influence of party considerations which have served to limit the effectiveness of the Bar poll in elective systems.

The members of the legal profession in Missouri have recognized the importance of providing voters information on how the Bar feels about the capabilities of the various judges. In the early years of the Plan, the rival Bar Associations in Kansas City and St. Louis conducted separate polls that occasionally resulted in the electorate's receiving conflicting advice on some judges.[36] To avoid this possibility, and to regularize the gathering of lawyers' attitudes on the judges, beginning with the 1948 elections, the Missouri Bar Association (the official body of the state Bar) has conducted a poll among all lawyers practicing in the jurisdictions affected by the Plan. The polls involve sending ballots to these lawyers several weeks before the general election, listing all judges who are up for reelection, and asking them simply to indicate

---

[34] Party affiliation is considered to be the more important factor. For a thorough analysis of the voting behavior of Americans in Presidential elections, see Angus Campbell, Phillip Converse, Warren Miller and Donald Stokes, *The American Voter* (New York: John Wiley and Sons, 1960).

[35] For an excellent discussion of the effect of such rules in judicial elections, see Jack Ladinsky and Allan Silver, "Popular Democracy and Judicial Independence: Electorate and Elite Reactions to Two Wisconsin Supreme Court Elections." *Wisconsin Law Review* (1967), 128–169, reprinted as Number 22 in *The Law and Society Series* of the University of Wisconsin.

[36] As might be expected, the "plaintiffs'" bar associations were more likely to vote to retain "hold over" elective judges in office than were the "defendants'" groups.

by a "Yes" or "No" vote whether each of the judges should be retained in office. The ballots are mailed in sealed envelopes to the clerks of the respective courts. They are counted, and the results are published in newspapers prior to the elections.

However, an analysis of the results of these elections indicates that the official poll has provided little guidance for the electorate in deciding whether individual judges should be retained in office. In the period from 1948 to 1964, polls involving 75 separate trial and appellate judges were held; all the judges involved obtained a majority vote of approval from the Bar. Two received affirmative votes in the range of 50 to 60 percent, three in the 60 to 70 percent decile, and the remainder all scored 70 percent or better. Thus the Bar polls over the years indicate to the public that all the judges under the Plan should be retained in office, including these that were originally elected to the bench and were held over in office when the Plan went into effect in 1940.

The personal interviewees that we questioned about this matter gave several reasons for the high affirmative vote in the Bar polls. Some said it occurred because many lawyers are not convinced that the ballots are actually secret,[37] and do not want to risk casting a negative vote for fear that a judge may learn of their attitude toward him and may not give them fair treatment in his courtroom. Others suggested that a general sentiment exists among members of the Bar that once a lawyer gives up his practice to go on the bench, it is sort of "dirty pool" to turn him out of office and force him to build up a clientele again after most of his clients have taken their legal business elsewhere. Therefore, all doubts about a judge's capabilities are generally resolved in his favor. This means that unless an attorney, or a close associate, has an unsatisfactory personal experience with a judge, he tends to vote in favor of the judge's retention. Since most members of the Bar have relatively little trial experience, the perfunctory "Yes" votes predominate over the negative ballots of attorneys who are actually familiar with a judge's incompetency. The validity of these various suggestions is open to question, but the fact remains that the Bar poll has not been a discriminating one to which voters can turn for information on the merits of the incumbent judges who are up for reelection.

Another obvious source of potential influence in Plan elections is the press. Although newspapers often enjoy operating in situations that mini-

---

[37] Ballots are returned in sealed envelopes which, in turn, are placed inside return envelopes. Although the ballot envelopes are removed and segregated from the return envelopes, so as to prevent the identification of the two, and the opening process takes place before representatives of the press and Bar, some attorneys are uneasy about the fact that their names appear on the outside envelope.

mize the effect of political parties on public decisions (in part, at least, because this tends to increase their own role in the political process), an examination of the newspapers of the two major cities over the years of the Plan indicates that they seldom have attempted to influence the electorate to vote a judge out of office. Only in the Waltner incident described below, did the press launch an all-out effort at unseating an incumbent judge. In addition to this case, two other circuit judges in Kansas City, and three in St. Louis, have been criticized adversely in the press. (Three of the five were criticized for association with criminals, or for showing leniency in the treatment of criminal offenders in the matter of paroles, suspended sentences, etc.) In the overwhelming number of cases, however, the newspapers have merely reported the results of the Bar polls and elections, with the general comment that they reflect the high caliber of the judges. It is difficult to determine why the press has not played more of a watchdog role in such elections, but it may well be that the newspaper owners' basic commitment to the Plan causes them to avoid taking any action that might be construed as being critical of its operation. In this connection, it is interesting that no judge who has been appointed under the Nonpartisan Court Plan (in contrast to those who were held over in office) has ever been opposed or even commented on critically by the press in connection with Plan elections.

Another type of organization that can benefit from the absence of party labels on the judicial ballots are interest groups. However, we could discover very few incidents in which these groups took an overt role in attempting to prevent incumbent judges from being reelected to office. The most notable exception to this pattern of inactivity was the campaign described below, which was conducted by a citizen's group to unseat Judge Waltner in 1942. In addition, a group known as the Council for Community Preservation, which sought to prevent the entrance of Negro residents into certain neighborhoods in St. Louis, campaigned against two of the circuit judges in that area in 1946 because of decisions rendered by them against white plaintiffs in litigation attempting to exclude the Negroes. And, in 1956, certain A.F. of L. unions in the St. Louis area tried to defeat three Supreme Court judges who were up for reelection that year because of certain decisions of the Court which the labor leaders considered to be antilabor in nature.[38]

---

[38] There were reports that the labor organizations went so far as to distribute sample ballots to their members indicating what they had to do to vote "No" against the Supreme Court judges involved. No attempt was made to defeat other Plan judges up for reelection that year.

However, except for this one instance, labor has made no attempt to campaign against the reelection of judges, even though as a movement, it claims publicly to be opposed to the Plan, and to favor popular elections of members of the bench. When questioned about the matter in a personal interview, one of the state labor leaders explained that working to unseat Plan judges was "like trying to move city hall; there is no point to it," and that labor can expend its efforts more fruitfully in other areas of public affairs.

In the absence of the familiar voting clues of party, candidate, and issues, and with the failure of the Bar, of the press, and of interest groups to play a significant role in assessing the capabilities of the various judges, it is not surprising that the Plan elections have, indeed, been plebiscites rather than meaningful decisions by the electorate. During the period from 1942 to 1964, 179 separate elections were held involving 87 different judges; only one candidate (Judge Waltner) has ever been voted out of office, and he came within a few percentage points (46.4 percent, affirmative vote) of receiving the majority vote necessary to remain on the bench. No other judge has come close to being defeated, and only 7 of them have failed to obtain at least a 70-percent favorable vote. Moreover, the trend over the years has been in the direction of higher majorities; the one negative vote occurred in 1942, the first year that Plan elections were conducted, and the 7 elections mentioned above were all restricted to the first three Plan election years of 1942, 1944, and 1946. The new era, commencing with the 1948 elections when the voters began to give such strong support to all the candidates, coincides with the advent of the official Bar poll which also approved every one of the judges up for reelection.

A closer analysis of the election data also indicates that the voters have not been very discriminating in their ballots on individual judges. The overwhelming proportion of the judges poll majorities in the 80 to 90 percent range, and only occasionally does the affirmance rate fall into the 70 to 80 percent category. There are no marked differences in the voting results for circuit and appellate judges (the average affirmance rates for the two groups of judges are 82 and 78 percent, respectively), nor between circuit judges in St. Louis City and Jackson County (the comparable figures are 83 and 78 percent, respectively). These results lead us to conclude that there is a core of voter resistance to the Plan in general which consists of about one-fifth of those casting judicial ballots, and it makes little difference which particular judges are up for reelection; all of them tend to receive about the same response from the electorate.

As might be expected, there is also considerable voter apathy concerning the elections as evidenced by the fact that the number of persons casting ballots in judicial elections is considerably lower than the number that votes for other public officials who are running in the same elections.[39] This has caused some supporters of the Plan to fear that groups which are opposed to it generally (or to particular judges because of their decisions) can take advantage of the light vote in such elections to mount a concerted campaign that will lead to the defeat of the judges concerned.[40] However, as the above results indicate, this has occurred only once in the history of the Plan. An analysis of that particular incident provides some insight into the kinds of circumstances that must be present in order to overcome the forces that operate to perpetuate Plan judges in office.

The Defeat of Judge Waltner

Along with the previously discussed Donnelly incident, the removal of Judge Marion Waltner from the Jackson County circuit bench by the voters in 1942 has become a *cause célèbre* of the Nonpartisan Court Plan. Plan supporters applaud the incident as a demonstration of the fact that an incompetent and intemperate judge can be removed under the elections provided for under the Plan; Waltner's defenders are just as adamant in their opinion that a "good" judge was railroaded out of office simply because he incurred the wrath of a number of conservative vested interests in the Jackson County area. It is difficult to arrive at a judgment on the merits of the case about twenty-five years after it occurred; but, for our purposes, the important consideration is not whether the various charges and countercharges of the two sides of the controversy are true but, instead, how persons at the time regarded the incident. To get an insight into this latter consideration, we examined the newspaper accounts of the events, leading up to Waltner's removal, and then interviewed some of the major principals involved in the dispute, including Judge Waltner himself.

---

[39] For example, the two Supreme Court Justices who were up for reelection in 1964, received some 54 percent of the votes cast in the Attorney General's race that year. The Jackson County circuit judges as a group polled 45 percent of the Attorney General's ballots, while in St. Louis City, the circuit judges' vote total fell to 37 percent of the latter figure.

[40] The St. Louis Bar Association called for its members to stimulate voting for judges in the 1950 elections as a means of making the Nonpartisan Plan work. The President of the Association warned that, "When only half of the persons voting in recent elections cast their judicial ballot, they are inviting punitive raids on the Judiciary by partisan groups." *St. Louis Post Dispatch*, October 28, 1950.

An analysis of the incident indicates that the various forces described above, which are normally absent or quiescent in Plan elections, were brought to the surface by the particular circumstances of the case. Although no party label appeared beside Judge Waltner's name on the ballot, he was prominently identified in the newspapers and in political circles as a member of the Pendergast organization. He had been a precinct captain in this party faction at one time, and was originally appointed to the circuit bench in 1934 by Governor Park as a favor to Pendergast. His connection with the organization continued to receive public notice when he was charged with choosing a number of Pendergast men to serve on two grand juries during 1940 and 1941.[41] Also, the press carried accounts during the 1942 election to the effect that the organization had passed the word to its party lieutenants to work for the reelection of Judge Waltner to the circuit bench.[42]

It would be a mistake, however, to attribute Waltner's defeat to his identification with the Pendergast organization alone; other judges who got on the bench through its efforts were reelected to office under the Plan. Judge Waltner also incurred the enmity of a number of prominent attorneys, particularly those who represented the Kansas City Public Service Company. A dispute arose over changes of venue which were sought by the company's lawyers who considered Waltner to be prejudiced against their client; ultimately the matter was taken before the Supreme Court where a commissioner appointed by the Court found that Waltner was actually prejudiced against the Kansas City Public Service Company and recommended that two damage suits filed against the company not be tried in his court.[43] Beyond this incident, allegations were made that Judge Waltner was abusive of attorneys representing the company and of other lawyers who sought changes of venue from his court. He was also accused of criticizing the efforts of some attorneys to get their business-firm clients to encourage their employees to serve on juries by paying them their regular salaries during the period of such service. The judge denied that he mistreated lawyers in his court, and defended his criticism of the jury-service practice on the grounds that it tended to place on juries persons who were sympathetic to the point of view of business.

The Waltner case split the Bar down the middle. A number of attorneys appeared at the hearings held in connection with the change of venue matter to testify that he was an impartial judge. Moreover, he

<hr />

[41] *Kansas City Star,* October 26, 1942.
[42] *Kansas City Times,* October 29, 1942. (The *Times* is the morning edition of the paper; it has the same ownership as *The Star.*)
[43] *Kansas City Star,* July 9, 1942.

received an affirmative vote (270 to 172) in a poll conducted by the Kansas City Bar Association to determine whether he should be retained in office. In marked contrast, another such poll, held by the Lawyers' Association of Kansas City, resulted in a 187 to 47 ballot against him.[44] Thus the plaintiffs'-defendants' division in the Bar had direct relevance for lawyers' attitudes on Judge Waltner. Political overtones were also present in this Bar division, since there was a feeling that lawyers close to the Pendergast organization were more prominent in the Kansas City Bar Association (some attorneys suggested that they controlled it in his behalf) than they were in the Lawyers' Association of that city.

The Kansas City Star which, as suggested above, has usually taken a "hands-off" position in Plan elections, also openly entered the controversy by publishing anti-Waltner accounts of the dispute and by urging voters not to retain him in office. The newspaper coverage of the matter was particularly heavy in the month immediately preceding the elections. Some persons that we interviewed attributed the paper's great interest in the Waltner case to the fact that the same law firm that represented the Public Service Company also handled the legal affairs of *The Star*. Others connected it with the paper's long-time feud with the Pendergast organization, as well as its staff's considered judgment that Waltner was not worthy of judicial service and that his mere presence on the bench tended to discredit the Plan. But whatever the motives of the Star's owners might have been, parties on both sides of the dispute gave the newspaper considerable credit (or blame) for helping to bring about Judge Waltner's defeat.

One final force that entered the picture were interest groups. A citizens' group composed of 45 business and professional men and women was formed to lead a campaign to bring about Waltner's defeat.[45] Known as "The Committee for the Rejection of Judge Marion D. Waltner," the group leveled a series of charges (primarily the ones discussed above) against the judge, which were carried in *The Star*. Directly opposing this business-oriented organization in the election was the Central Labor Union, representing 135 A.F. of L. unions, which unanimously voted to endorse Judge Waltner, and asked all persons connected with organized labor in Jackson County to work in behalf of his vindication and reelection.[46]

The Waltner case, then, was unique in setting into motion a number of forces (political, legal, as well as those of the press and the economic

---

[44] *Kansas City Star,* October 28, 1942.
[45] *Kansas City Times,* October 22, 1942.
[46] *Ibid.,* October 28, 1942.

community), all of which converged on the question of his reelection to the bench. It involved not just the fate of one judge, but carried within it the imprint of all the social forces and conflicting values that contended initially over the establishment of the Plan. The case represented an important victory for the Plan movement because, along with the defeat of the previously-discussed Lauf amendment at the same election, it demonstrated that the newly-conceived system was secure against attempts of its enemies to destroy it before it became firmly established. But precisely because the Waltner case involved such larger issues, it does not really demonstrate that under more normal circumstances, judges can be removed from office under the procedure of the Plan.

Partisan Elections of Judges in Missouri

In contrast to judges selected under the Nonpartisan Court Plan, those who run on partisan ballots face the prospect of electoral defeat at the hands of rival candidates in either the primary or general election. The kinds of problems that this presents for an incumbent judge are described by a judicial candidate in Davis' study of judicial selection in West Virginia. As one judge put it:

All in all, it's a harrowing experience to have to go through a political campaign for a judgeship to succeed yourself when you have arrived at an age that any thought of trying to practice law again is frightening and after you have given so many years to being neutral that your skill as an advocate has all but left you, and when you have held an office that does not, because of the smallness of the salary, permit you to build up an estate to tide you on, and when you have developed the fault of being so proud that it would be repulsive to you to beg or to sell pencils on the street. You reach the place where you could well feel that you just had to win. And this is not a wholesome attitude to be in for one has to maintain his dignity and equilibrium in all areas of being fair and unprejudiced.[47]

While feelings of insecurity undoubtedly plague many popularly elected judges who must periodically go before the electorate to have their terms of office renewed, studies of such elections in a number of states indicate that these fears are usually unfounded; incumbent judges are seldom defeated in electoral contests. Moreover, the studies indicate that in many instances judicial elections are not even contested. Although state data on the matter are incomplete, the same situation has been found to apply in a variety of electoral contexts, including

---

[47] Davis, op. cit., p. 37.

states using both nonpartisan and partisan ballots to select judges; it also characterizes partisan judicial elections in one-party states, as well as those in more competitive jurisdictions.[48]

To determine the nature of competition in partisan judicial contests in Missouri, we investigated both primary and general elections. The analysis includes the electoral situation in the Jackson County and St. Louis City circuits and the appellate judicial races in the quarter-century preceding the institution of the Plan in 1940, as well as contests in St. Louis County and outstate circuits in comparable periods preceding and following that date. The degree of competition in the primary and general election is divided into four categories: "uncontested;" "token opposition," which is used to describe the situation in which the combined vote of opponents of the incumbent judge is less than one-third of the total vote cast; "serious opposition," which represents a situation in which the combined opposition vote amounts to more than one-third of the total ballot cast;[49] and "defeat," which means that the incumbent judge was beaten. Since we were concerned with the electoral situation faced by popularly-elected judges vis à vis those chosen under the Plan, we disregarded those elections in which judges were originally chosen

<hr />

[48] For an analysis of nonpartisan judicial elections in Wisconsin, see Herbert Jacob, "Judicial Insulation–Elections, Direct Participation, and Public Attention to the Courts in Wisconsin," *Wisconsin Law Review* (1966), 801–819. Malcolm Moos analyzes similar elections in Minnesota in his article, "Judicial Elections and Partisan Endorsement of Judicial Candidates in Minnesota," *The American Political Science Review,* 35 (1941), 69–75. Henderson and Sinclair, op. cit., and Vines, op. cit., came to similar conclusions in their analysis of one-party judicial politics in Texas and Louisiana, as does John Wood in Oklahoma in his article, "Reform of Judicial Selection Procedures in Oklahoma" (Oklahoma Bar Association, 1964). Kenneth Vines in his chapter, "Courts as Political and Governmental Agencies," which appears in a book by him and Jacob entitled, *Politics in the American States: A Comparative Analysis* (Boston: Little, Brown and Company, 1965), at p. 265, presents data on judicial elections in Kansas and Tennessee which also indicate a lack of competition in these one-party states. Davis, op. cit., reports a similar occurrence in the more competitive state of West Virginia, while Wallace Sayre and Herbert Kaufman indicate that the same general development occurs in the two-party state of New York. See their *Governing New York City* (New York: Russel Sage Foundation, 1960), p. 534 f.

[49] We used the same criteria for determining degree of electoral competition which Julius Turner employed in his analysis of nomination contests in Congressional elections. See his article, "Primary Elections as the Alternative to Party Competition in 'Safe' Districts," *The Journal of Politics,* 15 (1953), 197–210. However, many persons would probably regard a 40 or 45 percent vote for the losing person or persons as necessary to constitute a serious threat to the incumbent, at least in general election races. Therefore, our analysis may, if anything, make some of the judicial general elections appear more competitive than they really are.

for the bench; thus our analysis is restricted to contests in which judges already in office (whether by prior election or by gubernatorial appointment) sought to remain on the bench.

Table 6.5, which contains the data on partisan contests for circuit judgeships in Missouri, reveals a fairly high degree of competition between the two major parties for seats on the lower court bench. The competition has been particularly spirited in the St. Louis area; incumbents in city elections prior to the institution of the Plan, as well as county elections in both periods studied, faced serious competition from contenders of the opposite political party. Moreover, in about one of three elections held during the early period, judges were actually defeated in their efforts to remain on the bench. During this same era, Jackson County and outstate incumbents also met considerable opposition from contenders in the opposition party, and were actually unseated in more than one of five elections. Of the various groups studied, only the judges who went on the trial bench in the outstate areas in the period since 1940 have generally escaped serious competition in judicial elections. Apparently, it is only in such jurisdictions that a kind of gentleman's agreement has developed whereby the parties agree not to oppose each other's incumbents in judicial races.[50]

The table also shows, however, that while competition usually has been the prevailing pattern in general elections for trial judges in Missouri, incumbents have not been seriously threatened by rival candidates from their own party. The major exceptions to this situation were the St. Louis area judges in the early period (particularly those in the city, but judges in the county as well), who encountered major opposition in their own primaries.[51] However, this intraparty competition has waned in the county in the more recent period, and judges there typically are concerned with threats to their incumbency only in general elections. There has also been a decline in primary competition for outstate judgeships during this latter era.

An analysis of competition for seats on the appellate bench in the period from 1917 through 1940 shows the same general patterns as prevailed in this period for circuit judgeships. All of the Supreme Court judges and the intermediate courts of appeals judges faced serious competition in general elections: in fact, 7 of the 12 elections to the highest court

[50] Davis, and Sayre and Kaufman, op. cit., report the existence of such agreements in some areas of West Virginia and New York.
[51] One possible reason for the greater primary competition in the St. Louis area is that in the earlier period, judges in the City and County (both of which had multiple divisions), ran "at large" rather than by divisions. In contrast, those in Jackson County contested by division, while most outstate circuits were single-judge circuits.

TABLE 6.5

Competition in Partisan Judicial Elections[a] for Circuit Judges in Missouri by Geographical Location and Period When Selected for Court[b] (Percent)

Election	Jackson County (N = 24) 1st Period	Jackson County (N = 0)[c] 2nd Period	St. Louis City (N = 50) 1st Period	St. Louis City (N = 0)[c] 2nd Period	St. Louis County (N = 7) 1st Period	St. Louis County (N = 24) 2nd Period	Outstate (N = 97) 1st Period	Outstate (N = 106) 2nd Period
Primary								
Unopposed	79	—	0	—	29	76	74	88
Token Opposition[d]	17	—	0	—	29	12	5	2
Serious Opposition[e]	4	—	84	—	29	12	18	7
Incumbent defeated	0	—	16	—	13	0	3	3
Total	100	—	100	—	100	100	100	100
General Election								
Unopposed	4	—	0	—	0	0	36	75
Token Opposition[d]	54	—	0	—	0	4	1	0
Serious Opposition[e]	21	—	65	—	67	92	39	17
Incumbent defeated	21	—	35	—	33	4	24	8
Total	100	—	100	—	100	100	100	100

[a] Does not include election in which incumbent first went on bench. Also does not include elections involving judges whose tenure spanned both periods of study.

[b] The first period is 1917 to 1940. The second is 1941 to 1964.

[c] Plan judges not subject to partisan elections.

[d] Combined vote of opponents of incumbent is less than one-third of total vote.

[e] Combined vote of opponents of incumbent is one-third or more of total vote.

ended in the defeat of incumbents, while 4 of the 12 intermediate court races resulted in the unseating of judges on this bench. Thus, if anything, the competition in general elections was stiffer than that which generally prevailed in circuit court races.[52] In contrast, only 1 in every 3 intraparty contests at both levels of the appellate bench saw the incumbent face serious competition from a member of his own party, and in no instance was a sitting judge defeated in a primary election.

An overall analysis of partisan judicial elections in Missouri indicates that competition in such races has generally been greater than that found in other states. At the same time, the trend in both St. Louis County and the outstate areas has been in the direction of fewer and less meaningful contests in both primary and general elections. This means that, to an increasing extent, the tenure of Missouri judges has been terminated by causes other than defeat at the polls. Other procedures that end judicial careers are discussed below.

Removal, Retirement, and Resignation of Judges

In addition to death in office, three nonelectoral means by which judicial services are terminated are removal, retirement, and resignation. Each of these methods can take several forms; for example, judges can resign from office under pressure, seek another public position, or return to the private practice of law. Moreover, the procedures are closely related to each other, and often it is difficult to assign a particular instance by which a judge leaves the bench to one of the three categories. Thus, a judge's resignation under pressure, or his forced retirement, may actually constitute an indirect means of removing him from the bench. Because of these interrelationships and complexities, all three of the procedures are dealt with together. Our discussion provides background information for the final section of the chapter, which gives a statistical analysis of the particular circumstances that resulted in judges leaving the bench in Missouri.

There is no unique method for *removing* trial and appellate judges from the bench in Missouri. They come under the same general provisions regarding impeachment as all elective executive officials of the state, that is, they are subject to being charged by the state House of Representatives with "crimes, misconduct, habitual drunkenness, wilful neglect of duty, corruption in office, incompetency, or any offense involving moral turpitude or oppression in office," and subsequently being

---

[52] Henderson and Sinclair, Jacob, and Wood, *op. cit.*, report the same situation in judicial elections in Texas, Wisconsin, and Oklahoma, respectively.

tried by the state Supreme Court.[53] But despite the potentialities of the impeachment weapon for removing public officials, the Missouri experience, like that of other jurisdictions,[54] indicates that the remedy is too drastic to be effective. This is evidenced by the fact it has seldom been used—a total of about *six* instances in the history of the state. A recent impeachment case involved a circuit judge in St. Louis County who was accused of filing a fraudulent state income tax return, tampering with a grand jury, and borrowing money from an attorney who had won a favorable judgment in his court. In 1963, the Missouri House of Representatives voted impeachment charges against him, but he resigned five days before his trial was to have begun in the Supreme Court. Thus impeachment did result in the indirect removal of one judge from office during our period of study. The only instance of direct removal from judicial office during this time occurred when a judge of an outstate circuit was ousted as a result of conviction for a crime.

Retirement from the bench occurs in various ways. One is the simple decision of a candidate not to seek reelection for political reasons. More often, however, retirement is related to the factors of age and health. Under the Missouri Constitution, all judges of the Supreme Court and the intermediate courts of appeal must retire at the age of 75.[55] There is no compulsory retirement age for lower court judges, but they, along with all other judges in the state (including appellate ones), can retire voluntarily at age 65, provided that they have served for six continuous years prior to 1959 or have a total twelve years service. Following voluntary retirement, or that connected with reaching the statutory age, judges receive a pension of one-third of their final salary, but are forbidden to engage in the practice of law. They are subject, however, to being recalled for temporary duty as commissioners or referees, in which case they receive compensation during the period of their actual service.[56]

In view of the relatively modest retirement benefits (one-third of the salaries of $19,000, $21,500, and $22,500 for circuit judges, courts of appeals, and Supreme Court judges, respectively),[57] and the strictures

---

[53] *Constitution of the State of Missouri*, 1945, Art. VIII, Secs. 1 and 2. If the governor, or a member of the Supreme Court is involved, a special commission of seven "eminent" jurists is elected by the state senate to hear the case.

[54] For a discussion of judicial removal, see Jack E. Frankel, "Removal of Judges, Federal and State," *Journal of the American Judicature Society*, 48 (1965), 177–183, and an article by the same author entitled, "Judicial Discipline and Removal," which appears in *The Texas Law Review, op. cit.,* 1117–1135.

[55] *Constitution of the State of Missouri*, 1945, Art. V, Sec. 25.

[56] *Revised Statutes of Missouri*, 1959, Sec. 476.450 et. seq.

[57] In lesser populated circuits of Missouri, the salary for circuit judges is $16,000 rather than $19,000, unless the counties concerned choose to make up the difference out of their own funds. *Revised Statutes of Missouri*, 1959, Sec. 478.013.

against supplementing such income through private practice, it is not surprising that appellate judges under the mandatory retirement age of 75, and trial judges of more advanced years, have not been inclined to voluntarily step down from the bench. The constitution of 1945 did create a Committee on Retirement of Judges and Magistrates composed of nine judges, which is empowered to retire any judges unable to discharge the duties of their office because of sickness or physical or mental infirmity of a permanent nature.[58] However, as Braithwaite, a close student of the subject, has indicated, the committee from its inception took the position that it could not move on its own motion, but had to wait until information was filed in writing either by a judge himself or by some third party.[59] In the decade following the creation of the committee, it was not very active, since judges themselves were not generally inclined to come forward to seek retirement, and attorneys were not disposed to take the initiative in such a delicate matter as forcing a senior citizen of the legal profession from the bench.

In time, the state Bar Association decided to take action to convert the Judges' Committee on Retirement into a meaningful body. By resolution of its Board of Governors adopted on September 10, 1954, the association created its own Committee on Judicial Retirement, which was authorized to investigate cases of alleged incapacity for judicial service, and if it found such incapacity to exist, to file a formal information with the Judges' Committee. Thus the Bar committee took upon itself the responsibility for activating the procedure for forced retirement provided for by the Committee of Judges.

Since that date, the Bar Committee has worked out a *modus operandi* for dealing with the delicate problem of getting judges who are unable to carry on their duties for health reasons to retire from the bench. The seven-man body (it was expanded from five members in 1963), which contains a balance of members from various geographical areas of the state, works through such members to obtain information on judges from their particular areas who are reported to be incapacitated for judicial duties. If, after checking with attorneys who appear in the concerned judge's court, or on occasion with his doctor, it is determined that he is unable to carry out his judicial responsibilities, attempts are

---

[58] *Constitution of the State of Missouri,* 1945, Art. V, Sec. 27, and Supreme Court Rule 12.

[59] William Braithwaite, Research Attorney for the American Bar Foundation, is currently conducting a comparative study of the problems of judicial removal and retirement in the United States. He very graciously made available to us prior to the publication of his study, the data he gathered in Missouri on these matters. We have relied heavily on his data in discussing the operation of the system that has evolved for retiring judges who are incapacitated for their duties.

made to persuade the judge to retire from the bench. The particular committee member involved may call upon the judge himself to accomplish this result, or he may attempt to work through the judge's family, colleagues, or friends to that end. In the event that such overtures do not bring the action desired, the committee always has the "shotgun behind the door" in the nature of a threat to file an information with the Committee of Judges, and thus to set the formal proceeding on retirement into motion. However, out of deference to the dignity of the judges involved, as well as a desire to avoid any appearance that it is too zealous in its efforts, or is acting beyond the bounds of propriety, the committee has never chosen to file such an information. In some cases, it has waited almost a year for a judge himself to act, and in one instance the individual involved did so just fifteen minutes before the time at which the committee threatened to file its own information in his case.

Braithwaite's study of the work of this Bar Committee indicates that its approach has generally been effective in persuading judges with health problems to step down from the bench. An analysis of the official records of the Judges' Committee indicates that 30 judges in the state have been retired by the Committee for physical or mental incapacity, and in another 10 instances, the Committee did not take official action because the judges involved either died, or retired voluntarily prior to the time their cases reached the final stage.[60] Moreover, some judges decided to leave the bench voluntarily rather than go before the Committee at all, even though their retirement benefits are not as great if they pursue this course of action. (Judges who are retired by the Judges' Committee receive one-half of their salary for the remainder of their term, and one-third thereafter, while those whose cases do not go through the Committee are placed upon the one-third pension immediately upon retirement.) Thus some judges place pride before financial considerations, as far as their own retirement is concerned.

Despite the effective work of the Bar and Judges' Committees, it should be pointed out that they only have authority to deal with cases

---

[60] Of the 40 judges involved, half were Plan judges, (4 at the appellate level, 7 from the Jackson County Circuit Court, and 9 from the St. Louis City trial bench), even though such judges constituted only 22 percent of the state's total number of judges at the time Braithwaite conducted his study. He suggests that cases involving incapacitated judges in outstate circuits may be less likely to come to the attention of the Judges' Committee because attorneys and other concerned persons in less populated areas are more tolerant of litigation delay and are also more likely to be close personal friends of the judges involved. They may thus prefer to "make do" with a situation (such as having clerks, with the help of local attorneys, assume many of the judge's duties), rather than bring the matter to the Retirement Committee.

involving mental or physical incapacity. Like most states, Missouri has no effective remedy for removing judges from the bench for general incompetence or misconduct in office,[61] and as suggested in the following chapter, many attorneys consider this to be a major weakness of the Plan. The third major method by which a judge leaves the bench is by *resignation* of his post. Like retirement, the decision to resign may be prompted by several circumstances. One is resignation under pressure as occurred with respect to the St. Louis County judge previously discussed. Another is resignation for health reasons. A third is a decision to resign in order to take some other position. As indicated in Table 6.6, this occurs most frequently when judges resign to accept another judicial post, but on occasion they also decide to leave the bench for another type of governmental office or to return to the practice of law.

Circumstances Under Which Missouri Judges Have Left the Bench

As suggested above, the analysis of departures from the bench on the basis of removal, retirement, and resignation is not only confusing but also tells one very little about the particular circumstances that are associated with the termination of judicial careers. To get a clearer and fuller picture of why judges leave their posts, we divided the circumstances into four major categories: electoral, corruption charges, changes of career, and incapacity for their duties. The first category includes such matters as the decision not to seek reelection;[62] defeat in a primary or general election; or the failure to be retained under a Plan election.[63] Corruption involves criminal charges made against a judge which lead directly or indirectly to his leaving his position. Career changes refer

---

[61] In 1960, California created a Commission on Judicial Qualifications, consisting of 5 judges, 2 lawyers and 2 laymen, which has the power to recommend to the Supreme Court the removal or retirement of judges who cannot properly perform the duties of their office. In the period from 1960 to 1964, 344 complaints were filed with the Commission; the body directly caused the resignation or retirement of 26 judges. See Louis H. Burke, "Judical Discipline and Removal—the California Story," *Journal of the American Judicature Society,* 48 (February 1965), 167–173. (The entire issue of this journal is devoted to the subject of "judicial misconduct.") For comments on the problems of judicial removal by the Executive Director of the California Commission, see Frankel, *op. cit.*

[62] In some instances, it is not possible to determine from the state manuals why an incumbent judge chose not to seek reelection. It is conceivable in such cases that the decision may have been prompted by one of the other reasons we identified in Table 6.6. However, it should be noted that the problem is not a serious one, since the "not seek reelection" category is virtually nonexistent in the latter period, even in the St. Louis County and outstate circuits.

[63] It should be noted that while we previously analyzed electoral situations in Table 6.5, there the unit of analysis was elections, while in Table 6.6, it is judges.

TABLE 6.6

Tenure Circumstances of Circuit Judges in Missouri by Geographical Location and Period When Selected for Court (Percent)[a]

Circumstance	Jackson County 1st Period[b] (N = 21)	Jackson County 2nd Period[c] (N = 19)	St. Louis City 1st Period[b] (N = 54)	St. Louis City 2nd Period[c] (N = 15)	St. Louis County 1st Period[b] (N = 9)	St. Louis County 2nd Period[b] (N = 12)	Outstate 1st Period[b] (N = 87)	Outstate 2nd Period[b] (N = 78)
Still on Bench	5	57	9	72	0	84	2	50
Electoral								
Not seek reelection	5	0	13	0	22	0	23	7
Defeated in primary	0	—	13	—	11	0	9	4
Defeated in general election	28	—	26	—	45	8	31	10
Not retained under plan	5	0	0	0	—	—	—	—
Corruption								
Prison sentence	0	0	0	0	0	0	1	0
Impeachment	0	0	0	0	0	8	0	0
Career Change								
Other judicial post	5	11	6	14[d]	0	0	10	12
Other public post	5	0	0	0	0	0	1	0
Private practice	0	0	2	0	0	0	2	4
Incapacity								
Age or ill-health	15	11	14	7	0	0	4	4
Death	32	21	17	7	22	0	17	9
Total	100	100	100	100	100	100	100	100

[a] The first period is 1917 to 1940. The second is 1941 to 1964.
[b] Elective judges.
[c] Plan judges.
[d] One person in this group took an administrative position with a national association of judges. We placed him in the judicial post

238

to a judge's decision to seek or accept another public position, judicial or otherwise, or to return to the private practice of law. Finally, incapacity includes such matters as a judge's giving up his duties because of ill health or dying while still in office. Table 6.6 analyzes the relative importance of these various circumstances in terminating the judicial careers of circuit judges in Missouri. For comparative purposes, the judges are again categorized by the geographical area of the state in which they served and the period during which they went on the bench.

The table indicates that two of the general categories of circumstances have not been important factors in the departure of circuit judges from the bench. Scandals growing out of charges of criminal corruption have been virtually nonexistent in Missouri. Career changes have also had relatively little to do with judges leaving their positions. To the extent that such changes occur, they have done so almost entirely within the judiciary itself as persons sought or accepted positions at higher levels of the state system or, in some instances, federal court posts. Only two circuit judges during our period of study resigned their posts to seek some other elective office (one ran for governor and the other for a Congressional seat), and only a few have ever left the bench for private practice. Thus, in effect, a career judiciary has developed in Missouri. While it is most evident as far as Plan judges are concerned (none of them has ever resigned to seek another public post or to return to private practice), similar patterns have occurred under the partisan election system that was formerly employed in Jackson County and St. Louis City and continues to be used in St. Louis County and outstate circuits.

Table 6.6 also reveals the decline in the importance of electoral circumstances in eliminating incumbent judges. While this is to be expected under the plebiscites by which Plan judges are retained in office, it is also interesting to note that fewer elective judges in St. Louis County and outstate circuits in the latter period left the bench due to defeats in primary or general elections. The major circumstance that remains as a potential factor in ending judicial careers is incapacity but, as the table also shows, relatively few judges left the bench in the latter period for this general reason, and the ones who did were more likely to have died in office rather than to have relinquished their duties for reasons of ill health or advanced age. The data also indicate that a considerable number of judges who went on the bench sometime during the recent period still remained in office at the end of 1964. Thus the major conclusion derived from the table is that circuit judges in Missouri consider the judiciary a permanent career, that they have secure tenure, and that many of them remain on the bench until their deaths.

A similar analysis of the tenure circumstances of appellate judges in Missouri, selected both before and after the adoption of the Plan, shows generally the same situation as prevailed for members of the state's trial bench. None of the upper court judges has ever been forced off the bench because of corruption charges. The appellate judiciary has been even more of a permanent career than the lower court judiciary: none of the judges has ever sought another type of elective office; only three of them (all of whom went on the bench in the period before the institution of the Plan) have ever returned to private practice; and the same limited number of appellate judges have resigned their positions in the state judicial system to accept appointments on the federal bench. Moreover, the considerable degree of electoral uncertainty that appellate judges faced in the earlier period (one of four did not seek reelection and one in five was defeated in the general election) has been eliminated in favor of the plebiscites held under the Plan. The end result is again what amounts to life tenure on the Missouri bench, although proportionately more appellate than circuit judges left the bench for reasons related to incapacity, perhaps because they are required by law to retire at age 75. Their somewhat more advanced age at time of appointment (see Table 6.4) means that appellate judges selected in the latter period were more likely to have died by the end of 1964 than were trial judges who also went on the bench some time between 1941 and that date.

Our analysis of the general background and tenure situation of Plan and elective judges thus indicates that, while variances exist between the two sets of judges, in many respects the similarities in these matters outweigh the differences.[64] Our study now shifts to a broader type of inquiry, and one that involves not objective facts but rather subjective perceptions, namely, attitudes of lawyers in the state on methods of selecting judges.

---

[64] An interesting by-product of the decline in electoral defeats in the outstate circuits between the two periods is the fact that a greater proportion of the judges in the latter era went on the bench by gubernatorial appointment rather than by winning an election. (In the early period, only 15 percent of the judges were appointed; in the latter period, the figure rose to 44 percent.) The reason for this development is that when an elective judgeship becomes vacant because of the removal, retirement, or resignation of its occupant, the office is filled by gubernatorial appointment. (*Revised Statutes of Missouri*, 1959, Sec. 105.030.). Thus, as an elective system becomes more like the Plan one in providing electoral security for judges, it also begins to resemble the Plan in the method by which judges first go on the bench. For an analysis of this development on state courts in the United States, see James Herndon, "Appointment as a Means of Initial Accession to Elective Courts of Last Resort," *North Dakota Law Review*, 38 (1962), 60–73.

7

LAWYER ATTITUDES ON METHODS
OF JUDICIAL SELECTION

As previously mentioned, there has been no shortage of comments from the Bar concerning the operation of the Nonpartisan Court Plan. In fact, since the Plan was originally conceived, a deluge of hortatory articles has appeared in legal periodicals[1] and in the press, singing its praises and urging its adoption in various jurisdictions of the nation. And despite the fact that lawyers might be expected to respond favorably to a selection system that gives them a dominant role in choosing judges, there have also been attacks on the Plan, a few of which have been expressed in print.[2] While some of these evaluations of the Plan have been helpful and suggestive, for the most part they represent impressions of individuals or comparatively small groups of lawyers, or fail to explore

---

[1] Recent examples of such articles include W. W. Crowdus, "Twenty Years of the Missouri Nonpartisan Court Plan," *Oklahoma Bar Association Journal*, 31 (1960), 2270 ff.; Forrest Hemker, "Experience Under the Missouri Nonpartisan Court Plan," *Journal of the American Judicature Society*, 43 (1960), 1959 ff.; Laurance Hyde, "The Missouri Method of Choosing Judges, *ibid.*, 41 (1957), 74 ff.; Robert A. Schroeder, "Twenty Five Years Under the Missouri Plan," *ibid.*, 49 (1965), 105 ff.; and Glenn Winters, "One-Man Judicial Selection," *ibid.*, 45 (1962), 198 ff.
[2] For an attack on the Plan by a member of the Illinois Bar, see George Moran, "Counter-Missouri Plan for Method of Selecting Judges," *Florida Bar Journal*, 32 (1958), 471 ff. Other criticisms of it include William Anderson, "Reorganization of Minnesota's Judiciary," *Minnesota Law Review*, 27 (1943), 383 ff., and Francis D. Wormuth and Rich Grover, "Politics, the Bar and the Selection of Judges," *Utah Law Review*, 3 (1953), 459 ff.
Some of the lawyers we interviewed in our study also claimed that many attorneys who actually oppose the Plan are hesitant to go on the record as being against it. We found little reluctance in this regard, perhaps because the questionnaire protected the identity of the respondents and we promised all our personal interviewees that their comments would be kept confidential.

the subject in any depth.[3] The one study that examines the question closely focuses on the attitudes of state legislators and judges in Pennsylvania rather than the Bar as a whole; moreover, it represents the thinking of persons who presumably have no first-hand experience with judicial selection under the Nonpartisan Court Plan.[4]

Our approach to gaining insight into lawyer attitudes on the operation of the Plan compared to that of an elective system was to explore the matter broadly in our personal interviews, so as to allow members of the Bar to offer comments within their own frames of reference. We then used these comments in developing inquiries for our questionnaire designed to test the thinking of the Missouri Bar as a whole on these matters.[5]

This chapter is divided into three major parts: (1) the preferences of lawyers concerning methods of selecting circuit and appellate judges; (2) an analysis of the reactions of members of the Bar to certain consequences that are commonly associated with the operation of the Nonpartisan Court Plan; and (3) a discussion of improvements in the operation of the Plan as viewed both by members of the Bar and judges selected under its provisions.

PREFERENCES OF LAWYERS ON METHODS OF JUDICIAL SELECTION

Our responses from lawyers concerning the best method of choosing judges indicates that the Missouri Bar is, for the most part, concerned

---

[3] A study made some years ago of attitudes of Missouri lawyers toward the Plan by William Shafroth was based upon replies from only 22 respondents who were not chosen in any systematic manner. For an account of the results of that inquiry, see "Missouri and California Lawyers Appraise Judicial Selection Methods," *Journal of the American Judicature Society*, 31 (April, 1948), 176–184. Henderson and Sinclair, *op. cit.*, Vol. 2, p. 126, received replies from 177 Texas lawyers concerning their preferences on methods of judicial selection (45 percent of them favored the Missouri Plan compared to 30 percent who preferred the elective system in the state), but a detailed analysis of the issue lay beyond the scope of their study.

[4] See William J. Keefe, "Judges in Politics: The Pennsylvania Plan of Judicial Selection," *University of Pittsburgh Law Review*, 20 (1959), 621–631. The latter limitation also applies to the Henderson and Sinclair study.

[5] In eliciting responses from lawyers on their preferences concerning judicial selection, we used as suggested choices on the questionnaire those that were mentioned most often in our personal interviews. These included, in addition to selection under the Plan, popular election with either partisan or nonpartisan ballots, and appointment by the governor alone. Respondents were also asked to add other suggestions besides those specifically mentioned.

with only certain limited selection possibilities: the Nonpartisan Court Plan and popular election using partisan or nonpartisan ballots. (For example, only 1 percent supports straight gubernatorial appointment and a similarly small proportion desire selection by the Bar alone.)[6] However, there are important variations among lawyers practicing in various parts of the state concerning which of the selection methods is superior with respect to the choosing of circuit judges. Moreover, some attorneys prefer one method for selecting members of the trial bench and another for determining who will sit on the state's appellate tribunals. Therefore, the analysis that follows explores these variations, first among attorneys concerning the choice of circuit court judges, and second, their preferences regarding the selection of members of the appellate benches. Included in this latter section is an examination of the reasons that prompt some elements of the Bar to prefer different election methods for the two kinds of courts.

Preferences of Jackson County and St. Louis City Attorneys on the Selection of Circuit Judges

Our survey results indicate a clear preference of metropolitan lawyers in the state for using the Nonpartisan Plan to select circuit judges before whom they presently practice. Seventy-nine percent of the Jackson County attorneys support this method of choosing judges, while the Plan's advocates in St. Louis number about 70 percent of the members of the Bar. These ratios compare with the figures of 4 and 9 percent, respectively, which favor a return to the partisan election method of choosing trial judges that was used in both these communities prior to 1940.[7]

An analysis of the attitudes of the Bar along practice lines, however, indicates that attorneys in certain fields are more inclined to favor the Plan than are those who specialize in other areas of the law. Table 7.1 reveals that those groups of lawyers who originally favored the Plan

---

Straight gubernatorial appointment was specifically listed as an alternative on the questionnaire, while selection by the Bar alone was not. The attorneys favoring this latter method added it under the "other" category provided for on the questionnaire. Several attorneys, whom we personally interviewed, said that selection by the Bar alone was not "practical" because the public would not accept it; and, at any rate, the legal profession is the primary influence in the system as it presently operates because the lawyer and judge members dominate the nominating commissions.

The proportions favoring nonpartisan elections are somewhat higher: 7 percent among Jackson County lawyers, and 13 percent among those practicing in St. Louis.

TABLE 7.1

SELECTED FIELDS OF LEGAL PRACTICE OF JACKSON COUNTY
AND ST. LOUIS LAWYERS AND PREFERENCE
ON JUDICIAL SELECTION METHODS

Field of Practice[a]	Non-partisan Court Plan	Popular Election[b]	Other[c]	Not Ascer-tained	Total	N
Defendants'	83%	9%	5%	3%	100%	129
Corporation and business	81	10	7	2	100	335
Real estate	81	10	4	5	100	86
Probate, trust and taxation	76	14	7	3	100	253
Domestic relations	72	23	2	3	100	78
Labor	58	32	10	0	100	19
Plaintiffs'	55	30	13	2	100	162
Criminal	54	41	5	0	100	37

[a] Includes lawyers listing the field exclusively, or as one of the two or three major fields of their practice.

[b] Includes partisan and nonpartisan elections.

[c] Includes straight gubernatorial appointment, gubernatorial appointment with Senate confirmation, selection by lawyers only, and a scattering of other suggestions.

when it was first proposed (that is, those representing defendants in personal injury cases and corporations in general) continue to be its major supporters, while the plaintiffs' and criminal attorneys, who fought the Plan in the 1930's, are much less enthusiastic about it. However all groups favor it over the method of popular election. This may indicate that it has not turned out to be as adverse to plaintiffs' and criminal attorneys' interests as they originally feared.

An analysis of the data also indicates that the social status differences in the profession that served to divide metropolitan lawyers into the rival bar associations discussed in Chapter 1, are also quite relevant for preferences on judicial selection. Lawyers most favorable to the Plan are employed on the legal staffs of corporations and are partners in the larger law firms. Solo practitioners[8] are least disposed toward it

[8] Paul Freund notes that solo practitioners in the United States and Great Britain are at the opposite poles of the profession. In Great Britain, he is the barrister who may not enter into a partnership, who deals with clients only through solicitors and who enjoys a special prestige. Moreover, older, successful barristers have the highest earnings in the profession. See his selection, "The Legal Profession," *Daedalus,* 92 (1963), 689.

while small firm and government lawyers hold an intermediate position. Similarly, persons who received their legal education at an outstate institution (there are no differences, however, between those who went to prestige and nonprestige schools there) favor the Plan most, while those who attended local law schools with a nighttime curriculum react the least favorably toward it. The attitudes of lawyers who are educated at instate, full-time law schools fall between the two positions. Income levels of lawyers also generally relate, as anticipated, to attitudes toward the Plan, with the exception that many young attorneys who currently earn less than $10,000 a year are among its strongest supporters.[9] Many respondents in this group are presently associates in law firms, and undoubtedly identify with senior partners and their firms' clients on the selection issue.

A precise measure of the association that exists between social status in the legal profession and preferences on judicial selection can be determined by combining the factors discussed above which relate most closely to such preferences, namely, practice arrangement and legal education. An index, reflecting both these indicators of status, was constructed by assigning points to respondents on the basis of their characteristics on these two matters.[10] Table 7.2 shows that the index is very relevant for preferences on judicial selection, with the percentage of the very high status respondents favoring the Nonpartisan Court Plan being almost twice that of those with very low status. Moreover, between these extremes, preferences correlate with status.

The above analysis indicates the relevance of kind of legal practice for lawyer preferences on methods of judicial selection. Another potential factor to be considered is the partisan affiliation of attorneys. The often-heard assertion that Democrats have more faith in the "common people" than Republicans might lead Democrats to be less favorably disposed toward the Plan than Republicans. Also, there are practical political considerations present, since both Jackson County and St. Louis are

---

[9] Sixty-seven percent of the lawyers earning less than $10,000 a year are under 40 years of age, compared to 38 percent of the total sample who are in this age group.

[10] A three-point scale was used for each factor with three points assigned to partners of law firms with six or more members, associates of law firms, and attorneys employed by corporations; two points to partners in firms from two to five members and attorneys employed by the government; and one point for solo practitioners. Similarly, three points are assigned to respondents who attended law schools outside the state; two points to those who went to instate, full-time law schools; and one point to those who attended instate, night law schools. A combination of these two scales means that the largest possible number of points is six, and the smallest, two. The five categories of social status ranging from six through two points are designated, "very high," "high," "medium," "low," and "very low."

TABLE 7.2

SOCIAL STATUS (PRACTICE ARRANGEMENT AND LEGAL EDUCATION)[a]
OF JACKSON COUNTY AND ST. LOUIS CITY LAWYERS
AND PREFERENCE ON METHOD OF JUDICIAL SELECTION

Social Status Levels	Non-partisan Court Plan	Popular Election	Other	Not Ascer-tained	Total	N
Very high	92%	3%	3%	2%	100%	108
High	87	7	4	2	100	151
Medium	80	12	7	1	100	184
Low	60	27	12	1	100	139
Very low	47	41	12	0	100	76

[a] Respondents for which there was no information on either practice arrangement or legal education were eliminated from the analysis.

heavily Democratic and, therefore, the popular election of judges would probably result in the selection of all Democratic judges in contrast to the situation under the Plan whereby some Republicans have been appointed to the circuit courts of the two cities.[11] One might also expect lawyers who participate more in party activities to be more favorable to an elective system, particularly one using partisan ballots, than their less-involved colleagues.[12] Table 7.3 indicates that while both these assumptions are true, the party-related differences among lawyers are not as marked as they were for social status variables.[13] Thus preferences on judicial selection among metropolitan lawyers in Missouri relate more closely to professional factors than to political party loyalties.

One final professional matter that we explored relative to preferences on judicial selection was that of trial experience. Our general hypothesis was: the more often attorneys appear in court, the more likely it would

[11] The Republicans have not held the governorship in Missouri since 1944. From 1953 to 1964, however, six Republicans were appointed to the circuit courts in Jackson County and St. Louis by three Democratic governors.
[12] The index of party activity is the same as that explained in footnote 12 of Chapter 2.
[13] The differences between the Republican and Democratic lawyers tend to "wash out" almost completely when social status is held constant. In other words, a more favorable attitude of Republicans toward the Plan is actually a reflection of the fact that more of them practice in larger firms and went outstate for their legal education, while more Democrats are in solo practice and attended a local night law school.

be that their general attitudes on judicial selection would be intensified. For example, those attorneys in practice specialties generally disposed toward the Plan (such as defendants' and corporation lawyers) would be even more favorable to the Plan if they had had extensive trial experience than if they had not. Conversely, attorneys in fields of practice that did not support the Plan as much (such as those handling criminal and plaintiffs' work) would be even less favorable to it if they had been in court frequently. Table 7.4 contains data to test these assumptions.

Our hypothesis concerning the effect of trial experience on attorneys in fields of practice generally less favorable to the Plan was confirmed. The contrast in attitudes between labor, plaintiffs', and criminal lawyers who have tried more than 100 cases, with those who have not, is striking. Preference for the Nonpartisan Court Plan falls below the 50 percent level for active trial attorneys in all three fields, and in the case of active labor and criminal lawyers, more of them prefer popular election of judges than the Nonpartisan Plan. However, the preferences of the

TABLE 7.3

PARTISAN AFFILIATION[a] AND AMOUNT OF PARTY ACTIVITY[b]
OF JACKSON COUNTY AND ST. LOUIS LAWYERS AND
PREFERENCE ON METHOD OF JUDICIAL SELECTION

	Non-Partisan Court Plan	Non-Partisan Elections	Partisan Elections	Other	Not Ascertained	Total	N
Partisan Affiliation							
Republicans	83%	7%	4%	5%	1%	100%	324
Democrats	68	12	8	10	2	100	381
Independents[c]	73	7	9	10	1	100	26
By Amount of Party Activity							
Republicans							
Inactive	90	8	1	1	0	100	133
Active	73	7	8	9	3	100	114
Democrats							
Inactive	70	12	7	9	2	100	136
Active	58	16	13	6	7	100	148

[a] Those respondents whose partisan affiliation or amount of party activity is not known are not included in the analysis.
[b] For the index of party activity, see footnote 12 of Chapter 2.
[c] Since there are so few respondents in this category, they are not included in the sub-analysis by amount of activity level.

TABLE 7.4

SELECTED FIELDS OF LEGAL PRACTICE AND TRIAL EXPERIENCE[a]
OF JACKSON COUNTY AND ST. LOUIS LAWYERS AND
PREFERENCE ON METHOD OF JUDICIAL SELECTION

Field of Practice	Non-partisan Court Plan	Popular Election	Other	Not Ascertained	Total	N
Defendants'						
Less than 100 cases	86%	10%	3%	1%	100%	88
100 cases or more	77	11	9	3	100	35
Corporation						
Less than 100 cases	85	8	5	2	100	238
100 cases or more	67	18	10	5	100	79
Real Estate						
Less than 100 cases	86	8	4	2	100	51
100 cases or more	67	19	7	7	100	27
Probate and Trust						
Less than 100 cases	81	10	7	2	100	169
100 cases or more	60	28	7	5	100	67
Domestic Relations						
Less than 100 cases	72	23	3	2	100	39
100 cases or more	50	44	3	3	100	38
Labor						
Less than 100 cases	73	18	0	9	100	11
100 cases or more	38	50	12	0	100	8
Plaintiffs'						
Less than 100 cases	64	23	11	2	100	90
100 cases or more	41	39	11	9	100	70
Criminal						
Less than 100 cases	81	19	0	0	100	16
100 cases or more	30	60	5	5	100	20

[a] Trial experience refers to that before the circuit court. Respondents whose trial experience was not ascertained are not included in the table.

active trial attorneys in fields generally disposed toward the Plan (such as defendants' and corporation specialties) are precisely the opposite of what we had anticipated: those in court frequently are less likely to favor the Plan than attorneys in the fields without such an extensive trial practice. In fact, this was true in all the fields analyzed, including real estate, probate and trust, and domestic relations. Why this should be true is not known at this point, since we have thus far merely identified certain factors as being associated with preferences on methods of judicial selection, but reasons for this attitude are suggested by the subsequent section of this chapter dealing with specific features of the Plan's operation.

Preferences of St. Louis County[14] and Outstate Lawyers on the Selection of Circuit Judges

The high degree of consensus that exists among metropolitan lawyers in favor of the Plan does not apply to Missouri lawyers who presently practice before elected judges. The general support levels are only about one half of the previously noted 79 and 70 percent figures for Jackson County and St. Louis City attorneys, respectively. Nevertheless, St. Louis County lawyers clearly favor it over their present partisan system by a 44 to 55 ratio, with 30 percent supporting nonpartisan elections. On the other hand, outstate attorneys prefer some kind of elective system with 30 percent choosing partisan ballots and 27 percent choosing nonpartisan ballots. However, a substantial group of "outstaters" (the largest proportion favoring any one method, about 36 percent) would like to see their jurisdictions adopt the Plan, a possibility indicated previously, that has never been authorized by the Missouri legislature.[15]

While the support levels for the Plan thus vary considerably between lawyers who presently practice before Nonpartisan judges and those who do not, both general groups of attorneys show similar preferences based upon social divisions within the Bar. The St. Louis County and outstate attorneys who are most favorable to the Plan are those with defendants' and corporate practices (55 and 46 percent, respectively); those least favorably disposed toward it are plaintiffs' and criminal lawyers (22 and 23 percent). The preference patterns also show that at-

---

[14] Our analysis of St. Louis County lawyers is restricted to the 81 respondents who have their main practice of law in the county. Another 53 respondents indicated on their questionnaires that they had about an equal amount of their practice in St. Louis County and St. Louis City. We did not include this latter group of lawyers in our analysis by geographical area of practice because of the problem of categorizing them.

[15] The Constitution of the State of Missouri, 1945, Article V, Section 29(b), provides for the adoption of the Plan by voters in other judicial circuits but, as previously noted, the Missouri Supreme Court has ruled that this section is not self-executing and requires legislation to make it effective. *State ex rel. Millar v. Toberman,* 360 Mo. 1101, 232 S.W. 2d 904 (1950). The 1967 General Assembly granted St. Louis County residents the right to vote on the Plan.

torneys employed by corporations and those practicing in medium-sized law firms[16] are more supportive of the Plan (68 and 47 percent) than are solo practitioners and those in two-man partnerships (28 and 31 percent). Similarly, the Plan is most favored by attorneys who went out of state for their legal education (42 percent) and least supported by those who attended night law school (33 percent), with attorneys who went to full-time institutions within the state holding an intermediate position (40 percent).

It will be recalled that Jackson County and St. Louis lawyers with extensive trial experience were less supportive of the Nonpartisan Court Plan and more favorable to an elective system than were their colleagues who appeared in court less often. Moreover, this was true in all fields of practice analyzed, including such areas as defendants' and corporation specialties which generally involve lawyers who are favorably disposed toward the Plan. Interestingly enough, Table 7.5 shows that the same pattern of preferences appear among St. Louis County and outstate lawyers, who practice under elected judges;[17] this means that unlike the Plan situation, among these latter attorneys, those whose practices are most affected by their selection system are its greatest supporters. Thus one cannot conclude that familiarity breeds contempt, that is, that lawyers most experienced with any selection system are necessarily opposed to it. Instead, as discussed later, some lawyers feel that certain consequences affecting litigants and themselves flow from the operation of the Plan which are not as likely to occur under an elective judicial system.

Table 7.6 tests the associations that exist between the partisan affiliations of St. Louis County and outstate lawyers and their preferences concerning judicial selection. The suburban St. Louis attorneys have little use for their present system of choosing judges by means of a party ballot. Their low level of support for partisan judicial election parallels that previously shown to exist among attorneys practicing in Jackson County and St. Louis. Also like the city attorneys, the county lawyers favor the Plan over any of the alternative selection methods,

---

[16] The law firms in St. Louis County and outstate areas are generally in the range from 3 to 5 men; only about 3 percent of our respondents from these areas practice in firms with more than 5 men.

[17] A smaller proportion of plaintiffs' lawyers with an extensive trial practice favor popular elections than do their less-experienced colleagues. However, this is not because of a greater preference of the active practitioners for the Plan, but rather because more of them either favor another selection method altogether, or did not make their preferences known. Moreover, experienced plaintiffs' attorneys are more favorable to partisan (as compared to nonpartisan) elections than are their less active colleagues.

TABLE 7.5
SELECTED FIELDS OF LEGAL PRACTICE AND TRIAL EXPERIENCE[a]
OF ST. LOUIS COUNTY AND OUTSTATE LAWYERS AND PREFERENCE
ON METHOD OF JUDICIAL SELECTION

Field of Practice[b]	Nonpartisan Court Plan	Popular Election	Other	Not Ascertained	Total	N
Defendants'						
Less than 100 cases	61%	30%	7%	2%	100%	43
100 cases or more	46	46	4	4	100	26
Corporation						
Less than 100 cases	51	37	10	2	100	59
100 cases or more	40	50	5	5	100	40
Real Estate						
Less than 100 cases	42	50	2	6	100	50
100 cases or more	22	70	6	2	100	49
Probate and Trust						
Less than 100 cases	45	51	1	3	100	84
100 cases or more	26	60	8	6	100	85
Domestic Relations						
Less than 100 cases	48	36	4	12	100	25
100 cases or more	23	65	6	6	100	31
Plaintiffs'						
Less than 100 cases	24	67	5	4	100	58
100 cases or more	21	54	15	10	100	48
Criminal						
Less than 100 cases	22	61	4	13	100	23
100 cases or more	22	72	6	0	100	18

[a] Trial experience refers to that before the circuit court. Respondents whose trial experience was not ascertained are not included in the table.
[b] There are too few labor lawyers for analysis.

but they are not nearly so enthusiastic about it as are their colleagues who presently practice before Plan judges. A substantial proportion of the suburban attorneys in both political parties prefer nonpartisan elections for choosing judges even though their particular method has never been used to choose judges in Missouri. Nonpartisan elections may represent a "half-way house" for many county lawyers, since this method permits them to retain popular elections but yet avoid the unfavorable

TABLE 7.6

PARTISAN AFFILIATION[a] AND AMOUNT OF PARTY ACTIVITY[a] OF
ST. LOUIS COUNTY AND OUTSTATE LAWYERS AND PREFERENCE
ON METHOD OF JUDICIAL SELECTION

	Non-Partisan Court Plan	Non-Partisan Election	Partisan Election	Other	Not Ascertained	Total	N
By Area and Partisan Affiliation							
St. Louis County							
Republicans	39%	30%	0%	25%	6%	100%	44
Democrats	49	31	11	9	0	100	35
Outstate							
Republicans	24	37	31	0	8	100	116
Democrats	42	21	30	3	4	100	208
Outstate Lawyers By Amount of Party Activity[b]							
Republicans							
Inactive	39	39	22	0	0	100	18
Active	22	36	35	5	2	100	88
Democrats							
Inactive	52	26	17	5	0	100	46
Active	36	21	33	2	8	100	141

[a] Those respondents whose partisan affiliation or amount of party activity are not known are not included in the table.
[b] There are too few St. Louis County lawyers of either party to permit a subanalysis by level of party activity.

aspects of judicial electoral contests which they associate with party political machines. Such an attitude is consistent with the favorable attitude that suburbanites display toward nonpartisanship as a general political principle; moreover, the fact that St. Louis County has been so politically competitive in recent years means that neither party has a clear advantage when partisan ballots are utilized.[18]

---

[18] Eugene Lee, *The Politics of Nonpartisanship: A Study of California City Elections* (Berkeley: University of California Press, 1960) and Robert Wood, *Suburbia: Its People and Their Politics* (Boston: Houghton-Mifflin, 1958) are two general studies dealing with nonpartisanship. The political competitiveness of St. Louis County is reflected in the 4 to 3 ratios that have tended to characterize the partisan composition of the 7 member county council in recent years with both parties alternately holding majority states.

The selection preferences of outstate lawyers also reflect partisan factors. Republican attorneys tend to be less enthusiastic about the Plan and more inclined to favor nonpartisan elections than are Democratic lawyers. Such attitudes may relate to calculations of minority party lawyers that they have relatively little chance of capturing the governorship and the judicial-appointing power the office represents, but might fare better under nonpartisan ballots that conceal their party affiliation.[19] The outstate lawyers of both political persuasions are much more receptive to continuing the partisan method of choosing their judges than are the St. Louis County lawyers.[20] Moreover, the lawyers who have been active in the affairs of either party are more supportive of partisan elections than are their less-involved colleagues.

Lawyer Attitudes on the Selection of Appellate Judges

The preference patterns regarding the selection of judges of the state's four appellate courts (the three intermediate courts of appeal and the Supreme Court) parallel those for choosing members of the trial bench.[21] The attorneys who tend to be most favorable to the Plan practice in Jackson County and St. Louis, come from the upper social strata of the profession, are less-involved in party affairs, and are affiliated with the Republican party in the two urban communities and the Democratic party in St. Louis County and in outstate areas. However, the support level for the Plan for choosing appellate, as compared to circuit judges, rises among all groups. (On a state-wide basis the figures are 72 and 61 percent, respectively.) The contrast is most dramatic among outstate

---

[19] Lee, *op. cit.*, and other students of the subject have concluded that Republicans generally benefit from a nonpartisan system of elections because with the "clue" of partisanship for voters missing from the electoral system, political resources like newspaper endorsements and business and civic organizations become more crucial to the election outcome, and Republicans as a group are more likely to possess these resources than are Democrats.

[20] As the subsequent discussion indicates, partisan politics in outstate areas is not considered to be as subject to political machines as it is in urban communities. Also, many counties tend to be fairly stable in their party voting habits and thus both Democratic and Republican lawyers can expect persons of their partisan persuasion to sit on given circuit benches. For example, in 1963–1964, there were 35 Democrats and 10 Republicans serving as judges in "outstate" circuits; in 1961–1962 the ratio was 33 to 12 and in 1959–1960, it was 34 to 10 a favor of the Democrats.

[21] One exception to this pattern is the fact that the amount of trial experience attorneys have before appellate courts does not affect their selection preferences for judges of these courts as it does at the trial court level. See footnote 27, *infra.* for a possible explanation of this matter.

attorneys: almost two-thirds of them prefer the Plan for upper court judges, almost twice the proportion that favor it to select those sitting on the lower courts.

Reasons for Lawyer Preferences for Elected Circuit and Appointed Appellate Judges

To determine why some lawyers prefer to elect circuit judges, but want to use the Plan for appellate ones, we asked such persons to indicate their reasons for choosing different selection methods for the two kinds of courts. As might be expected, the open-ended question evoked a variety of explanations, but essentially they involve a few major arguments relating to political considerations and the different functions performed by trial and appellate courts. There is also some feeling that the quality of persons appointed by the governor to the two levels of courts differs considerably.

Some lawyers distinguish clearly between the kind of politics that exists in rural areas as compared to the large cities in Missouri and fear the effect the politics of the latter areas would have on political contests for appellate judgeships. One outstate lawyer active in political affairs stated:

Urban area primaries are controlled by party machinery which would have too great an effect on appellate judge nominees. In rural circuits, the attorneys are personally known to the voters and votes are cast with some degree of intelligence and certainly with independence.

Interestingly enough, some urban lawyers also share this view of the disparate political worlds of the city and outstate areas. One Republican attorney practicing in Jackson County suggested that "in large cities the election is controlled by factions—in rural areas people vote their convictions and are not led by factions." A related factor bearing on the rural-urban matter is the fear expressed by a politically-active, outstate Democrat that state-wide elections for appellate judges would result in the selection of few judges from less-populated sections of the state.

Other reasons advanced for preferring different systems at the two levels are associated with different conceptions that lawyers have of the functions performed by trial and appellate courts. Some attorneys feel that trial judges are "closer to the people" than appellate judges, and that they should be made more responsive to public sentiment than higher court judges. One Jackson County firm lawyer with a corporate and probate practice suggested that the judges of the lower courts "must feel the pulse of the people in order to accomplish justice according to current circumstances," and that "making judges more accountable to the people tends to insure this result." Another young politically-active Democrat, also from Jackson County, described the fact that in his area the circuit judges "have a tendency not to be responsible to anyone or to a political party." A St. Louis attorney in solo practice said he wanted circuit judges "to be subject to political pressures" and felt that making them "subject to election makes them more reasonable." Another lawyer from that area suggested that "circuit judges work harder and are not so arbitrary if selected by the people at an election." Thus these lawyers conceive of the work of the trial judge as being "the hearer of the facts and the applier of the law." They consider it as being of such a nature that it benefits from an infusion of public attitudes, a result that can best be obtained by making such judges responsible to the people through elections.

In contrast to this conception is the one that attorneys usually have of the function performed by appellate judges in the state judicial system. A respondent suggested that appellate judges "pass on a cold record and look solely to legal precedent for their decisions; as the determiners of the law, they need to be removed from the voters and interest group and political party pressures." Another pointed out that "appeals are almost exclusively on legal questions and require experience and knowledge most laymen do not possess." Another respondent expressed the viewpoint that while circuit judges pass on issues of local concern such as divorce, annexation, adoption, and juveniles, and should reflect local attitudes on such matters, "higher courts should not be subject to the influence of circumstances of a particular locality." Thus these attorneys emphasize what they conceive to be the legal, nonpolitical nature of the work of the appellate tribunals and the necessity of insulating such judges from the pressures and attitudes of the general public.

Related to this same difference in function of the two courts is the view of some attorneys that the people are in a better position to evaluate judges for the lower courts because they observe these judges in action and also because the conduct of trial proceedings does not involve as much legal expertise as work on an appellate tribunal. An outstate solo practitioner suggested that "a circuit judge needs to be more understanding of human nature and observant of people, while an appellate applies more legal theory." Under this reasoning, lay persons are capable of determining qualities needed for a trial judge, while only lawyers and judges can properly evaluate those of candidates for the higher courts. As a St. Louis County attorney put it, "The people as a whole are not aware of the intellectual capacity required at the appellate level."

Moreover, there is a tendency for some attorneys to view the two kinds of courts as having different constituencies. This is reflected in the comment of a young outstate attorney that "circuit court judges deal directly with the people who should directly control the selection of the judge; appellate judges deal with lawyers who should control their selection."

Some attorneys feel that the combination of elected trial court judges and appointive appellate ones is desirable. As it works in operation, the lower court experience acts as an apprenticeship for possible subsequent service at the higher levels of the state judicial system. In other words, the elective system provides an opportunity for many capable young attorneys to run for office and prove their worth. Those who lack competence will be eliminated by the public. At the same time, attorneys and Supreme Court judges who play the crucial role in the appointment of appellate judges have the chance to assess the qualifications of trial court judges for the upper benches. Moreover, if errors are made by circuit judges they can be corrected by the appellate judges who review the proceedings of the lower courts.

It is interesting to note that lawyers' conceptions of the respective roles the upper and lower courts play in the judicial process are at variance with the way that some political scientists view the functions of the two kinds of courts. While members of the Bar tend to think of the work of appellate tribunals as "pure law," as one attorney put it, it is also possible to view it as the part of the judicial system where public policy is made, that is, where general rules are formulated that affect the future disposition of social conflicts. Developing such rules becomes the particular province of the appellate courts, while the trial courts are chiefly concerned with applying these general rules to particular cases involving specific fact situations.[22] Under this conception of the judicial process, a case can then be made for reversing the preferences of the Bar, that is, letting the people play a role in public policy-making by electing appellate judges, while insulating the trial judge against undue pressures of persons for favored treatment in individual

---

[22] Herbert Jacob in his study, *Justice in America, op. cit.*, p. 26 f., distinguishes between "policy-making," which he considers to be developed primarily by appellate courts, and "norm-enforcement," which is the major function performed by lower courts in the state judicial system. He suggests that "Policy decisions are intended to be guideposts for future actions; norm-enforcement decisions are aimed at the instant case alone." Davis, *op. cit.*, p. 34, states that "The higher the court is in the hierarchy, the more it is likely to be concerned with policy." He further suggests that the idea of choosing appellate judges (rather than lower court ones) through the Plan "contradicts the idea that policy-makers should be elected and non-policy-makers should be appointed."

cases by protecting him under the system of appointment and tenure provided under the Plan.

Be that as it may, the Bar primarily conceives of the work of the appellate courts as being of an objective, technical nature that requires legal expertise if it is to be handled properly. Some lawyers also feel that the Plan is particularly desirable at the upper level, because experience has shown that the governor is more apt to select able persons to the appellate than to the trial bench. As a St. Louis large-firm Republican attorney expressed it, "The Governor usually appoints some political hack for circuit judge, whereas high-caliber lawyers are chosen for the appellate courts." Some persons attribute this tendency to the fact that the governor is able to have first-hand knowledge of the relatively few men who are qualified for selection as appellate court judges, but is frequently not acquainted with individuals nominated for the circuit benches, and hence must take someone else's recommendation on their respective merits.

The foregoing analysis provides suggestive comments of certain lawyers regarding their reasons for favoring the popular election of circuit judges and Plan appointment of appellate judges. However, to obtain a fuller understanding of how lawyers generally view the Plan, it is necessary to assess the attitudes of a substantial segment of the Bar concerning its functioning. The next section explores such attitudes by analyzing how those attorneys who are most familiar with the Plan (that is, those practicing in Jackson County and St. Louis)[23] react to certain consequences most often associated with its operation.

LAWYER ATTITUDES TOWARD OPERATION OF THE PLAN

In our personal interviews with lawyers, we sought not only their preferences concerning methods of judicial selection but also their attitudes on how the Nonpartisan Court Plan had operated over the years. By probing with open-ended questions, we tried to determine the reasons why lawyers supported or opposed the Plan, and specifically how they

---

[23] Lawyers practicing outside the two metropolitan communities do have some experience with Plan judges which they acquire in practice before appellate courts. However, our survey data indicate that 80 percent of them have tried fewer than 10 cases before courts of appeals judges; the proportion with this limited amount of litigation before the Supreme Court is 83 percent. This compares with 27 percent of our Jackson County and 30 percent of our St. Louis respondents who tried less than 10 cases before the circuit courts of their respective communities.

felt it functioned compared to the elective system. From their responses, we were able to identify certain common consequences that lawyers associate with the operation of the Plan. These consequences relate to three major aspects of the Plan's operation: the process by which persons are chosen for the bench; the kinds of individuals who are selected under this process; and the effect the Plan has on the behavior of judges once they are in office.

With respect to the selection process, two general reactions occurred again and again in the interviews. One was that the Plan had succeeded mainly in doing what the Bar leaders who developed it had sought to do: it had taken "politics" out of the selection of judges. However, other lawyers saw the process differently. Many of them suggested that changing the selection system from popular elections to the Nonpartisan Court Plan had not eliminated "politics," but merely had substituted Bar politics and gubernatorial politics for the traditional politics of party leaders and machines.

With respect to the kind of persons who became judges under the Plan, again the lawyers we interviewed hold two disparate conceptions. Supporters of the Plan are inclined to think that it recruits "better" judges than the elective system. The major reasons advanced for this result include the greater willingness of able lawyers to seek positions on the bench under a system that spares them the rigors, expense, and uncertainties of election campaigns, as well as the more rational nature of the selection process itself. Many attorneys who oppose the Plan agree that it results in the selection of different kinds of lawyers to the bench than the elective system does, but believe that defendants' lawyers and those representing corporate clients are favored by the system.

Again there is agreement among lawyers that the election provisions of the Plan whereby judges run "on their records" against no opponent, in effect, give members of the Bench life tenure, and that this fact has important consequences for their behavior in office. However, supporters and opponents of the Plan emphasize different aspects of the independence that Nonpartisan Plan judges enjoy. The former see it as permitting them to make decisions based on the merits of the case rather than subjecting them to pressures that elective judges must often face; the latter say it tends to make judges arbitrary in the treatment of lawyers and laymen with business before the courts.

We took these general reactions to the operation of the Plan on which there appeared to be substantial disagreement among supporters and opponents of the Plan whom we personally interviewed, and framed six statements containing these assertions. Each respondent in our sample

was asked to indicate his reaction to each statement, utilizing a five-cate-
gory response ranging from "strongly agree" to "strongly disagree." Thus,
general attitudes of favorableness, neutrality, or unfavorableness toward
the operation of the Nonpartisan Court Plan are measured by a six-item,
Likert-type scale.[24]

The results indicate that lawyers, as a group, vary considerably in
their reactions to the six statements concerning the Plan. Their attitudes
are fairly clear about those aspects of its operation concerned with the
kinds of individuals chosen under the process. Thus 73 percent think
that the Plan has recruited better judges compared to 13 percent who
believe it has not;[25] only 21 percent feel the Plan favors the selection
of defendants' and corporation attorneys as judges, while 56 percent
think this consequence has not occurred. Likewise, their views tend
to coincide on the effect the Plan has on the behavior of judges once
they are in office. Attorneys support the idea that the Plan permits
judges to make decisions on the merits of the case by a 68 to 12 percent
ratio, and reject the negative comment that it tends to make them arbitrary in the treatment of lawyers and laymen by a 52 to 24 percent
margin.

Lawyers are much less agreed about the functioning of the selection
process itself. The respondents are fairly evenly divided on the issue
of whether the Plan has taken the "politics" out of judicial selection
with 37 percent feeling it has, compared to 44 percent who think it
has not. Moreover, more attorneys agreed than disagreed (51 to 21
percent) with the statement concerning Bar and gubernatorial politics,
even though it was considered to be unfavorable to the Plan on the
basis of its source. (It came primarily from persons we personally interviewed who opposed the Plan.) One explanation for the result (suggested by comments respondents added to the questionnaire) is that
some attorneys do not regard this feature of the operation of the Plan
as unfavorable if it is compared with what they consider to be the
only alternative possibility, namely, the use of traditional party politics
to select judges. In other words, they feel that politics of some kind

---

[24] Agreement with the assertions concerning the Plan's taking "politics" out of judicial
selection, its recruitment of "better" judges, and its permitting judges to make
decisions based on the merits of the case are considered as favorable attitudes
toward the Plan, as are disagreement with its alleged negative features, namely,
substituting Bar and gubernatorial politics for party and machine politics, favoring
the selection of defendants' and corporation lawyers as judges, and contributing
to the arbitrary treatment of lawyers and laymen by members of the bench.
[25] The categories of "strongly agree" and "agree" are combined for purposes of
this analysis, as are those of "disagree" and "strongly disagree."

is inevitable ("politics unavoidably exists whenever people are involved, since the personal element can never be discounted"), but they prefer politics engendered by the Plan over politics produced by an elective system. As one attorney put it, "Plan politics is the lesser of two evils inasmuch as party politics entails the additional demand of monetary expenditures." Therefore, this latter statement regarding Bar and gubernatorial politics should be considered the least helpful in distinguishing lawyer attitudes toward the operation of the Plan, even though it meets the test of discriminating sufficiently between the attitudes of persons who are generally favorable or unfavorable to the Plan.[26]

It will be recalled that lawyers practicing in certain fields of law clearly preferred the Plan as the best method of selecting judges, while others are considerably less disposed toward it. For example, defendants' and corporation lawyers, who handle the legal affairs of upper-class clientele, are its greatest advocates, while plaintiffs' and criminal lawyers, who represent lower class clients, support it far less. Moreover, it will be remembered that lawyers with extensive trial experience in all practice specialties (those highly favorable to the Plan, as well as those less favorable) are less inclined to prefer the Plan for the selection of judges than attorneys in the same specialties with less time in the courtroom. A comparison of the attitudes of these various groups toward specific consequences of the Plan indicates what particular aspects of its operation they regard with most favor and disfavor. Table 7.7 provides these data for the statements that relate most closely to matters

---

[26] To test whether the six statements are internally consistent, that is, the extent to which the attitudes on each of them are consistent with those on the others, a score ranging from 1 to 5 (from least, to most favorable, to the Plan) was assigned for each statement, and then a total score on all six items was compiled for each respondent. The respondents were then divided into high and low scoring groups (approximately the upper and lower quintiles) on the basis of their total scores. The discriminatory power of each statement, determined by comparing the mean scores of the high and low scoring groups on each item, is as follows:

| | \multicolumn{6}{c}{Statement Number*} |
	1	2	3	4	5	6
Mean score of upper 1/5	4.8	4.8	4.3	4.4	4.4	3.8
Mean score of lower 1/5	2.4	2.7	1.8	2.4	2.0	1.7
Discriminatory power	2.4	2.1	2.5	2.0	2.4	2.1

* 1. Recruits better judges.
  2. Permits decisions on merits of case.
  3. Takes "politics" out of judicial selection.
  4. Favors selection of defendants' and corporation lawyers as judges.
  5. Tends to make judges arbitrary in treatment of lawyers and laymen.
  6. Substitutes Bar and gubernatorial politics for party politics.

TABLE 7.7

SELECTED FIELDS OF PRACTICE, TRIAL EXPERIENCE[a] AND ATTITUDES[b]
OF JACKSON COUNTY AND ST. LOUIS LAWYERS TOWARD CERTAIN
ASPECTS OF OPERATION OF NONPARTISAN COURT PLAN

	Recruits Better Judges		Permits Decision on Merits of Case		Favors Selection of Defendants' and Corporation Attorneys as Judges		Tends Toward Arbitrary Treatment of Lawyers and Laymen		
	Agree	Disagree	Agree	Disagree	Agree	Disagree	Agree	Disagree	N
Field of Practice									
Defendants'	83 %	8 %	81 %	10 %	11 %	78 %	16 %	64 %	129
Corporation	81	7	78	6	14	64	15	64	335
Plaintiffs'	54	29	62	22	44	33	43	33	162
Criminal	54	22	51	27	43	41	49	27	37
Trial Experience									
Less than 100 cases	76	9	76	10	18	57	19	56	485
100 cases or more	62	26	64	18	29	53	38	41	217

[a] Trial experience refers to that before the circuit court. Respondents whose trial experience was not ascertained are not included in the table.
[b] A favorable attitude to the Plan is indicated by agreement with the first two statements and disagreement with the latter two statements. Responses of "strongly agree" and "agree" are combined in the table, as are those of "disagree" and "strongly disagree."

of legal practice, namely, the kinds of judges chosen under the Plan, and its effect on the behavior of the judges once in office.

Table 7.7 indicates that attorneys who are less supportive of the Plan as a method of selecting judges (that is, plaintiffs' and criminal attorneys, as well as those in all practice specialties who appear in court more often) are less favorable toward all four aspects of the Plan's operation than are corporation and defendants' lawyers, and those who have more limited trial experience. However, all the groups examined agree that the Plan results in the recruitment of better judges and permits decisions to be made on the merits of the case. The most obvious differences of opinion concerning the Plan's operation involve the assertions that it favors the selection of defendants' and corporation attorneys as judges and tends to make judges arbitrary in their treatment of lawyers and laymen. Attitudes toward the former statement definitely reflect the practice specialties of the respondents. Defendants' and corporation lawyers, the groups alleged to be favored as judges by the Plan, feel that this is not the case, while the plaintiffs' and criminal attorneys believe it is; moreover, the two groups that have the most disparate views on this matter (the defendants' and the plaintiffs' lawyers) are also the ones most directly involved in it, since they are courtroom rivals in personal injury litigation. The charge of arbitrary treatment of lawyers and laymen draws most support from criminal lawyers, but also is generally believed by plaintiffs' lawyers, as well as by a number of lawyers in all practice specialties who have an extensive trial experience. Comments of respondents indicate that some lawyers resent the fact that the independence circuit judges enjoy under the Plan gives them "the power to press attorneys to trial prematurely," and feel that such judges "should be responsive to the convenience of litigants and the Bar." Thus it appears that attorneys who are in court the most frequently, are more sensitive to the way judges treat them and laymen than are their colleagues who do not come in contact with judges as often.[27]

Table 7.8 tests the associations that exist between the partisan backgrounds of Jackson County and St. Louis attorneys and their attitudes toward the two statements regarding the Plan's operation which relate to the effect that political factors have on the selection of judges. Republicans, who it may be remembered favored the Plan more than the Democrats (see Table 7.3), are more likely than Democrats to think that the Plan has taken "politics" out of judicial selection, and, on the other hand, are less disposed to feel that it has merely substituted Bar and gubernatorial politics for the traditional politics of party leaders and machines. Thus support of the Plan is associated with a tendency to view it favorably as far as partisan factors are concerned. The table also indicates, however, that the more politically-active attorneys in both parties are more likely to see political factors at work in the operation of the Plan than are their colleagues who are not so involved in party affairs.[28]

---

[27] It will be recalled that among attorneys practicing outside Jackson County and St. Louis, support for their present elective system tends to rise with the amount of trial practice of the respondent. Presumably, elective judges are more inclined to take the desires of these groups into account on such matters. Moreover, an analysis of reactions of both metropolitan and outstate attorneys toward the allegation of arbitrariness of Plan judges shows no essential differences in attitudes among respondents with extensive experience before *appellate* courts and those without such experience. Apparently, then, attorneys are most sensitive to their treatment by judges in trial courts where there are witnesses and spectators present.

[28] Among attorneys practicing outside Jackson County and St. Louis, the partisanship factor operates in the opposite direction. Democratic lawyers (who it will be recalled are *more* supportive of the Plan than Republicans) are less likely to see political factors at work than are Republicans. The amount of party activity among these attorneys, however, has the same association with attitudes toward these political factors as it does among metropolitan attorneys, that is, the outstate respondents who are active in both parties are more likely to see such factors at work in the operation of the Plan than are their less politically involved colleagues.

TABLE 7.8
PARTISAN AFFILIATION, AMOUNT OF PARTY ACTIVITY, AND ATTITUDES
OF JACKSON COUNTY AND ST. LOUIS LAWYERS[a] TOWARD CERTAIN
ASPECTS OF OPERATION OF NONPARTISAN COURT PLAN

	Takes "Politics" Out of Selection of Judges		Substitutes Bar and Gubernatorial Politics for Traditional Politics		
	Agree	Disagree	Agree	Disagree	N
Party Affiliation					
Republicans	48%	32%	41%	29%	324
Democrats	40	42	54	23	381
By Amount of Party Activity					
Republicans					
Inactive	54	25	33	33	133
Active	41	43	47	27	114
Democrats					
Inactive	42	39	50	24	136
Active	30	53	60	18	148

[a] Those respondents whose practice affiliation or amount of party activity is not known are not included in the table.

The above analysis reveals the perceptions attorneys have of certain consequences commonly associated with the functioning of the Nonpartisan Court Plan. The final section of the chapter extends the analysis of their attitudes toward the Plan a step further by exploring suggestions made by members of the Bar concerning possibilities for improving the operation of the Plan.

SUGGESTED IMPROVEMENTS IN THE PLAN

Attorneys whom we interviewed personally suggested a number of ways of improving the operation of the Plan. We selected seven of the specific proposals that were mentioned most often and asked each of the respondents in our sample survey to indicate which of them he favored. Beyond this, we asked each of the respondents to indicate other improvements that he favored besides the seven mentioned in the questionnaire. This combination of approaches provides a determination of how the Bar as a whole reacts to specific proposals for change, as well as information in depth on the attitudes evinced by particular lawyers concerning various weaknesses in the Plan's operation.

The following discussion first analyzes the improvements in the Plan suggested by our lawyer respondents,[29] dividing them into those that relate primarily to the tenure of judges and those associated with the process for recruiting and selecting persons for the judiciary. These improvements are then compared with those proposed by judges themselves to determine the extent to which members of the bench and Bar tend to evaluate the Plan similarly.

Improvements Relating to Tenure of Judges Under the Plan

The responses of the Bar indicate that, for most attorneys, the gravest weakness in the Plan is its inefficacy for removing judges from the bench who are not capable of performing the duties of the office. The problem is particularly serious for older judges. As one attorney stated, "We now have some judges who are good fellows but who need to retire."

Apparently many lawyers are either unfamiliar with the operation of the Bar and judges' committees on retirement (described in the previous chapter) or feel that their efforts are not entirely successful, because more than four-fifths of our respondents said they favored the specific proposal that circuit judges be required, like appellate jurists, to retire at 75, and some even indicated in their questionnaire comments that they would like to see the retirement age lowered to 65 or 70 for all judges.[30] At the same time, about three-fifths of the survey respondents agreed with the proposal that the financial effects of retirement for judges be cushioned by increasing their retirement benefits beyond the present level of one-third of the annual salary at time of retirement.[31]

---

[29] Again, as with our discussion of lawyer attitudes toward the operation of the Plan, we have restricted our analysis of suggested improvements to those made by lawyers most familiar with the Plan, namely, ones practicing in Jackson County and St. Louis. Generally, the opinions of outstate attorneys on improvements parallel those of the metropolitan lawyers. Significant differences in attitudes of the two geographical groups of lawyers on specific proposals for improvement are noted in footnotes 31 and 33, *infra*.

[30] Some of our respondents stressed the value of having experienced men on the bench and preferred not to make an iron-clad rule on retirement, but rather favored permitting judges of retirement age who are physically and mentally capable to continue their judicial service, providing that the appropriate nominating commission or lawyers practicing in their jurisdiction voted to retain them in office.

[31] Among those in practice outside the two metropolitan communities, only one-third favored this proposal. This suggests that financial factors do not loom as large

Some also mentioned in questionnaire comments the desirability of utilizing more extensively the services of retired judges as special commissioners in court cases.[32]

While the issue is most acute for older judges, there is also a general concern among members of the Bar for developing some workable procedure for removing incompetent judges regardless of their age. A variety of "solutions" for the problem of removing such judges from the bench were suggested by lawyers included in our survey. About one-third of them favored the specific proposal of raising the "Yes" vote necessary to stay in office from a simple to a two-thirds majority. A number of attorneys prefer getting at the problem through another approach, namely, revising the present arrangement described in the previous chapter whereby lawyers practicing in Plan jurisdictions vote in a special bar poll, the results of which are published as a guide for the voters in the subsequent general election. Some attorneys would like to make the Bar vote on the retention of judges determinative rather than merely advisory, thus eliminating the public completely from the reelection process. Others are critical of the character of the Bar poll as it is now conducted on the grounds that it includes perfunctory "Yes" votes by many attorneys who have no first-hand experience with the judges upon whom they are passing judgement, the end result being that virtually all sitting judges, regardless of merit, are endorsed by the Bar. As a means of making the Bar poll more meaningful and discriminatory, these critics suggest that it be restricted to attorneys with trial practices who have personal knowledge of the abilities of the various judges, or that open meetings of lawyers be held to discuss the qualifications of the judges up for reelection, with a secret ballot taken of those participating in the meetings.

One final suggestion made for dealing with the problem of judges who are unable to perform their duties properly is to vest the responsibility for removing them in some committee of the Bar. Some lawyers expressing this general sentiment singled out the nominating commission as the appropriate body for this task, but most of them were not specific concerning the composition of such a committee. The important point

---

in the minds of outstate attorneys, perhaps because living costs are not as high as in the two major cities.

[32] As indicated in the previous chapter, present legal provisions permit retired judges at all levels of the state judicial system to serve as special commissioners or referees in court proceedings. However, the fact that there is no compulsory retirement age for circuit judges means that few retire until an advanced age. Therefore, the provision has not been as effective for lower court judges as it has been for appellate judges who must retire at age 75.

for this group of attorneys was that some administrative procedure be devised that would remove incompetent judges without dependence upon elections to accomplish this purpose.

Improvements Relating to the Recruitment and Selection Process

Generally, lawyers are not as critical of the Plan's recruitment and selection process as they are of its tenure provisions. However, a number of specific proposals in this general area drew considerable support from the Bar. One such improvement, designed to facilitate the recruitment process by attracting more capable candidates for the bench, is that of raising the compensation of judges to make it competitive with income received by leading members of the Bar. About two-fifths of our respondents favored this proposal.[33]

Our personal interviewees and survey respondents also offered certain improvements designed to mitigate what they consider to be unfair advantages which some groups enjoy in the selection process. As might be expected, Republican attorneys, in particular, support the specific proposal that the courts under the Plan should be made bipartisan, that is, should be required to represent, as equally as possible, both major political parties.[34] Moreover, Republican lawyers who are active in politics are more likely to support this proposal than their less-involved colleagues; among Democratic attorneys, the trend runs in the opposite direction.[35]

A number of attorneys also feel that the commissioners of the Supreme Court are in a favored position as far as judgeships on that court are concerned. They charge that the members of the Supreme Court, in effect, choose their future colleagues by first appointing them as commissioners and then using their influence on the nominating commission, channeled through the Chief Justice who serves as *ex officio* chairman, to get the commissioners nominated for Supreme Court judgeships. To break up this closed selection system (which they feel operates against the candidacies of lawyers in private practice), a variety of suggestions are made including the specific proposal, favored by about two-fifths

---

[33] About one-third of St. Louis County and outstate lawyers favored the proposal, again indicating that financial considerations are apparently not as salient to nonmetropolitan lawyers. See footnote 31, *supra*.

[34] Forty-eight percent of Jackson County and St. Louis Republican lawyers favor this proposal compared to 15 percent of the comparable Democratic respondents.

[35] Sixty-two percent of the politically-active Republicans practicing in the two major metropolitan communities support the proposal compared to 10 percent of the politically-active Democrats.

of the Bar, that appellate commissioners be chosen under the provisions of the Nonpartisan Court Plan rather than being appointed by the Court itself.[36] Other attorneys prefer different approaches to the problem, including making commissioners ineligible for judgeships, or eliminating them altogether in favor of either additional judges (to be chosen under the Plan) or law clerks. A few respondents even suggest that the Chief Justice be removed from the nominating commission to avoid the possibility of using his position to favor commissioners as candidates.

While suggestions like that above for eliminating judicial members of the commission were rare[37] (and nonexistent for the lawyer members), a sizable proportion of the Bar, more than one-quarter of our respondents, favor the specific proposal of removing lay members from the nominating commissions. The reasons behind this sentiment include the feeling of many attorneys that lay persons are not qualified to pass judgment on the judicial capabilities of practicing lawyers, as well as the suspicion that such persons tend to be too receptive to the desires of the governor (particularly if he appoints them) on the matter of choosing nominees. In fact, some respondents suggested that if some other method of selecting lay members besides appointment by the chief executive could be devised (for example, popular election), the major objection to their presence on the nominating commissions would be obviated.

This concern with gubernatorial control of the selection process (known as "wiring," "rigging," or "loading" the appointment in lawyer parlance) was reflected in comments made by individual attorneys in personal interviews, as well as the sample survey. Only a handful of attorneys suggested eliminating the governor from the process altogether,[38] but some checks on gubernatorial appointments were recommended, such as fuller consultation on his part with the Bar Associations, or a potential veto by the Supreme Court sitting *en banc* as a means of preventing a "gubernatorial fix," as one wary respondent put it.

Our interviews and sample survey also elicited a number of other improvements designed to make the selection process more "open" and

---

[36] Party differences are also significant with respect to this proposal, with 74 percent of the metropolitan Democratic lawyers supporting it compared to 41 percent of the Republicans. One possible explanation for this difference is that as members of the state's majority party, Democratic lawyers are more hopeful of being appointed to the appellate courts than are Republicans and, therefore, are more concerned about possible advantages that commissioners enjoy in the selection process.

[37] Less than 1 percent of our respondents added this suggestion to their questionnaires as a means of improving the operation of the Plan.

[38] Only about 1 percent of the respondents added this suggestion to their questionnaire as a method of improving the Plan.

"public." Included were suggestions that all attorneys be advised of vacancies and how to apply for consideration as a judge;[39] that the list of candidates and their qualifications be made public; that both the commission and the governor be required to interview all candidates and nominees respectively and that the votes of all nominating commissioners be published. Some attorneys also suggested that the size of the nominating commissions be increased to make them more representative and to reduce the opportunities for both internal commission politics (trading nominations, for example), as well as control by any outside pressure group.

Finally, some of our respondents would like to see an increase in the influence of the organized Bar in the selection process. A few even suggested the elimination of the commission system itself in favor of selecting judges through lawyer elections. However, more common was the suggestion that the commissions take into greater account the wishes of local bar associations when they make nominations for the bench.

Judges' Suggestions for Improving the Plan

Judges tend to see eye-to-eye with our lawyer respondents when it comes to improving those features of the Plan that relate to tenure.[40] An overwhelming proportion of them (over nine-tenths) favor the proposal of requiring all judges to retire at 75, and some would like to see the retirement age lowered to 70. About four-fifths of them share the prevailing sentiment of the Bar that the retirement benefits should be increased beyond the present level of one-third of the annual salary at the time of retirement. Some of them also expressed the desire to be able to play some kind of judicial role after retirement, such as sitting in on special cases where their experience would be helpful.

Interestingly enough, some of the judges also volunteered comments relating to the problem of removing incompetent members of the bench. These judges expressed the general sentiment that a method be developed to accomplish this purpose without the necessity of impeachment proceedings. Also, quite understandably, they all opposed the proposal that the "Yes" vote required to stay in office be raised from a simple

---

[39] Vacancies are announced in the newspaper and attorneys are invited to submit names for consideration by the nominating commission, but apparently some attorneys feel that the process is somehow covert. Also, as suggested previously some attorneys mistakenly think that persons cannot submit their own names; actually, protocol, rather than legalities, account for the fact that usually, names suggested for the commission's consideration do come from other parties.

[40] The number of Plan judges from whom we obtained responses on improvements was 41.

majority to a two-thirds majority. The concern that this kind of proposal creates for sitting judges is revealed in the following comment made by a member of the St. Louis circuit bench:

Statistics show the "No" votes on Judges in St. Louis range from 12 to 15 percent of the votes cast.

By requiring a two-thirds vote, we would have a judge defeated by a "No" vote of 34% of the votes cast. This means that 19% of the vote could be organized and delivered against a judge to defeat him (34% minus 15%). There are several political groups in St. Louis who could influence 19% of the voters against non-campaigning judges. Therefore an organized minority could campaign actively against a judge who cannot campaign or engage in political activity.

This suggestion to require an increase in the judges vote to two-thirds to be retained was first conceived in St. Louis by some lawyers who have actively opposed the Nonpartisan Court Plan, in a spirit of wrecking the plan (subjecting judges to political pressure) and not in the interest of improving the Plan.

A measure of self-interest is also reflected in the desire of about two-thirds of the judges to have the present compensation of judges raised to make it competitive with income received by leading members of the Bar. However, some of the judges stated in their comments that this proposal was unrealistic, since it would require increasing judicial salaries to more than $50,000 a year, and that they would be satisfied if their compensation would be made comparable to that received by federal district judges.

The attitudes of judges differ most markedly from those of the Bar on improvements associated with the selection system for choosing members of the bench. Having successfully run that winnowing process themselves, it is quite natural that few of the judges favor any changes in the status quo. For example, only 2 of the 41 judges (and 1 of the 10 Republican judges) among our respondents favored the specific proposal that the courts under the Plan be made bipartisan, that is, be required to represent, as equally as possible, both major political parties.[41] Also, none of the appellate judges favored the proposal for selecting their court commissioners under the Plan, a suggestion that would have eliminated the courts' present power to select such commissioners themselves.[42] In fact, none of the judges made any comments whatever relating to the concern expressed by many lawyers that the

---

[41] One judge commented that while he did not regard an equal party representation on the bench as necessary, he thought that the dominant party should not have more than two-thirds of the judgeships at any time.

[42] One-third of the circuit judges did favor the selection of such commissioners under the provisions of the Plan.

Supreme Court commissioners have a preferred position as far as judgeships on the Supreme Court are concerned.

Nor do the judges generally favor suggestions that would change the participants in the selection process. For example, only one wanted to remove lay representatives from the nominating commissions, his reasons being the usual ones of their unfamiliarity with the judicial qualifications of lawyer candidates and receptivity to gubernatorial wishes on nominations. One judge defended his opposition to the proposal on the grounds that, whatever its merits, the suggestion lacked "practicality"; another stated that it was necessary to retain lay members on the nominating commissions as a means of keeping the general public interested in the courts. And, quite understandably, none of the judges suggested that the judicial members be removed from the commissions.

The only hint of dissatisfaction of the Plan judges with the selection system, as it now operates, relates to the delay that sometimes develops between the time the nominations are sent to the governor and his initial appointment of a judge. Some judges suggested that a time limit be imposed (such as 60 days) and, if the governor did not make his appointment within that period, that some other appointing agency (one proposed the Supreme Court itself) be empowered to make the appointment. Presumably, such a procedure would tend to mitigate the amount of pressure that builds up on the governor during the interim period and also to insure that the services of the newly-appointed members of the bench would be available to the Court sooner than otherwise.

A number of changes in the Plan discussed above have been incorporated by a Citizens' Committee on Courts in a proposed constitutional amendment governing the state judiciary, which favors the extension of the Nonpartisan Court Plan to all courts in the state.[43] Included among its provisions is one that requires all judges to retire at age 70, with voluntary retirement at age 65 permitted for those with 12 years of service. In either case, retirement benefits would constitute

---

[43] The Citizens' Committee on the Courts, composed of lay, lawyers and judicial participants, has proposed extensive changes in the state's judicial department as set forth in Article V of the Missouri Constitution. The constitutional amendment proposed by the Committee would abolish all present magistrate, police, municipal corporation, probate and common pleas courts and vest their powers in circuit and district courts. These two general courts, together with four courts of appeals districts (a new one for the central district in Jefferson City is added to the present three districts in St. Louis, Kansas City and Springfield), together with the Supreme Court, would constitute the state's court system.

two-thirds (rather than the present one-third) of salary at the time
of retirement and judges would be subject to assignment as special
judges.[44] The new judicial article also provides for a Committee on
Disability, Removal, and Discipline, which is empowered to recommend
to the Supreme Court that action be taken against judges who are incapable of carrying out the activities of their office.[45] In addition to
these new provisions governing tenure, the amendment proposes the
elimination of appellate court commissioners,[46] and also stipulates that
if the governor makes no judicial appointment within 60 days after
receiving the three nominees from the commission, one of the three
is to be selected by a majority vote of the Supreme Court.[47]

With this overall assessment of the Plan's operation in mind, we now
turn to a key consideration in determining the consequences of any
judicial selection system: Does the Plan tend to produce a higher quality
judge than an alternative method such as popular election? This specific
issue, together with broader matters relating to the evaluation of judicial
performance, is explored in the following chapter.

---

[44] Article 5, Sec. 27 of the proposed amendment.
[45] Ibid., Sec. 25.
[46] Under the proposed amendment, present Supreme Court commissioners would
become judges of the central district of the Court of Appeals, while the present
commissioners of the St. Louis and Kansas City divisions of the court of appeals
would become judges of those divisions. Ibid., Schedule.
[47] Ibid., Sec. 26.

8

❧

LAWYER RATINGS OF JUDICIAL

PERFORMANCE

Assessments of the results of any judicial selection system inevitably involve the question of the quality of persons who are elevated to the bench. Certainly the members of the legal profession make this their number one consideration in discussions of the relative merits of different methods of selecting judges. The leaders of the Bar who developed the Nonpartisan Court Plan, as well as those who have praised it in print over the years, have used as their major argument the fact that it results in the choice of judges who are superior to those produced by an elective system. Our own study revealed the same emphasis on "better" judges in personal interviews with attorneys and, as indicated in the previous chapter, the Missouri Bar as a whole is most agreed upon this particular consequence of the Plan. Moreover, laymen, including members of the circuit and appellate nominating commissions, as well as civic and political leaders, constantly couch their comments in terms of the quality of the judges that the Plan engenders. On the other hand, persons opposing the Plan sometimes defend the caliber of elective judges as being equal to, or even superior to, the caliber of judges chosen by the Nonpartisan Court Plan.

Since all of the above groups place such a high priority on the quality of members of the bench, we attempted to deal with the issue of evaluating judicial performance. Admittedly the problems involved in doing so are difficult, and probably no means can be devised for evaluating the quality of judges that will satisfy all persons. Nevertheless, the importance of the matter led us to explore the issue.[1] Naturally, our efforts and findings must be considered as exploratory rather than definitive.

---

[1] In doing so, we borrow the argument of a Professor of Mathematics, John W. Tukey, that it is better to obtain "an approximate answer to the right question,

272

The following discussion investigates various facets of the problem of evaluating judicial performance. The initial section explores and evaluates various approaches that may be employed to judge the quality of members of the bench. This is followed by an analysis of the relative caliber of Missouri judges based upon the most satisfactory of these criteria. The third section examines another matter closely related to the whole question of evaluating judicial performance: the qualities of a "good" judge, as viewed by practicing lawyers, as well as members of the judiciary themselves. The final portion of the chapter explores the issue of whether there are certain judicial qualifications in the nature of background experiences and attributes of individuals that are associated with superior performance on the bench.

METHODS OF EVALUATING JUDICIAL PERFORMANCE

Lawyers, political leaders, newspaper editors, and other persons who take an interest in the activities of the courts, are quick to volunteer the information that Judge A is a "good" judge, while Judge B is a "bad" one. However, a search of the literature indicates that very few attempts have been made to develop methods of measuring judicial performance. Rodney Mott constructed an index reflecting background characteristics of state and federal judges which presumably bore on their capabilities for a judgeship.[2] He then investigated the significance of these materials for measuring judicial performance by relating the cumulative indexes developed for the various state supreme courts in the United States to prestige ratings developed for these same courts.[3]

---

which is often vague, than an exact answer to the wrong question, which can be made more precise." See his "The Future of Data Analysis," *Annals of Mathematical Statistics* 33 (1962), 13, cited in Arthur Banks and Robert Textor, *A Cross-Polity Survey* Cambridge, Mass., (M.I.T. Press, 1963), at p. 7. We also take solace from the statement by Rodney Mott that "We may not be able to measure the goodness of a judge, but it is very possible to measure the extent he is thought to be good." See his, "Measurement of Judicial Personnel," *New York University Law Review*, Vol. XXXIII (1948), p. 274.

[2] As indicated in the previous chapter, sixteen characteristics were involved. See Rodney L. Mott, Spencer D. Albright and Helen R. Semmerling, "Judicial Personnel," *Annals of the American Academy of Political and Social Science*, 167 (1933), 143–155.

[3] Three separate prestige ratings were developed for the state supreme courts. One was based upon evaluations of the various courts by law professors, and the other

However, this latter evaluation of performance was based on the activities of entire courts, not of individual judges. The recent study of the Texas judiciary by Henderson and Sinclair also restricts its assessments of the judiciary to measuring the relative prestige of various kinds of courts, rather than distinguishing the performances of single justices.[4]

The only previous studies we found that attempt to evaluate individual judicial performance are one in the mid-1930's by Neitzert[5] and a recent exploratory effort by Olson.[6] The former sought to determine whether the quality of the metropolitan trial bench in Illinois had deteriorated in the twentieth century. The author utilized four criteria to test the issue: the percentage of lower court cases that were reversed on appeal to higher courts; the volume of cases disposed of; judicial election returns; and evaluations of judges by Bar associations.[7] Olson experimented with rating judges of the Federal District Court for the District of Columbia through the use of subjective evaluations of their performance by lawyers practicing before the Court,[8] as well as the volume of litigation handled by the various justices.

With these studies as guidelines, we explored several approaches for evaluating judicial performance. Two involve subjective evaluations of

---

two, on the number of times each state tribunal was cited by other state supreme courts, and by the United States Supreme Court, respectively. The personnel index correlated significantly with all three such prestige indexes.

[4] Seven courts were involved, including four levels of Texas courts and three of the United States courts. The Texas Supreme Court was rated the highest by the Texas lawyers and the United States Supreme Court the lowest. See Bancroft C. Henderson and T. C. Sinclair, *Judicial Selection in Texas: An Exploratory Study,* University of Houston Studies in Social Science (Houston: Public Affairs Research Center, 1964), Vol. 2, pp. 90 ff.

[5] Howard Neitzert, "The Judges of the Nisi Prius Courts of Illinois," *Illinois Law Review,* 30 (1935–1936), 469–486.

[6] Edwin E. Olson, "Problems in Rating Judges: A Demonstration of Some Criteria and Methods." This unpublished working paper was prepared by Professor Olson in connection with a study of the selection of federal judges conducted by Professor Harold Chase under the auspices of the Brookings Institution. It was kindly made available to us by Professors Olson and Chase.

[7] The analysis calculated the percentage of elected judges who were considered to be candidates of the Chicago Bar Association on the basis of a straw vote of the members concerning their judicial preferences. A separate analysis was also made using answers to letters sent to members asking whether or not they favored the renomination and reelection of incumbent judges.

[8] Olson drew his sample of lawyer-evaluators from the list of the District Court's appointees to represent indigent criminals. He also had newspaper reporters covering the courts for the three large Washington, D.C. metropolitan newspapers assess the performances of the judges.

individual judges by members of the Bar.[9] We listed the names of circuit and appellate judges in the state alphabetically without regard to the system under which they were selected,[10] and asked each of the respondents in our sample survey to rate those before whom he had personally appeared, the rating to be based on the judges' best work years on the bench.[11] Two separate evaluations for each judge were requested. One involved his overall performance as a judge (outstanding, good, average, poor, and very poor), which we developed into a five-point index based upon a weighted average of the various evaluations.[12] The other assessment was of his degree of objectivity (very pro plaintiff; pro plaintiff, neutral, pro defendant and very pro defendant) which, for our present purposes, we reduced to a three-point index by combining the ratings of very pro plaintiff and very pro defendant, as well as pro plaintiff and pro defendant, with a neutral rating constituting the

---

[9] Of course, other persons besides lawyers, such as newspaper reporters and individuals with frequent business before the courts, have some inkling of how various judges perform, but attorneys have the most direct and sustained contact with the courts.

[10] The names of all appellate judges in the state who served during the period from 1940 to 1964 were included on the questionnaire, along with Jackson County, St. Louis City, and St. Louis County judges who were on those benches during the same period. Outstate respondents were requested to write in the names of circuit judges before whom they had practiced.

[11] The reason for asking that the rating be based on the judges' best work years on the bench was to avoid the possibility that the evaluations of some of the older judges would suffer because they no longer were as capable as they had been in former years. An analysis of the ratings by judges' ages at the time of the survey revealed no tendency for older judges to receive low scores, so apparently the respondents complied with our request.

[12] The index for each judge was computed by multiplying the figure assigned the various ratings (outstanding—5; good—4; fair—3; poor—2; and very poor—1), by the number of respondents giving him each such rating, and then dividing the total figure by the number of raters. Thus, for example, if a judge received 200 outstanding ratings; 150 good ones; 100 fair ones; 75 poor ones and 75 very poor ones, his index would be

$$\frac{(200 \times 5) + (150 \times 4) + (100 \times 3) + (75 \times 2) + (75 \times 1)}{600}$$

or

$$\frac{1000 + 600 + 300 + 150 + 75}{600} = \frac{2125}{600} = 3.54.$$

This means that the higher a judge's index number is, the better our respondents consider his overall performance on the bench to be.

third category.[13] The two resultant evaluations of individual judge's over-all performance and degree of objectivity constitute two criteria by which we sought to measure the quality of members of the bench.

Two other tests of judicial performance incorporate the use of Bar poll results and election returns pertaining to judges under the Non-partisan Court Plan.[14] As previously noted, voting in both such elections overwhelmingly supports the incumbents. Nevertheless, some differences do appear in assessments of individual judges by lawyers, as well as the general electorate and, therefore, we explored such evaluations as providing some measure of the relative quality of members of the Bench. To do so, we computed a percentage of "Yes" votes in such Bar polls over the years;[15] a similar statistic was calculated for the affirmative votes of the general public in the elections in which the individual judges ran on their records.[16]

The final approach we used to measure the caliber of judges was based on the appeal records of circuit court judges. All cases appealed either to the three intermediate courts of appeal or to the state Supreme Court in the last twenty-five years[17] were examined to determine the identity of the circuit court judge whose ruling was questioned, and the outcome of the appeal, that is, whether it was affirmed, reversed, or affirmed in part and reversed in part.[18] A percentage of affirmance was then computed for each lower court judge in the state whose decisions were so appealed. This constituted our fifth criteria for assessing the quality of individual judges.

Thus the five approaches[19] utilize a number of techniques of measure-

---

[13] Our immediate concern being that of judicial quality, we were interested only in the amount, not the direction, of a judge's bias as perceived by our respondents. (The latter matter will be explored in the following chapter.) The 3-point index was computed in the same manner as the 5-point one explained in the previous footnote, with the figures assigned the ratings being 3 for neutral, 2 for pro plaintiff or pro defendant, and 1 for very pro plaintiff or very pro defendant.

[14] No comparable data are available for elective judges since they run in competitive partisan contests.

[15] Circuit judges run for reelection every six years, probate judges every four years, and appellate judges every twelve years. The affirmative votes were averaged for judges involved in more than one Bar poll.

[16] Again, when a judge came up for reelection under the Plan more than once during the period under study, the affirmative votes for all elections were averaged.

[17] For those cases taken from the intermediate court of appeal to the state Supreme Court, the finding of the latter determined the status (affirm, reverse, etc.) of the circuit court ruling.

[18] The relatively few decisions that were affirmed in part, and reversed in part were eliminated from the analysis.

[19] We decided not to include the volume of work disposed of by individual judge.

ment, different groups of evaluators, and apply to various kinds of judges. The first two tests (overall performance and degree of objectivity) involve subjective evaluations of judges (on five- and three-point scales, respectively) by a sample of the Missouri Bar and pertain to all judges in the state. The third and fourth (Bar poll and general election) use a dichotomous rating (Yes or No on retention in office) by members of the Bar and the general public as revealed by voting returns, and are available only for judges who come under the provisions of the Nonpartisan Court Plan (those appointed under the Plan as well as those elected judges who were "held over" under its provisions when the Plan was adopted in 1940). Finally, the fifth evaluative technique is again of a dichotomous nature (affirm or reverse); it also constitutes a kind of rating, since it involves a judgment by upper court judges of how accurately their colleagues on the lower courts have understood and applied the law to cases before them which were eventually appealed. Of course, it can only be applied as a test for the performance of judges of these lower courts.[20]

We next compared these various measures of judicial performance to determine the extent to which judges tended to be rated similarly on the various approaches, that is, whether those scoring well on overall performance also received favorable assessments on their degree of objectivity, Bar poll, election results, and the like. The ideal tool for such a determination is correlation analysis, which indicates the relationships that exist among variations in the different measures of judicial performance. A positive correlation between two variables means that judges rated high, medium, or low on one variable have proportionately high, medium, or low ratings on the other; a negative correlation means the opposite situation is present. A no-correlation result between two variables means that they are not related to each other in any significant way. Numerically, correlation is expressed as a coefficient which runs from zero, no correlation, to +1.00 or −1.00, which designates a perfect positive or negative correlation, respectively.[21]

Because of the disparate functions performed by lower and appellate court judges in the judicial process, we separated the circuit and appellate judges in our analysis. Table 8.1 shows the correlations that exist among the five measures for evaluating the performance of lower court

---

s a measure of judicial performance because we felt that the quality (not the quantity) of output was the more important factor in the judicial process.
The lower courts included, in addition to the circuit ones, the probate courts of Jackson County and St. Louis City and the St. Louis Court of Criminal Correction.
The particular correlation technique used was product moment, not one based merely upon the rank order of the variables.

TABLE 8.1
CORRELATION MATRIX FOR FIVE DIFFERENT MEASURES OF EVALUATING
JUDICIAL PERFORMANCE OF LOWER COURT JUDGES

	Overall Performance		Objectivity[b]		Bar Poll		Election	
	Corr.	N^a	Corr.	N^a	Corr.	N^a	Corr.	N^a
Objectivity[b]	.55	(113)						
Bar poll	.86	(47)	.71	(47)				
Election	.31	(57)	.51	(57)	.59	(50)		
Affirmance	.32	(104)	.19	(104)	.49	(47)	.49	(56)

[a] The number of cases varies because of differences in the data available for the five measures. The number of cases for each correlation is the number of judges for whom there are data for *both* the variables being correlated.

[b] The five-point objectivity scale was reduced to a three-point scale for correlation purposes: 1-very pro plaintiff or very pro defendant; 2-pro plaintiff or pro defendant; 3-neutral. It thus reflects the amount, but not direction, of the judges' biases as perceived by members of the Bar.

judges. It indicates that the five variables are significantly related to each other,[22] that is, the evaluations of judges in each of the tests used tend to parallel those on the others. The highest correlation, .86, exists between the results of the Bar poll and the survey evaluation of the overall performance of judges; this is to be expected since the same matter (general judicial performance) is being assessed by essentially the same group of raters. Close associations also exist between each of these measures of overall judicial performance and the degree of objectivity ratings made by lawyers in the survey. The election results are most clearly connected with those of the Bar poll. This may indicate that the voters pay some attention, at least, to the opinions of the Bar when they cast their judicial ballots. The fifth variable, the affirmance rate of the judges, relates most significantly to the Bar and election results. Lawyers in the sample survey apparently used other criteria besides the appeal record of lower court judges in evaluating their performance on the bench.

A similar correlation of the four measures for assessing the performance of appellate judges (of course, no affirmance variable exists for such judges) is made more difficult by the limited number of cases

---

[22] This is true at the .05 level of significance. At the .01 level, all the relationships are statistically significant except the one which exists between the degree of objectivity and appeal variables.

TABLE 8.2
CORRELATION MATRIX FOR FOUR DIFFERENT MEASURES OF EVALUATING
JUDICIAL PERFORMANCE OF APPELLATE COURT JUDGES

	Overall Performance		Objectivity[b]		Bar Poll	
	Corr.	N^a	Corr.	N^a	Corr.	N^a
Objectivity[b]	.21	(28)				
Bar poll	.75	(23)	.01	(23)		
Election	.15	(26)	.07	(26)	.31	(26)

[a] The N's vary because of differences in the data available for the four measures. The N for each correlation is the number of judges for whom there are data for *both* the variables being correlated.

[b] The five-point objectivity scale was reduced to a three-point scale for correlation purposes: 1-very pro plaintiff or very pro defendant; 2-pro plaintiff or pro defendant; 3-neutral. It thus reflects the amount, but not direction, of the judges' biases as perceived by members of the Bar.

involved, compared to those available for analysis at the lower court level.[23] Nevertheless, Table 8.2, like Table 8.1, indicates that a high correlation exists between the evaluation of overall judicial performance by our sample of lawyers and the results of the Bar polls. Also, there is again some correspondence between the way lawyers voted in the Bar poll and the results of the judicial elections in which the general public participated.[24] However, there is no statistically significant association between the overall performance and degree of objectivity assessments by our sample of lawyers; moreover, there is none at all between the latter variable and the Bar poll one which also assesses the all around capability of a judge. This may suggest that the plaintiff-defendant factor is not as salient for lawyers in evaluating the overall performance of appellate judges as it is in their assessment of persons who serve on the lower courts.

Having explored and correlated the various approaches to measuring

---

[23] The fewer the number of cases involved (in the case of the appellate judges, from 23 to 26 of them, depending upon the availability of data on *both* variables being correlated), the more likely it is that a correlation will be the result of chance. For this reason, higher correlations are required than for the comparable analysis of circuit judges (where the cases ranged from 47–113) before statistically significant relationships between variables can be established.

[24] The .31 correlation falls just short of the .33 figure necessary to establish a relationship at the .05 level of significance between two variables involving 26 cases.

judicial performance, we then assessed their relative merits for our subsequent analysis, taking into account the strengths and weaknesses of each. Of the five measures, only the first two (overall performance and degree of objectivity) are available for evaluating the performance of all judges, since the third (Bar poll) and fourth (election returns) relate to Nonpartisan Plan and holdover judges only, and the fifth (affirmance rate) can be used only for lower court judges. The first two measures of judicial performance have other obvious advantages. They both use scales that are more refined than the dichotomous measure (Yes or No) rating for the Bar poll, election, and affirmance record approaches;[25] moreover, the fact that the overall performance and objectivity ratings were obtained from a sample survey, not only means that they are representative of the Bar's evaluations but also that they can be fruitfully analyzed by the various characteristics of the respondents involved in such evaluations.

We also feel that the basis of judgment for the first two approaches, namely, the experiences of lawyers actually practicing before the judges concerned, is better than that involved in the other three evaluation techniques. As suggested previously, lawyers often vote in the Bar poll without regard to their personal appearance before the judges concerned. Moreover, relatively few members of the general public, particularly in the metropolitan communities, have any real information about the activities of the courts, and may (as the correlations between Bar and general elections results suggest) take their cues on voting in judicial elections from the lawyers' poll.

The fifth evaluative technique, that of the affirmance rate of trial court judges, is obviously based on an excellent source of judgment (that of appellate justices) but we feel there are some serious questions concerning the value of what is being judged, that is, application of the law, primarily as it has been enunciated by the courts in the past. Some of the lawyers we personally interviewed pointed out that a judge who knows the law, but feels that it should be changed, is penalized by this test if his brethren on the upper courts disagree with him. A member of the bench also suggested that a judge who is very conscious of his appeal record (this is particularly true, one informant said, of a person when he first assumes office) tends to be too cautious in his rulings, that is, he does everything he can to avoid the possibility that his judgment on a matter will be legally questioned. Thus he may send the case to the jury rather than risk an overruling on a directed verdict

---

[25] As previously explained, the index for overall performance is based on a five-point scale while the one for degree of objectivity involves a three-point scale.

motion.[26] If these allegations are true, the affirmance rate test would appear to work to the benefit of the lower court judge who is conservative, rather than one who welcomes changes in the law and who is willing to take a very active role in the trial proceedings.[27] The fact that the correlations shown above in Table 8.1 between affirmance record and the overall performance and objectivity ratings of trial judges are fairly low indicates that lawyers who practice before the courts do not consider appeal results as very determinative of the quality of a judge.

With respect to the relative value of the overall performance and objectivity ratings, for our purposes the former proved to be the superior one. First, it is a better measure of a judge's all around capabilities because it takes into account a broader range of considerations than his attitudes on the plaintiff-defendant issue. Important as this latter factor is in litigation, it is not an element in all cases, particularly those at the appellate level. Second, because the overall performance evaluation involves a five-point scale rather than a three-point one, it is a more discriminating measure of judicial performance, with ratings ranging from a high of 4.71 to a low of 1.58, compared to 2.87 and 1.77 ratings for the degree of objectivity assessment.[28] Moreover, a comparison of the overall performance ratings of judges in the survey with those made by lawyers in personal interviews indicates considerable agreement in the results of the two assessments. And, as indicated by Table 8.1, the overall performance rating of circuit judges correlated with all of the other measures of their judicial quality that we explored.[29]

---

[26] In ruling on a directed motion by the defendant, the judge is asked to determine that even if the evidence for the plaintiff is accepted as true, as a matter of law, he is still not entitled to recover under his cause of action.

[27] Clarence Morris makes the same general point in his article, "Law, Reason and Sociology," *University of Pennsylvania Law Review,* 107 (December, 1958), when he states at page 159 that "Trial judges with crowded dockets can be sometimes harried into legalistic thought at the expense of substantive justice. Many trial judges overdread appellate court reversals; some of them rightly or wrongly think that their appellate courts hold to formal considerations—especially when that court has clearly enunciated an applicable doctrine. The attitude of trial judges is partly an attitude on separation of functions—an allocation of roles; trial judges are likely to think that correction or qualification of supreme court pronouncements is properly done only by supreme court judges and that their own role requires them to apply the law laid down by the supreme court."

[28] The mean and standard deviation for the overall performance rating are 3.87 and .57; for the degree of objectivity evaluation the comparable figures are 2.48 and .19.

[29] All correlations are at the .01 level. For circuit judges, the only evaluation measure that has a higher average correlation with the other four variables is the Bar poll results.

ASSESSING THE RELATIVE PERFORMANCE OF MISSOURI JUDGES

Applying the lawyer ratings of overall performance as our criterion, we turned to the basic question referred to at the beginning of the chapter: Do different methods of selecting judges result in placing persons on the bench who can be distinguished from each other on the basis of quality? We again separated our analysis by level of court. Table 8.3, which deals with lower court judges, compares the rankings of various groups of trail court judges in Missouri: those from Jackson County and St. Louis City who were appointed under the Nonpartisan Court Plan; those from the same jurisdictions who were originally chosen under the former elective system used in those areas, and who were "held over" in office when the Plan came into effect in 1940; and those from suburban St. Louis County and outstate areas of Missouri who are presently elected. The comparative analysis shows the number of judges from each of these categories who are included in quartiles based upon ratings of all trial judges in the state combined.

Focusing initially on the three broad categories of judges (Plan, "holdover" and elective) shown by the underlined data, Table 8.3 indicates that the greatest differences in the ratings of judges in the state exist

TABLE 8.3
COMPARISON OF QUARTILE RANKINGS OF CIRCUIT COURT JUDGES IN MISSOURI BY SELECTION SYSTEM AND GEOGRAPHICAL LOCATION

	Nonpartisan Plan Judges			Holdover Judges			Elected Judges			
	Jackson County	St. Louis City	Total	Jackson County	St. Louis City	Total	St. Louis County	Out-state	Total	Total
First quartile (4.25–4.71)[a]	6	1	7	1	2	3	5	13	18	28
Second quartile (3.85–4.24)[a]	4	8	12	3	2	5	3	8	11	28
Third quartile (3.43–3.84)[a]	5	4	9	2	6	8	5	5	10	27
Fourth quartile (1.58–3.42)[a]	2	1	3	3	9	12	5	9	14	29
Total	17	14	31	9	19	28	18	35	53	112
Mean[a]	3.93	3.92	3.93	3.58	3.39	3.45	3.68	3.96	3.86	3.77

[a] Based upon a possible rating of 5.00. The rating for each judge is a weighted average of all lawyers rating him. The number of lawyers rating individual judges varies.

between the two sets of Jackson County and St. Louis City judges. The Plan judges in these communities have a mean rating of 3.93, and 19 of 31 (about 61 percent of them) rank in the upper two quartiles of all the lower court judges in the state. In contrast, the holdover judges have a mean of 3.45, and only 8 of 28 (about 29 percent) are in the upper two quartiles of all members of the circuit bench. The elective judges hold an intermediate position between the Plan and holdover judges (somewhat closer to the former than the latter), with a mean of 3.86, and 29 of 53 judges (about 55 percent of them) are included in the upper two quartiles of all lower court judges.

The table is also revealing with respect to the variation in ratings among judges within each of the three major categories. The assertion made frequently by supporters of the Plan that it tends to eliminate the selection of very poor judges[30] tends to be supported by the data. Only 3 of 31 (about 10 percent of the Plan judges) are ranked in the lowest quartile, while about 43 percent (12 of 28) and 26 percent (14 of 53) of the holdover and elective judges, respectively, received such a ranking. Also the differences in quality of elective judges are considerable. In fact, this latter group has a higher percentage of judges in the highest quartile than has the Nonpartisan Plan group, the proportions being 34 percent (18 of 53) and 23 percent (7 of 31), respectively.

A further examination of Table 8.3 reveals that within the three broad categories of judges, there are differences in the ratings of judges serving in different geographical areas. The outstate elected judges are rated better than their counterparts in St. Louis County. Generally, the judges in Jackson County have somewhat better ratings than those in St. Louis; the differences are most pronounced between the Nonpartisan Plan judges of the two communities in the highest quartile,[31] and between the holdover judges in the lowest quartile.

One of the problems involved in comparing the ratings of the various judges in the state is the fact that differences between them may be attributable to divergent standards applied by the separate groups of raters. This is not an issue in the evaluations of Plan and holdover judges

---

[30] For example, an editorial in a Kansas City newspaper commenting on the Plan suggests that while some excellent judges were produced by the former elective system, it also produced some bad judges. The writer concludes that "Under the Nonpartisan procedure, the range has been from excellent down to reasonably good." See *Kansas City Times*, October 13, 1949.

[31] It should be noted, however, that the means of the Kansas City and St. Louis Plan judges are virtually the same, and proportionally fewer of the latter than the former judges are located in the lowest two quartiles of all circuit judges in the state.

TABLE 8.4

COMPARISON OF QUARTILE RATINGS OF ST. LOUIS CITY AND ST. LOUIS
COUNTY CIRCUIT JUDGES BY LAWYERS RATING BOTH GROUPS OF JUDGES

	St. Louis City	St. Louis City	St. Louis County	
	Plan Judges	Holdover Judges	Judges	Total
First quartile	3	4	6	13
(4.12–4.53)				
Second quartile	8	1	4	13
(3.73–4.11)				
Third quartile	3	6	4	13
(3.26–3.72)				
Fourth quartile	0	8	4	12
(1.59–3.25)				
Total	14	19	18	51
Mean	3.92	3.38	3.67	3.70

within each of the two major cities, since the same attorneys practice
before both kinds of judges there, but it does have a potential effect
upon the relative assessments of judges in St. Louis County and outstate
areas where only the elective method of judicial selection is employed.
A comparison can be made in the St. Louis area, however, involving
both city and county judges and a common group of raters; this is
possible because many lawyers living in this metropolitan community
practice before both benches.[32] Table 8.4 analyzes the ratings of judges
by lawyers evaluating the personnel of *both* the St. Louis City and
St. Louis County circuit courts.

Table 8.4 shows the distinct differences that exist among the ratings
of the three kinds of judges. Those selected under the Plan clearly rank
the highest; they have a mean rating of 3.92, and 11 of 14 (about 79
percent of them) are included in the upper two quartiles of all the
St. Louis area circuit judges, as contrasted to a mean of 3.38 and 5
of 19 (or 26 percent) for their holdover colleagues who are located
in these same quartiles. The elected county judges are "average" in
comparative terms, as indicated by their fairly even distribution among
the four quartiles and their mean rating of 3.67. However, the elected
group has a greater proportion of persons in the highest quartile (6
of 18, or 33 percent, compared with 3 of 14, or 22 percent) than has

---

[32] Our analysis shows that 397 of the respondents practicing in the St. Louis area
rated both city and county judges, while 72 rated city judges only and 23 rated
only St. Louis County judges.

TABLE 8.5

COMPARISON OF QUARTILE RANKINGS OF APPELLATE COURT JUDGES IN
MISSOURI

	Courts of Appeal Judges		Supreme Court Judges		All Appellate Courts		
	Plan	Holdover	Plan	Holdover	Plan	Holdover	Total
First quartile (4.40–4.56)	6	1	2	1	8	2	10
Second quartile (4.18–4.39)	3	2	3	1	6	3	9
Third quartile (3.96–4.17)	1	3	3	2	4	5	9
Fourth quartile (2.64–3.95)	3	3	0	3	3	6	9
Total	13	9	8	7	21	16	37
Mean	4.20	3.88	4.25	4.06	4.22	3.96	4.11

the Plan group serving in the City. In contrast, 4 of the county's 18 judges were ranked in the lowest quartile, while none of the Plan judges are in the category, further supporting the contention that the Plan method of selection tends to eliminate very poor judges.

The fact that the evaluations of the three kinds of St. Louis area judges in Table 8.4 so closely parallel those of the same categories in Table 8.3[33] (where the groups of evaluators are not necessarily composed of the same lawyers) suggests that the relative judicial rankings are based upon actual differences in perceived capabilities of the judges themselves, rather than on disparities resulting from divergent standards employed by different raters. It is not possible to test this matter in other areas of the state, since there are no significant groups of attorneys who practice before circuit judges in both major cities, or in outstate areas and also before any of the other lower court benches. There is no reason, however, to expect that attorneys in these areas behave differently in evaluating judges than those practicing in the St. Louis area, and, therefore, we would infer that differences between the various categories of trial court judges in the state are meaningful.

Table 8.5, which contains data for appellate judges similar to those already analyzed for trial courts, shows that the same general pattern exists for the relative ratings of Plan and holdover members of the upper courts. The former judges have higher mean ratings than the latter and

---

[33] Notice that the means of the three groups of St. Louis area judges in the two tables are virtually identical.

are generally concentrated in the upper two quartiles of rankings of both the intermediate appeal and state Supreme courts. A comparison of the overall mean ratings of judges of the two appellate courts, together with those shown in Table 8.3 for trial judges in the two urban communities, also indicates a progressively higher evaluation for the members of the three levels of courts. This is true for those chosen under both selection systems, the mean ratings of the Plan ones being 3.93, 4.20 and 4.25, and the holdover judges, 3.45, 3.88, and 4.06, respectively.

The Effects of Selection Preferences and Background Characteristics of Lawyers on the Ratings of Judges

The examination thus far has shown that judges chosen under the Plan score higher than their colleagues in ratings of overall performance by members of the Bar.[34] The analysis, however, has been based on the ratings of lawyers as a group, and, therefore, does not reveal possible differences in evaluations of judges by different segments of the legal profession. One important question in this connection is whether linkages exist between lawyers' evaluations of judges chosen under different selection methods and their preferences concerning such methods. If they do, then the higher ratings of Plan judges in Missouri should come from attorneys who support the Plan, while the more favorable evaluations of elective judges should come from those who advocate partisan ballots to choose judges.[35] Table 8.6 provides the relevant data for the evaluation of circuit judges in Missouri.

The table indicates that correlation between the support for the Plan as a selection method and the evaluations of its judges is clear. Lawyers favoring the Plan rate its judges higher than do attorneys who prefer partisan election. Also, Plan advocates in both Jackson County and St. Louis rate Plan judges more favorably than they do their holdover colleagues who originally went on the bench through partisan elections. Moreover, in the St. Louis area, Plan supporters evaluate the City's Plan judges as being superior to the elective St. Louis County judges.

[34] The Plan judges also score higher than the other judges on other kinds of measures of judicial performance. The Bar poll results show a 92 percent affirmative vote for Plan judges as compared to a 79 percent figure for holdover ones. The corresponding affirmative votes of the electorate for the two groups are 82 and 80 percent. The affirmance records on appeal are 71 percent, 62 percent and 66 percent, for the Plan, holdover and elected judges, respectively.

[35] Although we have comparable data on ratings of judges by lawyers who favor judicial elections utilizing nonpartisan ballots, we have not included them in our analysis because none of the judges in Missouri have ever been chosen under that system.

TABLE 8.6

Comparative Ratings of Circuit Judges[a] Selected Under Different Systems by Lawyers Favoring Plan or Partisan Elections

Method Favored by Lawyer Raters	Nonpartisan Plan Judges			Holdover Judges			Elected Judges		
	(N = 17) Jackson County	(N = 14) St. Louis City	(N = 31) Total	(N = 9) Jackson County	(N = 19) St. Louis City	(N = 28) Total	(N = 18) St. Louis County	(N = 30)[b] Outstate	(N = 48) Total
Plan	3.98	4.05	4.02	3.48	3.39	3.43	3.70	3.97	3.89
Partisan elections	3.75	3.61	3.69	3.76	3.44	3.54	3.62	4.19	3.97

[a] The rating in each cell is an average of all applicable ratings. For comparative purposes, the ratings of St. Louis City and County judges are based upon evaluations of lawyers practicing before both benches. See footnote 32, *supra*.
[b] When the lawyer respondents were divided by selection method favored, there were an insufficient number of raters for 5 outstate judges.

However, the reverse side of the coin (that is, the linkage between preference for an elective system and the ratings of its judges) is not so obvious. The Jackson County holdover judges and the outstate elective ones do receive higher ratings from the lawyers who prefer partisan elections over the Plan. However, the difference between the evaluations of the St. Louis holdover judges by the two kinds of lawyer raters is minimal, and the St. Louis County judges actually receive more favorable ratings from attorneys who prefer the Plan, rather than those who support the present partisan election system under which such judges are chosen. Table 8.6 also shows that supporters of the elective system do not evaluate its judges higher than those chosen under the Plan: their ratings of Plan and holdover judges in Jackson County are virtually identical, as are their ratings of St. Louis City Plan and St. Louis County elective judges, and they actually rate the St. Louis City Plan judges as being considerably better than their holdover colleagues.

It is not possible to determine from the data why preferences for partisan elections do not correlate more closely with the evaluation of judges.[36] Conceivably, those attorneys who favor the elective method do not feel that the holdover judges in Jackson County and St. Louis are really representative of the kinds of judges that such a system would produce today, or that the present St. Louis County elective judges can be fairly compared with city judges who operate in a different political and judicial arena. It is also possible that preferences on methods of judicial selection relate more closely to ideological considerations growing out of political and social divisions in the Bar than they do to perceptions of actual performance on the bench.[37]

One such factor that might affect lawyers' evaluations of judges is partisan affiliation. Do Republican and Democratic lawyers tend to rate their colleagues on the bench higher than they do judges who come from the opposition party? Related to this question is another consideration: Does partisanship affect assessments of judicial performance more

[36] An analysis of the overall performance of appellate judges produces similar results: preferences for the Plan correlate with the evaluations of its judges but the same pattern is not so clear with respect to support for partisan elections and ratings of judges originally chosen under that system. However, those who favor such elections do rate the holdover Supreme Court judges higher than they do those selected under the Plan.

[37] It should be pointed out that even where a correlation exists between high ratings of judges chosen under a particular selection system and preference for that system, it does not necessarily follow that the system was chosen by lawyers on the basis of the evaluation of these judges. The reverse tendency might also be true, that is, lawyers may tend to perceive judges as being "good" because they are chosen under a selection method which they favor for some other reason.

under one system than under another? It will be recalled from the previous chapter that many lawyers feel that the Nonpartisan Plan has "taken politics out of judicial selection." If this is true, we might then expect that comparative ratings of Plan judges by Republican and Democratic lawyers would be less influenced by such judges' partisan affiliations than lawyers' evaluations of persons who went on the bench under an elective system. However, Table 8.7, which categorizes judges' ratings by both selection system and partisan factors, reveals no distinct party patterns with respect to the evaluation of judges. Republican Plan judges in Jackson County and St. Louis City, as well as elected Republican St. Louis County judges, are rated higher than their Democratic colleagues on the bench by lawyers of both political persuasions while, in the outstate areas, the reverse situation exists (that is, elective Democratic judges are considered superior by both Republican and Democratic attorneys alike). Nor are there clear correlations with respect to the Democratic holdover judges (no comparable group of Republican judges exists): those in Jackson County are rated higher by their fellow partisans but the opposite is true in St. Louis where Republican lawyers give the Democratic judges slightly higher ratings. Moreover, the type of selection system has little relevance for the evaluations as far as partisanship is concerned. Democratic attorneys do rate Republican Plan judges higher in both cities, but they also give St. Louis County elective judges of the opposite political persuasion better performance scores than they do those from their own political party. The same tendency is true outstate, where Republicans assess Democratic elected judges somewhat more favorably than judges of their own partisan background.[38]

Previous chapters have demonstrated the importance of social divisions in the Bar for judicial selection in Missouri. Such divisions not only affect lawyers' preferences concerning selection methods, but also shape Bar politics operating within the framework of the Plan: plaintiffs' and defendants' lawyers and their respective allies, criminal and corporation attorneys, seek to elect candidates to the nominating commissions on the assumption that this will tend to insure that the judges who are ultimately chosen will be sympathetic (or at least not antagonistic)

---

[38] The ratings of the appellate court judges also show no distinct partisan patterns. Lawyers of both parties assess Republican Plan judges of the intermediate court of appeals and the Supreme Court more favorably than their Democratic counterparts, while the Democratic holdover judges on the Courts of Appeals are rated higher than are their Republican colleagues. (There are no Republican holdover judges on the Supreme Court so a two-way comparison of the latter group of judges is not possible.)

TABLE 8.7

RATINGS OF CIRCUIT JUDGES SELECTED UNDER VARIOUS SYSTEMS[a] BY PARTISAN AFFILIATION OF JUDGES AND RATERS

Partisan Affiliation of Raters	Nonpartisan Plan Judges				Holdover Judges				Elected Judges			
	Jackson County		St. Louis City		Jackson County		St. Louis City		St. Louis County		Outstate	
	(N = 5) Republican	(N = 12) Democrat	(N = 5) Republican	(N = 9) Democrat	(N = 0) Republican	(N = 9) Democrat	(N = 0) Republican	(N = 19) Democrat	(N = 6) Republican	(N = 12) Democrat	(N = 8) Republican	(N = 27) Democrat
Republicans	4.14	3.95	4.09	3.94	—	3.50	—	3.45	4.11	3.40	3.90	3.94
Democrats	4.03	3.83	3.91	3.72	—	3.62	—	3.40	3.96	3.55	3.72	4.00

[a] The rating in each cell is an average of all applicable ratings. For comparative purposes, the ratings of St. Louis City and County judges are based upon the evaluations of lawyers practicing before both benches. See footnote 32, supra.

290

TABLE 8.8
RATINGS OF NONPARTISAN PLAN JUDGES WITH CERTAIN PRIOR PRACTICE EXPERIENCE[a] BY LAWYERS WITH COMPARABLE PRACTICE EXPERIENCE

| | Judges' Backgrounds[b] | | | | | | | | | | | |
| Lawyers' Backgrounds[c] | Defendants' | | | Corporation | | | Plaintiffs' | | | Criminal | | |
	(N = 7) Circuit	(N = 2) Appellate	(N = 9) Total	(N = 10) Circuit	(N = 5) Appellate	(N = 15) Total	(N = 4) Circuit	(N = 3) Appellate	(N = 7) Total	(N = 4) Circuit	(N = 1) Appellate	(N = 5) Total
Defendants'	4.05	4.39	4.14	3.93	4.14	4.00	3.84	3.77	3.81	4.04	4.43	4.12
Corporation	4.15	4.41	4.21	4.06	4.29	4.13	4.08	4.11	4.09	4.18	4.39	4.22
Plaintiffs'	3.80	4.10	3.87	3.90	4.28	4.03	3.81	4.14	3.98	4.10	4.35	4.15
Criminal	3.86	4.30	3.96	3.89	4.26	4.01	3.59	4.14	3.83	3.94	4.30	4.01

[a] The rating in each cell is an average of all applicable ratings.
[b] Information on prior experience is restricted to those Plan judges who returned questionnaires. Includes those who listed field exclusively or as one of two or three major fields of practice.
[c] Includes those lawyers who listed field exclusively, or as one of two or three major fields of practice.

to their clients' interests. Table 8.8 is designed to test whether such perceptions continue to persist after judges go on the bench, that is, whether lawyers with a particular kind of legal practice (the four groups analyzed represent the extremes of the Bar's social spectrum) tend to rate Nonpartisan Plan judges[39] who had a similar prior practice experience more highly than they do jurist who came from the opposite side of the profession from themselves.

The data indicate that the evaluation of judges by defendants' lawyers most clearly reflects Bar rivalries. They rate both circuit and appellate judges with their own practice specialty higher than they do judges with a prior plaintiffs' practice. However, the reverse tendency is not as clear, since plaintiffs' attorneys score judges at both levels who come from a defense practice only slightly lower than they do members of the bench with their own specialty. The table also shows that beyond the immediate plaintiffs'-defendants' rivalry, the comparative evaluations of judges bear little relationship to broad social divisions in the Bar. Judges who once had a criminal practice receive their lowest scores from their attorney counterparts, while corporation lawyers tend to give high evaluations to all judges regardless of their kind of prior experience.

Nor do the data show especially favorable orientations by attorneys toward judges with specialities akin socially to their own: defendants' lawyers rate judges with a criminal practice background higher than they do those who had previous corporate experience, while criminal attorneys evaluate judges with a corporate practice experience more favorably than they do erstwhile plaintiffs' attorneys with whom they are supposedly allied in broad social divisions of the Bar. Corporation lawyers also regard judges with a prior criminal practice as well as they do those from the defense side of the Bar. Only the plaintiffs' attorneys' favorable ratings of judges with a criminal practice background compared with those formerly in corporate work accords with expectations based upon social status differences within the legal profession.

The analysis thus demonstrates considerable consensus among attorneys in Missouri concerning who is and who is not a good judge. Moreover, such evaluations have limited relationships with either judical selection preferences of attorneys or political and social divisions of the Bar. The following section explores another facet of evaluating judicial performance: Do attorneys agree or disagree on what are the most important qualities of a judge, and how do their preferences compare with those of persons who themselves sit on the bench? Prior to the

---

[39] Our data on judges' prior practice experience is restricted to the 41 Plan judges who returned questionnaires sent to them.

analysis of these questions, there is a short discussion of the procedures that were used to elicit information from members of both the bench and the Bar on the matter of judicial qualities.

THE QUALITIES OF A GOOD JUDGE

About 35 years ago Mott observed that "The virtues which should be combined in a perfect judge have been extolled in platitudes which are more literary than accurate; the functions this ideal creature must perform have long been the subject of bar association addresses which are more debatable than penetrating."[40] A perusal of the literature that has been written on the subject in the intervening years indicates that, for the most part, the situation that he described still prevails. Law review articles, and, particularly speeches and writings of lawyers and judges that constitute the major sources of information on the issue, generally suffer from the same kinds of defects to which Mott alludes: the qualities mentioned are stated in broad generalities and also often fail to focus on the attitudes that a judge, as compared to persons in other pursuits in society, should possess if he is to do his job properly.[41] Moreover, even when some precision is achieved in terms of identifying specific judicial qualities, the sources for such judgments are usually the opinions and observations offered by individual practitioners and jurists.[42] At the time we began to investigate the issue of judicial qualities, only Olson's exploratory study represented a systematic effort to obtain views on the subject from a group of lawyers and judges;[43] since

---

[40] Mott, Albright and Simmerling, loc. cit., 143.
[41] Harry W. Jones has recently analyzed various facets of the work of a trial judge. See his selection, "The Trial Judge—Role Analyses and Profile" which appears in The Courts, The Public and The Law Explosion (Englewood Cliffs, N.J.: Prentice-Hall, 1965), 124–145.
[42] Examples of such literature include Charles T. McCormick, "Judicial Selection—Current Plans and Trends," Illinois Law Review, 30 (December 1935), 446–469; Robert A. Leflar, "The Quality of Judges," Indiana Law Journal, 35 (1955–1960), 289–306; and Trial Courts of Several Jurisdictions in the Forty Eight States (Chicago, Council of State Governments, 1951), p. 9, which cites a list of qualities used by the Cleveland Bar Association in evaluating judicial candidates.
[43] See footnote 8, supra. Olson is careful to point out at page 16 of his paper that his sample of lawyers is not a representative one and contained a disproportionate number of white attorneys from law firms who had high incomes. Nevertheless, at the time he conducted his exploratory study, it represented the most systematic effort to elicit attitudes of the Bar on judicial qualities.

that time, Rosenberg has also analyzed the desirable qualities of judges as seen by a number of trial judges in the United States.[44]

These previous studies, plus helpful comments made in our personal interviews with lawyers and judges, provided us with some guidance as to how to deal best with the admittedly difficult problem of identifying the most important qualities of a judge. We decided initially that we would ask members of both the Bar and the bench which judicial qualities they thought were crucial so that the perspectives of the two groups could be compared. As far as the lawyer respondents were concerned, we thought it wiser not to question them about such qualities until after we had already solicited their evaluations of individual judges; thus, instead of requiring them to answer the somewhat abstract question concerning the desirable qualities of a judge in general, we requested them to designate the important qualities that were most often found in the *particular* judges they themselves had rated as outstanding or good. In the case of the Plan judge respondents, the frame of reference for their judgment concerning important judicial qualities was their own service on the bench. We thus sought to anchor the opinions of both lawyers and judges in specific personal experiences relating to qualities *actually* found in judges, rather than depending on an idealized picture of what qualities *should* be found in members of the bench.

We also decided to develop a list of potentially important qualities of a judge, which we could use as a common reference point in eliciting reactions from a broad range of lawyers and judges in Missouri on the subject. The list we drew up contained the qualities that writers identified in common, as being important for a judge; to these qualities, we added others that lawyers and judges in Missouri mentioned most often in personal interviews.[45] Members of our sample of lawyers were then asked to use this list (as well as to add any other preferred qualities of their own) in identifying the five qualities (ranked in order of importance) they felt were most often found in the judges they rated as outstanding or good. Judge respondents were given a similar list in

---

[44] Maurice Rosenberg, "The Qualities of Justices—Are They Strainable?" *Texas Law Review*, 44 (June 1966), 1063–1080. His sample of 144 included 94 trial judges with limited experience on the bench who were attending the 1965 session of the National College of State Trial Judges in Boulder, Colorado as students in a four-week orientation program, and 50 veteran trial judges who assembled in August in Miami Beach, Florida for the annual meeting of the National Conference of State Trial Judges. The survey indicated that the views of the two groups on judicial attributes were nearly identical.

[45] The most helpful list of such qualities was the one developed by Olson. We found that many attorneys we interviewed in Missouri mentioned the same qualities that his group of Washington, D.C. practitioners did.

ranking the five qualities they had found from their experience to be most crucial in a judge.

With respect to the qualities themselves, we made it a special point in this part of our study to focus on such qualities alone, and not to confuse the issue by also soliciting information on judicial qualifications as well.[46] In other words, we were looking for matters associated with on-the-bench performance, not for kinds of background experiences and attributes that were thought to be helpful in preparing a person to be a good judge. We shall explore this latter matter as a separate issue in the concluding portion of this chapter.

We also excluded certain qualities from our list which we thought were so obvious that persons would take them for granted; involved were such attitudes as integrity, honesty, and physical and mental health. Beyond this, we attempted to make more precise and specific the kinds of matters involved in what members of the legal profession loosely refer to as "judicial temperament."[47] In doing so, we separated two distinct ideas usually included together under that term. One is objectivity or what we termed "open-mindedness and the ability to listen patiently to both sides of the case." The other is consideration for others or what we called more specifically "courtesy to lawyers and witnesses." To these two qualities we added seven others, including "common sense," "knowledge of the law," "native intelligence," "hard working," "basic understanding of people and human nature," "ability to make prompt decisions," and "ability to keep control of the case being tried."

One matter that we did not provide for in our survey involves possible differences between the important qualities of trial judges, compared to those of persons occupying seats on the appellate bench. Several of our respondents commented on this fact in their questionnaires and, in retrospect, it would probably have been better had we asked for separate lists of qualities for the two kinds of judges. Although there was no way to completely rectify this oversight, in the analysis that follows, we did take this possible distinction into account by separating the responses of lawyers by the kinds of judges whom they rated, and

---

[46] The tendency to combine these two matters is quite common in the literature dealing with judicial qualities.

[47] Rosenberg, *loc. cit.*, at page 1079, cites the case of a Bar committee in New York City which, in the course of developing a set of minimum judicial standards, defined judicial temperament as "a condition of courtesy, dignity, patience, tact, humor and a personality free from arrogance, pomposity, irascibility, impatience, loquacity, bias, prejudice and ability to listen and keep an open mind." One Florida journalist who heard the list exclaimed, "Why, that man was crucified 2,000 years ago!"

Judges Rated by Lawyers	Common Sense		Knowledge of the Law		Courtesy		Open-Mindedness	
	Score[a]	Rank[b]	Score[a]	Rank[b]	Score[a]	Rank[b]	Score[a]	Rank[b]
Trial judges only	2.45	3	3.36	1	1.52	4	2.70	2
Appellate judges only	2.82	3	3.82	1	1.19	5	3.02	2
Both trial and appellate judges	2.73	3	3.83	1	1.41	4	2.76	2
All raters	2.69	3	3.75	1	1.41	4	2.77	2

the judges' replies by the level of court on which the respondent served. This was done on the assumption that attorneys who practiced exclusively before either trial or appellate judges would take such judges as their frame of reference for the question on important qualities, and that judges sitting on the two kinds of courts would also use their own personal experience as the basis for their evaluation of judicial qualities.

Lawyer Assessments of Important Judicial Qualities

Table 8.9 indicates the way our lawyer respondents rate the most important qualities of superior judges before whom they practiced.[48] With relatively few exceptions, they tended to restrict their evaluations to the nine specific qualities that were listed on the questionnaire.[49] Moreover, as the table demonstrates, there is considerable consensus within the Bar concerning the five qualities that were found most often in the judges whom they rated highly. Those attorneys practicing before either the trial or appellate benches, as well as those who rated judges at both levels, all list the same five qualities as being the most important:

[48] An index or weighted average was developed for each quality on the basis of five points for a number one ranking among important judicial qualities, four points for a number two ranking, etc., with one point assigned to qualities ranked as fifth in importance.
[49] The relatively few qualities added to the questionnaire included some of those we decided to exclude such as integrity, honesty, and health. In addition, some attorneys wrote in the term "judicial temperament" which, as explained above, we tried to define more precisely.

8.9
QUALITIES OF SUPERIOR JUDGES

Native Intelligence		Hard Working		Understands People		Prompt Decisions		Control of Case		
Score[a]	Rank[b]	Score[a]	Rank[b]	Score[a]	Rank[b]	Score[a]	Rank[b]	Score[a]	Rank[b]	N
1.12	6	1.38	5	.68	8.5	.68	8.5	.87	7	162
.84	6	1.55	4	.77	7	.33	9	.41	8	63
1.21	6	1.35	5	.84	7	.63	9	.80	8	646
1.17	6	1.37	5	.80	7	.62	9	.79	8	871

[a] Based upon a possible 5-point score.
[b] Relative importance of quality compared to other qualities.

"knowledge of the law," "open-mindedness and willingness to listen to both sides of the case," "common sense," "courtesy to lawyers and witnesses," and "hard working."[50] (Of the other four qualities listed, only "native intelligence" achieves close to a comparable rating to the fifth preferred quality.) Moreover, even the priorities within this group of five qualities are fairly consistent: "knowledge of the law" enjoys a considerable edge over all the other qualities, while "open-mindedness" and "common sense" are ranked second and third by all groups of raters analyzed. The only differences in relative rankings of the five qualities are the interchange of "courtesy" and "hard working" as the fourth and fifth preferred items by those practicing at the circuit and appellate court levels. Thus attorneys appear to look for the same general qualities in both trial and appellate judges.

Even though consensus exists within the Bar generally on important judicial qualities, there is the distinct possibility that lawyers with varied backgrounds will have somewhat different priorites with respect to such qualities. For example, one might anticipate that corporation and defendants' lawyers (who represent generally the established institutions in society) might have a high regard for a judge's knowledge of the law on the assumption that such law tends to support the status quo, while plaintiffs' and criminal attorneys (who generally defend the rights

---

[50] The most important judicial qualities as seen by Olson's sample of lawyers in Washington, D.C. contained many of the same qualities. Included were objectivity, knowledge of the law, common sense, hard working and courtesy. His respondents rated intelligence higher as a preferred judicial quality than ours did.

TABLE

LAWYERS' RATINGS OF MOST IMPORTANT QUALITIES OF SUPERIOR

Characteristic of Rater	Common Sense		Knowledge of the Law		Courtesy		Open-Mindedness	
	Score[a]	Rank[b]	Score[a]	Rank[b]	Score[a]	Rank[b]	Score[a]	Rank[b]
Kind of Practice[c]								
Defendants'	2.68	3	3.58	1	1.03	7	2.87	2
Corporation	2.59	3	3.51	1	1.21	6	2.98	2
Plaintiffs'	2.95	2	3.46	1	1.57	4	2.72	3
Criminal	2.81	2	2.88	1	1.83	4	2.49	3
Partisan Affiliation[d]								
Republicans	2.59	3	3.45	1	1.32	5	2.78	2
Democrats	2.70	3	3.59	1	1.47	4	2.77	2

of "underdogs") might place more importance on a judge's basic understanding of people and human nature. The same kind of basic orientation conceivably could shape the attitudes of Republican and Democratic lawyers, since a part of our conventional political wisdom presumes that Republicans are solicitous of property rights, while Democrats generally care more about people, particularly the so-called "common man." Table 8.10 is designed to test these assumptions, as well as other associations that exist between practice and partisan backgrounds of attorneys and their assessment of important qualities of judges whom they rate highly.

The table indicates that while some differences regarding preferred judicial qualities exist among attorneys with varied backgrounds, these differences are minor compared to the attitudes they share in common. Defendants' and corporation attorneys do rate knowledge of the law somewhat higher than do plaintiffs' lawyers and criminal lawyers, and the reverse pattern is true of attitudes toward a judges' understanding of people and human nature. However, the more significant factor revealed by the data is the fact that all four groups evaluate "knowledge of the law" as the most important judicial quality, while an "understanding of people" is not included in the preferred five qualities of even the criminal lawyers whose ratings vary most in the anticipated direction

8.10
JUDGES BY PRACTICE BACKGROUND AND PARTISAN AFFILIATION OF RATERS

Native Intelligence		Hard Working		Understands People		Prompt Decisions		Control of Case		
Score[a]	Rank[b]	Score[a]	Rank[b]	Score[a]	Rank[b]	Score[a]	Rank[b]	Score[a]	Rank[b]	N
1.16	6	1.65	4	.77	9	.68	8	1.18	5	156
1.27	5	1.43	4	.73	8	.57	9	.81	7	344
1.12	6	1.20	5	.83	7	.48	9	.75	8	245
.98	7	1.37	5	1.25	6	.68	9	.88	8	59
1.20	6	1.43	4	.81	7	.67	9	.74	8	361
1.08	6	1.35	5	.81	8	.58	9	.82	7	479

[a] Based upon a possible 5 point scale.
[b] Relative importance of quality compared to other qualities.
[c] Listed exclusively or as one of two or three major fields of practice.
[d] Independents have been excluded from the analysis.

from those of lawyers with the other practice backgrounds. In fact, the general ratings assigned the nine qualities by attorneys in all four practice groups are remarkably similar,[51] despite some correlation in priorities of corporation and defendants' attorneys on the one hand, and plaintiffs' and criminal lawyers on the other. The attitudes of Republican and Democratic attorneys concerning judicial qualities also show little variation except that the former value "hard working" judges somewhat more, and "courteous" jurists somewhat less, than do the latter.

Judges' Assessments of Important Judicial Qualities

The foregoing analysis indicates that there is a remarkable degree of consensus within the Missouri Bar concerning key qualities possessed by superior judges. The question remains, however, whether judges themselves assess judicial ability on the same basis. In other words, do both major participants in the judicial process (those who argue the cases and those who hear them) look at the process similarly, or

---

[51] One exception is the higher evaluation that defendants' attorneys give to keeping control of the case. This probably reflects the desires of such lawyers to have the judge exclude from the jury's consideration prejudicial and questionable evidence that may help the plaintiff's cause.

do the separate roles they assume cause them to apply different criteria to determine whether the man on the bench is doing a good job? Another related question is whether trial and appellate judges employ similar standards for superior judicial performance. Table 8.11, which adds information on Plan judges' evaluations to that previously analyzed for lawyers in Table 8.9,[52] compares the ratings of the bench and the Bar on the five most important judicial qualities.

The comparative data on lawyers' and judges' evaluations of preferred judicial qualities indicate that while some differences in perspective occur, for the most part, the two groups see eye to eye on the matter. "Knowledge of the law" is the most highly rated quality for all groups analyzed· except for appellate judges who rank it a close second to "common sense"; this latter quality has a particular appeal for members of the upper bench[53] compared to its third ranking among lawyers and trial court judges. "Open-mindedness" scores highly as a quality with all groups, although somewhat less so with the appellate judges. The most important difference between the attitudes of the Bar and the bench on judicial qualities relates to interpersonal relationships between the two. Courtroom courtesy, which is valued rather highly by the practicing attorney who is on the receiving end of such treatment, is not so salient a matter for the judge who is directly involved on the other side of the process.[54] On the other hand, a judge's "understanding of people" is considered more important by members of the bench themselves than it is by lawyers who appear before the courts.

BACKGROUND QUALIFICATIONS
AND JUDICIAL PERFORMANCE

Having explored the qualities thought to be possessed by a "good" judge, we turned to another question often asked by students of the judiciary:

---

[52] The analysis is restricted to the Plan judges who returned our questionnaire. Like the lawyers, the judge respondents tended to stay with our list with the exception of those qualities such as honesty, integrity, health, and judicial temperament, etc., which we had previously decided to exclude.

[53] This priority runs counter to the notion we discussed in the previous chapter that the appellate courts are concerned more with the law in rather pure terms, while trial judges are supposed to be "close to the people" and thus presumably more influenced by practical, common sense considerations.

[54] It is possible, of course, that elective judges might have given courtesy a higher evaluation since, as was suggested in the previous chapter, there is some feeling that the necessity of facing the electorate makes such judges more sensitive than Plan judges to the attitudes of lawyers and the public.

TABLE 8.11
COMPARISON OF LAWYERS' AND NONPARTISAN PLAN JUDGES' RATINGS OF MOST IMPORTANT QUALITIES[a] OF SUPERIOR JUDGES

	Common Sense		Knowledge of the Law		Courtesy		Open-Mindedness		Hard working		Understands People		Number of Cases
	Score[b]	Rank[c]	Score[b]	Rank[c]	Score[b]	Rank[c]	Score[b]	Rank[c]	Score[b]	Rank[c]	Score[b]	Rank[c]	
Lawyers' Ratings													
Raters of trial judges only	2.45	3	3.36	1	1.52	4	2.70	2	1.38	5	.68	8.5	162
Raters of appellate judges only	2.82	3	3.82	1	1.19	5	3.02	2	1.55	4	.77	7	63
All raters	2.69	3	3.75	1	1.41	4	2.77	2	1.37	5	.80	7	871
Judges' Ratings													
Trial judges	2.44	3	3.72	1	.60	8	2.96	2	2.08	4	.80	5	25
Appellate judges	3.38	1	3.25	2	.62	7	2.44	3	1.91	4	.93	5	16
All judges	2.80	2	3.54	1	.61	7.5	2.78	3	2.01	4	.85	5	41

a Restricted to those listed as one of five most important qualities by any group of raters. Native intelligence, promptness of decisions, and ability to control case were 6th, 7th, 8th, or 9th on all such lists.

b Based upon a possible 5-point scale.

c Relative importance of quality compared to other qualities.

Are there certain kinds of qualifications that one can link with superior accomplishment on the bench? Here we were interested not in the personality and character traits of judges that allow them to perform well in the courtroom but, instead, in the kinds of background experiences that might be helpful in preparing a person to become a good judge or the particular attributes of lawyers that one could look for in identifying potentially able candidates for the bench. We thus sought to distinguish between judicial *qualities* and judicial *qualifications* because we felt they involved essentially different matters and might profitably be analyzed with separate approaches.

Previous studies investigating judicial qualifications have asked lawyers and judges themselves what kinds of background experiences and attributes a person *should* have if he is to do well on the bench. The method used to investigate the issue has, therefore, been one calling for the subjective opinions of the members of the bench and the Bar. We employed what we believe is a more objective approach to the problem by investigating the kinds of background experiences and attributes that were possessed by judges whom we had already identified as performing well on the bench. Thus the emphasis was not on determining what people *thought* the background qualifications of good judges should be, but rather upon ascertaining, on the basis of experience, what the qualifications of such judges *had actually been*.

Our approach to the problem involved comparing the background characteristics of judges who had been rated highly by the Bar with those who had received low evaluations by lawyers. The particular characteristics chosen for initial analysis were those discussed in Chapter 6 (age at time of appointment, legal education, place of birth, party affiliation, and previous judicial and political experience) which, as previously noted, cover a variety of important factors. The specific judges included in the "high" and "low" groups were those who ranked in the upper and lower quartiles of all those rated by members of the Bar (see Table 8.3). Because of differences in the nature of the work performed by trial and appellate judges, and the effect such differences might conceivably have on the qualifications of persons serving on the two kinds of benches, we again separated our analysis by level of court.

Table 8.12 indicates that there are few marked differences in the background characteristics of circuit judges in Missouri who are rated superior and inferior by lawyers practicing before them. More of those in the higher- than the lower-rated group went outstate to law schools and the reverse is true of attendance at an instate, night institution. Localism, as measured by place of birth, is also more prevalent among

TABLE 8.12

COMPARISON OF BACKGROUND CHARACTERISTICS OF MISSOURI
CIRCUIT JUDGES RANKED IN THE UPPER AND LOWER
QUARTILES OF ALL JUDGES EVALUATED

Background Characteristics	Upper Quartile[a] (N = 28)	Lower Quartile[a] (N = 29)
Age		
Under 40	10	9
40–49	11	12
50–59	7	6
Over 60	0	0
No information	0	2
Total	28	29
Legal Education		
Outstate prestige	2	0
Outstate, other	2	1
Instate, full-time	11	10
Instate, night	9	15
Law office	4	3
Total	28	29
Place of Birth		
In judicial district	11	16
Outside district	9	8
Outside state	8	4
Not ascertained	0	1
Total	28	29
Party Affiliation		
Republican	6	5
Democrat	22	24
Total	28	29
Judicial Experience		
Minor court	0	3
Court of record	4	1
None	24	25
Total	28	29
Political Experience		
Law enforcement	18	17
Legislative	2	4
Other	3	3
None	10	10
Total[b]	33	34

TABLE 8.12 (*Continued*)

Background Characteristics	Upper Quartile[a] (N = 28)	Lower Quartile[a] (N = 29)
Office Held at Time of Selection		
Judicial	1	3
Political	4	3
None	23	23
Total	28	29

[a] See Table 8.3 for the quartile rankings of all circuit judges in Missouri.
[b] Total equals more than number of judges because some judges held more than one kind of political office.

the inferior judges. To the extent that the members of the circuit bench had judicial experience at all, those in the upper quartile are more likely to have served on another court of record, and their less esteemed colleagues, on a minor court. The other factors analyzed (age at time of appointment, party affiliation, and previous political experience) bear no appreciable relationship to performance on the bench.

A similar analysis of appellate judges in Missouri (see Table 8.5 for their quartile rankings) also revealed few significant differences in background characteristics of those rated as superior and inferior by members of the Bar. In fact, the localism and prior judicial experience factors that had some relevance for performance at the circuit court level were not related to judges' abilities in appellate court work. Moreover, none of the highly rated appellate judges went to an outstate law school whereas 3 of the 9 judges in the lower group did; unexpectedly, the reverse situation was true of attendance at a night law school.[55] The only characteristic investigated that differentiated the good from the poor judges was partisan affiliation, with 8 of the 9 lower-rated group composed of Democratic judges, compared to a 6 to 4 Republican majority among the appellate jurists most esteemed by their colleagues.

Since the six characteristics we analyzed for all judges in Missouri showed so little relationship to performance on the bench, we explored the matter further by comparing high and low ranking judges appointed under the Plan with respect to a number of other background qualifications. This analysis was made possible by the much fuller data we had assembled on such judges as a result of questionnaire information that many of them gave us. We were thus able to analyze associations be-

---

[55] Three of the highly rated judges went to a night law school, while none in the lower group did.

tween judicial performance and such diverse matters as the type and financial status of a judge's practice prior to his going on the bench; how he was rated professionally as a lawyer by Martindale-Hubbel;[56] the extent to which he participated in political party,[57] Bar,[58] and civic affairs;[59] and the political circumstances surrounding his appointment, that is, the governor who appointed him, and the year of the chief executive's term in which he went on the bench. Table 8.13 compares these attributes for Plan judges considered superior and inferior as evidenced by their ranking in the upper and lower third of all such judges rated by lawyers practicing before them.[60]

---

[56] Martindale-Hubbel is a private organization that evaluates lawyers' abilities on the basis of information provided by other attorneys. Such matters as age, practical experience, and nature and length of practice, are taken into account in such ratings. A lawyer first becomes eligible for a "c" (fair) rating after practicing for three years. At least five years of practice is required for a "b" (high) rating, and at least ten years is required for the "a" (very high) rating. Not all eligible attorneys receive ratings, but most well-regarded lawyers in private practice do.

[57] The index of party activity is the same one that was used in previous chapters. We assigned one point to each act of participation beyond voting, including attending political rallies; working for parties or candidates by getting people registered to vote, canvassing, passing out literature, poll watching, etc.; making speeches for candidates; contributing money to a party or candidates and serving as a campaign manager. Two points were assigned for holding a party office at the city and county level, and three points for serving in a state or national party office. A total point count was computed for each respondent; those scoring three points or higher were considered as being "active" in party affairs, and those with two points or less, as "inactives."

[58] A list of pertinent national and local Bar associations was provided on the questionnaire and respondents were asked to check those to which they had ever belonged as well as to add the names of other organizations not listed. They were also requested to indicate the offices they had ever held in any of such organizations. In devising an index of Bar Association activity, one point was assigned for each association to which a respondent belonged, and two points for each office he held in such organizations. A total point count was computed for each respondent; those scoring four or more points were considered as being "actives" in Bar Association matters, and those with three points or less, as "inactives."

[59] Respondents were asked to list various types of civic groups (public affairs, public service, social-fraternal, business, veterans and religious) to which they ever belonged or in which they had held an office. An index of civic or community participation was constructed by assigning one point for each such group listed and two points for each office held in them. Those scoring a point total of six points or higher were considered as being "active" in civic affairs, and those with five points or less as "inactive."

[60] A total of 36 Plan judges returned questionnaires that were usable for this analysis. Because of the limited number of judges involved, we grouped together circuit and appellate judges; for the same reason we also studied the upper and lower third rather than the highest and lowest quartiles of such judges.

TABLE 8.13

COMPARISON OF BACKGROUND CHARACTERISTICS OF PLAN JUDGES
RATED IN THE UPPER AND LOWER THIRD OF ALL PLAN JUDGES

Background Characteristics	Upper Third[a] (N = 12)	Lower Third[a] (N = 12)
Practice Arrangement		
Solo	1	4
Partnership, 2 to 5	6	3
Partnership, 6 or over	3	0
Law firm employee	1	2
Corporation employee	0	1
Government employee	1	2
Total	12	12
Type of Practice[b]		
Defendants'	2	3
Corporation	5	3
Probate and trust	3	4
Plaintiffs'	2	3
Criminal	2	1
Total[c]	14	14
Income Prior to Going on Bench		
Less than $10,000	2	4
$10,000–19,999	3	5
$20,000 and over	6	2
No information	1	1
Total	12	12
Martindale Hubbel Rating		
Eligible for a, rated a	9	0
Eligible for a, rated b	1	5
Eligible for a, rated c	0	0
Eligible for a, not rated	2	7
Total	12	12
Political Party Activity[d]		
Active	9	11
Inactive	3	1
Total	12	12
Bar Activity[e]		
Active	9	6
Inactive	3	6
Total	12	12
Civic Activity[f]		
Active	7	8
Inactive	5	4
Total	12	12

TABLE 8.13 (Continued)

Background Characteristics	Upper Third[a] (N = 12)	Lower Third[a] (N = 12)
Governor Who Made Appointment		
Donnell	2	0
Donnelly (first term)	1	1
Smith	2	4
Donnelly (second term)	4	4
Blair	2	1
Dalton	1	2
Total	12	12
Year of Governor's Term When Appointed		
First	2	4
Second	3	0
Third	4	4
Fourth	3	4
Total	12	12

[a] The ratings for those in the upper third ranged from 4.27 to 4.62; those in the lower third ranged from 3.30–3.94.

[b] Includes those who listed field exclusively or as one of two or three major fields of practice.

[c] Total equals more than number of judges because fields are not mutually exclusive.

[d] See footnote 57.

[e] See footnote 58.

[f] See footnote 59.

The data indicate some distinct associations between practice background factors and performance on the bench. The clearest relationship exists between lawyers' incomes prior to becoming judges,[61] with those earning less than $20,000 a year more likely to come from the lower-rated group, and those with net incomes above that figure, from their more highly esteemed colleagues. (Of the 12 highly evaluated judges, 8 experienced a loss in income when they went on the bench; only 3 of the lower group did.) There is also some tendency for judges who once practiced law as partners in firms to be considered superior to those who were solo practitioners. (On the other hand, no clear-cut pattern emerges with respect to type of practice—defendants', plaintiffs', etc.— and courtroom performance.) Also closely associated with judicial per-

---

[61] As previously noted, the income figure used is the average net earnings of a judge in the three years immediately preceding his appointment to the bench.

formance is the professional evaluation that judges received when they were in private practice from the Martindale Hubbel organization: all 9 of those receiving the highest rating of "a" are included in the upper group of judges, while 7 of the 9 who received no rating, are in the lower category.[62]

The remaining factors analyzed do not bear as close relationships to judicial performance as do those relating to practice background. There is some association between Bar Association activities and superior performance on the bench, but no such linkage appears with respect to prior participation in political party or general civic affairs. The distribution of superior and inferior appointees among the various governors is fairly uniform with the possible exception of Donnell and Smith who tended to select persons from the upper and lower groups, respectively. The frequent assertions that governors tend to make poorer appointments when they first go into office as a result of paying off political debts is supported by the data as far as those made in the first year are concerned. On the other hand, the opposite situation prevails with respect to second-year appointments. Moreover, no appreciable differences appear in the caliber of appointments made in the first half of four-year terms compared with those in the last two years of governors' service in office.

Although there are some limiting circumstances present in the analysis in Table 8.13,[63] it does suggest that professional factors are more closely linked with subsequent performance on the bench than are other kinds of experiences and attributes. The next chapter discusses another question relating to judicial selection: Has the Plan selection method tended to put on the bench men who are disposed to favor certain social and economic interest in the judicial arena at the expense of others?

---

[62] The two judges in the upper group who received no ratings immediately prior to their appointments to the bench held public positions, and hence were not subject to such an evaluation. Three of the seven non-rated judges in the lower group were in the same situation.

[63] Our data for this particular analysis are restricted to Plan judges who, as indicated in Table 8.3, rated more highly as a group than did holdover and elective judges. Therefore, the differences in evaluation of the upper and lower third of Plan judges is not as marked as were the quartiles of all circuit judges analyzed in Table 8.12. Moreover, the total number of judges involved in Table 8.13 is 24 (12 in the upper and lower thirds), compared to the 57 (28 and 29 in the upper and lower quartiles) which constitute the subject matter for Table 8.12. We mention these matters to indicate that the analysis of Plan judges should be considered suggestive rather than determinative of the matters explored.

9

DECISIONAL PROPENSITIES OF
PLAN AND ELECTED JUDGES

One of the major charges leveled against the Nonpartisan Court Plan is that it tends to place on the bench men who are conservative in their orientation. An example of this attitude is the suggestive comment made recently by the late Justice Charles E. Clark of the United States Court of Appeals that the Plan has a "unique bias toward professional competence."[1] He explains:

Since in our economy the rewards of professional competence are, quite naturally and properly, the confidence of and employment by all the settled institutions of our society—the banks, the insurance companies, the mammoth business combines, and so on—the imbalance toward mere preservation of the status quo and notably its aristocratic elements is a potential danger for the courts. Thus if an executive can make his judicial choice only from a limited roster supplied him by a commission composed of the successful and conservative members of the community, then it is obvious that no one who deviates from the professional norm—labor lawyers, for example—need apply.[2]

Previous chapters have indicated that the stereotype of the Plan judge does not accord with the facts on their actual social backgrounds: they are not the "bluebloods" of the profession that they are assumed to be. Nevertheless, a considerable number of Plan judges (the largest single group in terms of practice specialty) did handle corporate and business matters prior to going on the bench, and conceivably this experience background could shape their decisional propensities along the lines suggested by Judge Clark. It is also possible that Plan judges,

---

[1] Charles E. Clark and David M. Trubek, "The Creative Role of the Judge: Restraint and Freedom in the Common Law Tradition," *Yale Law Journal*, LXXI (1961), 272. (Trubek was Judge Clark's law clerk in 1961–62.)
[2] *Ibid.*

regardless of their particular practice backgrounds, may be affected in their attitudes by "professional" considerations so as to favor unconsciously the "settled" institutions of which the Judge speaks. The purpose of this chapter is to test whether Plan judges are really more conservative in their orientation toward litigation than are elected judges.[3]

There are a number of problems involved in trying to test this proposition. One is the criteria that should be used to determine "liberal" and "conservative" decisions in cases at the state court level. Stuart Nagel, one of the earliest students to explore this general area, suggests that the term liberal be applied to the "viewpoint associated with the interests of the lower or less privileged economic or social groups in one's society and (to a less extent) with acceptance of long-run social change; and the term conservative to the viewpoint associated with the interests of the upper or dominant groups and with resistance to long-run social change."[4] As examples of the liberal position on issues drawn from state litigation in both trial and appellate courts, he includes the following:

1. The defense in criminal cases.
2. Administrative agencies in business regulation cases.
3. The private party in cases involving regulation of nonbusiness entities.
4. The claimant in unemployment compensation cases.
5. The libertarian position in free speech cases.
6. The finding of a constitutional violation in criminal cases.
7. The government in tax cases.
8. The divorce seeker in divorce cases.
9. The wife in divorce settlement cases.
10. The tenant in landlord-tenant disputes.
11. The labor union in union-management cases.
12. The debtor in debt collection cases.
13. The consumer in sales of goods cases.
14. The injured party in motor-vehicle accident cases.
15. The employee in employee injury cases.[5]

Others have applied similar criteria in examining voting propensities of state supreme court judges in workmen's and unemployment compen-

[3] For a review and analysis of a series of studies relating social backgrounds of judges with their decision-making, see Joel B. Grossman, "Social Backgrounds and Judicial Decision-Making," *Harvard Law Review*, **79** (June, 1966), 1551–1564.
[4] Stuart Nagel, "Political Party Affiliation and Judges' Decisions," *The American Political Science Review*, **55**, (1961), 846 f.
[5] *Ibid.*, 844.

sation claims on the basis that conflicts taking place in these areas have overtones of a class struggle.[6]

Even if one accepts the validity of this general liberal-conservative dichotomy based on the "underdog-topdog" status of the respective parties to the litigation (here one might well quarrel with Nagel's designation of the wife's side as the liberal one in divorce–settlement cases!),[7] other problems remain with respect to testing the question of whether Plan judges tend to be less liberal in Missouri than elective ones. Particularly troublesome is the matter of investigating the situation in the trial courts of the state where the overwhelming amount of the litigation is heard.[8] Trial judges hear cases alone, not as a group. Therefore, one cannot simply determine the proportion of times that Judge A rules on the "liberal" side of a particular kind of case, compared to Judge B, and conclude that differences between them are based upon their divergent attitudes toward the position of the underdog in our society. Instead, it might be attributable to the fact that they are hearing separate cases with different fact situations.[9] Beyond this, the examination of trial court decisions made by about 112 Plan and elected judges in the state over the twenty-five year period of our study was beyond our resources of either time or money.[10]

The analysis of Supreme Court decisions presents neither of the above problems. The Court is a collegial one in which several judges hear the same case,[11] and it hears a fairly limited number of cases.[12] However, determining the effect of the Plan on the outcome of appellate litigation raises other kinds of methodological issues. Only nonunanimous cases

---

[6] See S. Sidney Ulmer, "The Political Party Variable in The Michigan Supreme Court," *Journal of Public Law*, 11 (1962), 352–362. Glendon Schubert also states that positions on workmen's compensation cases are an acceptable criterion of judicial liberalism-conservatism in the United States. See his, *Quantitative Analysis of Judicial Behavior* (The Free Press of Glencoe, 1959), pp. 129–141.

[7] Grossman makes this same point, *loc. cit.*, at p. 1563, footnote 48.

[8] See Chapter 1, footnote 47, for the most recent statistics on the number of cases heard by trial and appellate courts in Missouri.

[9] Stuart Nagel makes this same point in his article, "Testing Relations Between Judicial Characteristics and Judicial Decision-Making," *The Western Political Quarterly*, 15 (September, 1962), 425–438.

[10] As previously indicated in footnote 47 in Chapter 1, the lower courts in Missouri disposed of 63,866 cases during the period beginning June 16, 1966 and ending June 15, 1967.

[11] The Missouri Supreme Court hears cases by division as well as *en banc*. See footnote 19, *infra*, for an explanation of this matter.

[12] The Report of the Judicial Conference of Missouri for the period beginning June 16, 1966 and ending June 15, 1967 indicates that the Supreme Court disposed of 847 cases that year.

can be used to determine differences in decisional propensities between the various judges and, in Missouri as in other states, such cases constitute a fairly small percentage of the total caseload of the Court.[13]

We considered the above problems in developing methods to test the decisional propensities of Plan and elective judges. We focused on personal injury litigation in the lower court for two major reasons. First, such cases constitute a major share of the litigation of such courts.[14] Second, they also involve, to a greater degree than most litigation, a conflict between groups with different social status, since usually a person in the lower classes is suing some "settled" institutions such as public utilities (railroads, bus lines, etc.), insurance companies, or other corporations. As previously noted, Nagel and others who have analyzed cases at the state level designate personal injury matters as one of the major categories of cases by which one can distinguish liberal and conservative positions in litigation arising in the state courts.

Having determined to focus only on personal injury litigation, there remained the problem of properly assessing the attitudes of trial judges in such suits when they hear separate cases involving different fact situations. As a means of avoiding this methodological issue, we decided not to examine the actual results of such suits, but rather to have practicing attorneys assess the extent to which each of the trial judges before whom they practiced had a plaintiffs' or defendants' orientation. We reasoned that the personal experience of members of the Bar with injury litigation involving all kinds of fact situations would enable them to take this factor into account when they compared the orientation of the various judges before whom they had cases.

We followed a similar procedure in analyzing the attitudes of appellate judges in personal injury cases, as those attitudes were perceived by the Bar. In addition, we studied all kinds of cases heard by the Supreme Court during our period of study. Our approach involved analyzing

---

[13] See Table 9.4 *infra*, for an analysis of dissenting opinions in Missouri Supreme Court decisions during our period of study. For a general discussion of the lack of dissenting opinions in state supreme court cases, see Kenneth N. Vines, "Courts as Political and Governmental Agencies," in Herbert Jacob and Kenneth N. Vines, eds., *Politics in the American States* (Boston: Little Brown and Company, 1965), pp. 268 ff.

[14] See Chapter 1, footnote 48, for the most recent statistics on this matter in Missouri. Studies in other states have shown even a higher proportion of the court docket to consist of personal injury litigation, namely, 60 percent in New York and over one half in New Jersey in recent years. See Maurice Rosenberg and Michael J. Sovern, "Delay and Dynamics of Personal Injury Litigation," *Columbia Law Review*, 59 (1959), 1117.

actual decisions since, in this collegial court, judges hear the same litigation and, therefore, differences between their voting patterns cannot be attributed to disparities in the specific case they are examining. In particular, we scrutinized nonunanimous decisions of the Missouri Supreme Court to determine whether any "blocs" developed among the judges on the Court, that is, whether any groups tended to vote together in cases before the Court and, if so, whether they involved judges with common characteristics, particularly method of appointment (Plan or elective) or partisan affiliation.

We also explored another facet of state Supreme Court voting behavior to which Grossman has drawn the attention of the profession: Do common background experiences contribute to consensus and unanimity among judges?[15] (In view of the overwhelming tendency for judges of collegial courts below the U.S. Supreme Court to vote together, his query is a salient one.) In our particular study we attempted to deal with this issue by comparing the record of the state Supreme Court with respect to the extent of dissenting opinions in the periods when it was composed entirely of elective judges, when there were both holdover and Plan judges on the Court, and when its membership consisted primarily of judges appointed under the Plan.

THE PLAINTIFFS'-DEFENDANTS' ORIENTATION
OF PLAN AND ELECTIVE TRIAL JUDGES

As indicated in the previous chapter, we listed each of the state judges on our questionnaire without regard to the system under which they were selected and asked each of our respondents in the sample survey to assess the degree of objectivity of those judges before whom he had personally appeared. Five separate categories were provided: very pro plaintiff; pro plaintiff; neutral; pro defendant; and very pro defendant. For our present purposes[16] we developed this evaluation into a five-point index based on a weighted average of the various evaluations.[17] Thus the indices ranged from a potential score of 1 for the most pro plaintiffs' judge to a 5 for the most pro defendants' one.

The data in Table 9.1 point to one overriding fact: the absence of

---

[15] See Grossman, *loc. cit.*, 1564.

[16] It will be recalled that in the previous chapter we reduced the data to a 3 point index to indicate the amount, but not the direction, of the judges' biases in personal injury litigation.

[17] The index was developed in the same manner as the one for overall performance used in Chapter 8. See footnote 12 of that chapter for an explanation.

judges on the trial bench in Missouri who are considered by attorneys to be very biased on the plaintiffs'-defendants' issue. Of the 112 lower court judges, none received an overall rating of below 2, or over 4, evaluations used to designate pro plaintiffs' or pro defendants', attorneys, respectively. In fact, the indices ranged from 2.16, for the most pro plaintiff judge, to 3.44, the score received by the judge considered the most pro defendant by the practicing attorneys. The greatest number of judges were considered to lean slightly towards the plaintiffs' side in personal injury litigation; less than 1 in 5 received more pro defendants' than pro plaintiff's ratings. The data show that none of the general categories of trial judges in Missouri were considered, as a group, to be biased toward the defendants' side of personal injury litigation. Even the judges appointed under the Plan are generally evaluated by attorneys as slightly plaintiff-minded, although somewhat less so than either the "holdover" ones, or those elected in St. Louis County or the outstate areas of the state. (The greatest range of scores occurs among the last group of judges.) The major conclusion to be drawn from Table 9.1 is that most judges are essentially neutral on the plaintiff-defendant issue, and the variation among the different groups of judges is quite small.

Although evaluations of the Bar generally with respect to objectivity may not show marked differences between Plan and elective judges, it is possible that practice backgrounds of attorneys may affect their perceptions of the orientation of judges in personal injury cases. Thus lawyers who are in court more often may discern more variations among such judges than do their colleagues who do not try as many law suits. Moreover, particular specialties (especially those of attorneys on the extremes of the practice spectrum) may shape their views of the plaintiffs'-defendants' orientation of judges before whom they have cases. Table 9.2 is designed to test both of these possibilities.

The data indicate that lawyers who have been active in the courtroom rate all categories of judges as somewhat less plaintiff-oriented than do their colleagues without such extensive trial experience. However, the variation in the comparable ratings of the two groups of attorneys is not marked. Practice background appears to have more of an effect on the perceptions of attorneys concerning the orientation of judges before whom they practice. Generally, defendants' attorneys and their Bar allies (the corporate lawyers) rate judges as somewhat more pro plaintiff than do lawyers with a plaintiffs' or criminal practice. (The major exception to the pattern are the criminal attorneys in Jackson County who are closer to the defendants' and corporation attorneys in their perceptions than they are to their usual Bar allies, the plaintiffs' lawyers.) The greatest differences in the ratings of the four categories

TABLE 9.1
Degree of Objectivity Ratings of Trial Judges in Missouri Selected Under Various Systems[a]

	Nonpartisan Plan Judges			Holdover Judges			Elective Judges		
	Jackson County (N = 17)	St. Louis City (N = 14)	Total (N = 31)	Jackson County (N = 9)	St. Louis City (N = 19)	Total (N = 28)	St. Louis County (N = 18)	Outstate (N = 35)	Total (N = 53)
Mean	2.86	2.88	2.87	2.67	2.73	2.71	2.82	2.79	2.80
Most pro plaintiff	2.61	2.54	—	2.16	2.50	—	2.48	2.16	—
Most pro defendant	3.44	3.09	—	3.05	3.17	—	3.06	3.33	—
Range	.83	.55	—	.89	.67	—	.58	1.17	—
Judges with defendants' rating[b]	18%	28%	23%	11%	5%	7%	17%	20%	19%

[a] The rating in each cell is an average of all applicable ratings. For comparative purposes, the ratings of St. Louis City and St. Louis County judges are based upon evaluations of lawyers practicing before both benches.

[b] A defendants' rating is 3.01 or higher. Judges receiving more pro defendants' than pro plaintiffs' ratings.

TABLE 9.2
DEGREE OF OBJECTIVITY RATINGS OF TRIAL JUDGES IN MISSOURI SELECTED UNDER VARIOUS SYSTEMS—BY AMOUNT OF TRIAL EXPERIENCE AND PRACTICE BACKGROUND OF LAWYER RATERS[a]

	Nonpartisan Plan Judges			Holdover Judges			Elected Judges		
	(N = 17) Jackson County	(N = 14) St. Louis City	(N = 31) Total	(N = 9) Jackson County	(N = 19) St. Louis City	(N = 28) Total	(N = 18) St. Louis County	(N = 35) Outstate	(N = 53) Total
By Amount of Trial Experience									
Under 100 cases	2.87	2.83	2.85	2.68	2.72	2.71	2.79	2.77	2.78
Over 100 cases	2.88	2.94	2.91	2.71	2.76	2.76	2.88	2.80	2.82
By Lawyer's Practice Background[b]									
Defendants'	2.76	2.89	2.82	2.54	2.63	2.60	2.81	2.72	2.75
Corporation	2.88	2.85	2.86	2.64	2.70	2.68	2.85	2.83	2.84
Plaintiffs'	3.11	3.02	3.07	2.98	2.92	2.94	2.99	2.84	2.89
Criminal	2.60	2.98	2.77	2.63	2.86	2.78	2.97	2.95	2.95

[a] The rating in each cell is an average of all applicable ratings. For comparative purposes, the ratings of St. Louis City and St. Louis County judges are based upon evaluations of lawyers practicing before both benches.

[b] Includes those lawyers who listed field exclusively, or as one of two or three major fields of practice.

TABLE 9.3

DEGREE OF OBJECTIVITY RATINGS OF NONPARTISAN PLAN
CIRCUIT JUDGES WITH CERTAIN PRIOR PRACTICE
EXPERIENCE BY LAWYERS WITH COMPARABLE
PRACTICE EXPERIENCE[a]

	Judges' Practice Background[b]			
	$(N = 7)$ Defendants'	$(N = 10)$ Corporation	$(N = 4)$ Plaintiffs'	$(N = 4)$ Criminal
All lawyers	2.97	2.83	2.73	2.74
By Lawyers Practice Background[c]				
Defendants	2.90	2.78	2.66	2.71
Corporation	2.92	2.85	2.75	2.75
Plaintiffs	3.16	3.02	2.89	2.86
Criminal	2.78	2.69	3.04	2.84

[a] The rating in each cell is an average of all applicable ratings.
[b] Information on prior experience is restricted to those Plan judges who returned questionnaires. Includes those who listed field exclusively or as one of two or three major fields of practice.
[c] Includes those lawyers who listed field exclusively, or as one of two or three major fields of practice.

of lawyers occur generally between those attorneys who are most directly involved in personal injury litigation: plaintiffs' and defendants' attorneys. Moreover, such differences are greater between Jackson County and St. Louis lawyers than they are between such Bar rivals in St. Louis County and outstate circuits.

Another pertinent issue is whether the backgrounds of Plan judges[18] prior to their going on the bench are reflected in their ratings, that is, whether judges who came from a plaintiffs' background, for example, are more likely to be considered pro plaintiff than those who were defendants' attorneys before they ascended to the bench. A related matter is whether the practice backgrounds of attorneys evaluating these separate groups of judges also affect such ratings. Table 9.3 provides the data to test the perceptions of objectivity that exist, based upon the practice backgrounds of both judges and the attorneys who rate them.

Table 9.3 indicates that the prior practice of Plan judges does bear

---

[18] Our data on judges' previous experience are restricted to the Plan judges who returned questionnaires sent to them.

some relationship to how they were rated on degree of objectivity by members of the Bar. The former plaintiffs' attorneys are considered the most pro plaintiffs judges, and those who came out of the defendants' practice as leaning more toward that side in personal injury cases. However, the differences among the various judges are not great, and even the group of judges that came out of a defendants' background is evaluated by the Bar as being very slightly pro plaintiff in its orientation. The data also indicate that the practice backgrounds of attorneys help shape their perceptions. This is particularly true of plaintiffs' and defendants' attorneys who, more than other practitioners, tend to view judges with backgrounds opposite from their own as being oriented toward the other side in personal injury litigation. Thus the most pro plaintiffs' rating is given by defendants' attorneys to those judges who came out of a plaintiffs' background; concomitantly, the most pro defendants' rating is the one assigned by plaintiffs' lawyers to their former courtroom opponents who have now ascended to the bench.

Nonetheless, the general conclusion to be drawn from the data is that the plaintiffs'-defendants' dichotomy, which plays such a major role in shaping rivalries among members of the Metropolitan Bar, is not nearly so salient with respect to perceptions of actual courtroom behavior. Contrary to the claims of many of the critics of the Plan, it has not placed on the bench pro defendants' attorneys; if anything, most trial judges are thought by practicing attorneys in both Jackson County and St. Louis to be slightly pro plaintiff in their orientation. In the concluding chapter we shall examine some possible reasons for this paradox. First, however, we shall consider another judicial arena—the appellate courts—to determine the decisional propensities of judges sitting on those tribunals during our period of study.

DIMENSIONS OF APPELLATE COURT DECISION-MAKING

In addition to charging that Missouri Plan judicial selection has produced a conservative appellate bench, critics of the Plan also allege that it has resulted in a high degree of conformity among appellate judges, particularly among members of the state Supreme Court bench. One critic of the Plan remarked in this connection:

The reason we have a multiple member court is so that we may get an amalgam of opinion. You need to have people on the bench who think differently, who can look at questions from a different standpoint. Of course, I'm not denying that judicial decisions are frequently the result of compromise among the judges. Nor am I saying that there shouldn't be such compromise.

But if the judges on the court all have the same set of views, then you don't get the benefits that are supposed to be produced by a collegial court. The point is that the Missouri Plan will not produce a maverick. On the other hand, if you select your judges under the elective system, you may get all kinds of wacky characters going on the bench, who will frequently dissent from the views of their colleagues, and who will air different viewpoints and thus let a little ventilation into the process of justice.

From this point of view, the low frequency of dissent among Supreme Court justices may be ascribed to the cooptative nature of the process of appellate judicial selection described in an earlier chapter.

Defenders of the Missouri Plan agree that there is relatively little dissent at the appellate court level in Missouri. But they do not consider this to be an undesirable state of affairs; nor do they feel that the low frequency of dissent is in any way attributable to the Missouri Plan system of judicial selection. Instead, as was noted earlier, the Plan's strongest supporters contend that the issues that usually come before state supreme courts do not raise the kinds of fundamental social and economic questions that would be apt to precipitate dissent. Moreover, supporters of the Plan who profess acquaintance with the decision-making procedures utilized by the Supreme Court say that dissent rates alone are misleading, since many differences among the justices are resolved through consultation prior to the issuance of the Court's decisions.

Furthermore, many proponents of the Missouri Plan, while agreeing that the appellate bench is conservative in its orientation, feel that this conservatism is a product of the general political climate prevalent in the state, rather than a result of the Missouri Plan per se. Indeed, supporters of the Plan feel that the most significant contributions of the Nonpartisan Court Plan do not flow from the process by which judges are initially chosen for membership on the bench, but from the system's provisions for retention in office.

Thus, many Plan supporters recognize that partisan political considerations still have great relevance for the judicial selection process; defenders of the Plan also admit that attorneys with a "conservative" legal orientation tend to have an advantage in the competition for appellate judicial office. Yet, in the view of the Plan's proponents, any bias that is operative in this phase of selection tends to be more than offset by the effects of the mechanism through which judges seek new terms of office under the Plan. The fact that the judges stand for reelection on the basis of their "records," and without opposition or partisan label, means that they are relatively unaffected by pressures from party leaders and interest groups—the sorts of pressures that impinge on judges chosen under partisan elective systems. In this view, such "vested interests" have no ready means of retaliating against Missouri Plan judges, and the security and tenure provided by the Plan permit them to be completely independent from *ex parte* pressures upon the decision-making process.

These contrasting views of Plan critics and supporters raise a more general question: Precisely what are the effects on the appellate judicial decision-making process of the Missouri Plan method of judicial selection and retention? A fully satisfactory answer would require a systematic comparative analysis of judicial selection and decision-making in a number of states employing different selection systems—a task far beyond the scope of this particular study. A less satisfactory (but nonetheless feasible) alternative entails the analysis of voting behavior of judges on the Missouri appellate courts.

That analysis is limited in two major respects. First, it deals only with voting behavior on the Missouri Supreme Court bench. This limitation should not introduce serious distortions into the analysis, since the Missouri Plan would appear to have similar effects on the decisional processes of both the courts of appeals and the state's Supreme Court. Moreover, there are distinct advantages in focusing on the Supreme Court rather than the three Courts of Appeals. The limited jurisdiction of the latter courts results in cases of relatively minor importance being channeled to these intermediate-level tribunals. The comparatively small number of cases handled by these courts, together with the fact that only three judges sit on each court of appeals bench, also limits drastically the possibilities for analysis of voting behavior in the appeals courts. For these reasons, the analysis below deals only with nonunanimous Supreme Court decisions.

The second major limitation of the decision-making analysis is that it does not examine voting behavior in terms of the substantive issues that come before the Supreme Court. The relatively small number of nonunanimous decisions handed down by the Supreme Court in any given year precludes analysis by type of case. Therefore, the assessment of the Plan's impact upon decisional processes must be of a more general nature. Principally, it focuses on the extent to which dissent within the Court, and patterns of agreement among the justices, vary as a result of changes in court membership, or changes in the decision-making process, following the adoption of the Missouri Plan.

Although the Court Plan went into effect in 1941, it was not until late 1942 that the first Missouri Supreme Court justice was chosen under the Plan. At this point, the remainder of the Court membership consisted of justices who had been originally elected to the Court under the partisan elective method, but who had been "held over" in office by provisions of the Missouri Plan. On the expiration of their terms of offices, these justices were eligible to seek new terms of office under the retention provisions of the Plan. Not until 1950 did a majority of the seven-man Supreme Court consist of judges chosen initially through the provisions of the Nonpartisan Court Plan; and it was not until 1964 that all members of the Supreme Court bench had been originally chosen through the Missouri Plan method.

The question to be considered here is the extent to which changes in the composition of the Supreme Court during the period from 1942 to 1964 have been reflected in the decision-making process. The concern is, first, with changes in the frequency of dissent that might be related to changes in court membership. Next, consideration will be given to the extent of interagreement among Supreme Court justices of different kinds of background, including those "held over" in office in 1941, as opposed to those chosen for their initial terms under provisions of the Missouri Plan. Finally, in lieu of information about the voting behavior of Supreme Court justices in terms of substantive issues, evidence will be introduced with respect to lawyer evaluations of the Supreme Court justices' orientations on one limited but key issue: the plaintiffs'-defendants' issue posed in personal injury cases.

Table 9.4 gives data that are germane to the question of whether the level of dissent on the Missouri Supreme Court bench has changed during the period of the Plan's operation. The data are presented for four different periods. In the first, (1930–1942), none of the judges on the Supreme Court had gone on the Court through provisions of the Plan. For most of the second period (1943–1949), only two justices on the Court had been selected under the Plan for their initial terms of office. During most of the third period (1950–1954), a bare majority

TABLE 9.4

FREQUENCY OF NONUNANIMOUS EN BANC DECISIONS
BY THE MISSOURI SUPREME COURT, 1930–1964

Nature of Split Vote	1930–1942		1943–1949		1950–1954		1955–1964	
	Number	Percent	Number	Percent	Number	Percent	Number	Percent
Solo	29	4.6	14	3.6	16	8.7	27	8.9
Marginal	23	3.6	5	1.2	8	4.3	18	5.9
Other	23	3.6	21	5.6	12	6.6	32	10.6
Total	75	11.8	40	10.4	36	19.6	77	25.4

of the seven-member Court were Plan judges, with the remainder having been held over in office upon adoption of the Plan. In the fourth period, (1955–1964), all but one of the members of the Supreme Court were Plan judges.

Table 9.4 indicates the frequency of nonunanimous decisions in those cases decided by the Supreme Court *en banc;*[19] it reveals that the highest proportion of such decisions occurred in the last period, when all but one of the Supreme Court justices were Plan judges. Furthermore, the increase in the frequency of nonunanimous decisions was reflected in higher rates for all kinds of split votes: solo dissents (where a single justice comprised the minority); marginal splits (when cases were decided by a one-vote margin); and other divisions where, if the full Court membership participated, the minority consisted of two justices. Finally, members of the partisan elective court, serving in the 1930–1942 period, disagreed with each other far less than did the judges in the years from 1955 to 1964 when Plan judges dominated the Court. On the basis of this evidence, the Plan led to the selection of Supreme Court judges who were *less* conformist in their orientation than were the judges chosen under the elective system utilized prior to 1941.

Table 9.5 presents data on the agreement rates among different categories of Supreme Court justices. For any specific category of justices (for instance, those affiliated with the Democratic party), the agreement rate is the percentage of times in which all pairs of Democrats voted in agreement out of the total joint participations of all pairs of Democrats in nonunanimous *en banc* decisions. Analysis of these data leads to the following conclusions about the bases of voting behavior within the Supreme Court: (1) with the exception of divisional affiliation, the judicial characteristics being considered are related to voting propensities in only one period, 1930–1942; and (2) divisional affiliation has a significant but limited effect upon voting behavior in all the periods under consideration.[20]

---

[19] *En banc* decisions comprise only a small percentage of the total handed down by the Supreme Court. Most cases are heard and decided in division, with four justices sitting permanently as Division 1 and three justices as Division 2. Some cases initially heard in division are transferred to the Court *en banc,* primarily on the request of a dissenting justice in the division, or on the request of a losing party to the litigation. Slightly over nine-tenths of all dissents occur in the cases disposed of by the court *en banc,* with the remainder occurring in the cases handled by the two divisions.

[20] A breakdown of the voting alignments of justices on the basis of residence (metropolitan versus outstate) shows no significant patterns with the exception that, since 1950, outstate judges have tended to vote somewhat more cohesively than have those from the metropolitan areas.

TABLE 9.5
AGREEMENT RATES AMONG SUPREME COURT
JUSTICES IN NONUNANIMOUS EN BANC DECISIONS, 1930–1964

	1930–1942		1943–1949		1950–1954		1955–1964	
Categories of Justices	Number	Percent	Number	Percent	Number	Percent	Number	Percent
By Partisan Affiliation								
Democrat–Democrat	441	56	765	57	313	63	496	59
Democrat–Republican	310	53	141	62	137	63	429	62
Republican–Republican	85	70	—ᵃ	—ᵃ	1	50	33	55
By Division								
Division 1–Division 1	280	65	137	66	145	69	294	66
Division 1–Division 2	439	52	261	57	250	61	533	59
Division 2–Division 2	117	56	59	50	56	58	131	58
By Method of Selection								
Plan–Plan	—	—	8	40	137	68	673	60
Plan–Non-Plan	—	—	201	61	255	62	284	63
Non-Plan–Non-Plan	—	—	248	56	59	56	1	50

ᵃ Only one Republican served on the Court during this period.

During the pre-Plan period (1930–1942), both partisan affiliation and the divisional assignment of the judges affected voting alignments on the Court. The highest interagreement rates occurred among Republican justices and those assigned to Division 1 of the Court. Thus, in the period when all justices of the Court were selected under the partisan elective method, there was a consistent but moderate relationship between voting behavior, on the one hand, and partisan and divisional affiliation, on the other.[21]

After 1943, when the first justice chosen under the Missouri Plan assumed office, none of the background characteristics investigated was significantly related to the pattern of agreements obtaining among members of the Court. The effect of party was no longer reflected in Supreme Court voting behavior during the Plan era, nor did the method by which the justices were initially chosen for membership on the Court affect such behavior, since the agreement rates among Plan justices, and among those held over in office, were generally no higher than the agreement rates between those two categories of justices. Moreover, the effect on voting behavior of the Supreme Court justices' divisional affiliations was of reduced significance during the Plan era. As they had in the early

---

[21] The effect of partisan affiliation remains when divisional assignment is held constant.

period, however, Division 1 judges continued to display more cohesion in *en banc* cases than did those justices assigned to Division 2.[22]

On the basis of the evidence examined here, it appears that the kinds of cleavages that were factors in Supreme Court decision-making in the pre-Plan years no longer affected voting alignments among Supreme Court justices in the Plan era. After 1942 neither partisan affiliation nor the method by which the justices were chosen had any significant bearing upon voting behavior in nonunanimous decisions. Nor were there any other identifiable voting blocs on the Court in the Plan period, although divisional affiliation did have some effect upon voting patterns in the Court. Yet, the absence of any meaningful blocs within the Court did not result in a lessening of dissent within the Court. In general, dissent levels were slightly higher in the Plan years than in the pre-Plan period.

The final question to be examined is that of the alleged conservatism of the Missouri Supreme Court and the courts of appeals, and the extent to which such conservatism might be attributable to the kinds of appellate court judges chosen under the Missouri Plan method of judicial selection. The evidence presented with relation to this issue is drawn from the lawyer survey responses rating members of the appellate benches in terms of their objectivity with respect to the handling of personal injury or negligence litigation. Table 9.6 gives data on rating of appellate judges, data which is comparable to that contained in Table 9.1 on circuit court judges. As in Table 9.1, the objectivity rating scale ranges from 1 to 5, with 1 indicating an extreme bias on the plaintiffs' side, 5 an extreme pro-defense bias, and 3 a neutral or "objective" position.

Only one member of the entire appellate bench received more pro defendants' than pro plaintiffs' ratings from Missouri attorneys; all the rest were adjudged as leaning towards the plaintiffs' side of litigation. In general, courts of appeals and Supreme Court justices chosen under the Missouri plan are somewhat less plaintiffs-inclined than are the judges who were held over into office upon adoption of the Missouri Plan. Moreover, the court of appeals and Supreme Court judges chosen under the Plan were evaluated, on the whole, as being more pro-plaintiff than the Plan judges on the two circuit benches of the state. As was the case for the circuit judges, there are slight differences in lawyer perceptions of appel-

---

[22] The differences in cohesion between justices assigned to Division 1 and Division 2 may be partially attributable to the fact that the divisions are of unequal size. If the four Division 1 justices vote together in *en banc* cases, they can prevail, since they comprise a majority of the seven–member Court.

TABLE 9.6
DEGREE OF OBJECTIVITY RATINGS OF APPELLATE JUDGES[a]

| | Nonpartisan Plan Judges | | Holdover Judges | |
	Appeals Court (N = 13)	Supreme Court (N = 8)	Appeals Court (N = 9)	Supreme Court (N = 7)
Mean	2.71	2.84	2.61	2.70
Most pro plaintiff	2.44	2.72	2.21	2.55
Most pro defendant	2.93	3.13	2.93	2.85
Range	.49	.41	.72	.30
Judges with defendants' rating	0%	12%	0%	0%

[a] The ratings are derived by the same method employed for the data reported in Table 9.1, *supra*.

late judicial objectivity, depending on the practice orientation of the lawyers. In general, as indicated by Table 9.7, corporate and defense lawyers assess the appellate judiciary as being more plaintiff-inclined than do the plaintiffs' and criminal practice attorneys. The differentials are even more pronounced when the practice backgrounds of the judges themselves are taken into account, as is shown in Table 9.8.

Although these data on lawyer ratings of appellate court judges pertain only to the degree of judicial objectivity in one area of decision-making, they are probably reliable indicators of the general ideological stance

TABLE 9.7
DEGREE OF OBJECTIVITY RATINGS OF APPELLATE JUDGES
BY PRACTICE BACKGROUND OF LAWYER RATERS

| Practice Background of Lawyer Raters[a] | Nonpartisan Plan Judges | | Holdover Judges | |
	Appeals Court (N = 13)	Supreme Court (N = 8)	Appeals Court (N = 9)	Supreme Court (N = 7)
Defendants'	2.80	2.83	2.82	2.65
Corporate	2.83	2.86	2.78	2.74
Plaintiffs'	2.88	3.18	2.88	2.97
Criminal	3.00	2.95	2.90	2.93

[a] Includes those lawyers who listed field exclusively, or as one of two or three major fields of practice.

TABLE 9.8
DEGREE OF OBJECTIVITY RATINGS OF NONPARTISAN PLAN
APPELLATE JUDGES WITH CERTAIN PRIOR PRACTICES
EXPERIENCE BY LAWYERS WITH COMPARABLE
PRACTICE EXPERIENCE

	Judges' Practice Background[a]			
	Defendants' (N = 2)	Corporate (N = 5)	Plaintiffs' (N = 3)	Criminal (N = 1)
All Lawyers	2.98	2.80	2.69	2.78
By Lawyer's Practice Background[b]				
Defendants'	2.92	2.89	2.70	2.82
Corporate	3.14	2.90	2.68	2.86
Plaintiffs'	3.26	3.07	2.74	2.99
Criminal	3.21	3.12	3.00	3.00

[a] Information on prior experience is restricted to those Plan judges who returned mail questionnaires. Includes those who listed field exclusively or as one of two or three major fields of practice.
[b] Includes those lawyers who listed field exclusively, or as one of two or three major fields of practice.

of Missouri Plan judges. Personal injury litigation would seem to pose the most fundamental kinds of issues along the conservatism-liberalism dimension. The lack of any significant difference in the position of Missouri Plan judges on these issues—whether comparison is made between Plan and holdover judges, or appellate and circuit judges—suggests that the Missouri Plan system of judicial selection has not resulted in a notably more conservative appellate judiciary. Rather, the data indicate that lawyers of all practice backgrounds regard appellate judges as being essentially neutral in personal injury litigation; to the extent that, such judges show any bias, it is generally toward the plaintiffs' side of such litigation.

PART III

AN ASSESSMENT OF
THE PLAN

10

◄◄◄·••ᴥ

CONCLUDING COMMENTS

Having analyzed the origins, dynamics, and consequences of the Non-partisan Court Plan, the task remains of drawing together our major findings so one can see the full picture, and not just the details of judicial selection under the Plan. We also assess the implications that our study has for broader issues involving the Bar, the judiciary, and the judicial process.

The first section of the chapter summarizes and relates our major findings with respect to the development and operation of the Plan recruitment and selection process. The second section uses the same approach in analyzing the consequences of the Plan compared to an elective system of choosing judges. In the third section we relate the specific findings of our study to basic issues involving the bench and the Bar. The final part of the chapter raises questions regarding the state judiciary that require future research.

DEVELOPMENT AND OPERATION OF THE PLAN
RECRUITMENT AND SELECTION PROCESS

As previously suggested, no other group of officeholders in American society are selected by such a variety of methods as are our state judges. No less than five distinct systems are currently in use: executive and legislative appointment; popular election by partisan and nonpartisan ballots; and the Nonpartisan Court Plan. The first four of these methods are linked to general political philosophies and constitutional practices prominent in different eras of our nation's history. Thus the original thirteen states provided for selection by executive appointment (usually with confirmation by a council or by the upper branch of the legisla-ture), or by the legislature itself, which was regarded in those days as the more popular and democratic body. These two methods are still employed by the same states today.[1] Other states, which were admitted to the Union later, tended to adopt the system of popular election of judges, particularly as the Jacksonian Revolution came to be accepted as the dominant political philosophy of the time. Still later, certain states, especially those in the Mid-West and West, fell under the influence of the Progressive movement and used nonpartisan ballots to choose judges along with other governmental officials.

Although these four methods involve different groups and types of ballots to choose judges, they are based on the common assumption that men who occupy judicial positions are like other governmental officials and, therefore, should be chosen by political figures such as governors or legislators, or should be elected directly by the people. However, in time, the feeling grew among members of the legal profession that judges were not in the same category as other officeholders, but were a special type of public official for which the Bar had a unique responsibility. The first modern Bar Association, the Association of the Bar of the City of New York, was founded in 1870 specifically to fight Boss Tweed's control over the courts and, since that time, the activities of the organized Bar have been closely linked to this issue.[2]

The Bar's concern with judicial selection grows out of professional values. Just as its members have sought to police the types of persons who become lawyers through legal education and admission standards, so they have considered the quality of the bench to reflect on the legal profession. Beyond this, the leaders of the Bar have taken the position that the expertise of the lawyer extends beyond the handling of legal affairs of society to matters of judicial administration. This credo holds that the judgments of lawyers on the selection of members of the bench are likely to be more objective and more knowledgeable than those of political leaders and the electorate. In other words, they have "professed"[3] a special competence in evaluating which of their brethren should ascend to the bench.

---

[1] Hawaii is the only state which was not one of the thirteen colonies that presently uses gubernatorial appointment of state judges. All those states in which judges are chosen by the state legislature were included in this original group.

[2] Within the decade following the establishment of the Association of the Bar of the City of New York, a number of similar organizations, including the American Bar Association, were formed to improve the administration of justice. See Roscoe Pound, *The Lawyer from Antiquity to Modern Times* (St. Paul, Minn.: West Publishing Company, 1953), Chap. IX.

[3] Everett C. Hughes suggests that "professions profess. They profess to know better than others the nature of certain matters." See his "Professions," *Daedalus*, XCII (Fall, 1963), 656.

Over the years, the organized Bar has sought to bring its judgment to bear on the selection of members of the judiciary. Its main efforts have been directed at effecting changes in the partisan election method because of the "evils" that the leaders of the profession have associated with that system (that is, its domination by the political machines of the large urban areas). Initially, this involved attempts to minimize the power of political party organizations in electing judges through such devices as judicial nominating conventions, primaries, nonpartisan judicial ballots, and separate judicial elections. Also, the Bar sought to enhance its own influence by means of referenda in which Bar Associations evaluated the capabilities of the various judicial candidates and passed their recommendations on to the electorate.[4] When such efforts to work within the framework of popular elections failed to bring to the profession the influence its leaders desired, two national professional groups (the American Judicature Society and the American Bar Association) developed the Nonpartisan Court Plan which was first adopted in Missouri in 1940. This system, with its key feature of nominating commissions that include lawyer and judicial members, was specifically designed to give the legal profession a special voice in choosing members of the bench.

Despite the fact that the Plan does provide a unique role for the bench and the Bar, it also contains elements of traditional judicial selection methods. The public is provided some voice in the choosing of judges through the representation of lay members on the nominating commissions and the electorate can, at least in theory, vote Plan judges out of office, while the chief political figure in the state, the governor, actually appoints such lay persons, and also makes the final decision as to who will be selected for the bench. Thus the Plan purports to provide representation for four general interests concerned with judicial selection: the organized Bar, the judiciary, the general public, and the state political system.

Viewed in this context, it is naive to suggest (as some of the Plan's supporters do) that the Plan takes the "politics" out of judicial selection. Instead, the Plan is designed to bring to bear on the process of selecting judges a variety of interests that are thought to have a legitimate concern in the matter and at the same time to discourage other interests. It may be assumed that these interests will engage in the "politics" of judicial selection, that is, they will maneuver to influence who will be

---

[4] Chicago conducted its first Bar primary in 1887. For an analysis of this and subsequent primaries in this metropolitan community, see Edward M. Martin, *The Role of the Bar in Electing the Bench in Chicago* (Chicago: University of Chicago Press, 1936).

chosen as judges (1) because such judgeships constitute prestigious positions for aspiring lawyers, and (2) because, in the course of making decisions, judges inevitably affect the fortunes of persons and groups involved in the litigation process. Whether the Plan eliminates politics in judicial selection is a false issue. Instead, the key issue is whether the particular kind of politics that evolved under the Plan adequately represents the legal, judicial, public, and political perspectives thought to be important in determining who will sit on the bench.

In answering this broad question, we must analyze a number of dimensions of the judicial selection process as it has operated in Missouri over the period of a quarter of a century. First, what are the concerns of these various groups in judicial selection? That is, what considerations do lawyers, judges, the general public, and state political leaders take into account in deciding which person should become judges? Second, do spokesmen of these various groups involved in the actual selection process (the lawyer, judicial, and lay members of a nominating commission, and the appointing authority, the governor) adequately represent the perspectives of these various groups? And, finally, does the interaction of the various participants in the nomination and appointment process operate so as to protect the legitimate interests of all parties concerned—or are some such interests favored at the expense of others?

Members of the Bar have a direct and salient concern with the judiciary. Some attorneys have a personal stake in the judiciary because they would like to become judges. Our study indicates, however, that not all members of the Bar feel the "pull of the robe." Some lawyers frankly prefer the role of the "advocate" to the "referee" in the judicial process; moreover, many persons who have highly successful practices are not willing to suffer a loss of income associated with a move to the bench. Beyond this, formal legal requirements of residency render ineligible for circuit judgeships a considerable segment of the Bar, particularly those practicing in St. Louis City; informal "availability" factors also operate to discourage the trial court candidacies of young and aged attorneys, together with those who are not directly involved in the practice of law, or who have specialized practices which keep them out of the courtroom. Some attorneys are also deterred from seeking such judgeships because they feel that political considerations (their minor party affiliation or lack of political involvement) will eliminate them from serious consideration as candidates for the bench.

Our study indicates that different considerations are involved with respect to the candidacies of courts of appeals and Supreme Court judges; this means that there are, in effect, two pools of candidates for the trial and appellate benches. Relatively few attorneys are eliminated from appellate judgeships by legal requirements,[5] and the greater prestige associated with an upper court position means that more financially successful practitioners are willing to make a sacrifice to accept a seat on the appellate court. Moreover, the more intellectual and contemplative work of such courts appeals to some attorneys who do not relish the pressures associated with the trial judge's task of refereeing the verbal combat of the lower court chambers. Advanced age and lack of involvement in party affairs are also less likely to discourage appellate court candidacies than they are those for lower court positions. At the same time, a number of attorneys who seek to become judges at the lower level of a judiciary do not make themselves available for an appellate judgeship, because they prefer the job of a trial judge, or because they do not calculate their chances of obtaining the more prestigious upper court post as being very great.

But the interest of the Bar in a judiciary extends beyond the personal ambition of the lawyers who covet a position on the bench. The attorneys who are in court frequently have an obvious concern in seeing that lawyers ascend to the bench who are not only competent, but who have personalities and dispositions that make interpersonal relationships as pleasant as possible. Our study indicates that attorneys are sensitive to the treatment that they receive from trial judges in front of witnesses and the courtroom public; they also resent the judges who press them to trial before they feel they are adequately prepared.

An analysis of lawyer elections under the Plan also reveals the presence of general social and economic cleavages in the Bar, which have a direct relevance for judicial selection. Most immediately concerned are the plaintiffs' and defendants' attorneys who have a direct stake in personal injury cases which constitute such an important share of the caseload of the courts, particularly at the trial level. Both groups attempt to influence the choice of judges because, as shapers of the rules of the courtroom game, they are thought to affect vitally the outcome of personal injury litigation. Other members of the Bar also tend to become concerned with such litigation because their clients' affairs may end up in court even though they personally do not handle the cases. Moreover, difference in backgrounds of attorneys in different social strata of the Bar—those educated at prestige law schools, who are associated with large firms and handle the legal affairs of established economic institutions, versus night law school graduates in solo practice who service the legal problems of individuals and small businesses—en-

---

[5] These are the ones who live outside the state of Missouri. Only 52, or about 4 percent of our state sample of 1233, were included in that category.

courage rivalries within the Bar, which in turn lead each group to favor one of its men for a seat on a nominating commission as well as on the bench itself. While, undoubtedly, much of this Bar rivalry involves "we" and "they" feelings and thus relates more to symbolic stakes rather than concrete ones, it constitutes an important clue by which attorneys evaluate prospective candidates for both the nominating commissions and the judiciary itself.

Present members of the judiciary also have a keen interest in the question of which lawyers go on the bench. Those who occupy seats on the same court as the one for which candidates are being considered are concerned with these factors: the ability of new judges to absorb their fair share of the case load; whether new judges will add rather than detract from the court's prestige; and whether they will be amiable colleagues. While these considerations are present even for positions on the circuit court where the judges hear cases in separate divisions, they are more salient in the courts of appeals and the Supreme Court, which are collegial bodies. Here interpersonal relations are highly important, since decisions are collective ones on which judges must work together; the premium placed on unanimous decisions as a means of manifesting the certainty of the law makes it particularly important that persons come on the appellate courts who hold views on basic issues which are similar to those of the sitting judges, and that they be the kinds of individuals who are willing to compromise whatever differences may exist among members of the court in the interest of the judicial "team." Beyond this, the rather cloistered life many judges feel they must lead in order to demonstrate their independence and insulation from controversial social, economic and political matters that may eventually end up in their court, causes them to seek socially congenial companions with whom they can best share their common lot. Thus judges of appellate courts look for colleagues who can best fit into the "task" and "social" functions performed by these collegial bodies.[6]

Of the various groups that have a conceivable interest in the courts, the interest of the general public is the least substantial. Democratic theory notwithstanding, the plain fact is that the man in the street is, for the most part, blissfully unaware of the activities of the courts. If he is disinterested and uninformed about public affairs generally, as

---

[6] These are the concepts which David J. Danelski has used to demarcate the leadership roles the Chief Justice of the United States Supreme Court plays a promoting harmony among justices of that collegial body and expediting the work of the Court. See his selection, "The Influence of the Chief Justice in the Decisional Process" which appears in Walter F. Murphy and C. Herman Pritchett, eds., *Courts, Judges and Politics* (New York: Random House, 1961), pp. 497–509.

recent studies have found most persons to be,[7] he is even less concerned about judicial matters. Most individuals do not become personally involved in litigation; moreover, the courts, surrounded as they are with the trappings of majesty and suffused with ritual, are dimly understood by the average person. Nor are the usual signals and clues of party identification, personalities, and controversial issues present, which illuminate and order the legislative and executive worlds for the general public. Members of this public are likely to become interested in the courts only if there is a scandal in judicial administration or in the life of a judge. In the absence of such developments, the courts and the selection of judges have little or no salience for the electorate.[8]

There are, however, "attentive publics" which do take an interest in the courts and the judiciary. In addition to newspapers and civic groups, which become involved sporadically at the time of a judicial vacancy to insure that "good" men are considered and chosen, or which focus on the more notorious activities of the courts (usually criminal cases), there are a range of groups that are constantly concerned with the judiciary.[9] These constitute the clientele of the courts, that is, those involved in frequent litigation, such as public agencies handling civil or criminal matters, and established economic institutions such as banks, insurance companies, public utilities, real estate companies, general business organizations, and labor unions. Since judges make decisions that vitally affect such groups, they are attentive to the issue of judicial selection. Quite naturally, they hope to see persons go on the bench who are favorable to, or at least, not antagonistic to their interests.

Finally, the Plan judiciary is highly important for the chief political figure of the state, the governor. He is primarily interested in using such positions to reward his personal friends or former political supporters. Moreover, judgeships are also available as potential bargaining

---

[7] Studies indicate that most voters are not vitally interested in political matters or knowledgeable about public issues. They are more likely to take their "cues" on the political world from such factors as partisan affiliation and the personalities of the candidates. See Angus Campbell, Philip Converse, Warren Miller and Donald Stokes, *The American Voter* (New York: John Wiley and Sons, 1960).

[8] Jack Ladinsky and Allan Silver refer to the voters in judicial elections as the "acquiescent electorate" in their article, "Popular Democracy and Judicial Independence: Electorate and Elite Reactions to Two Wisconsin Supreme Court Elections." *Wisconsin Law Review* (1967), 128–169, reprinted as Number 22 in *The Law and Society Series* of the University of Wisconsin.

[9] For a study that develops a method of categorizing interest groups on the basis of the scope and regularity of their activities in the political process, see Wallace Sayre and Herbert Kaufman, *Governing New York City* (New York: Russell Sage Foundation, 1960).

weapons to obtain support for the governor's legislative program, or in lining up backing for future campaigns for public office. However, the one-party, "friends and neighbors" atmosphere of Missouri state politics, its relatively low level of concern with public policy, and the fact that the governorship has generally been a political "dead-end," all combined during our period of study to dispose most Missouri chief executives to use appointments more as rewards for past associations and political services than for legislative maneuvering or future electoral ambitions. Some, however, were more sensitive to charges of political favoritism or cronyism, and thus were more inclined to appoint persons who would make them look "good" in the eyes of the organized Bar.

The particular method for channeling the rewards of judicial appointments varies with the party organization situation in the Plan jurisdictions of Jackson County, St. Louis City, the three courts of appeals districts, and the state-wide constituency associated with Supreme Court appointments. Jackson County judgeships have usually been funneled through the mechanism of the Democratic party factions operating there, particularly as they relate to gubernatorial primary campaigns; the absence of such stable party divisions in St. Louis City opens up a wider range of potential influences, including legislators, local party and public officials, as well as individual political entrepreneurs active in state gubernatorial campaigns. The broader jurisdictions and the less structured situations associated with upper court appointments also provide the governor with a freer hand in choosing appellate judges—a desirable state of affairs for him in light of the more prestigious nature of such judgeships.

These four kinds of interests constitute what we have termed the broad "environments" surrounding judicial selection under the Plan. In analyzing its operation, it is necessary to assess the extent to which these various interests are "articulated"[10] by participants in the selection process, that is, the lawyer, judicial and lay members of a nominating commission and the appointing authority, the governor. The degree to which they articulate these interests depends on the perspectives these individuals bring to their task, together with the way they view their respective roles, that is, the interests they feel they are expected to represent when decisions regarding judicial appointments are made.

The polarization of the Bar, particularly in the two major metropolitan communities, and the fact that persons generally run in lawyer elections

---

[10] The word articulation is used by Gabriel Almond and James Coleman to designate the function by which claims and demands are made in a political system. See their study, *The Politics of Developing Areas* (Princeton: Princeton University Press, 1960), pp. 33 ff.

for the nominating commissions as representatives of the rival Bar organizations, make them sensitive to the plaintiff-defendant issue as it bears on judicial selection. However, this is not always true, as demonstrated by the fact that some lawyer members of the St. Louis Circuit commission who might have been expected to speak for the plaintiffs' lawyers actually tended to favor candidates from the other side of the Bar. (This situation has changed in recent years as lawyer members elected with support of the Lawyers' Association have spoken for their constituents' interests.) Moreover, the fact that both groups of lawyers were represented simultaneously on the Jackson County nominating commission during most of our period of study tended to cancel out any advantage either side might have exercised in the selection process. In contrast is the situation in the appellate commission where lawyer members have generally been pro defendant in their orientation, primarily because this segment of the Bar has viewed the upper court as more important to its clients' interests and has worked harder races to get their members elected to it than to the circuit nominating commissions. This circumstance, coupled with the fact that fewer of the defendants' group are disenfranchised for residency reasons in races for the appellate than the circuit commissions (particularly for the St. Louis one) means that the defendants' attorneys generally have been able to dominate the body that nominates candidates for the appellate courts.

However, lawyer commissioners represent other interests concerned with judicial matters besides those of the Bar itself. Indirectly, they articulate broader social concerns, since their perspectives are shaped to a great degree by the kinds of clients they serve: plaintiffs' attorneys want persons on the bench who they feel will be favorable or at least not hostile to the interests of injured parties, as well as "underdog" elements in society in general. The defendants' and corporation lawyers view matters from the vantage point of their upper class clientele.

It would be an exaggeration, however, to suggest that lawyers on nominating commissions assess candidates only from a social status standpoint. Since lawyers must work closely with judges, and also because they want to protect the reputation of the legal profession, they have a natural interest in seeing that competent individuals go on the court. Nor are their perspectives on judicial selection entirely professional in nature. Personal friendships affect their attitudes toward candidates. Beyond that, they are not political eunuchs: some have favored lawyers with a particular party or factional affiliation, sometimes in accordance with the governors' preferences and, in other cases, in spite of (or because of) a chief executive's antipathy toward them.

Of the various participants, the judges on the nominating commissions have evidenced the greatest variety of perspectives on judicial selection. They are the only members who may be expected to protect the particular interests of the judiciary; this is most important for the appellate courts because of their collegial nature. The wishes of sitting judges are best articulated in selections for the Supreme Court because in this instance an actual member of that court sits on the commission, while colleagues of newly selected circuit and courts of appeals judges are represented not by one of their own brethren, but rather by a judge at the next higher level of the state judicial system.

But judicial members of the commission bring other perspectives to bear on the selection process. They are also members of the legal profession and thus express some of the same previously noted concerns as do the lawyers on the commissions. (However, the fact that they are somewhat removed from the current plaintiff-defendant Bar rivalry makes this issue less salient to many of them.) Finally, some (particularly on the Jackson County circuit nominating commission), have been highly sensitive to the nuances of local politics as they relate to gubernatorial campaigns, and this has served to give added emphasis in the selection process to the political dimensions of candidate acceptability.

As previously suggested, there has been no sustained discernible interest of the general public in the courts, and hence the idea that the lay nominating commissioners represent such a point of view is a fiction. Instead, they have tended to articulate other environmental interests in the selection process. Most of them have been individuals in the business world, particularly from established financial institutions such as banks, insurance companies, realty firms, and public utilities. They have frequently viewed candidates from the perspectives of these "attentive publics." Moreover, since most of them turn to lawyers for advice on candidates, they also reflect the viewpoints of the Bar. The fact that they are best acquainted with attorneys representing their own businesses or others like them means that they have generally tended to articulate the attitudes of the defendants' segment of the legal profession.

Laymen on the commission have also served to channel political considerations into the selection process. In some instances, this has come at the specific request of the governor, transmitted directly or through an intermediary to the lay commissioner. More often, however, politically astute laymen have been able to bring gubernatorial attitudes on candidates to bear on the nominating process simply because they have known, without being told, who have been the friends and enemies of particular chief executives over the course of their political careers.

Generally, the Missouri governors have viewed selection under the Plan almost entirely from a personal or a political standpoint: they have used their appointments to reward friends or past political supporters. The perspectives of the Bar, the judiciary, and the courts' clientele on judicial appointments constitute outer limits on the governors' appointments, that is, chief executives in Missouri have not chosen individuals for the court who were anathemas to any of these groups, but within these broad confines, governors have been able to exercise considerable discretion in the direction of their personal and political preferences.

The question of how the various interests—legal, judicial, "attentive publics," and political—have fared in the ultimate selection of judges under the Plan has depended not only on their articulation by nominating commissioners and the governor but also on their "aggregation,"[11] that is, the way they have been combined, canceled, or compromised in the decision-making process. The mode of aggregation has been most affected by the extent to which the various participants have been influential in choosing members of the bench. While the nature of such influence naturally varies from appointment to appointment, certain overall patterns may be discerned.

One factor bearing on such influence is the personal effectiveness of the various participants. It is our judgment that the presiding judge has generally been most successful in interactions with other members of the nominating commission. He has a greater stake in the issue of who goes on the bench than do the other commissioners (this is particularly true of the case of the Chief Justice of the Supreme Court with respect to his future colleagues on that collegial body), and thus is inclined to devote more time and effort to affect that decision. He also possesses certain advantages in the negotiation process with other commissioners. The laymen are inclined to pay close attention to the presiding judge's views because they tend to have respect for the judiciary; beyond this, some believe that a judge knows better what that position involves, and the qualities it requires of practicing attorneys, than do other individuals. Also the presiding judge has common professional ties with lawyer members of the commission. Thus he can forge alliances with both kinds of nominating commissioners. Beyond this, he is also in a position to link the nominating and appointment phases of the selection process: he has often been involved in the political world (those serving in our period of study were either elected or appointed to the bench by the governor), and is therefore frequently able to understand and appreciate gubernatorial perspectives on judicial selection.

---

[11] Almond and Coleman, *ibid.*, pp. 39 ff., use the term "aggregation" to suggest the function whereby articulated interests are combined, accommodated and otherwise taken account of in a political system.

When such natural advantages are combined with particular skills of individual judges (this has been most obvious in the case of one presiding judge involved in a number of appointments to the Jackson County circuit court), the net effect is to make the presiding judge a preeminent figure in judicial appointments, a "first among equals." This is not always the case—some presiding judges have lacked the interest, knowledge, or skills to be effective in that role—but it is the general tendency.

We are also of the opinion that most Missouri governors have been fairly influential in judicial appointments under the Plan—even in the nomination stage of the process. This is because many lay and some lawyer commissioners have been sensitive to their wishes, as have some of the presiding judges. The politicization of the process has been particularly prominent in the case of the Jackson County circuit court, and has existed to a lesser extent in the St. Louis circuit, and for the appellate court positions as well.

We also believe that the lawyer commissioners as a group have been less influential on the selection process than many persons might believe. Cleavages between the members of the circuit commission, based on the plaintiffs-defendants split in the profession, as well as differences in party affiliation, have frequently made it difficult for attorneys to form alliances with each other. This has been less true as far as appointment to the appellate court is concerned, since most of the lawyer commissioners on that body have been from the defendants' side of the Bar.

As might be anticipated, lay members of the commission have not generally played the role in judicial selection which the theory of the Plan assigns them. Their supposed constituency, the general public, is meaningless when compared to the legal, judicial, and political worlds of the other participants. They have also generally lacked the knowledge and confidence in their judgments concerning capabilities of candidates for the bench and, therefore, have tended to defer to the views of the presiding judge, and to a lesser extent, the lawyers on the nominating commissions. For the most part, they have served the interests of others: the presiding judge, and the governor, and the political community. This does not mean that they have had no influence on judicial selection, or that the process would have been the same without their participation, but that most lay commissioners have been followers, rather than leaders, in the matter of choosing judges under the Plan.

In the final analysis the aggregation of interests that has occurred in the selection process depends not only on the relative influence of the various participants but also on the kinds of combinations that have been formed among the commissioners over the years. Another feature of the aggregation has been the extent to which the perspectives of the various nominating commissioners and governors have conflicted or converged on the matter of who should sit on the bench. The tendency for convergence has been most noticeable in the case of appointments to the Supreme Court where there has been substantial congruence among the interests of the defendants' lawyers who have tended to sit on the appellate nominating commissions, the presiding judge who represents the viewpoints of that collegial body, and the governor with his outstate political ties. All of these groups have tended to look for candidates with an essentially conservative orientation.

Judicial selection under the Plan can thus be conceived as a progressive, winnowing process reflecting a wide variety of factors. At one end of the process we have the particular subculture from which judges are drawn: the legal community consisting of persons admitted to the Bar. The recruitment phase of the process eliminates many of these attorneys for a number of reasons: legal requirements of eligibility; desire to stay in private practice; and informal availability factors relating to age, practice background, and political experience and involvement. Those who overcome the obstacles created by the recruitment mechanism are in turn affected by the myriad of factors associated with the nomination and appointment phases of choosing judges. In effect, candidates are required to "pass muster" with the nominating commissioners and the governor, who represent the interests and perspectives of the organized Bar, the judiciary, the "attentive publics" of the courts and the state political system. This further serves to winnow candidates for the bench until a chosen few emerge as the final products of the entire process.

Although every individual appointment necessarily involves a particular set of circumstances, it is possible to discern overall patterns of judicial selection, reflecting different combinations of the basic interests, that have evolved for the circuit courts of Jackson County and St. Louis City, as well as the appellate courts of the state. We have suggested the essential result of the aggregation process in the chapter headings dealing with the choice of judges in these areas of the state judicial system.

A number of factors have converged to politicize the selection process for the Jackson County circuit bench. The political environment has been structured by the Democratic factions, as well as the reform element in local politics, as they relate to the choice of Missouri governors. The fairly equal representation of plaintiffs' and defendants' lawyers on the nominating commission, together with the influence of firms representing a mixed practice, has tended to neutralize the effects of this cleavage on the selection process. Beyond this, many lay commissioners, together with certain presiding judges, have been sensitive to partisan factors relevant to candidate acceptability to Missouri governors, and this has also served to make political considerations important in judicial selection in Jackson County.

In contrast, the selection process for the St. Louis circuit bench has been essentially pluralistic. The political factors in choosing judges there have been less influential for several reasons. First, in that area there has been an absence of meaningful factions in the Democratic party by which one can identify the gubernatorial acceptability of the various candidates. Second, Republican lawyers have been more prominent in the Bar and on the nominating commissions, and this has served to broaden the pool of meaningful candidates for the bench. Beyond this, many lay commissioners have been more oriented to the values of the business community and less sensitive to political factors in the selection process than is true in Jackson County. Moreover, presiding judges with political knowledge and skills comparable to those associated with judicial selection in Jackson County have not been as much in evidence in the St. Louis area. In addition to these political differences that exist between the two circuits, other factors have brought different influences to bear on the choice of judges in St. Louis. The "attentive publics" have not been content with channeling their views exclusively through the Bar as they tended to do in Jackson County, but rather have acted on their own to try to influence who goes on the bench. Finally, the absence of influential St. Louis law firms with a mixed plaintiffs'-defendants' practice similar to those involved in the judicial selection of Jackson County has resulted in a greater representation of attorneys with a clear plaintiffs' or defendants' practice in the St. Louis community. The cumulative effect of these factors has contributed to the pluralism of judicial selection in St. Louis.

We have termed selection for the appellate courts in Missouri, and particularly the Supreme Court, as essentially cooptive in nature. The influence of the Supreme Court members themselves, as channeled through the Chief Justice of the court (who also serves as *ex officio* chairman of the appellate nominating commission), has made this factor the predominant one, as evidenced by the number of Supreme Court commissioners who have become nominees. Moreover, as previously indicated, there has been less conflict in the perspectives of the various participants in the appellate selection process than there has been in the choice of circuit judges under the Plan. The defendants' lawyers who have generally won seats on the commissions over the years, the governors in Missouri with their outstate political orientations, and the lay persons they have appointed to the nominating commissions, have all tended to reflect the values of Missouri's "traditionalistic" political culture, and the low key, don't-rock-the-boat political style, which has characterized persons active in public affairs in the state. This factor, in turn, has led them generally to select persons for the appellate bench who have also shared these values and orientations. The greater willingness of upper-status attorneys to accept a position on the appellate courts, as compared to the circuit ones, has also worked to the advantage of these groups.

THE CONSEQUENCES OF THE PLAN

One of the best ways to evaluate the kinds of interests that are represented in the operation of the Plan is to compare it with an elective judicial system. But in doing so, one must be sure the comparison is a valid one, that is, one that takes into account not only the realities of the Plan but also those of an elective judiciary as well, since the advocates of the popular election of judges have been as prone to idealize their preferred system as have the supporters of the Nonpartisan Court Plan. Fortunately, for comparative purposes, one can observe both systems in actual operation in Missouri. By analyzing the *consequences* associated with each system, one is in a position to determine what difference it made that the Plan was adopted in that state in 1940.

One of the most striking results of such a comparison relates to the kinds of persons who are elevated to the bench under the two selection systems. The stereotype of the Plan judge conjured up by the humorous ditty set forth in the Introduction of this study (that is, that only "men from fair old Harvard" will be considered for judgeships) could hardly be further from the truth. No Harvard man has been chosen for either the circuit or appellate benches in Missouri; the same is true of lawyers from the national prestige law schools of Yale and Columbia as well. Moreover, only one Chicago man and three Michigan men have made it. In fact, the trend has been in the other direction, that is, there has been a greater tendency for graduates of night law schools to ascend to the bench, particularly in the Jackson County and St. Louis City circuits, since the Plan was adopted in place of the elective system in 1940.

A further analysis of the backgrounds of the Plan judges negates other assumptions which are often made about their characteristics.

Rather than being "cosmopolitans" they are essentially "locals,"[12] that is, persons who were born and legally educated in Missouri, quite often in their own home community. Despite the Plan's claims of nonpartisanship, more of the lawyers who went on the bench in the post-Plan period were affiliated with the state's majority party (the Democrats) than was the case in the earlier period when judges ran in partisan contests. Moreover, those who went on the circuit bench in Jackson County and St. Louis City after 1940 had less previous judicial experience than did their elected predecessors.

There are, however, some trends in background characteristics of judges since the adoption of the Plan which support the allegations that are made by the Plan's supporters. It has pushed up the average age of judges from the 40's to the 50's, thus bringing a more mature lawyer to the bench. Plan appellate judges have had more service on the lower levels of the state's judicial system than was the case for judges who were elected to upper court positions prior to 1940.

The comparison also indicates certain basic similarities between the background characteristics of the Plan and elected judges in Missouri. There has been a growing trend for those who go on the bench in recent years to have had prior experience in a law enforcement position, primarily as a prosecutor. On the other hand, other kinds of political-office experience are fairly rare for all judges in Missouri, including those that are still elected in the St. Louis County and the outstate circuits. Moreover, few judges (Plan or elective) go directly from a political office (even a law enforcement one) to a judgeship.

Thus the differences in background characteristics of judges chosen under the two systems are not as marked as many persons assume. The Plan judges are not the "bluebloods" of the profession—a breed set apart from those chosen by partisan election. Actually, the two groups of judges appear to have more common than distinguishing characteristics.

A similar conclusion can be made concerning the decisional propensities of Plan and elective judges. Contrary to the charges of many critics of the Plan, it does not place on the bench persons who are notably more conservative than those chosen by popular election. The differences between lawyer ratings of Plan and elective judges with respect to their pro plaintiffs' or pro defendants' bias in personal injury cases are

---

[12] The concepts of "local" and "cosmopolitan" are used by sociologist Robert Merton to categorize persons whose primary orientations are to their immediate communities, and to a broader environment, respectively. See his selection on the subject that appears in Edward C. Banfield (ed.), *Urban Government: A Reader in Politics and Administration* (The Free Press of Glencoe, 1961), pp. 390–400.

minimal. Moreover, the Plan judges, including those who came out of a defense practice, are considered to be slightly pro plaintiff in their orientation. An analysis of the nonunanimous decisions of the Supreme Court also fails to indicate the presence of any blocs whereby Plan judges vote one way on cases and elective judges another. In fact, there have been more dissenting opinions rendered by the state Supreme Court since it became populated entirely by Plan judges than were handed down when both kinds of judges sat on the bench. In other words, as a group, Plan judges have tended to disagree on decisions more with each other than they formerly did with their elective colleagues.

One consequence of the Plan on which there has been general agreement by the Bar is that it results in putting "better" judges on the bench than are usually chosen under an elective system. Our survey data indicate that the Bar is most agreed on this result of the Plan: about six of every eight attorneys practicing in the two major cities of the state feel this result has occurred, compared to about one in eight who think it has not. Other independent data from our study on the same issue (the performance ratings of judges by attorneys actually practicing before them) show that, as a group, the Plan judges are rated more highly than those who are elected to the bench. (In particular, the comparative analysis demonstrates that the Plan has tended to eliminate highly incompetent persons from the state judiciary.) It has placed on the bench judges with the qualities that Missouri lawyers rate as most important in a "good" judge, namely, "knowledge of the law," "open-mindedness and willingness to listen to both sides of the case," "common sense," "courtesy to lawyers and witnesses," and "hard-working."

The Plan also has had an effect on the tenure of judges in Missouri. Although its judges are subject to being removed from the bench by the electorate, in reality this very seldom occurs. The fact that they run on their records with no opponents means that the elections become, in essence, plebiscites: only 1 of the 179 separate judicial ballots conducted during our period of study resulted in a judge's being turned out of office and that occurred under highly unusual circumstances posing larger issues than the case of the immediate individual involved. Under normal circumstances, a Plan judge has little to fear from the electorate.

The tenure situation of elective judges in Missouri has differed considerably from the one described above. In the quarter-century preceding adoption of the Plan in 1940, circuit judges in the two major cities, as well as appellate judges, met with frequent defeats, particularly in the general election. The same was true in St. Louis County and, to a lesser extent, in outstate circuits. More recently, the situation has improved for elective incumbent judges in Missouri with relatively few of them actually being turned out of office by the electorate. However, unlike many of the outstate judges who face little or no competition for office today, judges in urban St. Louis County continue to draw serious opposition in the general election. Their situation differs markedly from that of the Plan judge who need not concern himself at all with the thought of a campaign or the possibility of defeat at the polls.[13]

The attorneys in Missouri recognize that, in effect, Plan judges enjoy life tenure and this factor has important consequences for their behavior in office. A great number of them argue that this independence is desirable because it permits a judge to make decisions based on the merits of the case, rather than subjecting him to the pressures that elective judges must often face under threat of being voted out of office. However, some of them view this judicial independence as not entirely salutary, since it "federalizes"[14] some judges, that is, tends to make them arbitrary in the treatment of lawyers and laymen with business before the courts. (Attorneys who are active in trial courts are most likely to suggest this tendency; a number of them oppose the Plan for this reason.) Presumably, elective judges are more sensitive to the feelings of the Bar and public on such matters, because these groups are in a position to make their influence felt at the time of the next election.

It would be an exaggeration, however, to suggest that the tenure situations of Plan and elective judges are entirely different. In the recent period of our study (1941–1964), one marked by considerable political stability in the state, only about 1 in 12 of the circuit judges in St. Louis County and outstate areas actually met electoral defeat. What is more prevalent is for such judges, along with the Plan ones, to remain in office over a long period of time. Few judges in Missouri have left the bench voluntarily, and those that have, generally have done so to accept another judicial post. The judiciary in Missouri is a career position which few judges abandon unless they are forced to do so.

While this security of tenure has obvious advantages for the judges involved, it is considered to be a mixed blessing by members of the Bar. Our sample survey indicates that lawyers are concerned with the problem of the judge who is incapable of carrying on the duties of

---

[13] Plan judges are specifically forbidden by law "to take part in a political campaign." *The Constitution of the State of Missouri*, Art. V. Sec. 29 (f). Whether this prohibition applies to efforts to get themselves reelected to office or not, the electoral situation is such that no campaign is necessary for Plan judges.
[14] Some of our respondents used this term to refer to judges who are arbitrary in their conduct toward attorneys and litigants because they ascribe this type of behavior to federal judges who enjoy life tenure.

his office, but who remains on the bench because there is no effective means by which he can be removed from office. Despite the recent activities of the committees of both the Bar and judges designed to expedite the retirement of judges who are incapacitated, most of the lawyers in our survey felt that the problem of aged judges is an acute one, particularly for circuit judges who presently have no mandatory retirement age. Four-fifths of them would like to see all trial judges, like appellate ones, be required to retire at age 75 or earlier; at the same time, three of five favor raising retirement benefits of such judges above their present level of one-third of final salary. Considerable sentiment also exists for providing some effective means of removing incompetent judges from the bench regardless of their age.

However, despite the identification of such weaknesses in the operation of the Plan, the fact remains that it has considerable support among members of the Missouri Bar as revealed in our survey. The attorneys who are most inclined to favor it over an elective system are the ones who are most familiar with its operation, namely, those practicing in Jackson County and St. Louis City. Support for the Plan falls among attorneys practicing in St. Louis County and outstate areas which still elect their trial judges. Nonetheless, even in these elective circuits, the Plan is preferred by attorneys over either of the other two major alternative methods: nonpartisan and partisan elections. Only in the outstate circuits does the partisan election system draw any major support: less than 1 in 20 St. Louis County attorneys want to continue their present method of choosing judges by means of partisan ballots.

Also the survey indicates that the social status of attorneys shapes their attitudes toward the Plan. Those most inclined to favor it are the groups that originally worked for its adoption (defendants' and corporation lawyers), particularly those educated at prestige law schools who practice in large firms. The segment of the Bar that gives the Plan least support are the plaintiffs' and criminal attorneys, especially night law school graduates and those in solo practice, groups which fought the adoption of the Plan in 1940.

The partisan affiliation of attorneys is less closely connected with preferences regarding judicial selection than are social status considerations. There is a tendency for more Republicans than Democrats practicing in the two major urban communities to favor the Plan, and for the opposite situation to prevail in St. Louis County and the outstate circuits. Presumably, these preferences relate to calculations of party advantage, since Republicans would have little chance of electing circuit judges in Jackson County or St. Louis City, but stand a better chance of winning such contests in St. Louis County and in many outstate circuits. Concomitantly, Democrats might be expected to view the electoral situation from the contrary vantage point. Nonetheless, the fact that Democratic lawyers in the two major cities overwhelmingly support the Plan testifies to the fact that other considerations bearing on selection preferences are more salient to them than are matters of party advantage.

A final dimension of the Bar's attitude on the Plan revealed by the survey is the considerably higher level of support it enjoys for the selection of appellate, as compared to circuit, judges. Many attorneys, particularly those practicing in the outstate areas, are satisfied with the use of the elective system to choose their trial judges, but want to employ the Plan to select members of the appellate courts. They advance several basic reasons for this variation in their preferences. One is the ability of the voters to know and assess the capabilities of circuit court candidates in outstate areas, a situation they contrast with the politics of urban communities (the critical areas in appellate races), which leads to their domination by party factions and machines. Beyond this, many lawyers conceive of the two levels of courts as performing different functions in the state judicial system. They favor the popular election of trial judges, since these judges are involved in matters they feel should reflect public sentiments, particularly in the immediate localities concerned. In contrast, they consider the work of the appellate courts as being "pure law" in nature, that is, as involving matters of legal expertise over which the public should exercise no influence. These lawyers feel that it is necessary to insulate such judges from the pressures of the general public, as well as political parties and interest groups, and, therefore, the Plan, rather than popular election, should be the method utilized to choose and retain in office members of the appellate bench.

With this summary of our major findings in mind, we now turn to broader considerations. What general conclusions can be drawn from our study relating to the selection of judges in our society? Furthermore, what implications do our findings have for an understanding of the bench and the Bar?

GENERAL OBSERVATIONS ON THE BENCH AND THE BAR

As one assesses the basic conclusions that emerge from our study, it is apparent that they call into question a number of assumptions which are frequently made about both the bench and the Bar in this nation. One is the stereotyped notion that many persons have of the legal profession: the tendency to view the Bar as essentially monolithic and conservative in its orientation. Undoubtedly, a part of this misconception is attributable to the conservative views on public policy that the leaders of the American Bar Association have often taken over the years, and the natural tendency of many individuals to equate such views with those of the profession at large.[15] Beyond this, some students of the judiciary have painted a one-sided picture of the legal profession in their writings. Hurst has sketched the lawyer's role in American society through a series of historical stages as the impact of industrialism changed the attorney from a courtroom man representing individuals to a counselor for the corporate world.[16] In the same vein, Adolf Berle has referred to the lawyer as "an intellectual jobber and contractor in business,"[17] and a number of other persons have echoed that sentiment.[18] While none can deny the importance of these facets of legal practice in our corporate world, the development of NACCA and its state affiliates may portend a rise in importance and status of those who represent other economic interests in modern-day society, as a kind of revolution of the legal "proletariat" develops in the profession. Certainly our study demonstrates that such groups are beginning to develop a kind of "countervailing power" in the legal marketplace.

The Plan has operated to channel such basic cleavages in the legal profession into the issue of who should be chosen for the state bench. A practice has evolved in Missouri whereby rival Bar groups nominate candidates and mount campaigns to get their men elected as lawyer members to the circuit and appellate commissions which nominate candidates for the bench. These lawyers' elections have taken on many of the features of a general party system. The Bar organizations not only assume the role of parties in the selection process, but they also possess characteristics that differentiate them from mere "factions": they are durable and visible; they have not been dependent for their existence upon individual personalities or cliques; and they represent important

---

[15] For a discussion of the conservative public policy stands of the ABA over the years, see John Schmidhauser, *The Supreme Court: Its Politics, Personalities, and Procedures* (New York: Holt, Rinehart and Winston, 1960), Chapter 4.

[16] James Willard Hurst, *The Growth of American Law: The Law Makers* (Boston: Little Brown and Company, 1950), Chapter 13.

[17] A. A. Berle, Jr., "Modern Legal Profession," *Encyclopedia of the Social Sciences,* IX (1933), p. 340.

[18] Included are C. Wright Mills, *The Power Elite* (New York: Oxford University Press, 1956), p. 289; Fred Rodell, *Woe Unto You Lawyers* (New York: Reynal and Hitchcock, 1939), pp. 3 f.; Karl N. Llewellyn, "The Bar Specializes—With What Results?" *Annals of the American Academy of Political and Social Science,* **167** (1933), 177 ff.; and Harlan Stone, "The Public Influence of the Bar," *Harvard Law Review,* **48** (1934), 6 ff.

economic and social divisions in the Bar supported by conflicting ideologies.[19] Moreover, a competitive "two-party" system has developed, since no other group enters candidates, and both the Bar Association and Lawyers' Association have been able to elect their candidates at reasonably frequent intervals over the years.[20]

The development of this two party system within legal community means that diverse elements of the Bar are represented in the selection process. The concern of some persons that the Bar is inevitably conservative is disproved by the Missouri experience.[21] The fact that all attorneys, and not just the leaders of the American Bar Association, are involved in the selection process makes for a more adequate representation of the Bar than is involved in the profession's attempt to influence the choice of federal judges.[22]

What is suggested here is that the issue of the role of the Bar in judicial selection has been examined on the wrong basis. The question is not whether the legal profession as a group can serve as unbiased spokesmen for the "public interest"[23] in choosing judges, as its leaders sometimes claim to do; the fact that lawyers are lined up on opposite sides of economic and social issues in our society makes this hope unrealistic. Instead, the question is whether lawyers as "client caretakers"[24] adequately represent the various "publics" that utilize the courts, that is, the social and economic interests involved in litigation. It is our judgment that in Missouri the rival Bar Associations and Lawyers' Asso-

---

[19] V. O. Key talks of "factionalism" in his *Southern Politics in State and Nation,* (New York: Alfred A. Knopf, Inc., 1949), and William N. Chambers distinguishes between factions and parties in his *Political Parties in a New Nation: The American Experience* (New York: Oxford University Press, 1963).

[20] For methods of classifying state party systems on the basis of competitiveness see Austin Ranney and Willmoore Kendall, "The American Party Systems," *The American Political Science Review,* 48 (1954), 477–485; and Joseph A. Schlesinger, "A Two-Dimensional Scheme for Classifying the States According to Degree of Interparty Competition," *ibid.,* 49 (1955), 1120–1128.

[21] De Tocqueville, in his classic study, *Democracy in America,* referred to lawyers and judges as the American "aristocracy" which acted as a check on the democratic element in the society. For a discussion of the reasons underlying the alleged conservatism of lawyers, see Walter F. Murphy and C. Herman Pritchett, *Courts, Judges and Politics* (New York: Random House, 1961), pp. 126 f.

[22] Grossman's analysis of the composition of the Committee on Federal Judiciary in his study, *op. cit.,* shows that it represents primarily the conservative elements of the profession.

[23] For a critique of this concept, see Glendon Schubert, *The Public Interest* (New York: The Free Press of Glencoe, 1960).

[24] Pound uses the phrase, "client-caretaker," at p. 184, *op. cit.,* as does James Willard Hurst, *op. cit.,* p. 366.

ciations have acted as relatively effective spokesmen for many social and economic groups affected by Court decisions.

Of course, much remains to be accomplished in the matter of providing legal services for all elements of our society, particularly persons in the lower classes.[25] However, recent developments (including the Supreme Court's ruling that defendants accused of serious state crimes must be represented by counsel,[26] Congress' appropriation of money for legal services to low-income groups,[27] the development of public defender programs, as well as changes occurring in modes of legal practice)[28] all show considerable promise in assisting "underdog" groups with their legal problems. Such advances should thus favor some publics that utilize the judicial process, and increase the role of the Bar in

---

[25] One study of the use of lawyers by lower class persons showed that many of them were not aware of their need for legal services, and of those that were, only a small proportion actually went to a lawyer because of a concern with fees. See Earl Koos, *The Family and the Law* (Rochester: National Legal Aid Association, 1949, mimeographed). Personal injury matters, however, are an exception, since contingent fee arrangements mean that a client has everything to gain and nothing to lose by consulting a lawyer. A study in New York City showed that among automobile accident victims, lower class respondents were just as likely to retain a lawyer as higher class respondents. See Carlin, *Lawyers on Their Own, op. cit.*, p. 154, citing Roger B. Hunting and Gloria S. Neuwirth, *Who Sues in New York City* (New York: Columbia University Press, 1962).

[26] *Gideon v. Wainwright*, 372 U.S. 335 (1963). The courts are now involved in deciding a line of cases relating to the particular stages of the arrest and detention process for which counsel must be provided, and whether the principle of the case should be applied to criminal misdemeanors as well as felonies. One law professor has suggested that the decision will force more and more lawyers into criminal cases, and this will require that the organized Bar try harder to relate canons of ethics to criminal law practice. See B. J. George, Jr., "A New Approach to Criminal Law," *Harper's*, 231 (1965), 185.

A related development is the passage of the Criminal Justice Act of 1964, which provides for compensated counsel in federal courts for indigent defendants charged with felonies or serious misdemeanors.

[27] The funds are administered by the Legal Services Program of the Office of Economic Opportunity. The first annual report of the organization, dated August 1966, indicated that over 160 programs proposed by local communities and groups had been funded. Forty-three of the states had programs, as did 37 of the nation's 50 largest cities. Of the remaining 13 cities, 9 had applications pending at that time. The agency also reported that over 500 new law offices serving the poor were funded, and over 1000 full-time attorneys and an undetermined number of volunteer lawyers enlisted in the War on Poverty.

[28] This includes the increased usage of lawyer referral services, legal clinics and group legal service plans, as well as improvements in legal aid programs. See Lewis F. Powell, Jr., "The President's Annual Message: The State of the Legal Profession," *American Bar Association Journal*, 51 (1965), pp. 823 ff.

representing a broad spectrum of social and economic interests in judicial selection. To the extent that this occurs, the role that the Bar plays in judicial selection under the Plan will be even less likely to favor conservative interests than it did during our period of study.

But if the critics of the Plan have misconstrued the character and nature of the Bar, and the type of influence it exerts on the selection of judges, so the Plan's supporters have displayed little understanding of the role that political factors play in the operation of the Plan. As previously suggested, the Plan has not eliminated "politics" as the term is used in its broadest sense, that is, the maneuvering of individuals and groups to influence who will be chosen as judges. Rather, it has changed the nature of that politics to include not only partisan forces but also those relating to the interests of the organized Bar, the judiciary, and the court's "attentive publics." Nor has the Plan even eliminated partisan politics in judicial selection: vesting the final appointment power in the major political officer of the state is hardly calculated to have that result, particularly since state chief executives often have been able to influence the choice of the three nominees as well. What one can say is that the Plan has altered partisan factors in judicial selection so that ward committeemen and other local leaders and persons active in electoral politics are no longer the major figures in selecting judges as they were under the elective system formerly used to choose members of the bench in Missouri. Instead, it is now the governor who looms large in such decisions, and local and state political figures are only influential insofar as their political careers and fortunes are tied to his.

Thus the politics that has developed under the Plan is more complex, that is, takes into account a broader range of interests than that which is overtly associated with an elective system of choosing judges.[29] The Plan has also taken the partisan aspects of judicial selection out of the vortex of local political forces and leadership influence and projected them into the political world of the highest public official in the state. One might well argue that this new type of judicial selection politics is better than the old one because it is more pluralistic, or that the partisan considerations involved in it are likely to be broader and more enlightened because they emanate from the vantage point of the top man in the state political system rather than persons far down on the political ladder. But it is naive or misleading or both to suggest, as many of the Plan's supporters do, that it has taken the politics out of judicial selection.

---

[29] We have used the word "overtly" to indicate the possibility that a number of interests may affect the selection of elective judges by exercising their influence from behind the scenes.

Our study also raises doubts about another assumption which is often made about judicial selection, especially by critics of the Plan who champion the popular election of judges. That is the supposition that injecting partisan considerations into the choice of judges will result in the better representation of "liberal" interests (those associated with underdog groups in society). (This assumption is usually linked with the other one described above, namely, that the role of the Bar in judicial selection serves to facilitate the interests of the conservative, that is, the established institutions in society.) Our study indicates, however, that elective judges are not necessarily more liberal than Plan ones. If the political culture of the state or the political style of its leaders is conservative, as both tend to be in Missouri, then this type of influence is projected into judicial selection through the operation of partisan factors. The nature of the total state environment in which the selection process is located affects how the process works and the type of interests it takes into account. Therefore, it is quite possible that the Nonpartisan Court Plan might lead to different results in different states, or even in the same state over different periods of time.[30]

Our study indicates that even some of the persons most familiar with the actual operation of the Court Plan (the members of the Missouri Bar) tend to view judicial selection on the basis of ideological considerations and assumptions. As we have pointed out, lawyers' preferences on the method of choosing judges are shaped to a considerable degree by their social status, with those in the elite segment of the profession more inclined to favor the Plan than their less prestigious colleagues. Beyond this, these two groups battle it out in electoral contests for lawyer seats on the nominating commissions. Yet there is little in the way of hard evidence—the kind that lawyers are used to demanding in the course of their professional work—to link such preferences in status positions with concrete results or "payoffs" in the judicial process. Attorneys who favor the elective system in our survey did not rank judges chosen by that method as better than Plan judges; in fact, they rated the latter judges as the superior group. Nor were Plan judges considered defense-minded even by plaintiffs' lawyers. Rather, most Plan judges were thought to lean slightly toward the plaintiffs' side of personal injury litigation. Moreover, an analysis of the nonunanimous decisions of the state Supreme Court failed to uncover any blocs based upon differences in voting behavior of Plan and elective judges.

---

[30] Although the matter lay beyond the scope of our study, we have the general impression that some new developments have occurred in the dynamics of selection in Missouri since we terminated our analysis.

When one examines our findings regarding lawyers' attitudes toward the desirability of the Plan and their perceptions of how it operates, he is struck by the differences that appear on such matters in the thinking of various segments of the Bar. But when the same lawyers are questioned on matters that relate to judicial selection without specifically connecting them to the Plan or to the popular election of judges, their views tend to converge. Thus, the attorneys in our survey, regardless of their preferences on judicial selection methods, were in general agreement as to which particular judges performed well and poorly on the bench. Moreover, they look for essentially the same qualities in a "good" judge. Their perceptions of the plaintiff-defendant orientation of the various judges were even similar. Thus their preferences on judicial selection do not seem to be founded on disparate conceptions of who is a good judge, or what qualities are required of such a judge, or even whether judges tend to be biased one way or another in personal injury litigation, the issue that has been most instrumental in creating cleavages in the Bar. Faced with this conflict in evidence, one can conclude that lawyers' preferences on judicial selection tend to be triggered by ideological concerns rather than an assessment of actual differences in the consequences of the Plan vis à vis the partisan method of choosing judges.

As one ponders the interrelationships of the various aspects of our study, and their relevance for broader questions of the state judiciary, he soon realizes that much information that would help to clarify and set in perspective our particular findings is not available in the existing literature. There are a number of basic questions that require answers if we are to begin to understand the full implications of our own data and how they fit into the larger picture of the selection of judges and the operation of the courts at the state level. We suggest some of these largely unexplored areas that merit future research by persons interested in the field of the state judiciary.

SOME UNANSWERED QUESTIONS
ON THE STATE JUDICIARY

One major area of inquiry that needs illumination at the state level is the one we were directly concerned with in our study: How do individuals get recruited and chosen for the state bench? As previously suggested, the opportunities for comparative research in this field are particularly promising, since five separate selection methods are presently used by our states to pick their judges: executive and legislative appointment; popular election by partisan and nonpartisan ballots; and the Nonpartisan Court Plan. We are thus in a position to explore the dynamics of these various election methods to determine how they operate and which groups are influential in choosing judges under each of them. By doing this we can better know whether the institutionalization of the role of the bench and the Bar in judicial selection as provided for in the Plan markedly affects the influence of these groups, or whether they have essentially the same effect on the choice of judges when they are required by other selection methods to operate through informal channels to make their desires and wishes known.

Our findings would also have more significance if we knew how the Nonpartisan Court Plan has operated in other states that have adopted it in recent years, such as Alaska, Iowa, Kansas, and Nebraska. We have suggested that a different state environment might well affect the operation of the Plan, but we are not in a position to verify that general supposition, or to spell it out with more precision, until we have some comparative information on this subject.

By thus studying different methods of judicial selection, as they occur in various political environments, we shall be better able to understand just how much influence these respective factors have on the dynamics of the process of choosing state judges. A similar procedure would help to clarify the consequences that flow from using different methods to choose judges, together with the effect that disparate political and legal milieu have on the results of the judicial process.

Another area that would benefit from more systematic analysis is that of decision-making in the state courts. Although this particular matter was beyond the scope of our study, our curiosity was aroused by the fact that there was little differences in the plaintiff-defendant orientation of the various judges as perceived by members of the Bar; moreover, the practice background of the judges and lawyers concerned also had little effect on lawyer evaluations of judicial objectivity. This raises the possibility, at least, that attorneys who go on the bench are generally successful in abandoning the role of "advocate" in personal injury litigation in favor of a "referee" position, or that the fact situations in personal injury cases are such that there is generally little discretion available as to how individual judges will rule on such matters.

In fact, our findings with respect to the Missouri Supreme Court cases, which indicate an overwhelming amount of agreement among members of that body on all kinds of issues before that court, raise the broader question as to why there are so many unanimous decisions at the state level. Students of the judiciary have largely ignored this area of inquiry in favor of delineating differences among voting patterns of justices on the United States Supreme Court, perhaps because it is felt that their decisions are more important, or simply because they offer a greater opportunity to demonstrate that values do shape judges' opinions.[31] Whatever the reasons may be for this preoccupation with decision-making of the United States Supreme Court, it is equally important to determine why judges tend to vote alike in state litigation. A number of possibilities are present. First, similar background experiences (it will be recalled that our analysis showed relatively few differences in social backgrounds of Plan and elective judges), plus a common socialization process which all attorneys go through, may dispose them to view cases similarly.[32] Second, the collegial process for arriving at decisions in state appellate courts may operate to bring about consensus, particularly because a premium is placed on unanimity as a means of demonstrating the certainty of the law. Finally, there is the possibility that most state cases do not involve issues that allow much opportunity for philosophic differences to arise among members of the courts.[33] A thorough analysis of these various possibilities, and the respective parts they play in the formation of judicial opinions, will do much to illuminate the decision-making process, not only at the state level but also in the lower levels of the federal judicial system where dissents are also comparatively rare.[34]

Finally, we need to investigate much more thoroughly than we have, the part that courts play in the state political system. We lack an understanding of the kinds of interests for which the state tribunals are particularly important. To determine this, we require basic information on such matters as what kinds of persons are most involved in state litigation, the types of cases they bring, why they go to the courts to

---

[31] A pioneer student in this area was C. Herman Pritchett. In recent years, Glendon Schubert and Harold Spaeth have also pursued this line of inquiry. For a criticism of the approach employed by Schubert and Spaeth, see, Theodore L. Becker, *Political Behavioralism and Modern Jurisprudence* (Chicago: Rand McNally and Company, 1964), Ch. 1.

[32] Joel Grossman points out that common backgrounds may help explain similarities in judge's decisions. See his article, "Social Backgrounds and Judicial Decisions," *Journal of Politics,* 29 (May, 1967), 334–352. Becker, *ibid.,* feels that students of the judiciary have overlooked the effect which judicial role (that is, the expectation of judges that they should refer to established legal precedents) has on the decision-making process.

[33] Grossman, *op. cit.,* emphasizes the limitations placed on judicial discretion by the alternatives which are presented for dealing with situations raised by particular cases.

[34] For a study which found a low rate of dissents in decisions of the United States Courts of Appeals, see Shelton Goldman, *Politics, Judges and the Administration of Justice,* unpublished Ph.D. dissertation, Harvard University, 1965.

accomplish their purposes, and the results such litigation brings in terms of the distribution of values in our society.[35]

These, then, are some of the topics that merit further attention of students of the judiciary. They belong to a broad field of inquiry that might best be designated as the comparative study of judicial systems. Comparisons of courts at the national, state and local levels of the political process offer promise as a fruitful field of research for students of the judiciary.[36]

---

[35] Kenneth Vines has made some explorations of such matters in state courts. See his selection, "Political Functions of a State Supreme Court," which appears in a study edited by him and Herbert Jacob, *Studies in Judicial Politics*, Vol. VIII, Tulane Studies in Political Science (New Orleans: Tulane University Press, 1962). See also his chapter, "Courts as Political and Governmental Agencies" in another work edited by Jacob and him, *Politics in the American States: A Comparative Analysis* (Boston: Little, Brown and Company, 1965). The most intensive examination of such issues at the lower court level is Kenneth Dolbeare's, *Trial Courts in Urban Politics: State Court Policy Impact and Functions in a Local Political System* (New York: John Wiley and Sons Inc., 1967).

[36] A number of empirical studies of judicial systems of other nations are scheduled to appear in the near future. A volume edited by Joel Grossman and Joseph Tanenhaus, *Frontiers of Judicial Research*, to be published shortly by John Wiley and Sons of New York, contains individual selections on the judiciaries of Japan by David Danelski, West Germany by Donald Kommers, Switzerland by Fred Morrison, and Australia by Glendon Schubert. Walter Murphy and Joseph Tanenhaus are engaged in a analysis of public attitudes towards the courts in Argentina, Canada, Ireland and West Germany. The broadest comparative study of Judicial systems will be Theodore Becker's *Comparative Judicial Politics* (Chicago: Rand McNally and Company, 1969), which contains data to Asia, Africa, Latin America, Eastern and Western Europe, and the Middle East.

APPENDIX A

RESEARCH METHODS FOR

PERSONAL INTERVIEWS

Most of the data bearing on the process of judicial selection were collected through personal interviews with a wide variety of respondents, including nominees and appointees to the Missouri Plan benches and members of the judicial nominating commissions. Although newspapers and other public documents furnished valuable background information on the process, these sources rarely provided a sufficient understanding of the factors related to each nomination and appointment, or an understanding of the more general factors pertinent to judicial selection.

The primary objective of the interviews was to elicit information such that each nomination and appointment, and the general pattern of relationships prevailing in the selection process, could be "recreated" as completely as possible for each of the Missouri Plan courts studied. For this reason, it was deemed advisable to proceed from the specific to the more general in each interview. Only after respondents had recalled all that they knew about specific events relating to judicial politics were they asked to give their impressions as to the persons and factors that most influenced the selection process. Through such a procedure, we hoped to discourage the respondents from merely dealing in generalities or simply repeating "hearsay" information. Hopefully, this approach also prevented answers to questions calling for information about specific events from being structured or distorted by the initial injection of issues requiring the respondent to sum up his impressions of the entire process of judicial selection. The inclusion of questions on specific events also permitted us better to gauge the reliability and credibility of each interviewee, and thus to evaluate the worth of his more general observations.

Since a major objective of this study was the delineation of relationships between the judicial and political structures, it was essential that a reliable picture of the political system be obtained. It was impossible for us to make a separate, detailed analysis of partisan politics in each area studied. Such questions were therefore included in all the interviews about judicial politics, with only a few other respondents being interviewed specifically because of their presumed knowledge of partisan politics. Not only did we hope, through that method, to obtain a "shorthand" description of politics in each region, but we attempted specifically to learn whether those influential in judicial politics tended also to be influential in political affairs generally.

The portion of our study based upon data gathered in personal interviews is subject to the same limitations as are all studies that rely principally upon post-factum interviewing. The ability of respondents to recall past events declines markedly the farther back in time one goes. Moreover, the death of many participants in the selection process for the early Plan years made it impossible to acquire comprehensive information about the nominations and appointments during that era. In this connection, a most serious difficulty was posed by the fact that all but one of the governors serving during the 1940–1964 period were deceased or incapacitated at the time of our study.

The reliability of data gathered through personal interviews is directly dependent on the memory, knowledge, and honesty of those interviewed. Even after the normal precautions are taken—excluding data gained from respondents whose credibility is open to question, checking each interview for internal consistency, and comparing information obtained from a specific respondent with that given by other respondents—the method is less reliable than are some other techniques, particularly that of participant observation. Yet, if the researcher cannot assume the role of participant observer (it was impossible for this study because of the closed nature of the selection process), and if there are no documents or other public records containing the desired information, recourse to the retrospective type of interview is the only research tool available.

Fundamentally, as Selltiz and others observe, the personal interview is as reliable as are most other techniques for the collection of data.[1] Essentially the same sources of possible bias are present in reliance on written records. Indeed, data from the kinds of records and reports

---

[1] For a general comparison of the sources of bias in different kinds of data collection methods, see Claire Selltiz et al., *Research Methods in Social Relations* (New York: Holt, Rinehart & Winston, 1961), Appendix C, pp. 546–587.

generally used as source material by political scientists are often of more questionable validity than are data from interviews, since the sources of bias are frequently unknown and thus cannot be controlled. In the interviewing method, at least, one can attempt to compensate for the problem of respondent credibility, and for the equally difficult problem posed by the fact that most respondents speak from a very limited and partial perspective and rarely have insight into all the ingredients of the selection process. The remedy available to those using the personal interview method is to look for convergence in the statements of those who occupy diverse vantage points in the process. In the case of disagreement among respondents, it is often necessary to make a judgment as to whether some occupy more strategic positions and would therefore have greater credibility. In some instances it is impossible to resolve the discrepancies, and it is necessary to accept the inconclusiveness of the data.

Prior to conducting the bulk of our personal interviews, we prepared dossiers on each nominee and appointee to the Plan benches, and on each member of the nominating commission. Most of this information came from newspaper articles pertaining to the selection process, including articles on all individual nominees, judges, nominating commissioners, candidates for the nominating commission, and the governors. After these data were collected, background interviews were conducted with persons deemed to be knowledgeable about judicial selection, but who were themselves not participants in the selection process. Included in this category were academicians, newspaper columnists and reporters, and personal acquaintances of the authors who were assumed to be informed about the legal ecology, the political system, the factors relevant to the selection of nominating commissioners, or the judicial nominating and appointing processes. These respondents were asked not only for information about the foregoing dimensions of selection but also for suggestions as to persons who were influential in selection, or who were particularly well informed about it.

On the basis of these background data and interviews, we prepared a tentative list of respondents to be interviewed, a separate interview guide for each type of respondent to be interviewed (whether nominees, nominating commissioners, etc.), and a set of data forms to be utilized in the interviews. These data forms (on legal-sized pages) recorded the most pertinent information about the nominees chosen for each panel, and similar information about the nominating commissioners who selected them. As new information was acquired in the interviewing process, it was added to these data forms. By reference to these forms

TABLE A-1
DATA FORM FOR PERSONAL INTERVIEWS

| | Appointee | Nominee | Nominee | Nominee | Nominating Commission Members | | | | | | |
					Judge	Lawyer	Opponent	Lawyer	Opponent	Lay	Lay
Name and Party and Religion											
LEGAL BACKGROUND											
Bar Association											
Plaintiff or Defendant											
Type Practice											
Law Firm											
Bar Positions											
Law School											
Fraternity											
POLITICAL BACKGROUND											
Faction											
Party Posts											
Reform–Machine											
PUBLIC OFFICES											
BUSINESS AND CIVIC AFFAIRS											

during our personal interviews, we were able instantly to ascertain the information relevant to each selection. A sample of the form used is included as Table A.1.

The selection of further respondents for the study proceeded through a combination of the reputational and positional approaches. As we interviewed persons on the list compiled from the background interviews, we asked each respondent, in addition to questions about selection, to provide us with the names of persons either knowledgeable about or influential in judicial selection. For this purpose, we employed a "quota" system, through which we asked respondents for suggestions as to knowledgeables or influentials of the following types: lawyers whose practice was primarily of a corporate or defense nature; attorneys whose clientele was weighted toward the representation of plaintiffs; lawyers with a mixed plaintiffs-defense personal injury practice; leaders and influentials in the various Bar associations; legal counsel for various groups having a substantial volume of litigation before the courts; Democratic and Republican attorneys (with selection made in rough proportion to the partisan coloration of the Bar); lawyers who were especially active in partisan politics (at either the local or state levels); political party influentials; and confidants of each of the Missouri governors. If persons in these categories were mentioned by a sufficient number of our respondents, they were added to our interviewee list. In this respect, we followed what might be called a "cobweb" approach. In addition, we included on our interview list persons in certain positional categories: Bar association officials; political party officials; all candidates for lawyer seats on the nominating commission; all nominess for the bench; and all participants in the formal nominating process.

Each interview was of the partially-structured or focused variety. Working from a set interview agenda used for all respondents of a given type, we followed no fixed ordering of topics, but took up each item on the agenda at the time which seemed most appropriate for each respondent. The items dealt with in these interviews are typified by the topical format employed in the interviewing of nominees for the bench. An abbreviated version of the items included is as follows:

(1) How respondent happened to become a nominee.
(2) Sources of his support outside the commission itself.
(3) Activities, personal and by his supporters, designed to secure his nomination.
(4) Nature of contacts with members of nominating commission.
(5) Nature and extent of support for others nominated to panel along with him.

(6) Factors relevant to his nomination and to the choice of others named to the same panel, including party affiliation, factional affiliation, religious and ethnic considerations, family background, and fields of legal practice.

(7) The nature of cleavages in the legal profession and their relevance to the selection of lawyer nominating commissioners, and to judicial selection generally.

(8) Factors generally related to success in competition for judicial nomination, including lucrativeness of practice, trial experience and ability, legal craftsmanship, and knowledge of the law.

(9) Nominee's perceptions of the roles played by the different types of nominating commissioners.

(10) Nominee's perception of influentials in the nominating process.

(11) The governor's method of making a selection from the panel submitted to him—his contacts with the nominees and with others consulted for advice.

(12) Nominee's perception of the governor's basis for making the appointment he did, including the role of political party affiliation, factional affiliation, legal background, and personal relations with the governor.

(13) The kinds of persons selected by the governor for lay commissionerships, the factors he considers in making such choices, and the persons he consults about such appointments.

(14) Whether the governor tends to place more weight upon the lay commissioners' views than those of other participants in the process.

(15) Nominee's information about specific appointments made to levels of the Missouri Plan court system other than the one for which he was nominated.

(16) Nominee's perception of differences in the judicial selection process for the various court levels.

(17) Nominee's perception of involvement by the rank-and-file Bar in the selection process.

(18) Nominee's perception of lawyers or law firms that had been particularly active or influential in the selection of judges (with a check list of specific lawyers and firms inquired about following respondent's initial response).

(19) Nominee's perception as to whether persons involved and/or influential in judicial selection were involved and/or in-

fluential in certain other specific areas of public office politics, and in politics generally.

edgeable about, or who had been, or were then, influential with regard to judicial selection.

(21) Data on respondent's frequency of contact with the judiciary, the nature of his firm's and his own legal practice, his partisan affiliation, the extent of his partisan activity, and his involvement in public or civic affairs.

The interviewing, using the agenda appropriate for the type of respondent, proceeded generally through the following categories in the order listed: lawyers and other respondents not having roles in the formal selection process, nominees not appointed to the bench, the nominating commissioners and, finally, the judges chosen for the Plan benches. Such interviews ranged in length from 30 minutes to slightly over six hours, with the average interview lasting slightly less than one hour and a half. Altogether, 234 respondents were interviewed for the study.

APPENDIX B

THE SAMPLE SURVEY

Personal interviews were the appropriate means for gathering detailed data on individual judicial appointments and the specifics of the recruitment and selection process. However, they did not provide us with information on the attitudes of the Bar as a whole on the general operation of the Plan and the performance of all judges in the state. To tap the general thinking of Missouri lawyers on such matters, we conducted a mail survey of a representative sample of all attorneys in the state. Since this survey followed our personal interviews, we were able to use the interviews to help us develop the kinds and form of the questions to be asked in the survey. Beyond this, we utilized some of our personal interviews to pretest the questionnaire. In doing so, we benefitted from the constructive suggestions of our interviewees concerning the choice and wording of the questions to be asked in the survey.

In planning the mail survey, we were faced with the choice of using a short questionnaire to gather limited information from the Bar so as to maximize the rate of returns, or of utilizing a longer questionnaire to gather more information at the expense of reducing the percentage of lawyers responding to it. Because we were interested in a broad range of data, particularly the Bar's evaluation of the performance of individual judges, we opted for the latter alternative. To allow for the lower rate of return, we decided to send out questionnaires to a large number of lawyers in the state so that we would have enough responses to allow for fruitful use of the data along various lines of subanalysis.

Having decided on this course of action, we approached the leaders of the Missouri Bar Association about the possibility of using their membership list as our population of lawyers in the State. (Since the Missouri Bar was integrated by court order in 1944, all lawyers must belong to the official state Bar association.) The leaders not only agreed to allow us to do this but were kind enough to provide us also with the addressograph plates for the membership—a service that saved us the time of typing envelopes for individual lawyers to whom we were sending questionnaires. We randomly selected every other lawyer from the Missouri Bar Association's list (3303 of 6606) and mailed out questionnaires to them in May of 1964. Included with the questionnaire was a covering letter explaining the objective purposes of the study, the academic auspices under which it was being conducted, and the cooperation we had received from the Bar in developing and conducting the survey. The letter and questionnaire also stressed the anonymity of the respondents, and the fact that we would not identify by name in our study any of the judges whose performance they would be rating. A stamped envelope addressed to the Missouri Judiciary Study, the Research Center of the University of Missouri, was provided to facilitate the return of the questionnaires.

Fortunately for us, the response from the Bar was gratifying and served our purposes very well. Although the response rate was not high (37 percent, based upon 1233 usable replies of 3303 questionnaires sent), the total number of returns was large enough to permit subanalysis of the data without individual cells becoming too small for statistical comparisons. Even more important, the response was very representative of the Missouri Bar population as revealed by *The 1964 Lawyer Statistical Report* of the American Bar Foundation. For example, the Statistical Report showed that 32 percent of Missouri's lawyers practice in Jackson County; 30 percent of our respondents were from that county. The comparable population and sample figures for the St. Louis area were 41 and 42 percent, respectively. The Statistical Report showed 71 percent of Missouri lawyers to be in private practice, and we had an identical percentage of private practitioners in our sample. The comparison of age groups in the Missouri lawyer population and our sample were also very close with the exception that older lawyers were slightly underrepresented among our respondents.

We were pleased not only with the size and representativeness of the survey return but also with the quality of the responses we received from members of the Bar. There were only a few returns that were not usable, and the analysis of the data revealed that the replies were accurate and internally consistent. Beyond this, the open-ended questions elicited detailed and well-thought-out answers from most of our respondents; we were able to use such answers to supplement our statistical analyses of responses to the closed-end questions we also used in the survey. Undoubtedly the fact that our lawyers respondents were a highly educated group with considerable interest and experience in the subject matter of our study raised the quality of their answers beyond that which often attends surveys of the general public on matters of little salience to them.

The survey questionnaire not only served our purposes of eliciting information from the Bar; we also used essentially the same format in gathering data from nominees for the Plan bench over the years, as well as judges who were actually appointed to those courts. This enabled us then to compare the background characteristics and, in some cases, the attitudes of the Bar in general with the nominees and appointees of the Plan courts. The following is the questionnaire used for the general members of the Missouri Bar; with certain modifications, it was also used for the survey of nominees and judges.

APPENDIX C

❦

MAIL QUESTIONNAIRE

Most of the following questions can be answered by placing a check (✓) in the appropriate box or boxes. Please read through all the alternatives to a question before making your selection.

* * *

The first group of questions concerns the interest which practicing members of the Bar have in becoming judges.

1. Since the Nonpartisan Court Plan was established in Missouri in 1940, has your name ever been placed before a nominating commission for consideration as a judge?

☐ Yes   ☐ No

IF ANSWER IS *NO* TO QUESTION 1

(a) For what reason or reasons have you *not* allowed your name to be placed before a nominating commission? (Mark one *or more* boxes).

☐ I have not wanted to be a judge because I do not feel that I would enjoy the kind of work judges do as much as I enjoy the practice of law.

☐ I think I would enjoy being a judge but I can earn more money in practice than a judge does and am not willing to make the financial sacrifice necessary to go on the bench.

☐ I would like to be a judge but felt that I should not because of obligations to *lawyers* with whom I was practicing law.

☐ I would like to be a judge but felt that I should not because of obligations to *clients*.

☐ I would like to be a judge but never felt that I had a good chance of being nominated by the *nominating commission*.

☐ I would like to be a judge but never felt I had a good chance of being appointed by a *governor*.

☐ Other. Please be specific in your reason or reasons.

_____

_____

IF ANSWER IS *YES* TO QUESTION 1 (OTHERWISE SKIP TO PAGE 3).

(b) Indicate the *number of times* your name has been before:
　——— the nominating commission for circuit judges
　——— the nominating commission for court of appeals judges
　——— the nominating commission for supreme court judges

(c) How old were you when your name *first* came before any of these nominating commissions?

☐ under 35　　☐ 35–39　　☐ 40–44
☐ 45–49　　☐ 50–54　　☐ 55 and over

(d) How old were you when your name *last* came before any of the nominating commissions?

☐ under 35　　☐ 35–39　　☐ 40–44
☐ 45–49　　☐ 50–54　　☐ 55 and over

(e) For what reason or reasons have you wanted to become a judge? (Mark one or more boxes).

☐ Since very early in my legal career I have wanted to go on the bench because I thought the work of a judge would be more enjoyable and satisfying than that of practicing law.

☐ Although originally preferring the practice of law to becoming a judge, pressures and frustrations of that practice convinced me that being a judge would be more enjoyable than continuing in private practice.

☐ I enjoyed the practice of law for most of my legal career but wanted to go on the bench as a capstone to that career.

☐ I wanted to become a judge because of the honor and prestige of the office.

☐ I wanted to become a judge because I could earn more money.

☐ I preferred the fixed salary and retirement benefits which judges receive to the more uncertain income of private practice.

☐ Other. Please specify.

We would also like to get your views on the selection of judges in Missouri.

1. As far as *circuit court judges* are concerned, which way do you prefer to see them selected? (Select just *one* of the following.)
   ☐ Under the Nonpartisan Court Plan.
   ☐ Straight gubernatorial appointment.
   ☐ Popularly elected by the people on a *nonpartisan* ballot.
   ☐ Popularly elected by the people on a *partisan* ballot.
   ☐ Other. Please specify. ⎯⎯⎯⎯⎯⎯⎯⎯⎯⎯⎯⎯⎯⎯⎯⎯

   ☐ No opinion.

2. As far as *appellate judges* are concerned, that is Supreme Court judges and judges of the Court of Appeals, how would you prefer to see them selected?
   ☐ Under the Nonpartisan Court Plan.
   ☐ Straight gubernatorial appointment.
   ☐ Popularly elected by the people on a *nonpartisan* ballot.
   ☐ Popularly elected by the people on a *partisan* ballot.
   ☐ Other. Please specify. ⎯⎯⎯⎯⎯⎯⎯⎯⎯⎯⎯⎯⎯⎯⎯⎯

   ☐ No opinion.

IF YOU CHOOSE *DIFFERENT* ANSWERS FOR QUESTIONS 1 AND 2 ABOVE

3. Why do you prefer one method for the selection of *circuit court*

judges and another method for the selection of *appellate court* judges? Please be specific.

_____

_____

_____

_____

4. Many comments have been made about the selection and tenure of judges under the Nonpartisan Court Plan. To what extent do you *agree* or *disagree* with the following statements?

(a) The Nonpartisan Plan results in the recruitment of better judges than the elective system does.

☐ Strongly agree ☐ Agree   ☐ Not sure—it depends
☐ Disagree   ☐ Strongly disagree ☐ No opinion

(b) The independence judges enjoy under the Nonpartisan Court Plan tends to make them arbitrary in the treatment of lawyers and laymen with business before the courts.

☐ Strongly agree ☐ Agree   ☐ Not sure—it depends
☐ Disagree   ☐ Strongly disagree ☐ No opinion

(c) The Nonpartisan Court Plan has succeeded for the most part in taking "politics" out of the selection of judges.

☐ Strongly agree ☐ Agree   ☐ Not sure—it depends
☐ Disagree   ☐ Strongly disagree ☐ No opinion

(d) The Nonpartisan Plan favors the selection of certain kinds of lawyers to the bench particularly "defendants'" lawyers and those representing corporate clients.

☐ Strongly agree ☐ Agree   ☐ Not sure—it depends
☐ Disagree   ☐ Strongly disagree ☐ No opinion

(e) The Nonpartisan Court Plan encourages judges to make decisions based on the merits of the case rather than subjecting them to pressures which elective judges must often face.

☐ Strongly agree ☐ Agree   ☐ Not sure—it depends
☐ Disagree   ☐ Strongly disagree ☐ No opinion

(f) The Nonpartisan Plan has substituted Bar politics and gubernatorial politics for the traditional politics of party leaders and machines.

☐ Strongly agree ☐ Agree   ☐ Not sure—it depends
☐ Disagree   ☐ Strongly disagree ☐ No opinion

5. Several suggestions have been made for improving the operation of the Nonpartisan Court Plan. Which of the following would you favor? (Check *one or more* appropriate boxes).

☐ The retirement benefits of judges under the Plan should be increased beyond the present level of one-third of annual salary at time of retirement.

☐ The lay members should be removed from the nominating commissions.

☐ The courts under the Plan should be made *bipartisan*, that is, should be required to represent as equally as possible both major political parties.

☐ Judges of the circuit courts, like those at the appellate level, should be required to retire at age 75.

☐ Commissioners of the Courts of Appeals and the Supreme Court should be selected under the Nonpartisan Court Plan rather than being appointed by the judges of these courts.

☐ Judges running on their record at election time against no opponent, should be required to obtain a two-thirds, rather than a simple majority, favorable vote in order to stay in office.

☐ The compensation of judges under the Plan should be raised to make it competitive with income received by leading members of the Bar who are engaged in private practice.

☐ Other suggested improvements. Please specify. _____

❀ ❀ ❀

This next group of questions has to do with attitudes of lawyers toward judges and the qualities of a good judge. Of course, your personal reactions on these matters will not be identifiable; in addition, we will not designate individual judges by name in our study.

1. Since you first began to practice law how many cases would you estimate you have tried before each of the following courts in Missouri?

Circuit Courts	*Courts of Appeals*	*State Supreme Court*
☐ Less than 5	☐ less than 5	☐ less than 5
☐ 5–9	☐ 5–9	☐ 5–9
☐ 10–24	☐ 10–24	☐ 10–24
☐ 25–49	☐ 25–49	☐ 25–49
☐ 50–99	☐ 50–99	☐ 50–99
☐ 100–499	☐ 100 or over	☐ 100 or over
☐ 500 or over		

TO BE ANSWERED BY LAWYERS WHO HAVE APPEARED BEFORE JACKSON COUNTY AND/OR OUTSTATE MISSOURI CIRCUIT COURTS

2. How would you evaluate the following judges? (Please evaluate only those judges you have *personally* appeared before and rate them on the basis of their *best work years* on the bench.) Rating for *Overall Performance*: Outstanding—A; Good—B; Average—C; Poor—D; Very Poor—E. Rating for *Degree of Objectivity*: Very Pro Pl.—1; Pro Pl.—2; Neutral—3; Pro Def.—4; Very Pro Def.—5. Thus an average, pro def. judge would be rated C-4.

JACKSON COUNTY

Judge	Overall Performance (A,B,C,D,E)	Degree of Objectivity (1,2,3,4,5)
Broaddus, James W.		
Buzard, Paul A.		
Cook, John F.		
Cowan, Ray G.		
Hall, Harry A.		
Harris, Brown		
Hunt, Thomas R.		
Hunter, Elmo		
James, John R.		
Jensen, Richard C.		
Kirtley, J. Marcus		
Koenigsdorf, Richard H.		
Lucas, John H.		
McQueen, Joseph W.		
Moore, James A., Jr.		
Murphy, Donald		
Randall, Alvin		
Ridge, Albert A.		
Riederer, Henry A.		
Southern, Allan C.		
Strother, Duvaul P.		
Stubbs, Thomas J.		
Terte, Ben		
Waltner, Marion D.		
Welch, Leslie		
Wright, Emory H.		

OUTSTATE COUNTY

Judge	County	Overall Performance (A,B,C,D,E)	Degree of Objectivity (1,2,3,4,5)

374

TO BE ANSWERED BY LAWYERS WHO HAVE APPEARED BEFORE ST. LOUIS CITY AND/OR ST. LOUIS COUNTY CIRCUIT COURTS

3. How would you evaluate the following judges? (Please evaluate only those judges you have *personally* appeared before and rate them on the basis of their *best work years* on the bench.) Rating for *Overall Performance*: Outstanding—A; Good—B; Average—C; Poor—D; Very Poor—E. Rating for *Degree of Objectivity*: Very Pro Pl.—1; Pro Pl.—2; Neutral—3; Pro Def.—4; Very Pro Def.—5. Thus an average, pro def. judge would be rated C-4.

ST. LOUIS CITY

Judge	Overall Performance (A,B,C,D,E)	Degree of Objectivity (1,2,3,4,5)
Arnold, Glendy B.		
Aronson, Robert L.		
Boland, Thomas J.		
Buder, William		
Casey, John C.		
Connor, William S.		
Flynn, William B.		
Holt, Ivan Lee, Jr.		
Hyde, Laurance M., Jr.		
Killoren, William H.		
Kirkwood, Robert J.		
Koerner, William K.		
Mason, William L.		
Mayfield, Waldo		
McFarland, Alvin J.		
McLaughlin, James E.		
McMillian, Theodore		
McMullen, David A.		
Murphy, David J.		
Nangle, James F.		
Oakley, Ernest F.		
O'Malley, Frank C.		
Owen, Oswald P.		
Reagan, Franklin		
Regan, John K.		
Ruddy, Edward M.		
Russell, Harry F.		

Judge	Overall Performance (A,B,C,D,E)	Degree of Objectivity (1,2,3,4,5)
Sartorius, Eugene J.		
Scott, Michael J.		
Walsh, J. Casey		
Ward, Joseph J.		
Williams, Charles B.		
Williams, Francis E.		

ST. LOUIS COUNTY

Judge	Overall Performance (A,B,C,D,E)	Degree of Objectivity (1,2,3,4,5)
Barrett, Peter T.		
Brackman, Amandus		
Carroll, Michael J.		
Cloyd, George W.		
Ferris, Franklin		
Hoester, Robert G.		
Jones, Douglas		
Kelly, John J., Jr.		
LaDriere, Raymond E.		
Luten, Drew W.		
Mueller, Fred E.		
Murphy, Joseph		
Nolte, Julius R.		
Poelker, Virgil A.		
Schaff, George		
Weinstein, Noah		
Witthaus, John A.		
Wolfe, John J.		

375

TO BE ANSWERED BY LAWYERS WHO HAVE APPEARED BEFORE
MISSOURI COURTS OF APPEALS AND/OR MO. SUPREME COURT

4. How would you evaluate the following judges? (Please evaluate only those judges you have *personally* appeared before and rate them on the basis of their *best work years* on the bench.) Rating for *Overall Performance:* Outstanding—A; Good—B; Average—C; Poor—D; Very Poor—E. Rating for *Degree of Objectivity:* Very Pro Pl.—1; Pro Pl.—2; Neutral—3; Pro Def.—4; Very Pro Def.—5. Thus an average, pro def. judge would be rated C-4.

Ct.	Judge	Overall Performance (A,B,C,D,E)	Degree of Objectivity (1,2,3,4,5)
K.C.	Bland, Ewing C.		
	Bour, J. Coy		
	Boyer, John S.		
	Broaddus, James W.		
	Cave, Nick T.		
	Cross, Gerald		
	Dew, Samuel		
	Hunter, Elmo		
	Maughmer, Fred H.		
	Shain, Hopkins B.		
	Sperry, Floyd L.		
St.L.	Anderson, Lyon		
	Bennick, Walter E.		
	Brady, Robert G.		
	Doerner, Russell H.		
	Hughes, William C.		
	Matthes, M. C.		
	McCullen, Edward J.		
	Ruddy, Edward M.		
	Wolfe, John J.		
Spfd.	Blair, David E.		
	Fulbright, James F.		
	Hogan, Robert		
	McDowell, James C.		
	Ruark, Justin		
	Smith, Robert J.		
	Stone, A. P.		
	Vandeventer, William L.		

SUPREME COURT

Judge	Overall Performance (A,B,C,D,E)	Degree of Objectivity (1,2,3,4,5)
Barrett, Paul W.		
Bohling, Walter H.		
Bradley, John H.		
Clark, Albert M.		
Coil, Cullen		
Conkling, Roscoe P.		
Dalton, S. P.		
Douglas, James M.		
Eager, Henry I.		
Ellison, George R.		
Gantt, Ernest S.		
Hays, Charles T.		
Henley, Fred		
Hollingsworth, Frank B.		
Holman, Lawrence		
Houser, Norwin D.		
Hyde, Laurance M., Sr.		
Leedy, C. A.		
Lozier, Lue C.		
Pritchard, Jack		
Stockard, Alden A.		
Storckman, Clem F.		
Tipton, Ernest M.		
Van Osdol, Paul		
Welborn, Robert		
Westhues, Henry J.		

5. In assessing the judges above, what qualities do you feel were *most often found* in the judges you rated as outstanding or good? Please number *five* in order of importance (1, 2, 3, 4, 5, etc.)

———— common sense

———— knowledge of the law

———— courtesy to lawyers and witnesses

———— open mindedness and ability to listen patiently to both sides of case

———— native intelligence

———— hard working

———— basic understanding of people and human nature

———— ability to make prompt decisions

———— ability to keep control of the case being tried

———— Other. Please specify. ————————————————

——

——

☼ ☼ ☼

Finally we would like some information on your background. Of course, we are not interested in individuals as such, but rather in the general kind of lawyers that are included among our respondents.

1. Where do you presently have your *main* practice of law or other employment?

☐ In Jackson County ☐ In St. Louis City
☐ In St. Louis County ☐ Other

2. Where do you presently live?

☐ In Jackson County ☐ In St. Louis City
☐ In St. Louis County ☐ Other

3. In which general age group are you?

☐ under 35 ☐ 35–39 ☐ 40–44
☐ 45–49 ☐ 50–54 ☐ 55 or over

4. How long have you lived in Missouri?

☐ All my life
☐ All my life except for 1–4 years
☐ All my life except for 5–9 years
☐ All my life except for 10–19 years
☐ I have lived outside the state 20 years or more.

5. How long have you been *admitted to the practice of law* in Missouri?
   ☐ Under 5 years   ☐ 5–9 years   ☐ 10–14 years
   ☐ 15–24 years   ☐ 25–34 years   ☐ 35 years or more
6. What was your *father's occupation?* Please be specific. ⸻⸻⸻

⸻⸻⸻⸻⸻⸻⸻⸻⸻⸻⸻⸻⸻⸻⸻⸻⸻

7. Besides yourself, are or were there any other *lawyers* in your family? (Grandparent, parent, children, uncles, cousins).
   ☐ Yes   ☐ No

IF ANSWER TO 7 IS YES

   (a) How many *lawyers* are included in that family group?
        ☐ 1   ☐ 2   ☐ 3   ☐ 4   ☐ 5 or more
8. Did you:
   ☐ Graduate from law school
   ☐ Attend law school but did not graduate
   ☐ Study law in a lawyer's office
9. IF ANSWER TO 8 IS GRADUATE OR ATTEND LAW SCHOOL
   (a) What law school was that?

⸻⸻⸻⸻⸻⸻⸻⸻⸻⸻⸻⸻⸻⸻⸻⸻⸻

10. In which *one* of the following kinds of law practice arrangement have you spent *most* of your time since *being admitted to practice,* and in which of these are you *presently* engaged?

Most Time Since Admitted		*Presently Engaged*
☐	Solo practice	☐
☐	Two man partnership	☐
☐	Partnership 3–5 lawyers	☐
☐	Partnership 6–9 lawyers	☐
☐	Partnership of 10–19 lawyers	☐
☐	Partnership of 20 or more lawyers	☐
☐	Salaried employee of law firm	☐
☐	Salaried employee of corporation	☐
☐	Salaried employee of government agency	☐

11. *Since being admitted* to the practice of law, and *within the last year,* in which of the following fields have you earned *most* of your income or salary? (Please list up to 3 fields only).

Since Admitted		Within the Last Year
☐	General corporate and business (corporations, bankruptcy and commercial, public utilities, anti-trust, labor relations principally for companies).	☐
☐	Probate, trust, taxation	☐
☐	Criminal law	☐
☐	Domestic relations	☐
☐	Negligence and/or compensation law, principally for plaintiff	☐
☐	Negligence and/or compensation, principally for defendant	☐
☐	Negligence and/or compensation, about equally for plaintiff and defendant	☐
☐	Labor law, principally for unions	☐
☐	Real property	☐
☐	Municipal and administrative law	☐
☐	Other. Please specify.	☐

12. *Which of the following bar groups do you belong to and hold office in?* (Check *one or more* appropriate boxes). Include *past* memberships and offices held.

Membership	Office Held
☐ Jackson County Bar Association	_____
☐ Kansas City Bar Association	_____
☐ Lawyers' Association of Kansas City	_____
☐ Independence Bar Association	_____
☐ St. Louis Bar Association	_____
☐ Lawyers' Association of St. Louis	_____
☐ Mound City Bar Association	_____
☐ County Bar Association	_____
☐ American Bar Association	_____
☐ American Judicature Society	_____
☐ Missouri Association of Claimants Attorneys	_____
☐ National Association of Claimants Attorneys	_____
☐ National Association of Railroad and/or Insurance Attorneys	_____

☐ American College of Trial Attorneys   _____

☐ Other. Please specify. _____

13. Which of the following public legal offices have you held? (Check one or more appropriate boxes).

☐ City attorney or counselor's office   ☐ Law Clerk

☐ County prosecutor or counselor's   ☐ Circuit Court Judge

    office   ☐ Appellate Court Judge

☐ Legal staff of state or national agency   ☐ State Board of Law

☐ Justice of the Peace or Magistrate   Examiners

☐ Law school faculty member   ☐ Other. Please specify

14. In addition to legal offices, what other public offices have you held or sought unsuccessfully? (Check one or more appropriate boxes.)

	Office Held	Office Sought Unsuccessfully
☐ Elective city office	_____	_____
☐ Appointive city office	_____	_____
☐ Elective county office	_____	_____
☐ Appointive county office	_____	_____
☐ Elective state office	_____	_____
☐ Appointive state office	_____	_____
☐ Elective federal office	_____	_____
☐ Appointive federal office	_____	_____
☐ Other. Please specify.	_____	_____

15. In what ways have you participated in *political party activities?* (Mark one or more appropriate boxes.)

☐ Attending political rallies

☐ Working for parties or candidates by getting people registered to vote, canvassing, passing out literature, poll watching, etc.

☐ Making speeches for candidates

☐ Contributing money to party or candidates

☐ Serving as a campaign manager

                                Office

☐ Holding party office at city level   _____

☐ Holding party office at county level   _____

☐ Holding party office at state level   _____

☐ Holding party office at national level ———————————————
☐ Other. Please specify. ———————————————————

16. Generally speaking, do you think of yourself as
    ☐ A Republican   ☐ A Democrat   ☐ Neither, I'm an Independent

IF YOU ANSWER *INDEPENDENT*

(a) Which of the two parties do you *feel* closer to, that is, find yourself agreeing with most often?

    ☐ Republican   ☐ Democratic   ☐ Neither

17. During the last 3 years what would you estimate your *average yearly net income* to be?
    ☐ Less than $5,000   ☐ $5,000–$9,999
    ☐ $10,000–$14,999   ☐ $15,000–$19,999
    ☐ $20,000–$29,999   ☐ $30,000–$49,999
    ☐ $50,000 and above

18. What is your religious affiliation or preference?
    ☐ Protestant   Denomination ————————————————————
    ☐ Catholic   ☐ Jewish   ☐ Other   ☐ None

19. Which kinds of civic or community groups have you belonged to or held office in?

Kind of Organization	Name of Groups	Offices Held
☐ Public affairs (citizens, leagues, civic improvement, etc.)	———————	———————
☐ Public Service (Red Cross, Boy Scouts, etc.)	———————	———————
☐ Social-fraternal (Masons, Country Club, etc.)	———————	———————
☐ Business (Chamber of Commerce, Development Assn.)	———————	———————
☐ Veterans (American Legion, VFW, etc.)	———————	———————
☐ Religious (Knights of Columbus, etc.)	———————	———————

INDEX

383

judges, 213–215, 217–219; quality ratings and judges' previous, 302–305
Experience, public office: of elected and Plan judges, 213–219; of judgeship appointees, candidates, and nominees, 159–160, 197–198; of metropolitan attorneys, 129; quality ratings and judges', 302–305
Experience, trial, 34, 257n; and judgeship candidacy, 57, 70–71, 96; judicial objectivity ratings and lawyers', 314, 316–317, 324–326; and judicial selection methods preferred, 247–251, 253n, 260, 262n; and perceptions of Plan consequences, 261–262, 262n

Factionalism, 42, 350; and gubernatorial politics, 83–84; and judicial recruitment, 84; and judicial selection, 83–87, 91, 100, 112–122, 336, 341; and partisan judicial elections, 10
Factions, party, 6, 10, 81–87, 92–93, 100, 112–113, 115, 120, 254, 349; see also specific factions
Fenton, John H., 125n, 165n, 166n
Ferguson, LeRoy C., 58n
Focus of study, 3–7, 16–17
Form, William H., 78n
Foulis, Ronald J., 10n
Fragmentation in Jackson County politics, 82–83; of metropolitan areas in state politics, 164–165; in St. Louis nominating commission, 145; in St. Louis politics, 124–126, 140–142, 145
Frankel, Jack E., 234n
Freund, Paul, 244n
Friedrich, Carl J., 112n
Funds, state, 166, 172

George, B. J., Jr., 351n
Gideon v. Wainwright, 351n
Goldman, Sheldon, 16n, 206n, 356n
Governors, 45, 94, 185, 257, 331–332; attitudes toward Plan of, 99, 192, 194; conservatism of, 99, 166, 193–194; and judicial recruitment, 67, 69; legal practice backgrounds of, 194; and nominating process, 97, 100–101, 105–106, 108–109, 138, 186–189, 340, 352; outstate orientation of, 99, 144, 192–193; party affiliation of, 81, 97–98, 187, 246; patronage orientation of, 98, 335–336,

338–339; political orientation of, 85–86, 98–99, 166, 336; reaction of, to panel-loading tactics, 111, 115–120, 149, 188, 190–191; relations with Jackson County factions of, 84–86, 99–100, 112–113, 121; relations with lawyer commissioners, 108; relations with lay commissioners, 46–48, 88, 108, 137, 188–189; relations with presiding judge, 96, 108; relations with St. Louis party organizations, 126, 140; residential background of, 46, 144
Grossman, Joel B., 2n, 16n, 67n, 206n, 310n, 311n, 313, 350n, 356n, 357n
Grover, Rich, 241n

Hardworking, 295–301, 345
Hardy, David R., 118
Haynes, Evan, 3n, 7n
Hearnes, Governor Warren E., 166n
Hemker, Forrest, 241n
Henderson, Bancroft D., 2, 4n, 16n, 27n, 34n, 206n, 209n, 212n, 230n, 233n, 274
Herndon, James, 240n
Hobson, Robert P., 23n
Hodge, Robert W., 63n
Hofferbert, Richard, 43n
Honnold, John, 99n
Hoopes, Todd, 16n, 205n
Horowitz, Samuel B., 23n
Hughes, Everett C., 330n
Hunting, Roger B., 351n
Hurst, James Willard, 7n, 349, 350n
Hyde, Laurance, 241n

Ideology: and appellate selection, 185, 194; and Bar cleavages, 40, 43; and evaluation of Plan, 162, 353–354; of lawyer commissioners, 92, 135, 181–182, 185
Impeachment, 233–234
Income, 31, 56–57, 60, 64n, 266, 269, 332, 333; and Bar association membership, 26–28; and judgeship candidacy, 70–71, 73; and judicial selection methods preferred, 245; median, of lawyers, 26n; quality ratings and Plan appointees', 306–308
Incrementalism, 164, 166
Index of: Bar association activity, 305; candidacy for nonlegal public office, 129, 129n, 160; civic participation, 305; judicial objectivity, 275, 278–279, 281, 313;

judicial performance, 275, 275n, 280n,
281; political party activity, 60n, 129n,
156n, 157–158, 195, 246–247, 252, 305;
public legal office holding, 159n, 160;
social status, 245, 245n, 246
Information, political: as factor in nominating process, 94–96, 102, 107, 110, 120,
138–139, 148
Intelligence, 295–301, 345
Interest articulation, 336, 336n
Interest groups, 335, 335n; and appellate
selection, 170–173, 335; and circuit
selection, 79, 130–131, 335; and retention elections, 224–225; and selection of
lawyer commissioners, 43; stakes in court
decisions, 77–79, 168, 170–172, 335; in
state politics, 98, 165–167

Jacksonian Revolution, 3n, 7, 330
Jacob, Herbert, 3, 4n, 15–16, 200n, 204,
205n, 206n, 211, 212n, 213n, 230n, 233n,
256n, 357n
Jones, Harry W., 293n
Judges, appeals court: age at selection of,
217–218; law enforcement experience of,
218–219, 344; lawyer ratings of, 285–
286, 288–289, 291–292; legal education
of 217–218; objectivity of, 324–326;
partisan affiliations of, 217–219; policy-
making role of, 254–257; practice backgrounds of, 195–197, 197n; prior judicial
experience of, 217–219; prior party activity of, 195, 197–198; public office experience of, 217–219; quality ratings and
backgrounds of, 304–308; residential
backgrounds of, 193, 217–218
Judges, circuit: affirmance rates of, 286n;
age of selection of, 207–209, 217–218;
factional affiliations of, 112–113; holdover, 282–292, 286n, 313–318; interest
in selection process, 80, 131, 334; and judicial recruitment, 67–68, 80–81; and
judicial selection, 13, 80; law enforcement
experience of, 215–216, 218–219, 344;
lawyer ratings of, 282–292; legal education of, 207–209, 217–218; objectivity
ratings of, 313–318; partisan affiliations
of, 156–158, 210–212, 217–219; policy-
making role of, 39–40, 254–256, 256n,
257; practice backgrounds of, 152, 154–

155, 195–197, 197n; prestige of, 63, 63n,
64; prior judicial experience of, 213–214,
217–219; prior party activity of, 85–86,
120–121, 141, 157–158, 195, 197–198;
public office experience of, 159–160,
213–216, 217–219; quality ratings and
backgrounds of 302–308; residency requirements for, 49, 50; residential backgrounds of, 209–211, 217–218; terms of
office, 276n
Judicial Conference of Missouri, 40n
Judicial recruitment, 6, 14, 341; and attractions of judgeship, 49, 60–64, 73,
332–333; candidate characteristics and,
53–60, 70–71, 73, 207; definition of,
16–17; effect of residency requirements
on, 49–54, 72; factors deterring lawyer
candidacies in, 55–60, 68, 332; financial
considerations in, 56–57, 60, 64, 332–
333; governors' role in, 67, 69; initiation
of candidacy in, 64–65; judges' role in,
67–68, 80–81, 131, 168, 334; nominating commissions' role in, 66–67, 103;
past studies of, 1, 2, 16; presiding judge
and, 66; strategies of candidates in, 65,
68–70; as winnowing process, 16–17, 49,
55, 70
Judicial selection, 1–4, 8, 14, 20, 43, 330–
331; applicants' ages as factor in, 206–207;
applicants' practice backgrounds as issue
in, 96, 153–154, 156, 173, 175–176, 179,
181, 185, 192, 194, 259, 261–262; attitudes on governors' role in, 267, 270;
bargaining in nominating phase of, 105–
107, 109–110, 145–147; business influence in, 11, 79, 130–131, 170–173,
335, 342; candidate campaigns in, 87, 131–
132; candidates' ideology as issue in, 173,
175–176, 179, 181, 185, 192, 194; chief
justices' influence in, 182–183; commissioner candidacies as issue in, 176–177,
179, 182, 192; convergence of interests in
appellate, 168, 182, 185, 194, 341–343;
as cooptative process, 174, 179, 185, 191–
192, 194, 197–198, 266–267, 319, 342–
343; courts' institutional interests and, 80–
81, 94, 131, 173–180, 334; criticisms of
procedures in, 268, 270; decision-making
procedures in, 102–107, 146; defined, 17;
fusion of nominating and appointing phases
of, 100–101, 110–111, 140, 144, 187–190,

332; of circuit candidates, nominees, and appointees, 151–154, 195–197; of circuit lawyer commissioners, 33–34, 92, 121, 132–135, 145, 153, 337, 340; and conceptions of judicial quality, 297–299; degree of, among metropolitan attorneys, 127, 154; favored in selection process, 258–259, 261; of Missouri attorneys, 127–129, 152–154, 168–169, 197, 197n; and perceptions of Plan effects, 261–262; and perceptions of selection process, 58–60; quality ratings and Plan judges' previous, 306–308; of raters, and objectivity ratings, 314, 316–318, 324–326; of raters, and performance ratings, 289, 291–292; and residential eligibility, 51–52; and selection methods preferred, 243–251, 260, 347

Presiding judge, 13, 19; bases of influence of, 93–95; and courts' institutional interests, 81, 94, 338; and judicial recruitment, 66; political background of, 96, 114, 120, 145; practice background of, 96, 139, 145; relations with governor, 96, 108; relations with lawyer commissioners, 93–94, 139, 145, 339; relations with lay commissioners, 88–89, 93–94, 97, 145, 339–340; political orientations of, 91, 95, 138–139, 338–339; role in nominations, 89, 93–97, 120, 122, 138–140, 338–340; role orientation of, 93–97, 138–140, 338–339

Press, Charles, 78n
Pressures: on judges, 319–320; of legal practice, 62–63; on nominating commission, 46, 87, 90, 108, 114, 117, 130–132
Primary, Bar, 8n, 331n; see Polls, Bar
Pritchett, C. Herman, 221n, 334n, 350n, 356n
Progressive Movement, 3n, 330
Promptness of decisions, 295–301
Public Opinion Survey Unit, University of Missouri, 29n
Pye, Lucian, 164n

Qualification, judicial, 295; defined, 301–302
Quality, judicial, 5–6, 80, 200, 276, 276n, 281; and appointing governor, 307–308; defined by lawyers, 293–301, 354; defined by Plan judges, 299–301; dimensions of 293–301; ideology and evaluation of, 162;

and judges' background characteristics, 302–308; method for ascertaining, 293–296; Plan's effects and, 258–259, 261, 272, 345, 353; previous studies of, 293–294; ratings of holdover, elected, and Plan circuit judges, 282–292; ratings of holdover and Plan appellate judges, 285–286, 288–289, 291–292; and year of gubernatorial term appointed, 307–308; see also Performance, judicial)

Ranney, Austin, 42n, 350n
Reciprocity, rule of, 146
Recruitment, 1, 15–16, 167; see also Judicial recruitment
Reddig, William M., 81n, 82n
Referenda, Bar, see Polls, Bar
Reform, judicial, 8–9, 12–13, 330–331
Reichstein, Kenneth, 42n
Remittitur, appellate, 174
Removal, judicial, 221, 256–266
Residency requirements, 38, 44, 49–50, 332, 341; and appellate judicial recruitment, 72, 333, 341; and types of lawyers eligible for circuit bench, 51–54
Residential background: of elected and Plan judges, 209–211, 217–218; and voting in Supreme Court, 322n
Retirement benefits, 234–235
Rich, S. Grover, Jr., 221n
Riesman, David, 29n, 60
Rodell, Fred, 349n
Role: defined, 87–88; diffuseness in St. Louis commission, 132–145; of judges, 34–40, 56, 61–62, 73, 254–257, 300n, 348; of lawyers as advocates, 56, 61; structures in nominating commissions, 95–97, 105–106, 109–110, 112–113, 121–122, 145–148, 180, 183, 189–192, 339–343
Role orientations: of appellate lawyer commissioners, 181–182, 337, 340; of appellate lay commissioners, 186–187, 338, 340; of chief justice, 182–186, 338–339, 340; of circuit lawyer commissioners, 91–93; 132–136, 337, 340; of circuit lay commissioners, 88–91, 136–138, 338, 340; of presiding judge, 93–97, 138–140, 338–339, 340
Rosenberg, Maurice, 294, 295n
Rosenzweig, Robert, 63n
Rossi, Peter H., 63n
Rushing, William A., 87n